DIVIDED HOUSES

DIVIDED HOUSES

Gender and the Civil War

Edited by
CATHERINE CLINTON and NINA SILBER

OXFORD UNIVERSITY PRESS
New York   Oxford

Oxford University Press

Oxford   New York   Toronto
Delhi   Bombay   Calcutta   Madras   Karachi
Kuala Lumpur   Singapore   Hong Kong   Tokyo
Nairobi   Dar es Salaam   Cape Town
Melbourne   Auckland   Madrid

and associated companies in
Berlin   Ibadan

Copyright © 1992 by Catherine Clinton and Nina Silber

Published by Oxford University Press, Inc.,
198 Madison Avenue, New York, New York 10016-4314

Oxford is a registered trademark of Oxford University Press

Library of Congress Cataloging-in-Publication Data
Divided houses : gender and the Civil War /
edited by Catherine Clinton and Nina Silber.
p.   cm.   Includes bibliographical references.
ISBN 0-19-507407-6   ISBN 0-19-508034-3 (pbk.)
1. Sex role—United States—History—19th century.
2. United States—History—Civil War, 1861–1865—Social aspects.
3. United States—Social conditions—To 1865.
I. Clinton, Catherine, 1952– .   II. Silber, Nina.
HQ1075.U6D58   1992   305.3'0973—dc20   91–47143

Grateful acknowledgment is made to the following for permission
to use copyrighted material:
Johns Hopkins University Press for Nina Silber, "Intemperate Men, Spiteful Women,
and Jefferson Davis,"
American Quarterly, vol. 41, no.4 (1989), 614–35. Reprinted by permission
of Johns Hopkins University Press.
Journal of American History for Drew Gilpin Faust, "Altars of Sacrifice:
Confederate Women and the Narratives of War," *Journal of American History*,
76 (March 1990), 1200–28. Reprinted by permission.
University of Massachusetts Press for David W. Blight,
"No Desperate Hero: Manhood and Freedom in
a Union Soldier's Experience," *When This Cruel
War Is Over: The Civil War Letters of Charles Harvey Brewster*,
edited by David W. Blight (Amherst: University of Massachusetts Press,
1992). Reprinted by permission.

8 9 7

Printed in the United States of America

FOR LOUIS HUTCHINS
AND
FOR DREW AND NED COLBERT

Acknowledgments

As co-authors, we frequently divided our labors, but otherwise we remained united on almost all other issues throughout this project. It has been our great good fortune that this book has moved us from acquaintance to friendship, especially during very disruptive and challenging times in our lives. Throughout all, our husbands, Daniel Colbert (Catherine) and Louis Hutchins (Nina), have been generous and good-spirited. Ned and Drew Colbert, as always, put up with the inconvenience of having a feminist scholar for a mother, and Benjamin Hutchins was cooperative enough to be born between copyediting and page proofs.

The idea for this book originated over lunch in the autumn of 1990. It was also fortuitous that Sheldon Meyer was enthusiastic and supportive of our efforts at the outset, and by early 1991 committed to this enterprise. His vision and support have been essential throughout the project. We also extend our special thanks to Joellyn Ausanka and Karen Wolny at Oxford University Press for all their efforts on our behalf.

Many of our colleagues must be thanked for their generosity and devotion. Above all, our contributors met several deadlines and demands with extraordinary care and cheer. Their talent is evident in the finished product, but we wish to praise their collegiality as well.

The author of our preface, James McPherson, must be singled out for his invaluable support for this project from its inception. We are grateful for his invaluable input. Also, Jean Baker took time out from her own work to provide us with thorough and thoughtful criticism of the entire manuscript for which we remain indebted.

We consulted many scholars and university presses for suggestions for our bibliography, and wish to thank you all for your sage advice, most especially Reid Mitchell and Emory Thomas. Jona Hansen, our research assistant, met our endless demands with unfailing accuracy and good humor. We salute him.

And last but not least, we would like to thank Eric Foner for his endless supply of encouragement, his unstinting support, his dedication to younger scholars within the profession. His generosity and wisdom over the years have been extraordinary.

We would each like to acknowledge the assistance we received individually. Nina Silber would like to thank the Boston University Humanities Foundation and the Smithsonian Institution for their financial support of this project. Catherine Clinton would like to thank the American Council of Learned Societies for their financial support of her project and the W.E.B. DuBois Institute of Harvard University for its continuing support of her research.

Like all literary enterprises, ours involved compromise—for example, Catherine was willing to abdicate her position on penarchy if Nina would relinquish the term patriarchy. And yet there were no compromises made in terms of quality. We agreed to rigorous standards and the result is the best new scholarship in our field.

Nevertheless, because of our tight schedule, our focus on the war alone, and our page limitation, some very fine work could not be included. Our bibliography features excellent dissertations and manuscripts forthcoming which we encountered while undertaking this book. We thank all who so generously shared their work with us.

Cambridge, Mass.   C. C.
April 1992

Boston, Mass.   N. S.
April 1992

Contents

Part III   Women at War

Part IV   The Southern Homefront

Part V   The Northern Homefront

Part VI   The War Comes Home

Foreword

JAMES M. McPHERSON

In their novel *The Gilded Age* (1873), which labeled an era of American history, Mark Twain and Charles Dudley Warner wrote that the Civil War had "uprooted institutions that were centuries old, changed the politics of a people, transformed the social life of half the country, and wrought so profoundly upon the entire national character that the influence cannot be measured short of two or three generations." A dozen years later, Albion W. Tourgée, novelist and crusader for black civil rights, expressed vexation with the flood of books and articles beginning to appear that celebrated the military pageantry and heroism of the Civil War but said little about its issues. Though a twice-wounded combat veteran himself, Tourgée declared in 1885 that what was most important about the war was *"not the courage, the suffering, the blood, but only the causes that underlay the struggle and the results that followed from it."*[1]

Over the past century, many historians have responded to Twain's and Tourgée's challenges. We have whole libraries of books on the causes and consequences of the Civil War, on the institutions that were uprooted, and on the politics that were changed. All serious students of the conflict recognize that it resolved two fundamental, festering questions that had plagued the country since its beginning. Would this fragile experiment in republican government, this house divided, survive? Or would it follow the dismal fate of most republics throughout history and collapse into tyranny or disintegrate into squabbling fragments? And even if the Union founded on a declaration of the equal right of all people to liberty were preserved, would it continue to exist as the largest slaveholding country in the world? Northern victory in 1865 resolved these questions. The United States survived as a single indissoluble nation that had experienced a new birth of freedom in which chattel slavery would be known no more. And in the process of preserving the Union of 1776 while purging it of slavery, the "Second American Revolution" of 1861 to 1865 also profoundly transformed the political and economic balance of power. The institutions and ideology of a plantation society and slave system that had ruled half the country and dominated its national politics went down with a great crash. The institutions and ideology of free-labor entrepreneurial capitalism vaulted into the ascendancy. For better or for worse, the Civil War forged the framework of modern America.

Yet while these developments have attracted much scholarly attention, the great majority of books and articles that make the Civil War by far the most written-about event in American history have focused mainly on armies and generals, military campaigns and battles. A huge Civil War constituency exists outside the ranks of professional historians and the halls of academe. Serious books on the subject have reached best-seller lists, and the PBS video *The Civil War* has enthralled an estimated forty million viewers. But the core of that non-academic constituency, loosely organized in more than two hundred Civil War Round Tables, forty thousand reenactors, and various other groups such as the Sons of Confederate Veterans, are interested mainly if not exclusively in campaigns and battles.

At the same time, many professional academic historians ignore or disdain the military aspects of the Civil War. Two anthologies on the war era intended for college classes contain almost nothing on the actual fighting.[2] Likewise, an essay on the historiography of this period, sponsored by the American Historical Association and intended for teachers of history, says naught about the real *war*—the fighting and dying.[3] Just as the popular constituency of Civil War "buffs" seems indifferent to the huge and crucial social, cultural, economic, and political dimensions of the war, so the academics fail to recognize that all of these dimensions were inextricably bound up with events on the battlefield. Upon "the progress of our arms," said Abraham Lincoln truthfully, "all else chiefly depends." During the titanic battles of the Wilderness and Spotsylvania in May 1864, the New York lawyer George Templeton Strong wrote in his diary: "These are fearfully critical, anxious days, in which the destinies of the continent for centuries will be decided."[4] The destinies of the continent did indeed hang on these battles—and on many others. Most of the things that professional historians consider important during that era—the fate of slavery, the structure of society and social relations in both North and South, the direction of the American economy, the destiny of competing nationalisms in Union and Confederacy, the very survival of the United States—rested on the shoulders of those three million men in blue and gray who fought it out during four years of ferocity unmatched in the Western world between 1815 and 1914.

Perhaps nothing illustrates more starkly the two separate spheres of popular and academic Civil War history than the place of women in these spheres. In every respect except death and wounds in camp and battlefield, the Civil War affected the female half of the population as profoundly as the male half. Women played vital roles in economic and social mobilization for the conflict. Yet most Civil War Round Tables and similar organizations were initially all male. When this began to change, resistance in some quarters was vigorous. "To admit the ladies," said a member of the Chicago Round Table (the oldest and largest) in 1976, "would . . . inevitably lead to an erosion of the purpose of this organization. With all due respect to those few serious female students of the Civil War, the undeniable truth is that most women could [not] care less about the Battle of Antietam or Jackson's strategy in the Valley."[5] Whether or not this "truth" really was undeniable, the assumption underlying it— that the only concern of Round Tables should be campaigns and battles—seems to have been undeniable in 1976.

At the same time, the explosion of women's history in the 1970s and 1980s seemed almost to ignore the Civil War. An analysis of 603 books and doctoral dissertations on American women's history produced from 1980 to 1987 found that only thirteen of them—2 percent—dealt with the Civil War or Reconstruction.[6] This was a manifestation of a broader phenomenon in social history, in which women's history has been the most dynamic part of the most dynamic field of historical scholarship during the past two or three decades. The "new social history" arose in part as a challenge to the traditional focus of mainstream scholarship on white male elites who functioned in the worlds of politics, diplomacy, business, and warfare. Social history shifted the focus to ordinary people, including women and minorities, functioning in the home, the family, the workplace, and in the everyday urban or rural world they inhabited. The Civil War seemed almost irrelevant to this context—at least the Civil War as it was conventionally studied, as a story of political leaders, diplomats, generals, and battles. Thus Stephan Thernstrom's classic study of Newburyport from 1850 to 1880, which in many ways launched the new social history, did not even mention the Civil War, much less analyze the enormous demographic and social impact that it had on that community.[7] Surveying the prodigious output of community studies; labor histories; studies of women, family, culture, workplace; and similar studies that fall within the general category of social history that had appeared by the late 1980s, Maris Vinovskis asked in a now-famous article: "Have Social Historians Lost the Civil War?"[8]

Perhaps they had. But there are encouraging signs that the two spheres of popular and academic history are converging, at least a little, with respect to the Civil War. The Chicago Civil War Round Table did admit women more than a decade ago, and so have most other Round Tables that were once all-male preserves. And perhaps in part as a consequence, some of these Round Tables have broadened their perspectives beyond traditional military history. Several reenactor groups have admitted women, perhaps in recognition of the fact that several hundred women in the 1860s disguised themselves as men and went into the ranks. The largest reenactment ever, at Gettysburg on the 125th anniversary of the battle in 1988, included living history exhibits of life on the home front and in military hospitals that dramatized the important wartime functions of women and other civilians. At the same time, a wealth of recent superb studies that come under the rubric of social history focused on Civil War soldiers,[9] on soldiers and civilians,[10] on yeoman whites in the South,[11] on guerrilla warfare and class conflict in rural and urban areas,[12] on women and men on the home front in the Confederacy and Union,[13] and on slaves and freedpeople[14]—to cite only some of the important new works and their subjects.

If social historians did lose the Civil War, they are now finding it. Vinovskis himself edited a volume of seven essays published in 1990, suggesting some of the new directions this work is taking, *Toward a Social History of the American Civil War,* which focuses on the North. But the present volume of eighteen essays covering both South and North, *Divided Houses,* marks the full coming of age of social history for the Civil War era.

The editors of *Divided Houses* quite properly situate the essays in the field of gender studies, an expansion of women's studies that recognizes that women exist in relationship with a world that includes men and children of both sexes. Yet even "gender studies" seems too narrow a classification to encompass the richness and variety of these essays. It is true that seven of the essays focus mainly on women, four on men and concepts of masculinity, and seven on issues of gender and family. But as I write these words, I realize that such classifications are artificial and restricted. Several of the essays also deal with racial attitudes and relations; several delineate the crosscurrents of class as well as of gender; and in fact all of them analyze at least two, and some of them all three, of the main themes of the new social history—race, class, and gender. Nine essays focus mainly on the South, seven on the North, and two on both. But most important, all of them relate the experience of men and women and children, black and white, elites and ordinary people, to the overwhelming experience of a war that killed or wounded a million Americans, liberated four million from bondage, and changed forever the perspectives and social relations of most of the remaining twenty-seven million. "The war," wrote Ralph Waldo Emerson in 1861, "has assumed such huge proportions that it threatens to engulf us all—no preoccupation can exclude it, & no hermitage hide us."[15] The essays in *Divided Houses* will help us understand why.

DIVIDED HOUSES

PART I

xxxxxxxxxxxxxxxxxxxxxxxxxxx

Imperiled
Unions

*D*espite all pledges and vows, compromises and commitments, unions frequently dissolve. For some the very process of
unification plants the seeds of destruction; those who cherish independence and autonomy resent the mutual dependency imposed by bonding. Whether steeped in sentiment or cynicism, compacts represent
bargains struck. The done deal unravels when one or more of the
parties joined together pursues self-interest rather than those interests
allegedly comingled.

Whether principles or interests are involved, uniting involves a
lengthy process of definition. Responsibilities and rights are clearly
demarcated to provide systems of mutual benefit, but especially as
means to balance conflicts when future circumstances inevitably encourage a parting of the ways. If and when these partings develop,
dissolutions can tell us a great deal about how each party views itself,
as much as they do about the contract itself.

America at its revolutionary founding was surely a marriage of
convenience among competing parties. Despite the sectional conflicts
which had divided the colonial generation, the development of the
cotton trade and the expansion of slavery had consequences unforeseen
on the eve of unification. How could these fleeting attractions forge
disparate, far-flung, and fragile states into a single body politic? Declaring the nation as one—in God's eyes—did not diminish the
wrenching divides that rocked the world order at the end of the eigh-

teenth century: class in France, race in Haiti, and even Mary Wollstonecroft's plea of women's rights chimed in.

Several generations of historians have debated the events leading up to the American Civil War, in a scholarly deluge that defies summary. Because it has been characterized as "a brothers' war" and resulted in reunification rather than permanent disaffiliation, the war has often been portrayed as a "crisis of the Union." With over half a million war dead in a nation of thirty-two million, it was a crisis of enormous proportion. Yet these sectional divides, this imperilment of the nation-state profoundly shaped several other crises within the culture. The interlacing of themes involving gender, class, race, and sexuality creates a powerful framework within which pioneering work is being accomplished.

In many ways gender became a prism through which the political tensions of the 1850s were filtered. The rising tide of abolitionist movements and its waves of feminist sympathizing sexualized debate over sectionalism and eventually secession. Northerners and southerners frequently berated one another for violating what each believed were natural and immutable patterns of male and female behavior. Pictured as idle and useless aristocrats, slaveowners came under northern attack for their "peculiar institution" and its enfeebling aspects. Likewise, southerners believed that money-grubbing Yankees lacked the manly courage or feminine grace of the white gentlemen and ladies of their homeland. Both regions sniped at one another for the supposedly "effeminate" characteristics which flawed the other's menfolk.

LeeAnn Whites examines many of the ways in which gender figured into the prewar crisis and provides an overview of the war that allows us to factor crucial questions of race and gender into our re-rendering of war's impact. Gender also became enmeshed in the political developments of each section. In this light, Stephanie McCurry recasts our perceptions of the complex unification of southern interests through her exploration of contract and property, men and women, yeoman and planter. Like Whites, McCurry demonstrates gender's crucial and complex influence on class alliances and those divides which fragmented groups within the political economy.

Chapter 1

The Civil War as a Crisis in Gender

LEEANN WHITES

It was a cold winter's day and greenish ice flows clogged the turbulent river. Across its vast expanse, Eliza could see the far shore of Ohio and freedom. Behind her, coming ever closer, she could hear the baying dogs of the slavetrader, Haley. What could she do? On the one side was slavery and the certain loss of her child to the slavetrader. On the other was an impassable river and probable death. Looking down at her small son, Eliza knew only that she could not bear to lose him. And with one desperate burst of courage, she jumped onto the nearest ice flow. Scrambling and leaping from one teetering piece of ice to another, she struggled across the mighty Ohio and gained the far shore of freedom for herself and her child.

Laying down the collection of antislavery tracts she was reading, Harriet Beecher Stowe was deeply moved. In Eliza's desperate act of undaunted mother love, Stowe heard an almost irresistible call to action.[1] She would tell the world Eliza's story, for herein lay the true sin of slavery—the way in which it thwarted and repressed the maternal bond, separating mother and child, brother and sister, husband and wife, eroding the emotional fabric of the black family in the name of the vested property rights of white slaveowners. The emergence of the family as a separate sphere in the North, freed from the sordid economic concerns of men, had constituted the domestic realm of the mother as a sphere in its own right, allowing her older sister, Catharine Beecher, to claim a new and boldly autonomous role for women as the moral arbiters of social life.[2] Now Harriet Beecher Stowe would shine this newly emancipated light of the family and of the moral mother as the spokesperson of its interests upon what increasingly appeared to be a domestically retrograde southern slave system.[3]

The rest is history. *Uncle Tom's Cabin,* the novel that Harriet Beecher Stowe wrote as if driven to it, swept the nation by storm to become the most popular novel of the entire century.[4] Its claim for the domestic rights of slaves popularized the antislavery cause in the North in a manner that no abstract calls to the inherent equality of all mankind had ever succeeded in doing in the past. As Abraham Lincoln commented upon first meeting Harriet Beecher Stowe in the midst of the Civil War, "So you are the little woman who wrote the book that made this great war."[5]

If, however, popular antislavery sentiment in the North, and the war that followed from it, was grounded upon a new understanding of the domestic rights of the family, and in particular in the expansion of the private and public authority of the mother as the bearer and rearer of life, then we must ask, what did this war of domestic liberation mean for women of the South? How are we to understand the widespread support for the war among Confederate women, support for a War of Southern Independence that was understood by at least some of their northern sisters to be nothing less than the defense of the independence of Confederate men from the dictates of reproduction and the moral authority of motherhood? An independence that so subordinated the interests of reproduction and the family as a whole to the particular economic and productive interests of the individual planter that it gave him the right not only to own the child of some woman's heart and body but to dispose of it as *his* material interests would dictate.

While the readership of *Uncle Tom's Cabin* in the South was not as widespread as in the North, those who did read it were undoubtedly at least equally consumed by the critique of the southern slave household structure that it presented. Mary Boykin Chesnut, daughter of a prominent planter-class family and wife of a member of Jefferson Davis's staff, was haunted by the novel and returned to it time and again in her Civil War diary.[6] She took particular umbrage at Stowe's claim for the moral superiority of northern women. "What self-denial," queried Chesnut, did northerners like Stowe practice while sitting in their "nice New England homes—clean, clear, sweet smelling?" She contrasted this picture of the northern household, pristine in its isolation, with the experience of her female relations, living in households enmeshed in the institution of slavery.[7] These women of the planter elite were, according to Chesnut, educated in the same northern schools as their abolitionist critics. They read the same Bible and had the "same ideas of right and wrong," yet they were not so fortunate as to be safely ensconced in a separate familiar sphere dedicated to the domestic interests of their families alone. Instead they lived in "negro villages" where they struggled to "ameliorate the condition of these Africans in every particular."

> They set them the example of a perfect life—a life of utter self-abnegation. . . . Think of these holy New Englanders, forced to have a negro village walk through their houses whenever they saw fit . . . [these women] have a swarm of blacks about them as children under their care—not as Mrs. Stowe paints them, but the hard, unpleasant, unromantic, undeveloped savage Africans. And they hate slavery worse than Mrs. Stowe.[8]

Here the ultimate figure of domestic self-sacrifice and thus *the* "true woman" was not those abolitionist spokeswomen for the "cult of domesticity" and the family as a separate sphere, but rather the planter-class woman, who precisely *because* of the presence of slavery within the southern household was placed in a position to act as the mother of not only her own children but of her slave dependents as well. Of course, in Harriet Beecher's account, the most militant defender of motherhood was not in fact the northern abolitionist woman like herself, who risked only her good reputation in taking a public stance against slavery. Domesticity at its most insurgent was represented by those slave mothers, like Eliza, who in the very act of mothering their children could be called upon to subvert the institution of slavery itself. Chesnut's defense of the motherhood of the plantation mistress, on the other hand, spoke from within the confines of

the institution of slavery. For it was the very same slave system
that worked to deny Eliza her motherhood that gave Chesnut the
basis for claiming it as the slave mistresses' own. Ownership in
slaves not only made the planters the wealthiest men in the country through their appropriation of the productive labor of their
slaves, but it also served to make their women into "ladies" by
virtue of their own ability not only to "mother" their slaves but
more fundamentally to appropriate their domestic labor. It was
this ownership in slaves that empowered the white mistress, like
Mary Boykin Chesnut, to define the slave woman not as a mother
in her own right but as one of the many "children" under her
own maternal care.[9]

As slavery was an organic part of the southern household, it
became organic to the slaveowners' very conception of themselves as men and as women, as mothers and as fathers. It both
served to expand their own domestic claims as *individual*
mothers and fathers, while it served to subordinate, literally to
enslave, the sphere of reproduction and of domestic life as a
whole to the class interests of this same planter elite. Ultimately
the extent to which motherhood was rendered unfree within the
southern slave system served to undermine the domestic position
of even those women of the planter class who benefited from it
most in class terms. For whatever power they gained for their
own domestic position by having slave dependents, they lost by
the manner in which slaveownership further empowered their
own men. So while women of the planter class could claim to
"mother" their slaves, at least some of their husbands were literally fathers of slaves. The outcome, concluded Chesnut, was often far more devastating than even Harriet Beecher Stowe envi-
sioned. She recorded the conversation among one group of elite
Confederate women. ". . . I knew the dissolute half of Legree
well," asserted one of these women,

> He was high and mighty. But the kindest creature to his slaves—
> and the unfortunate results of his bad ways were not sold, had not
> to jump over ice blocks. They were kept in full view and provided
> for handsomely in his will. His wife and daughters in the might of
> their purity and innocence are supposed never to dream of what
> is as plain before their eyes as the sunlight, and they play their
> parts of unsuspecting angels to the letter.[10]

"Southern women," wrote Ella Gertrude Clanton Thomas, in her antebellum journal, "are I believe all at heart abolitionists."[11] When she made this claim, she in fact meant that all women of *her* class and race were abolitionists. Had she actually meant to refer to all southern women, her case would have been a stronger one. For to the extent that planter-class women were abolitionists, it was not in the first instance the consequence of their recognition of a common likeness among all women. It reflected instead their desire to be full-fledged members of their class, empowered like their men to dictate the cultural norms of their society.[12] Planter-class women burned, admittedly in private or in the company of other women, at the power that the ownership of slaves gave their men to create a double standard of sexual behavior within the planter class itself. As Rebecca Latimer Felton, a Georgia planter-class woman, wrote in her memoirs many years after the war, for the "abuses" that made "mulattoes as common as blackberries," the planters deserved to have their entire system collapse.

> In this one particular slavery doomed itself. When white men put their own offspring in the kitchen and the cornfield and allowed them to be sold into bondage as slaves and degraded them as another man's slave, the retribution of wrath was hanging over this country and the South paid penance in four years of bloody war.[13]

Hindsight is twenty-twenty, but where was this voice for the larger interests of southern motherhood in 1860? Jumping across ice flows? Not, certainly, coming from the likes of Rebecca Felton, who asserted in her memoirs that upon the outbreak of the Civil War, a war that she perceived to be a "battle to defend our rights in ownership of African slaves," there was "never a more loyal woman" than herself. "I could not," she wrote, "fight against my kindred." Besides, she concluded, she was "only a woman and nobody asked me for opinion."[14] The political voice of domesticity was silenced even among these most powerful of southern women, if only by the force of their own class interests. For at bottom was the undeniable fact that the slave plantation economy promoted their own material well-being. Therefore, no matter how frustrated they may have been in their own efforts to claim an enlarged sphere of authority in relation to the men of their class, they could not ignore the benefits that their own position as members of this class, however subordinated, gave them. If only out of their concern for their own children, women of the planter class were forced to recognize that the same planter who "defied the marriage law of the state by keeping up two households on the same plantation," as Rebecca Latimer Felton wrote, was also, as Mary Chesnut concluded, "the fountain from whom all blessings flow."[15]

In the face of mounting domestic criticism from the North, planter-class men and women, however, entered into an increasingly uneasy bargain.[16] Take for instance the courtship of Caroline Davis and Joseph Jones. In the spring of 1859, Caroline Davis made it clear in her correspondence with her suitor that marriage would in her estimation cost her her freedom as an individual, with which she was loathe to part. Joseph Jones replied by pointing to the benefits that her dependent position within his household would confer upon her. "Will the possession of a friend who will be your protector and defender when all friends and relatives fail, involve the loss of freedom?" he queried.[17] In exchange for her subordination, he promised that he would use his position to promote her own interests more effectively than she could ever hope to do in her own right. Caroline Davis did in fact accept Joseph Jones's suit, but while grudgingly relinquishing her own autonomy, she informed him that she would now be even more ambitious than ever for his success in life because, *"we poor women* have no name or existence of *our own,* we pass *silently* down the stream of time without leaving a single trace behind—we die unknown."[18] She would accept her subordinate status, but she would also expect him to maintain and enlarge his power to "protect and defend" her through his individual achievements in life.

The mid-nineteenth-century South presents the picture of a society teetering on the edge of a critical racial and gender imbalance, pushed to the brink by changes in the sectional social and economic structure. The incredible demand generated for cotton by the industrial revolution taking place in Britain and in the North made cotton the King of plantation staple crops and made the planter King as well—a King empowered by the profitability

of this crop to buy the reproductive capacity of ever larger numbers of slave women as well as to turn the domestic voice of the
women of his own class to his own self-empowerment. Almost
perversely, however, the very same industrial revolution which
served to fuel the expansion of the patriarchal power of southern planter-class men also created the basis for the emergence of
the family as a separate sphere in the North. Therefore while
reproduction remained enslaved within the plantation household economy and the voice of domestic politics was muted, it
burst forth with equally dazzling clarity in the North.[19] Northern
feminist and abolitionist women formed organizations and petitioned for fundamental changes within households and in the
society at large. Some of these women even claimed the right to
demand a single sexual standard of behavior from their men.[20]

While the emergence of a domestic critique of slavery served
to popularize the cause of abolitionism in the North by sidestep-
ping the unpopular issue of racial equality, it only served to
enflame white southern men by simultaneously attacking their
right to own slaves while threatening to empower their wives and
daughters. The North intended nothing less than to "subjugate
the South," as one southern newspaper editor wrote, "to a yoke
more intolerable than the bondage of the African." It was therefore, he concluded, the duty of every liberty-loving man to "close
the ranks, stand shoulder to shoulder as brothers animated by
one pure, patriotic impulse . . . to fight this fight out, come
what may . . . and never submit to the domination of a fanatic,
puritan horde of agrarians, abolitionists and free lovers, while
there is a dollar or a man among us."[21] After all, concluded one
planter upon the outbreak of the war, "The fight had to come.
We are men, not women."[22] For many southern men, as Bertram
Wyatt-Brown has written, the Civil War constituted a "simple test
of their manhood."[23]

Southern advocates for secession could actually argue that
northern abolitionism threatened southern white men with "a
yoke more intolerable than the bondage of the African," with no
recognition of the irony of the statement, because they truly did
not see their "African" slaves as having manhood to lose. Slavery
constructed the white man as *the* head of the household, and in
the process as the *only* legitimately independent, that is to say,

"free," member of southern society. Just as it robbed the black woman of her motherhood, so it robbed the black man of his fatherhood.

So as much as the Civil War constituted a test of white southern men's willingness to fight and die to protect their "manhood," it presented a much more fundamental challenge to enslaved black men. For as much as white southern men saw in northern abolitionist criticism a fundamental threat to the extent of their patriarchal prerogatives, for their slaves, the war opened up the possibility that they might be able to acquire the material basis for manhood in their own right. They might hope to gain the position of heads of their own economically independent households—the widely rumored outcome of Union victory among the enslaved population—forty acres and a mule for every black family. On that basis they could look forward to the day when they would be equally empowered with white southern men to protect and support their families, to become "fathers" and "husbands" in their own right.[24]

The stakes were high. The conflict was fundamental. Either the black man in his capacity as slave to the white man would go on making his master a *man,* or the white man would lose his slaves and with them his concept of himself as a free man, while the black man achieved his own manhood. The possibility that the black man might be empowered like any other was such a threat to the southern social hierarchy that some white southerners were inclined to fear not only for their position as slaveowners but for the entire basis for their claim to patriarchal power. They feared for their power not only over their slaves but over their women as well. As one white southern minister painted the likely outcome of emancipation:

> Then every negro in South Carolina and every other southern state will be his own master; nay, more than that, will be the equal of you. If you are tame enough to submit, abolitionist preachers will be at hand to consumate the marriage of your daughters to black husbands.[25]

Ever since the outbreak of the Civil War, Americans have been arguing over its causes, but rarely has the conflict been discussed as a crisis in gender relations.[26] There were, however, two groups of Americans at the time who saw its gendered face clearly. One was northern feminists such as Harriet Beecher Stowe, and the other was black Americans, especially black American men. As Frederick Douglass argued before northern audiences as early as 1858:

> The "vital question" at stake in the great sectional crisis is not whether slavery shall be extended or limited, whether the South shall bear rule or not . . . but . . . whether the four million now held in bondage are *men* [emphasis added] and entitled to the rights and liberties of men.[27]

Of course, as Frederick Douglass was painfully aware, it was not just black slaves who were denied the "rights and liberties of men." Even in the antebellum North, black men, although free in the sense of owning their own labor, were denied the political and economic prerogatives that created the basis for the antebellum social construction of manhood. Economically discriminated against, northern black men were rarely in a position to employ themselves, to therefore be the heads of economically independent households. Politically, they were frequently denied the vote, and they were *universally* denied membership in state militias and in the regular military. So the Civil War not only constituted a test of the southern black slaves' manhood, but it was also widely perceived by the northern black community as a test and an opportunity for the establishment of their own manhood as well. As one Philadelphia schoolteacher organizing black recruits told his audience:

> We have been denounced as cowards. Rise up and cast off the foul stigma. Shame on him who would hold back at the call of his country. Go with the view that you will return *free men*. And if you should never return, you will die with the satisfaction of knowing that you have struck a blow for freedom, and assisted in giving liberty to our race in the land of our birth.[28]

Surely leaders of the northern black community reasoned, if the black man was to stand by the Union in this critical juncture, if he was to offer up his life for the well-being of the nation, surely he could no longer be denied full membership in society? Frederick Douglass was convinced that the war offered the black man a rare opportunity to establish himself as truly free. He believed that a rebirth of the nation was finally at hand. Out of the destruction of the war would emerge a new nation and the glory of its founding would be shared this time·by *all* the fathers, and the inheritance would be enjoyed by *all* the sons.[29]

Upon secession and the outbreak of war, northern black men did seize their opportunity. They formed themselves into militia units and began to drill regularly. They petitioned their state governments to have the legislation removed that banned their active participation in the military. Their efforts on the drill fields were met by white mobs yelling: "We want you damned niggers to keep out of this; this is a white man's war." And according to the common northern perception of the war, the contest *was* a "white man's war."[30] It was a struggle between competing white men's visions of manhood, there was no room for the black man. Even in the face of northern military defeats and a critical shortage of Union manpower, the North refused to relent and allow black men to serve until late in 1862. They insisted, as Douglass put it, in "fighting with one arm tied behind their back." As he wrote:

> Our President, Governor, Generals and Secretaries are calling, with almost frantic vehemence, for men—Men, men! Send us men they scream, or the cause of the Union is gone . . . and yet these very officers . . . steadily and persistently refuse to receive that very class of men which have a deeper interest in the defeat and humiliation of the rebels than all other. . . . Why does the government reject the negro? Is he not a man? Can he not wield a sword, fire a gun, march and countermarch like any other?[31]

Of course, Douglass knew the answer to these questions. To take black men into the conflict was to acknowledge their manhood. The northern black community knew it and this is why they demanded the right to serve. The northern white community knew it as well, which is why they militantly claimed that it was a "white man's war." Ultimately northern white society was forced to choose—between recognizing their common manhood with black men or losing their own status as free men to the continued domination of white southern manhood, of the "slave-power," as they put it.[32] Finally, Lincoln issued the preliminary

Emancipation Proclamation in September of 1862. The Union War Department declared all slaves within captured Union territory freed and opened the door to the formation of black regiments.

The Confederate government responded to this newest challenge to their effort to defend what they saw as their liberties by making it clear that although the North might have decided to treat black men as *men* for the purposes of conducting the war, as far as they were concerned, blacks were all escaped property, and treasonous property to boot. If they were captured in Union uniform, they could receive none of the normal courtesies of war, but would instead be summarily executed.

This was truly a struggle to the death. By recognizing the slaves for their manhood, the Union was empowered with the very lifeblood of the Confederate cause. For here was the *ultimate* test of the southern social order. Would the white men's "dependents" forgo their own emancipation and continue to subordinate themselves to his empowerment? For now the war constituted not only a test of the white man's courage on the battlefield, it was also a test of his dependents' loyalty on which this courage was built. If his dependents failed to support him at this critical juncture, his cause was surely lost. The eager enlistment of ex-slaves in the northern military, the huge numbers that flocked behind Union lines whenever the opportunity to do so presented itself, was only the tip of the iceberg in the internal crumbling of the southern planter's world. Slaves that remained on the plantations slowed the work pace, and when the opportunity presented itself, they aided and abetted Union troops, leading them on back roads, supplying them with critical information.[33]

As the fiction of slave servility and childlike dependence upon the patriarchal planter dissolved in the crucible of war, it left only the subordination of southern white women—as the only dependents on whose loyalty the planter could continue to rely. As the racial and class basis for dependence slipped away, gender thus emerged as an ever more critical basis for the persistence of southern white men as "free men." Not surprisingly, Confederate men at the time and for years afterward have written in self-congratulatory tones of the loyalty that their women demonstrated during the conflict.[34] Confederate women, we are repeatedly told, constituted the "very soul of the war," offering up that which they did possess, their domestic attachments to those nearest and dearest to them, for that which they as individuals could never hope to obtain, the liberties of free men.[35] This was the discipline that the patriarchal slave system had reared them up to, to deny the interests of domesticity in the face of the interests of their class. Now, however, the necessity of placing class prerogatives over the interests of domestic life had come to their own families, rather than to those of their slaves. But they did not flinch. At least, not in public.[36]

After explaining at some length the reasons why his enlistment was necessary to defend "liberty and justice" and "true freedom," Joseph Jones closed his letter to his wife by saying, "I know my Dearest that you feel & appreciate all this, as a noble and true woman."[37] Joseph Jones relied on his wife's own sense of honor, the mirror of his own. And she did not, in fact, fail him in her reply, writing, "My beloved you are more to me than everything on earth, but I know & feel what you say is true that life would be valueless under such a rule as these miscreants would force upon us & that honor & feeling & everything else compels you to take part in this struggle."[38]

Some historians have gone so far as to argue that the women of the Confederacy were even more intensely committed to the war than were their men, packing the galleries of secessionist congresses, hissing at the delegates who opposed secession and cheering on its advocates.[39] One Selma belle was reputed to have broken off her engagement when her fiancé failed to enlist. She sent him a skirt and female undergarments with the message, "wear these or volunteer."[40] A letter of one young woman to her local newspaper upon the outbreak of war certainly reflected an intense identification with the cause:

> You will pardon the liberty I have taken to address you, when I tell you that my great inclination to do so assails me so constantly that I can only find relief in writing to you . . . My father and family have always been the strongest of Whigs, and of course not in favor of immediate secession; but as that has been the irrevocable act of the South I submit to it, and say "as goes Georgia, so go I." But at the same time I am conscious that that very act has increased our responsibilities tenfold. We have outwardly as-

sumed the garb of independence and now let us walk in the path
our state has chosen. And shall man tread it alone? . . . no, no a
thousand times no.[41]

Urging other Confederate women to join her in the cause, she
suggested that they "hurl the destructive novel in the fire and
turn our poodles out of doors, and convert our pianos into spinning wheels." Not only would this return to home manufacturing make a critical contribution to their male relation's pursuit of
political autonomy, the drive for political independence would
make Confederate women more independent as well. As she
concluded, "I feel a new life within me, and my ambition aims at
nothing higher than to become an ingenious, economical, industrious housekeeper, and an independent Southern woman."[42]
The demands of the war effort offered Confederate women a
rare opportunity. Through their contributions to the cause they
could enter into the heart of the struggle and like their men
define themselves as "independent" southern women. Women
who were independent because their privatized domestic pursuits were now thrust onto the center stage of southern life were
not in violation of their subordinated domestic status.[43] Confederate women in their role as mothers found themselves in a
particularly critical position. It was after all their children who
were the very stuff of the war machine. If men, especially young
men, were to participate in the war effort, women, especially
their mothers, would have to acquiesce in their departure. As
one newspaper noted, "The man who does not love his mother
and yield to her influence is not the right stuff to make a partiot
of, and has no business in a patriot army."[44]
With such influence came a newfound responsibility for southern women. Letters in southern papers therefore urged women
to consider the long-range impact the war might have on their
sons. "Let them not, in future years . . . be forced in sadness of
heart and reproaches of conscience, to say that in all this they
took no part." Mothers should, according to this writer, consider
with what "humiliation" sons would be forced to recognize that
they were "unworthy of the liberty and home secured for them
by the valor of others."[45] Motherhood should exert a public and
political presence.
Not only did the war serve to intensify the centrality of repro-

duction in southern society, it also gave public, political significance to the domestic manufacturing of women. For not only did
the war demand the contribution of women's reproductive product, their children, but critical economic problems now revolved
around essentially domestic questions of how the troops were to
be clothed, fed, and nursed. Cotton proved to be virtually useless
in this regard as it could not be eaten, made poor shoes, coats
and blankets, and could hardly be shot. Local newspapers urged
planters to turn their production toward subsistence crops instead and promoted the public organization of women into local
Ladies Aid Societies dedicated to organizing their previously privatized labor in order to more efficiently clothe, feed, and nurse
the troops.

From the perspective of Confederate women, patriotism took
on a peculiarly domestic cast. After offering up their children,
patriotism constituted a continued, and in fact an intensified,
commitment to the domestic labors women normally carried out
for them.[46] Upon receipt of uniforms from the Augusta Association in June of 1861, the Confederate Light Guards indicated
that such sentiments were understood and reciprocated. "Nothing can be more cheering to the soldier's heart," wrote Sergeant
Ells of the Corps, "than news from 'the loved ones at home,' but
when the news comes accompanied by such substantial tokens of
regard for him and his welfare . . . as have so recently reached
the members of this corps from the ladies of Augusta, our duties
are indeed lightened and our hearts made brave to battle for the
firesides of our noble countrywomen."[47]

While Confederate men may have gone to war in defense of
what they perceived to be their prerogatives as free men and in
rejection of the threatened domination of a "horde of agrarians,
abolitionists and free lovers,"[48] the actual demands of fighting
the war made them increasingly conscious of their own dependence upon women's love and labor. As a result the southern
soldier had to recognize, if only unconsciously, the extent to
which his manhood and independence was relational—a social
construction built upon the foundation of women's service and
love, out of the fabric of his women's "dependence." For the
more the war called forth women's domestic labor into the public
arena, making public those "small gifts of service," the more the
war itself was transformed from a struggle of men in defense of

their individual prerogatives into a battle for the "firesides of our noble countrywomen." Confederate women seized this opportunity to lay claim to an increased reciprocity in gender relations. As one woman wrote to the newspaper, ". . . do impress upon the soldiers, that they are constantly in our thoughts, that we are *working* for them, while they are *fighting* for us—and that their wants shall be supplied, as long as there is a *woman* or a *dollar* in the 'Southern Confederacy.'"[49]

Confederate women found that the war might support a newly independent stature on their part. As Rebecca Latimer Felton wrote, "Nobody chided me then as unwomanly, when I went into a crowd and waited on suffering men. No one said I was unladylike to climb into cattle cars and box cars to feed those who could not feed themselves."[50] Nor did the press find Amy Clark to be "unwomanly" when it was discovered that not only had she enlisted with her husband, but after he was killed she fought on alone in the ranks as a common soldier. She was described as "heroic *and* self-sacrificing" (emphasis added).[51] But then as Sarah Morgan recorded in her diary upon hiding a pistol and a carving knife on her person in order to defend herself against the invading Union soldiers in Baton Rouge, "Pshaw! There are *no* women here! We are *all* men!"[52]

As their women became more independent and, hence, more "male," Confederate men increasingly had to recognize their own dependence upon women, whether in managing their households in their absence, outfitting them in the field, or nursing them when wounded. Such men, in fact, became increasingly feminized. The male world of the camps was enough in and of itself to make many men think longingly of their lost domestic comforts. As Will Deloney wrote home to his wife, "Don't imagine that I have forgotten you—for I think of nobody else—and if you could see the discomfort my life held now you would conclude I could never forget. . . ."[53] Deloney had lost his mess and was forced to scramble for meals as best he could until he could get new gear. As he described his situation to his wife, "Here I am away from all I love sleeping on the wet ground, my horse poor, nothing to do, nobody to see, nothing to eat and not a pot to cook it in. . . . I smoke my pipe and think of home and try to bear it as best I may."[54]

William Deloney was shot from his horse while leading a cavalry charge in the fall of 1863. He died a hero to the cause, but he was lost to his family. He left his wife, Rosa, with four young children to carry on as best she might. In a letter written shortly after his death, a cousin urged Rosa to "take care of yourself for your dear children. Who can fill a *Mother's* place?"[55] Who indeed? Here was the expansion of the domestic autonomy of planter-class women with a vengeance, as impoverished widows.[56] For those Confederate men like Frank Coker, who were so fortunate as to survive the war and return to their homes, being a father and a husband was also at once more and less than it was before the War. For despite his wife's clever management and hard efforts at retrenchment during the war, the Cokers' finances were in great disarray.[57] The economy was devastated, their section was defeated, and their slaves were emancipated. Frank Coker was no longer the same "lord of creation" that he once was; no longer a veritable "fountain from whom all blessings flow."

The Cokers' economic loss was mirrored in their slaves' domestic gain. For the ultimate *structural* rebalancing of southern domestic relations began when the southern household was sheared apart with the emancipation of the slaves. As the freedmen departed en masse from the households of their ex-masters in search of members of their own families lost to them under slavery, they moved toward a new domestic integrity for *all* southern families. They established themselves as heads of their own households, fathers and husbands in their own right. As freedwomen turned their labor toward the needs of their own kin, withdrawing from the kitchens and the fields of the master class insofar as they were able, they laid claim to a common status with their white counterparts as wives and mothers.[58] In so doing they began to carve out what might have become a common ground for a future unity among southern women.

At the time, however, this newfound integrity of the southern family structure and the increased gender commonality of all women that it portended presented itself to planter-class women not as a victory for their gender interests but rather as the defeat of their men and of their class. For if the war served to intensify Confederate women's commitment to their men's class interests, their defeat served to set that commitment in concrete. "It was as though," in the words of one southern newspaper editor, "the mighty oak" was "hit by lightning" and only the "clinging vine" now kept it erect.[59] Planter-class women urged their men to take solace in their own family circle, a family circle which should be more valued for that which had been lost. "Your wives and children are around you," wrote one woman, "sharing your sorrows as well as your joys. Though you may not have as many luxuries as in former days, you still have enough to eat and wear and can repose in security."[60]

A retreat to familial life could make the sting of defeat more palatable, but it could not erase the necessity of subordination for defeated Confederate men. The "proud Southron" wrote one planter-class woman, Susan Cornwall, must now learn to "obey those laws which neither you nor yours had any hand in framing and those men who you fought four long years to be free from."[61] It was defeat at the hands of other men that would finally force these men to adopt a world view more like that of their dependents. For as both slaves and women of the planter class had recognized before the war, the way to accept such subordination to another man's will and yet retain some sense of self-respect was to acknowledge a master above the master—to believe that subordination on this earth was but a prelude to some ultimate self-realization in another. "Teach us Oh, Father," wrote Cornwall, "those lessons of patience and resignation which hitherto we have refused to learn and grant that once more we may lift our hearts to thee and cry *Our* father."[62]

Years later, the presiding minister at the funeral of one Confederate veteran, John Francis Shaffner, indicated the role that such religious faith could take on in the war's aftermath. He noted that it was in the daily trials of his postwar life that veterans like Shaffner had discovered the true warfare, by comparison with which the "great civil struggle was but as child's play." Though defeated, John Shaffner did not enter this deeper struggle unarmed, for he found solace in his family and "in faith" where "he committed himself to the mercy of his Savior." Through his faith Shaffner was able to achieve "a higher and blessed victory" than he could hope to attain in his daily life as a vanquished Confederate. Whatever trials worldly existence offered, "God," the mourners were reminded by the minister, had "no provision for an Appomattox." "That is not his plan. There shall be, God tells us, only victory, blessed, happy victory, ahead for all who are faithful."[63]

This lesson of victory in defeat—the proper place and power of the virtuous sufferers—was the lesson that Harriet Beecher Stowe meant to convey in the closing scene of her novel, through the story of Uncle Tom's fateful struggle with his rapacious owner, Simon Legree. For Harriet Beecher Stowe, Simon Legree represented the potentially devastating consequences of a male domination untempered by a recognition of the domestic claims of either his own family or that of his slaves. Running away to sea as a young man and abandoning his poor mother to die of a broken heart, Legree had eventually ended up in the South. There he acquired a plantation and many slaves, but never a home and a loving wife. Living in domestic squalor, he sexually exploited his female slaves while he worked all his field hands to exhaustion. Uncle Tom in fact sacrificed his own life to protect one of the slave women on the plantation from Legree's sexual abuse.

In the character of Uncle Tom, Harriet Beecher Stowe presented what she considered to be the highest exemplar of moral social behavior among men; men who, motivated by a keen sense of their own humility, turned their energies to upholding the human rights of those who were even more subordinated in the world than themselves. From this feminized vantage point, the defeat of the Confederacy and the economic difficulties of the region that followed upon it were perhaps not an unmitigated loss. The possibility of some gain ensued from the expanded significance and integrity that domestic life achieved. By sacrificing his own life, Uncle Tom had succeeded in forcing Simon Legree to recognize some limits to his power to dominate others. For although Legree won the battle and killed Uncle Tom, he was forced to acknowledge that he had lost the war for his soul. Through the moral power of his ultimate sacrifice, Tom found a better home, one in which he would be freed from the defeats and oppression he had endured in this world. "I'm right in the door," he gasped with his final breath, "I've got the victory."[64]

For one brief moment in the course of the war itself, as advancing Union forces intensified the erosion of slavery that was already occurring from within, it had appeared that the defeat of the Confederate war effort would underwrite the earthly victory of the enslaved southern black population. The land would be redistributed and freedmen would acquire their forty acres and a mule and thereby their status as "free men" as it had been constructed in the antebellum social order. At the same time, it appeared that the subordinated status of motherhood would also be at least mitigated as the abolition of slavery promised to ratify the increased public status and significance that domestic concerns had gained during the war. The collapse of the slave plantation household in war and reconstruction did indeed fundamentally limit the extent to which some men could define their own status as free men by the measure of the limits of freedom on others. It did set certain structural limits to the subordination of reproduction and the family to the interests of the market. Families could no longer be bought or sold. It did not, however, create the basis for racial or gender equality in this country. For although the planter class was defeated, it was not vanquished. They lost their ownership in slaves, but not their control of the land. As a result, the war left white southern men feeling like less than men. It left black men with a manhood that frequently continued to cost them their lives. It left white southern women clinging to what was left of white southern men's ability to provide, and, all too often, it left black southern women with no alternative but to work in some white woman's kitchen. All men were not created equal and few women found themselves even comparatively free.

Chapter 2

XXXXXXXXXXXXXXXXXXXXXXXXX

The Politics of Yeoman Households
in South Carolina

STEPHANIE McCURRY

Sometime in the fall of 1855, on the coast of South Carolina, Ralph Elliott, the son of a very wealthy planter, and a "vulgar" neighbor named Price came to blows over Price's relationship to the slaves on Elliott's "PonPon" plantation. Convinced that Price had been engaged in illegal trade with the PonPon slaves, Elliott had "knocked him down," an insult Price had answered with two pistol shots in Elliott's face, "so close as to burn him with the powder," but which missed their mark and "shot through his hat."[1] The yeoman Price had refused to play slave to Elliott's master.

Planters had always been touchy about the question of illegal trading with slaves, regarding it as the opening wedge of abolitionism. They were usually content to harass slaves and allegedly incendiary strangers. But in the 1850s, with sectional tensions heightened, they turned their formidable police powers on the vulnerable white men of their own communities, inviting the charge that theirs was "a combination to oppress the poor." It was a risky and sometimes explosive strategy. For yeoman farmers such as Price, who became the objects of planter suspicion, were touchy too—about the rights due them as freemen in a slave society.[2] And as the younger Elliott was to learn, yeomen brought to the struggle with planters considerable means, both legal and customary, with which to compel recognition of the social and political identity to which they laid passionate claim.

The neophyte Elliott thought the case against Price open and shut: the man had shot at him. His more experienced father, however, had no such illusions and proceeded to instruct him in the complex lineaments of power in lowcountry Carolina. The paramount legal issue, William Elliott informed his son, was whether he was justified in his attack on Price in the first place. And that, William explained, had nothing to do with the evidence against Price, and everything to do with the location of the assault: "If you had attacked him in his house, he would escape punishment on the plea that his house was his castle and that you had invaded him—but if the case happened as you write—and you can prove it—he must smart for it."[3] Elliott thereby exposed a key spatial dimension of class and, as we will see, of gender relations in the slave South: the virtually unlimited right of an independent man to mastery over his own household, or "enclosure," as it was often called.[4]

In South Carolina, as in the other slave states, the household was a spatial unit, defined as the property to which the owner not only held legal title but over which he exercised exclusive use rights. It was, however, much more than that, for in societies in which landed property comprised the chief means of subsistence, as it did in South Carolina, legal title to land had historically incorporated claims over the persons and labor of those who were dependents on it. The household thus was also the constituent unit of antebellum society, organizing the majority of the population—women, children, and slaves—in relations of legal and customary dependency to the propertied male head.[5] In this one crucial respect, it mattered not whether the household head was yeoman or planter, whether he owned 150 acres and no slaves or 1000 acres and 200 slaves. Even in the South Carolina lowcountry, the legendary land of southern "aristocracy," there were limits to planter power and the most powerful planter was bound to concede his neighbor's dominion over his own household, however modest.

The fundamental principle of masterhood and its complicated consequences embodied all the forces of conflict and cohesion between the region's planter elite and its yeoman majority. The yeomanry's commitment to the institution of slavery, nowhere deeper than in the black-belt South, to the household social relations it protected and the particular republicanism it permitted, was located in that most intimate and yet public of identities. A great deal was at stake in planter respect for the yeoman claim to independence and to masterhood, as William Elliott knew. The more experienced man had given his brash son a pointed introduction to the politics of yeoman households.

Ralph Elliott could not have been instructed by a more astute observer. As a politician, avid sportsman, early conservationist, and author of *Carolina Sports by Land and Water,* William Elliott had reflected deeply on property rights and class relations, particularly as they pertained to the politics of hunting. *Carolina Sports* has been interpreted primarily as proof of the persistence in the antebellum South of common rights to hunt on unenclosed land, a principle and practice that had been eradicated in the northeast, as in England in an earlier period, with the capitalist transformation of the countryside. But if customary respect for common rights was one side of the regional coin, then the religious respect for "the rights of private property . . . in our community," as William Elliott put it, was distinctly the other.[6]

In many ways, Elliott's text was an extended consideration of the ongoing problem of defining boundaries: between privately owned land to which proprietors had exclusive claim, and privately owned land to which the community customarily claimed use rights. The problem plagued not only Elliott but South Carolina's jurists and juries as well.[7] Amidst the confusion and conflict, however, one clear principle emerged: proprietors' rights followed their fences. The only spatially and temporally fixed boundary of private property was drawn by the fences that surrounded cultivated fields and dwelling houses on plantations and farms. As Elliott lamented, a man's land "is no longer his (except in a qualified sense) unless he encloses it. In other respects, it is his neighbors', or anybody's." What jury would convict, he noted conversely, "if the trespass was not committed by entering his own enclosure." The only thing as certain as the community's jealous regard for common rights to hunt, fish, and forage stock on unenclosed land was their jealous regard for that property bounded by the fence. "[I]t is the broad common law maxim," Elliott admitted, "that everything upon a man's land is his own . . . and he can thus shut it out from his neighbor without wrong to him." Jurists upheld that judgment in a series of trespass cases, etching the fence deeply in the legal cartography of power.[8] In the process, they defined the boundaries of the household, established its legal integrity as a private space, and rendered the authority of the master over it virtually absolute.

This principle undergirded the complex politics of yeoman households.[9] For when jurists ruled on the rights of proprietors they made no distinction between planters and yeomen. The relevant term in their vocabulary (as in political discourse) was "freemen," among whose ranks the yeoman majority, however poor, proudly numbered themselves. Freemen's rights were vigilantly guarded at law, as befitted a society that called itself republican, and they were indissociable from those which accompanied property ownership.

Among a "free man's" rights, all concurred, was the right to exclusive use of the property within his enclosure.[10] Property, however, took many forms in South Carolina, as it did in the rest of the slave South. Thus what jurists in effect outlined in their decisions were the legal parameters of a social and political system that might best be described as a propertied patriarchy. Yeoman heads of household were embraced within that system as surely as were their planter counterparts.

The medieval language jurists commonly used in their decisions—in references to "churlish" proprietors and "descendants of the Baron's bold," for example—suggested the relations of power that property law supported and fences enclosed.[11] Indeed, the law elided distinctions between forms of property, rendering a man's control over his enclosure synonymous with his control over the familial and extra-familial dependents within it. In one case, Judge Nott explained that assault and battery was justified if the defendant could prove that the victim "has traduced his character, had insulted his wife or daughter, or that he had found him within his enclosure attempting to steal his goods or to excite his negroes to insurrection." A man had the right to defend what was his own. So a man was justified in injuring one who attempted to dispossess him of his land and goods, just as "a parent may justify a battery in defence of the wife or the child."[12] Where the boundaries of enclosures were inviolable, property rights and power over dependents were inextricable. As property-holders—as freemen—yeoman farmers thus were masters, as surely as were the wealthiest planters. That was the valuable lesson William Elliott had taught his overweening son; that was the public identity Price had enforced with a pistol. The yeomanry's prerogatives as freemen and masters were rooted in the same principles and practices of propertied patriarchy as were planters'.

This common ground, and the tenuous alliance it nurtured among the enfranchised white male elite, left an indelible mark on all of the crucial political issues of antebellum South Carolina, and especially on slavery and secession. As masters of small worlds in the land of great planters, yeoman farmers admittedly inhabited a strangely privileged and compromised space. For if all men were masters, they were by no measure equally so. A larger and more complex world lay outside the fence and on that terrain yeomen found it more difficult to prevail. Yet in the fall of 1860, the enormity of the common struggle that confronted masters in defense of the slave republic rendered insignificant, for all but a few South Carolinians, the characteristic skirmishings of yeomen and planters. Then, common purpose overwhelmed particular interest as the free men of the state rose with unprecedented unity to carry secession and to lead the South in its tragic and reactionary quest for a permanent republic of slavery. Constrained and compromised as they were by planter power, the yeoman majority's political ideology and imperatives, out of which secession emerged as the only possible choice, were nonetheless resolutely moored in the politics of the household.

To view yeoman politics from this perspective is, however, to compel reinterpretation. For while historians have long acknowledged that planter politics were grounded in the experience of masterhood, which is to say in the domination of household dependents, few have considered the possibility that the yeomanry's politics were similarly grounded.[13] Instead, most interpretations have focused on the political meaning of independent proprietorship, and particularly on its egalitarian impulses with respect to planter prerogatives in the public sphere. Committed, above all else, to the reproduction of independence, and convinced that slavery buttressed their efforts, the yeoman majority, historians have insisted, was drawn into alliance with planters in defense of slavery and advocacy of secession. Thus have proslavery yeomen been represented as the democratic presence within the southern body politic.[14]

If relations of power within the household, and their public meaning, are fundamentally obscured by this perspective, as I would argue, so then is the yeomanry's politics. For yeomen, no less than planters, rested their claim to republican independence and equality in the public sphere on the command of dependents in the household. The everyday experience of personal domination—over the few slaves they may have owned, and just as importantly over the women they assumed it their natural right to rule—literally engendered the identity of masterhood in all of those independent freemen. And it shaped their politics as profoundly as relations with local and state elites. Viewed from the perspective of the household, the yeoman majority appear unlikely candidates to carry the torch of equality and democracy. Indeed, so located, their politics appear much more contradictory and much more purposefully complicit in the entrenchment of slavery than historians have previously allowed.

After all, yeoman households were, by definition, those in which familial and productive relations were almost indistinguishable, and in which both were defined by a series of dependencies that subordinated all members to the male head. For "self-working farmers," the term lowcountry plainfolk employed to distinguish themselves from planters, were landowning nonslaveholders and small slaveholders whose ownership of slaves was not sufficient to render their labor managerial. In yeoman households family members comprised the chief labor supply.[15] Discussion of the politics of yeoman households, logically begins, therefore, in the household with the organization of work, and particularly with its gender dimensions.[16]

Any number of factors shaped the particular configuration of labor on family farms, including the total number of household members, their sex and age, the stage in the family cycle, and, in antebellum southern households, the presence of slaves whether

hired or owned, and their sex and age. But in yeoman households the work done by wives, sons, and daughters was necessarily a part of the calculus of production. Reproducing independence involved a productive strategy designed to accomplish
self-sufficiency and limit market engagement.[17] In ways that historians have rarely acknowledged, however, it was achieved by a
gender division of labor in which women's work in the fields and
in the provision of subsistence and market goods proved a key
component.

Moreover, because sons could eventually reproduce their fathers' role as heads of independent households—a chief goal of
the yeomanry's strategy—the patriarch's more permanent power
over female dependents was an enduring legacy of the politics of
the household and one with perhaps more public significance.
The control and discipline of women's labor and the assumptions of natural authority that accompanied it sustained the
vaunted independence of the male yeomanry and their claim to
equality in the slave republic.

It is not so much that historians have denied the value of
women's labor in the yeoman household economy; it is, rather,
that they do not know what meaning to attach to it.[18] But as in all
households, then and now, complex structures and relations lay
within and gave definition to public postures. Antebellum political commentators knew the meaning of women's work in yeoman households. They knew, for example, that they had to encourage the products of women's labor to sustain self-sufficiency
at the level of the household and independence at the sectional
level as a proslavery strategy. The centrality of women's work in
such admittedly ill-fated strategies was clear. When in the heat of
Nullification the Pendelton Farmers' Society initiated an anti-
tariff campaign, they decided that their members should appear
at the next meeting "dressed *entirely in the Homespun of the
district,*"—a gratifying acknowledgment of the yeomanry's true
republican style and of women's traditional craft skills. But they
went further, voting to cancel the annual prizes for stock and
grain, believing that "the encouragement of our household industry [is] the only means within our reach to avert in some
measure the inferior effects of this . . . act." Instead, prizes
were awarded only for cuts of plain and twilled homespun of

cotton or wool, for linen diapers, coverlids, imitation gingham cloth, for wool and cotton stockings, and for butter and cheese. Women, then, received all of the premiums in recognition of their work in the reproduction of independence. And if yeoman women's work acquired added value in political crisis, it was not entirely neglected in quieter times.[19] What politicians had done in their romantic dreams of southern independence was to elevate to a sectional political strategy the practices that constituted the yeomanry's usual bid for independence.

Yeoman farmers, and the merchants who kept their accounts, knew the structural meaning of women's work better than politicians. For one thing, farmers knew that they managed to achieve an impressive degree of self-sufficiency because, in addition to the corn staple, virtually everything their families ate women grew or raised, preserved and cooked, and virtually everything they wore women spun and wove, dyed and sewed. By their industry wives and daughters ensured that nothing was purchased that could be produced at home, whatever the cost in labor and sweat. In antebellum yeoman households women contributed more than the services and skills that continue to represent the unpaid labor of wives and mothers; they contributed as well the production of goods for household consumption that had elsewhere already passed into the realm of the market. "I have been down at York today," yeoman wife Mary Davis Brown noted in her diary, and "I did not by much of enything."[20] If yeoman farmers escaped relations of serious debt and dependency with local merchants and planters, then they knew that the accomplishment was as much their wives' as their own.

Merchants knew, moreover, that yeoman families managed to keep their account balances manageable, not just with the annual influxes of credit from the sale of two or three bales of cotton or surplus corn, but also with the steady trickle of "country produce" that testified to women's ability to turn household production to market exchange. Although intended chiefly for the household, the products of women's labor regularly appeared on the credit side of the ledger in store accounts and petty trade with local planters; and presumably they figured as well in the informal exchanges, virtually impossible to document, between yeoman households. Eggs, chickens, feathers, butter, tallow, and especially homespun cloth were sufficiently important to local trade to figure prominently in the advertisements of village and crossroads merchants. "I feel like eating chicken and eggs, please bring me some," one enterprising rural Orangeburg merchant bantered in an illustrated advertisement.[21] The value of such transactions hardly approached that of the annual sale of the cotton crop, but the twenty-three dollars and fifty cents that Mary Davis Brown was paid for the "web of janes cloth" she sold in York in 1858 must have been a significant contribution to the perennially cash-poor household.[22]

There was one further contribution women made to the work of independence, one that contemporary southerners were less willing to acknowledge. And that was their labor, and especially that of their daughters, in the fields. Northern and European travelers, by contrast, invariably remarked upon the phenomenon. Frederick Law Olmsted, for one, insisted that he had "in fact, seen more white native American women at work in the hottest sunshine in a single month, and that near mid-summer, than in all my life in the free states, not on account of an emergency, as in harvesting, either, but in the regular cultivation of cotton and of corn, [but] chiefly of cotton." This almost anthropological interest in the subject reflected passionately held but newly constructed truths about women's physiology and nature, and about the "natural" gender divisions of spheres and labor that pertained among the ascendant American and European bourgeoisie. In the transgression against white womanhood that Northern and European observers claimed to have witnessed in the yeomanry's fields, they found confirmation of their faith in the superiority of free-labor society. Frances Trollope's harsh judgment of yeoman men and sympathy for their wives, those "slaves of the soil" as she called them, was thus a foreigner's gross misunderstanding of gender and class relations in the slave South.[23]

Trollope captured an essential truth, nonetheless. And it is one that has typically eluded historians, perhaps because they too remain captive to bourgeois ideas about separate spheres and the "natural" gender division of labor, insisting, despite the evidence, that field work was men's work, except, of course, for slaves. In taking this position, historians have inadvertently deepened a contemporary southern silence on the subject that owed to very different sensibilities about the gender conventions of slave society. Contemporaries of all classes were aware that the labor yeoman farmers commanded in the fields included that of their wives and daughters, but few public men showed the poor political judgment to acknowledge it.[24] A collusive silence surrounded one of the labor practices that most clearly distinguished yeoman farms from plantations, that set planter wives and daughters apart from their yeoman counterparts, that dangerously eroded the social distinctions between free women and slaves, and that could cut so deeply into the pride of men raised in a culture of honor. Out of respect for yeoman masters and particularly for their votes, planter politicians refrained.

The political meaning of the gender division of labor and authority, moreover, went beyond structures of independence to support the construction and reproduction of the identity of a "free man" in the master of the household. Historians have found it difficult to know with any certainty how yeoman farmers deployed their families' labor, and have been able only to speculate about how it shaped relations with household dependents, with the slaves whose labor they owned or hired, and with all manner of subordinates and superordinates in their black-belt communities. But one very rare treasure, a yeoman farmer's journal, confirms some of the labor patterns discernible in the more intransigent public records, and suggests how they supported the manly public identity of its author.

James F. Sloan's journals of the operation of his Spartanburg farm from 1854 to 1861 provide a tantalizing glimpse into the world of a hardworking yeoman farmer who assiduously recorded the tasks performed by each member of his household on the 60 improved acres that he cultivated. In 1854, that household consisted of himself, a 34-year-old native-born South Carolinian, his second wife, Dorcas Lee Sloan, three children from his first marriage (a son Seth who was 15 or 16 years old and two daughters Sarah-Jane and Barbara who were about 13 and 14 years old respectively), and at least two other children (James Haddon and an unnamed baby girl) from his marriage with Dorcas. For only one year, 1859, did that household include a slave, a girl named Manda, whom Sloan hired for $4 a month.[25]

If there ever was any doubt about the strategies by which yeoman farmers reproduced independence in the absence of significant numbers of slave laborers, Sloan's journal puts it to rest, along with any lingering notions that field labor marked an absolute class divide between southern women, slave and free. Sloan put his "wimmin" to work in the fields regularly throughout the year, from at least late spring to the end of picking season in December.[26] In June 1856, for example, while he and Seth harrowed the cotton and corn fields, "the wimmin commenced hoeing cotton in the lot field." Prior to that, since May, the "chilldren" had been thinning out the cotton, and in June they were joined by "the wimmin" who hoed first the corn and then the cotton fields. By July 5, Sloan noted, the "girls had finished the cotton," and by July 15 his crop was laid by. The children went to school briefly in August, but by September 2 they were back in the fields "pulling fodder," and by September 15 the cotton was "right smartly open," and picking season began. Sloan did not note the length of the picking season in 1856, but in 1858 it started on September 8 and continued until November 30, during which time the "chilldren" and the "balance of the family" picked cotton while he and Seth periodically attended to other tasks.[27]

Each year the tempo of work differed slightly. In June 1857, in one tragic interruption of the seasonal cycle, Dorcas Lee Sloan took "very bad," and later that day gave birth to "a still born babe"; she stayed out of the fields for a time after that. A little more than a year later she was again absent from the fields, but this time the reason was a joyous one. "Mrs Sloan sent out and presented me with a very fine girl child," Sloan recorded with evident pride on July 7.[28] What Dorcas Lee Sloan thought is left to the imagination.

Mrs. Sloan did not work in the fields for some time after the baby was born; in fact, it is possible that her husband decided to hire the slave girl to compensate for the field labor lost as a result. But conventional definitions of labor notwithstanding, in giving birth to a little girl, Mrs. Sloan made a fundamental contribution to the household economy. For the reproduction of independence required, above all else, the reproduction of the labor force. Children were, among other things surely, precious assets in the relentless struggle to keep the farm.[29]

The particular allocation of labor and tasks changed along with the family life cycle. Yet every year Sloan's family, including his teenage daughters and, with less regularity, his wife, worked in the fields steadily from May until December, enabling them to produce sufficient subsistence and market crops to maintain their status as a respectable yeoman family. And if, unlike some other yeoman farmers' daughters, Sloan's girls were spared the indignity of driving a plow, the farm chore perhaps most clearly demarcated as masculine, it was, at least in 1859, because another young woman assumed that burden: the slave Manda who joined Seth Sloan in the fields and matched him task for task the year round.[30] Manda's presence did not, needless to say, relieve the Sloan women of the burden of field work, never mind of housework.

It was startling how easily Sloan appeared to manage the adjustment to masterhood, however temporary, of a slave. Manda was introduced to his established labor system with little apparent disruption—extending it, but not transforming it. On the first day that Sloan put Manda to work, he simply noted "Seth and Manda hauled wood and rails," and thereafter she worked alongside Seth. Sloan's was an adjustment facilitated, no doubt, by years of commanding the labor of his other dependents, the "wimmin," "girls," "boyes," and "chilldren" who peopled his journal and cultivated the fields.[31]

The gender division of labor on Sloan's farm evinced a great deal more flexibility than the relations of power which apparently underlay it. Yet not all dependents were equally subordinated to the head; and not only because one was a slave. Manda did occupy a position of particular dependence within Sloan's household. But his wife and daughters did as well. Indeed, the very different trajectories of the coming of age of Sloan's eldest son and daughter suggest the generational reproduction of gendered relations of power, which had important implications for the assumptions yeomen brought to public political debate.

There can be no doubt that Sloan's eldest son, Seth, labored under his father's authority throughout the 1850s, finding himself "sent" to do specific tasks on and off the farm. But there can also be no doubt that he was being prepared to assume his father's role. Not only was Seth increasingly assigned independent jobs on the farm; he was gradually introduced to the community of independent men and that of their sons and heirs.

With increasing regularity, Seth took his father's place in labor exchanges with neighbors and kinsmen, and on trips to the grist mill and cotton screw, country store and tavern. These were the sites of male sociability, some of which, not incidentally, also provided the social location of electoral politics and the rituals of manhood within which they were enacted. Country stores, for example, commonly doubled as taverns, and purchases were rarely made without the company of a "dram" or two, some "segars," and a chat about the usual—the crops, the weather, the politicians. Since household accounts were kept in the name of the male head, marketing often coincided with militia musters, sale days, and court weeks, which deepened the connection with drinking and politicking. It all came together during militia musters and election season, when captains and politicians, often one in the same man, treated at the local store to shore up their men's loyalties. It was particularly handy when the store was also the polling station, which was often the case in rural lowcountry districts. It was all part, as one "retired private" put it, of the "Bust-head" system. Country stores, in short, were anything but the womanly and domesticated terrain they were fast becoming in northern cities.[32] This was one of the places yeoman sons were intitiated into the culture of freemen.

Although Seth still worked under his father, he gradually came to stand beside him as well, a coming of age perhaps ritually marked in Sloan's journal by the entry of April 6, 1859, when, for the first time, Seth accompanied him to court day at Spartanburg. It was almost certainly a moment of ritualistic significance when father and son first worked together cultivating cotton in the field called "Seth's patch," in April of 1860.[33] The economic and political foundations of his own claim to independence had been laid. The only coming of age Sloan marked for his daughter Barbara was a brief note of her marriage, a ritual that we can be sure conferred authority, but of a different, and much more circumscribed, kind.[34]

Yeoman daughters did not enjoy a long apprenticeship in the culture of freemen. Instead, their entry into adulthood was most commonly marked by evangelical conversion—the struggle to submit to God's will representing, perhaps, proper prologue to the submission demanded of Christian wives. Daughters came of age into their mothers' world, the world inside the enclosure, ushered in with a brief ceremony, commemorated with "sider," perhaps a few "wedding trimens," and a model of female excellence that made the submission of self the apotheosis of womanhood.[35]

Assumptions about gender and power thus were reproduced within yeoman households. Some, like Barbara Sloan and, in profoundly different ways, Manda, retained the identity of dependents permanently. They represented the foundations of masterhood for those, like Seth, who reproduced the paternal claim to independence and to the public recognition and privileged political position that accompanied it in the slave South. Manliness, masterhood, and republican citizenship were based upon the domination of dependents. The politics of the household *was* the politics of the public sphere in antebellum South Carolina.[36] For the yeomanry, that was at once an empowering and compromising truth.

Masterhood and its public recognition shaped the yeomanry's place in the political culture of slavery. The experience of independent proprietorship nurtured a fierce commitment to their legal and customary rights—such as those Ralph Elliott had been forced to concede. But it also engendered the belief that such rights were the privilege only of independent men, such as themselves. Yeomen did indeed press mighty planters for a greater share of power and resources. But they also, and more importantly, found common cause with planters in constructing and policing the exclusionary boundaries of the public sphere in the slave republic. After all, in their churches, marketplaces, courthouses, and electoral districts, black-belt yeomen moved as members of a privileged minority of independent and enfranchised men amidst a sea of dependent and disenfranchised people. As good republicans, they recognized domestic dependencies and inequalities as the necessary social conditions of public freedoms and equalities. And in the antebellum South, where the defense of "our domestic institution" was the paramount political issue, that recognition went a long way toward legitimizing slavery.

Nothing so quickly captures the public meaning of the politics of yeoman households than the uses to which proslavery ideologues and politicians put it. In seeking to legitimize slavery, ideologues constantly invoked domestic analogies, likening slaves' position in the "familial" order to that of women and children. Marriage took pride of place in the lexicon of metaphors for slavery: no other social relation was so universally embraced as both natural and divine, and none so readily evoked the state of enfranchised white men, yeomen and planters alike, in the defense of slave society. In settling on marriage as the dominant metaphor for slavery, ideologues recognized that the politics of the majority reflected domestic relations of power, and thereby made a bid to put the defense of slavery on the broadest possible social basis.[37]

That yeomen saw the connections between private dependencies, public freedoms, and the defense of slavery is hardly to be doubted. They were surely aware that their own patriarchal prerogatives were upheld by juries and legislators in the name of slavery. Yet unlike intellectuals and planter politicians, lowcountry farmers articulated their worldview piecemeal, in actions more frequently than in texts. The reconstruction of those values and judgments goes well beyond the purview of this essay. There is, however, little reason to assume, as historians have typically done, that yeomen were an insurgent democratic majority within plantation regions. To the contrary, they inscribed their own commitment to hierarchical social relations, political inequality, and slavery in every institution of community-life: in their own households, as we have seen; in evangelical churches where they reproduced secular household hierarchies in the name of "familial" Christian social order; in petitions to the legislature as "free men" for tougher policing of private property; in votes on state rights and conservative republicanism in national politics; and in the exclusionary character of the polity at home. The common ground of free men and masters produced a momentous alliance between yeomen and planters on the crucial issues of southern politics. Although unstable, it held its disparate elements together until the Civil War, when in many places it flew apart to be hinged again by an entirely different set of privileges and compromises.

To argue that the yeomanry's politics was moored in the

household is not, however, to argue for a gender determinism, and for a consensual and egalitarian public sphere of masters.[38] Even as it maintained an uneasy peace, the alliance of yeomen and planters did not constitute an egalitarian democracy, not even within the gerrymandered boundaries of the propertied and manly republican political sphere. For in the inevitable contest for authority outside enclosures, and for access to state power, yeomen found themselves overpowered. They had purchased their prerogatives at great cost indeed.

Yeoman farmers were committed to the defense of social hierarchy and political privilege—including slavery—in large measure because of the relations of personal domination on which their independence rested. But the very principles on which yeomen and planters found agreement—the rights of freemen and the prerogatives of masters—drew yeomen into a political culture and ideology in which planter power was difficult to deny. Planter control over vast tracts of land and legions of dependents left yeomen overmatched. They had gained masterhood, but they had also conceded the only ground on which they might have contested planters' claims as masters to rule over lesser men in the public sphere. They were left, as a result, with few resources to represent effectively their particular interests as small farmers in a state dominated by planters.

The yeomanry's passionate commitment to independence and equality betrayed an equally passionate commitment to dependence and desperate inequality. That was the nature of slavery republicanism. And the yeomanry's unwavering commitment to it was engendered in the politics of their own households. Egalitarian democracy would have been their undoing; slavery republicanism was the bedrock of their identity as masters. Yeomen, thus, were deeply complicit in the broad terms of antebellum southern politics—the defense of slavery and the rule of the planter class. Empowered by the politics of the household, they were simultaneously disempowered by it: masters of small worlds in the land of great planters.

In the reactionary revolution that South Carolina finally unleashed on the nation in the fall of 1860, yeoman farmers played the majority, if not the leading, part. Voting for secessionist representatives, resolving to renounce the Union and praying for God's blessing on disunion, joining vigilante societies and minute-men associations, and recording the rush of nascent Confederate pride, yeoman farmers revealed resolute faith in the necessity of secession. In the fall of 1860 South Carolina's masters, yeoman and planter, together struck a manly blow for the true and only Christian republic, the republic of slavery.

PART II

xxxxxxxxxxxxxxxxxxxxxxxx

Men at War

*T*he call to arms clearly divides any nation. Some of these divisions are matters of choice: civilian or soldier, ally or enemy, traitor or patriot. At the same time the onset of battle can sharpen other divides—such as those between children and adults, men and women. And war creates mythic boundaries: those who march off and those who remain at home, inextricably bound.

War made different demands on men and women and initiated a new discourse on gender roles. Although poets and scholars have celebrated men's wartime experience—exalting warrior, mourning fallen heroes—new discoveries about the Civil War's unique impact on nineteenth century manhood emerge afresh despite reams of previously published material. Absent husbands and fathers, facing battle, strike a chord among Americans even a century and a half later. The meaning of war and its dramatic shaping of individual men almost always conjure powerful responses, from Stephen Crane's **Red Badge of Courage** to Denzel Washington's award-winning performance in **Glory,** featured in Jim Cullen's essay.

The power of war to affect male identity, literally to define cultural perceptions of manhood, seems clear. Both Union and Confederate folklore are full of stories of women spurning suitors who do not prove their manhood through enlistment. The very act of donning the uniform connotes a change in status, one so keenly perceived by adolescent males that both armies contained boys who had barely entered their teens. The male pledge to protect home and hearth had to be channeled into a patriotic movement which tore men from households and carried the risk they might never return. These temporary separations from family and community were moments of rare reflection for many men.

When faced with a permanent separation from all they held dear—through death—they might reflect on their values and actions. War clarified for many men their own emotional responses; men's wartime letters and diaries offer us rare insight into not only the personal meanings of war but the new sense of manhood forged in battle.

The leap from boyhood into manhood, as Reid Mitchell illuminates, was accelerated by wartime. He emphasizes the fragile state of this newly evolved manhood—that those very boys turned into men might become less than men if the seasoning of battle became too harsh. As soldiers they were necessarily hardened, but in the process they might become de-humanized. The constraints of wartime entangled gender demands and with war's heightened pitch, Mitchell demonstrates, could provide for a more sensible balance: even manly men were able to cry, especially over thoughts of loved ones at home. Becoming a warrior might blur as well as sharpen the gendered responses for those caught up in war—as men were allowed to weep, women were expected to remain stoic and industrious, a near role reversal.

The tests of courage created by war were not the only trials endured by soldiers. One Massachusetts volunteer, examined by David Blight, faced ideological conflicts as well, as his vision of war's aims shifted over time. The impact of "contraband," Blight chronicles, was incalculable as men from Lincoln to the enslaved man himself were forced to redefine both manhood and the purpose of the Union. Race was, in many ways, a key component in war's redefinition of manhood, both North and South.

As Jim Cullen outlines, the way in which African American males exploited the opportunity to seize and refine the notion of manhood is one of the most dramatic chapters of wartime. The conflicted notions of status and class before and during the bloodshed created their own fearful battleground as politicians and disfranchised, as statesmen and soldiers, wrestled with these costly issues of right and wrong.

Gender was literally bound into conceptions of liberation for the emancipated man, just as race hedged gender definitions in mid-century America. Central to black men's sense of freedom were their experiences coming into manhood—a state emphatically denied by slave status. Ironically, as Cullen features, men's lives took on the most meaning as they risked death, a steep price for selfhood which thousands of former slaves paid.

Men caught in the whirlwind of battle not only experienced the *personal identity crises manhood engendered but explored kalei-doscopic changes which would transform the culture as well. The nar-ratives of men at war in some sense do not merely memorialize individ-ual experience or chronicle battles. Instead they represent the shared meanings of war which can even transcend racial and regional boundaries. As black and white, North and South, boys and men came together in the multiple and myriad experiences of war, those who survived did so unified by their baptism in blood. Thus redeemed, the warriors might not share loyalties or world-views, but the bonds of manhood.*

Chapter 3

XXXXXXXXXXXXXXXXXXXXXXXXXXX

Soldiering, Manhood, and Coming of Age: A Northern Volunteer

REID MITCHELL

When Abraham Lincoln first ran for President, Cyrus F. Boyd was already twenty-four years old. Nevertheless he would later say that he and the other Republican boys of Palmyra, Iowa, "organized a company of young men just young enough and strong enough to do some tall yelling." They must have been a sight—each one wearing blue overalls, white shirts, and "a chip hat," riding horseback to electioneer for Lincoln. "We were supposed to be assisting Abraham Lincoln to be elected President and everybody now knows that he was elected." The horses, he later confessed, were really colts. "We not only had to break and drill ourselves but had to break the *colts* also and at the same time."

This frolicking lot of young politicians became one of the companies Iowa contributed to the Union war effort. "When our man Lincoln called for men to suppress the insurrection we did not respond the first time but at the next call we left the colts at home and went almost to [a] *boy*." The word "boy" and indeed the emphasis are not mine but Boyd's himself, when he looked back years later at the events of the Civil War. Later in life, Boyd took his wartime diary and rewrote it into an account of his months in the Fifteenth Iowa Infantry Regiment, the regiment in which he served until he left to become an officer in another outfit. This autobiography, a mixture of a young man's diary and an old man's reflections, he sent to a friend of his who had soldiered with him in the Fifteenth Iowa. Cyrus F. Boyd self-consciously molded his autobiographical tale of service in the army into a story about a boy becoming a man—making soldiering a coming-of-age experience. He obviously expected his friend would recognize this story and share this understanding of their youthful joint service in the Union army.[1]

This vision, this credo of masculinity, maturation, and military service, was hardly unique to Cyrus F. Boyd or to the Civil War. Both during the years 1861 through 1865 and all through the postwar period, as Americans tried to make sense of their war, they linked the transformation of the civilian into soldier and the passage of a boy into adulthood. At the minimum, the relationship was twofold. First, with a great number of American youth—defined roughly as those still living within a parental household—joining the army, those who lived through the war emerged at the age traditionally associated with full manhood. They "came of age" during the war and the war had to be part of that experience. Second, the very ideas of man, soldier, and citizen were inextricably linked. Remaining a civilian was thought unmanly; going to war a proof of manhood. Since coming of age means not simply becoming an adult but assuming adult gender roles—becoming a man—popular thought sometimes conflated the two transformations. And so did many of the young men who served in the armies.[2]

Considering the age of many Union soldiers, as well as that of their Confederate counterparts, the stress on war as a maturing process is hardly surprising. Gerald Linderman notes that "in both armies, eighteen-year-olds constituted the single largest age group the first year of the war."[3] The men who served in the Union companies habitually referred to themselves as the boys, as did their officers and civilians, and nobody seems to have taken offense at the term. What strikes us now is how elderly Civil War armies were compared with the ones produced by mass conscription in the twentieth century. But nonetheless, from 1861 to 1865, many American men spent in the army the period of late adolescence and early adulthood usually associated with coming of age.

Cyrus F. Boyd felt the change begin in his initial weeks of service. The first sign that the young soldier was entering man's estate may have come from the flattering attention of the young women both back home and in other Iowa towns. In his diary, Boyd began noting how well the girls treated him. The company was mustered in Keokuk and there Boyd could scarcely make up his mind which young lady appealed to him most—"very shy" Lizzie Sullivan whose eyes were "sparkling black," or the Johnston girls, who gave him and his friends gingersnaps when the regiment went down river. When attending church, he principally noticed the women: "The people are very sociable—especially the young ladies who seem to take a great interest in the soldiers." All of his stepping out with Maggie, Aggie, and Lizzie seems to have been given zest by the fact that he was a soldier soon to be off to the war. One night, "We had a good dinner and a pleasant time not unmarred however by the ever present thought this might be the *last* time we should meet these kind people." The romantic soldier paying court before the army moves on was a role that Boyd took to with no trouble. While it may have marred the good times, it also added to their appeal. On the day the regiment boarded the boat that began their journey to the battle of Shiloh, they marched down the Main Street to Keokuk under the eyes of the women of the town. "1000 strong we marched that afternoon in the pride and glory of youthful soldiers The sound of the music—the cheering shouts of the people robbed [us] of all regrets and we marched proudly away. I saw some of our good friends on the side walks—but it would not do to look back."[4]

While Boyd and other decent young men were sparking the local girls, other Iowa soldiers enjoyed the saloons and brothels of Keokuk. Boyd complained of their fascination with the pleasures of the river town. But these unrepentant soldiers were claiming man's estate just as Boyd was, although in less respectable ways. These young men asserted their freedom from home and their new sense of masculinity with liquor and prostitutes. Soon Boyd recognized that this type of coming-of-age would be typical of his fellow soldiers, although he never learned to approve. "Whiskey and sexual vices," he claimed, "carry more soldiers off than the *bullet*."[5]

This escape from small-town morality seemed to be an inescapable part of soldiering. Old soldiers told a young recruit in another part of the Union army that "unless a man can drink, lie, steal, and swear he is not fit for a soldier." The men who pursued these vices and others—gambling and swearing were even more commonplace than drinking and fornication—disturbed Cyrus Boyd most by their enthusiasm: "How eager they seem to abandon all their early teachings and to catch up with everything which seeks to debase." Entering into the heavily masculine world of the army, they prided themselves on these thoroughly masculine vices. But to Boyd, who believed that true manhood required not release but restraint, the speed of his fellow soldiers' degradation was appalling.[6]

Part of masculinity was achieving a self-discipline within the institutional discipline of the army. Cyrus F. Boyd and other northerners were as proud of their ability to withstand the temptations to which other soldiers gave in as they were of their service to the Union. Indeed, virtuous self-discipline was in itself a kind of service. When secession and rebellion were perceived as hot-headed and impulsive—the result of unrestrained passion—self-discipline had political implications. During the war with the emotional, treacherous—feminine, childlike—South, the son of the rational, loyal—masculine, adult—North should be manly and upright.[7]

Yet part of the transformation necessary to become a soldier was hardening. While Boyd worried about men whose morals coarsened, he himself became less sensitive than he had been, more inured to suffering—both his own and others. Hardening was a process that ranged over all aspects of Boyd's life, from the commonplace to the most serious. It included getting used to a variety of discomforts and privations. His diet became coarser and simpler. "We have bid farewell to Bakers bread, cow's milk and such soft things. Had a piece of meat and a hard tack for breakfast—we are gradually breaking in." He learned to live outdoors; on the company's first night camping, "some of the boys began to think of their *mothers* and to talk of returning to their comfortable homes in the western counties."[8]

Hardening also included becoming accustomed to death and violence. The Fifteenth Iowa Infantry's introduction to bloodshed was perhaps more sudden than most. On April 6, 1862, they were aboard a steamer at Pittsburgh Landing, having breakfast, when the order came to go ashore. Once there, they ran into the battle of Shiloh. They hurried for three miles, "meeting hundreds—yes thousands of men on the retreat who had thrown away their arms and were rushing toward the Landing—most of these were *hatless* and had nothing on them except their clothes." Some of those who fled had been shot; some ran and others were being carried off on stretchers. As they passed, the Iowans could not help noticing that some of the men were "covered with blood from head to foot."

"Here we were a new Regt which had never until this morning heard an enemies gun fire thrown into this *hell* of a battle— without warning." This was what the Civil War generation and others before and since called "the baptism of blood"—a phrase that connoted not only sudden and complete maturation but a radical transformation in character and experience. In telling his story, Boyd deliberately contrasted the innocence of the recruits to the horror of the baptism.

The general horror of battle quickly became more specific. The Fifteenth Iowa came to the edge of a large field with a ravine at one end. They crossed the ravine and deployed into line of battle, all in clear view of the Confederates. The rebels fired on them. "Here I noticed the first man shot. . . . He was close to us and sprang high in the air and gave one groan and fell *dead.*" Then the hardening began. Boyd and his fellow soldiers each had to step over the newly dead man. "Each man as he came up seemed to hesitate and some made a motion to pick him up." But they could not stop to tend to the man. Instead, the officers "sternly" ordered a charge, the men responded with a cheer, and they moved forward—only to be pushed back and to retreat over that same open ground. Masculinity meant restraining both their instincts to flee—to be a coward was to be no man—and their instincts to minister to the corpse.

As they were recrossing the field, a soldier came to Boyd and told him that his brother Scott was being left behind. Exhausted, Scott had collapsed on the ground. Boyd ran back to rescue his brother, only to be told "he never could go any farther and that I had better save myself and let him go." Pleading with his brother had no effect, so Cyrus Boyd grabbed Scott Boyd "by the *nap of the neck* and jerked him upon his feet and told him to *come* or I should help him with my *boot.*" Scott stood up and Cyrus helped him seek cover in the ravine. There he left his brother, confident he could work his way to safety, and returned to his company.

They continued to fight and fall back, ending up on the bluffs back at the landing where they had disembarked that morning. From the bluffs, they witnessed the arrival of Buell's army—all, in Boyd's opinion, that saved Grant, his army, and themselves. There was a final rebel charge but the Union forces held. Then came night, in many ways more horrible than the day had been. As the rain came down, Boyd and his company tried to sleep, listening to the groans of the other men, wounded and dying, who surrounded them, and to the sounds of wounded horses "running through the darkness." Morning came and they were thankful to be held in reserve through the second day's fighting.

After the battle was finally over, Boyd and his friends went out and examined the field where they had fought. In just a few days war had changed them forever: "By this time we had become accustomed to seeing *dead* men and the *shock* had passed." They walked unmoved through the camp of the Fifty-second Illinois, looking at the bodies of dead and wounded soldiers, Union and Confederate, "alternately scattered over the ground." Some of the wounded were "so near dead from exposure they were mostly insane." Elsewhere on the field, Boyd came across a dead rebel lying "on his back with his hands raised above his head"; the man "had died in great agony. Boyd reached down and, for a memento, took a button off his coat.

"War is *hell* broke loose and benumbs all the tender feelings of men and makes of them *brutes.*" This was one conclusion Boyd drew after experiencing battle—presumably he included himself in his observations. He also concluded, "I do not want to see any more such scenes and yet I would not have missed this for any consideration." Being a man meant risking horrors that might unman an individual—not by feminizing him but by making him inhuman. The hardening process was painful but it was well begun.[9]

Boyd noticed his own hardening most when it centered on his reaction—or growing lack of reaction—to suffering and death.

He also found himself, despite his fears of moral degradation, taking food—chickens, pigs, roasting ears—from southern civilians. This was a more traditional form of masculine assertion that usually characterized the modest Boyd: being one of a group of armed men invading a homestead and taking what they wanted because nobody there could stop them. For Boyd, this food was due to the soldiers because they were loyal and self-sacrificing, while southerners were neither, and because, well, because they were soldiers. But he still responded to peacetime values that held foraging was theft. When Company E slaughtered a rebel sheep, Boyd noted approvingly that, "Major Purcell gave them a healthy old lecture and told the men they would not be allowed to *kill sheep* even if they were away from *home* and that hereafter such men would be severely *punished.*"[10]

Finally, the hardening required a kind of mental vigor. Even as he inveighed against whisky and fornication, Boyd believed the real enemy to the soldier was internal. "More men *die* of homesickness than all other diseases—and when a man gives up and lies down he is a *goner.*" His strategy for surviving the war was not simply military discipline—the ability to march, fight, obey orders, and keep oneself clean—not just moral discipline—the avoidance of temptation and degradation—but mental discipline as well. "Keep the mind occupied with something new and keep *going all the time* except when asleep." This pursuit of action and Boyd's practice of positive thinking was another duty required by manliness.[11]

That Cyrus F. Boyd should look back and choose to shape his life in the Union army into a tale of his coming-of-age is hardly surprising. This understanding of manhood, with its complex layers of definition, was commonplace among northerners of the Civil War era. Ideas about true manliness were central to the experience of northern men enlisting in the army, serving through the war, and remembering their service. In fact, the image of the young soldier coming of age was so central to later understanding of the war that it became, through a kind of cultural metonymy, a figure for both true manhood and for the nation itself.

Becoming a man was no simple step for a middle-class northerner like Cyrus F. Boyd. Sexual assertion by itself was insufficient; indeed, the young man might regard it as a sign that he was unmanly because he failed to exercise manly restraint. Physical violence—hunting and killing his fellow man in what seemed to be an extension of a primitive, perhaps savage, role—might be masculine, but true manhood required self-discipline and civilized morality. Both sexuality and violence had to be domesticated before a male became a true man—the one could be fulfilled only within the family, the other had to be directed purposefully toward a licensed enemy. Yet the demands of familial duty—defending family, home, and country—threatened to undercut the emotive ties that should bind a man to wife, parents, children, and friends: could a man harden himself enough to survive the war yet remain a son and a husband? True men recognized the role of emotions. An Illinois soldier confessed to his wife, "I cannot sing yet those songs such as, the vacant chair, the tears come." He went on, however, to invoke the ideal of manliness to justify his tears. "A man that cannot shed a tear when he thinks of those he left at home, is no man." Shedding a tear might be easy or painful or meaningless; what should a man do when his brother is lying exhausted on the battlefield of Shiloh while his company is rushing on? Is he first a sergeant or a sibling?[12]

Volunteering in itself was a sign of coming into manhood—it meant accepting a man's duties to defend his home and country. It was also, for many soldiers, the first time they had been away from parental supervision. Besides, military service had long been regarded as a climacteric. Sidney O. Little, an Illinois soldier, sounded as if he doubted his mother could believe in his transformation—he told her "you may think me jesting"—but he assured her that "my coming into this war has made a man of your son." As Benjamen F. Ashenfelter put it, deciding not simply to enlist but re-enlist in August 1863, "A man that is afraid to face his Countries foe on an open field would not Defend A wife & children from the Midnight Assassin." Another, boringly predictable attitude toward the relationship of soldiering and manliness was the claim that those who refused to fight weren't men at all—they might as well be women. As one soldier said, "Any young man who is drafted now and forgets his manhood so far as to hire a substitute is'nt [*sic*] worthy the name of man and ought to be put in petticoats immediately." When the soldier Wilbur

Fisk, an unofficial correspondent of his newspaper back home, explained why he sometimes wrote at length on the minutiae of soldier life, he spoke to the children of the community. "I thought perhaps some of the boys who read the *Freeman,* but are not old enough yet themselves to be soldiers, and some of the little girls too, perhaps, who never can be soldiers, but who almost wish sometimes they had been born boys so that they could, would be interested to read all about the little affairs in a soldier's common everyday life."[13]

Soldiers and other northerners frequently talked about fighting for the Union in specifically familial terms. Burage Rice, a New York captain, predicted the sure defeat of rebellion. "By the sacrifice and blood of our fathers was the Republic founded and by the treasure, faith, honor, and blood of their sons shall the same glorious flag forever wave over us." The Union was a fragile legacy handed down by the fathers of the Revolutionary generation; their sons owed it protection.[14]

But the long chain of familial responsibility did not end with the Civil War generation. The soldier's manhood required him to be a dutiful father as well as an obedient son. Henry H. Seys attributed his patriotism to "all the teachings of my boyhood— the very milk that nourished me in my infancy." This childhood education forced him to serve; otherwise "I should despise myself and be *ashamed to answer the questions of my children."* Preserving the Union was the duty he owed both the generation behind him—particularly, it would seem, his mother—and the generation to come. He further told his wife, "teach our children that their duty to the land of their birth is next to their duty to their God. And that those who would desert *her* in the hour of danger, should be deserted by Him when *their* final calamity comes." Fathers expected mothers to inculcate their children with patriotic values; the feminine, domestic sphere was the ground for the masculine, public world.[15]

Henry H. Seys—and many others like him—saw himself as part of an extensive family, one that included generations of Americans, not just his own parents and children. To put it simply, many northerners considered the Union itself a family. Fighting for the Union was, in that sense, much like fighting for one's family.

This metaphor influenced more than just the experience of

the young men of the North who joined the Union army. It underlay a lot of thinking about the Union's war goals. One way to sum up Union war motivations succinctly was to say that the South needed to be taught a lesson. The North was the schoolmaster, the army the rod, and the South the disobedient child. The Vermont Yankee Wilbur Fisk, looking back in 1894, remembered the enthusiasm with which "we boys" had greeted the war. "We were ready to shout hurrah because now there would be a chance to teach the South a lesson, but we didn't realize how much it would cost us to teach it."[16]

Americans had a habit of talking about the body politic in terms of family relationships. Even antiwar northerners used familial imagery—"let the erring sisters depart in peace." Sisterhood, in this case, wasn't powerful—the image provoked a sad aura of weakness. Northerners who were prowar used the image of unruly children who had to be made to obey. Sometimes this way of thinking about the South even reached the battlefield. Usually the specific familial imagery was hidden—northerners discussed southerners in terms of irrationality, emotion, savagery. One soldier wrote after the battle of Shiloh, "We showed them on the 2d day that northern obstinacy and coolness was more than a match for southern impetuosity"—northern obstinacy and coolness making up a critical part of manliness. Occasionally, northern imputations of southern childishness could be detected overtly. Henry C. Metzger wrote his sister, "I hate to hear the Rebles cheerre when they make a charge, they put me in mind of small schoolchildren about the time school is out." And indeed, sometimes men at war sound as if they have schoolboy notions of honor behind all the bloodshed and policy. A perfectly sensible Wisconsin soldier wrote his wife this, as he visited with defeated Confederate soldiers in Johnston's army in 1865: "They are willing to admit that we have whipped them, and that is all that we want of them, is to acknowledge that we are too much for them, and we will also get along very finely." The soldier knew that behind the war had been issues of the nature of the American Republic, the fate of democratic institutions, the place of slavery in a free society—yet he was able to write as if getting the Confederates to cry uncle had been the whole point of the conflict.[17]

The family analogy for understanding southern rebellion and northern response—the notion that the southern states might best be understood as disobedient children, the northern ones as filial—was woefully inadequate, indeed nonsensical. I am not suggesting that anyone who seriously thought about politics entertained it for a minute or ever pushed the analogy into an identification. But in a period when political duties were so often expressed in familial imagery, it is striking that an armed rebellion of grown men was sometimes made to sound like a squabble in a kindergarten. The family metaphor provided perhaps the most common image by which people thought about the political world.

Volunteer soldiers were dutiful sons of both their parents and their Revolutionary forefathers. Rebels challenged the mild parental authority of the national government—and thus defied the Revolutionary generation as well. In that sense, the good sons of 1861 went to war against the bad sons. Perhaps there is a hint of this, however attenuated, in the way we continue to call the Civil War "the Brothers' War." And if there is not, at least there is little doubt we still think of the war as a family tragedy.

Thinking about the Civil War experience as a rite of passage also continued into the next generation, as the sons of 1861 became the fathers of the Gilded Age. Once war becomes the defining experience for manhood, how can sons grow up in its absence? Just as the sons and grandsons down the line of the revolutionary generation knew that they might never measure up to the heroes of 1776, the children of the postwar era faced the knowledge that the ultimate courage was shown not by them but by their fathers. (Or perhaps worse—as in the lifelong case of Theodore Roosevelt—had *not* been shown by their fathers.) Mrs. C. E. McKay, a Civil War nurse, said in 1876, "And ought we not carefully to teach the children of the present generation,— charging them not to let their children or their children's children forget what it cost their fathers to leave to them a united country?"[18]

Men who had suffered through and survived the war told their children that military experience was crucial to manhood— in fact, they spoke of war not only as a burden to be borne manfully but as a piece of luck. "Through our great good fortune," Oliver Wendell Holmes, Jr., said, "in our youth our hearts were touched with fire." Both the veterans and the younger men coming after them worried that with no equivalent experience, the youth of America would never grow into men. College athletics—played, at Harvard, on Soldier's Field—were just one way that postwar society tried to reproduce the manly experience of war for their children. Stephen Crane, in his great novel *The Red Badge of Courage*, imaginatively seized the Civil War— and can we not hear, in its subtle ironies, a rebellious protest against turning frightened young men into heroes? Theodore Roosevelt literally seized upon war, pursuing the strenuous life up the slope of Kettle Hill. It took a generation of men uncertain of their manhood to find in the quick and nasty war with Spain in 1898 "a splendid little war."[19]

Talking about and presumably thinking about Civil War soldiers coming of age eventually influenced thinking about the war itself. Some saw—and still see—the Civil War as a coming-of-age experience for the nation entire. The war unified the country; it created strong institutions, including a powerful if short-lived army, and a long-lived sense of American power; it made Ohioans and New Yorkers as well as South Carolinians and Alabamians realize that they were Americans. It is as if the nation could not really mature without a massive bloodletting inflicted on itself, as if six hundred thousand deaths were some kind of adolescent rite of passage.

And Cyrus F. Boyd? He completed the romance of war by returning to Keokuk after Appomattox and marrying Maggie Johnston, one of the young ladies who had presented him gingersnaps. He had already become a soldier and an officer. Becoming a husband and a father—becoming in that sense, as well, a man—was for him part of his Civil War experience. Nothing in the diary he left us suggest that he would have been surprised that his years spent fighting for the Union could be interpreted as years he spent growing up. He wrote as if the war that swept down on him and his companions was as natural and expected and necessary as childbirth, love, and death. This synchrony of public and private lives was how a generation of soldiers—and their children who followed—made sense of the painful, fumbling, demotic heroism and the remarkable unremarkableness of the men who fought for the Union.

Chapter 4

xxxxxxxxxxxxxxxxxxxxxxxx

No Desperate Hero: Manhood and Freedom in a Union Soldier's Experience

DAVID W. BLIGHT

> The soil of peace is thickly sown with the seeds of war.
> Ambrose Bierce

With the First World War as his model, Paul Fussell wrote that
"every war is ironic because every war is worse than expected."
As national calamity and as individual experience, certainly this
was the case with the American Civil War. That slavery could be
abolished only by such wholesale slaughter, and that national
unity could be preserved only through such fratricidal conflict
provide some of the most tragic ironies of American history. On
a grand scale, such ironies are easily summarized, but as Fussell
observes, all "great" wars consist of thousands of "smaller constituent" stories, which are themselves full of "ironic actions."[1] One
of those stories is recorded in the more than two hundred Civil
War letters of Charles Harvey Brewster of Northampton, Massachusetts. As Bell Wiley first observed in the 1940s and 1950s, the
letters of Civil War soldiers are an extraordinary source for the
social history of nineteenth-century America. Brewster's single
cache of letters illuminates a remarkable range of attitudes and
experience of an ordinary American man caught up not only in
the sweeping events of the war but also in the values of his age
and the challenge of his own self-development. The emotions

and ideas he expressed range from naïveté to mature realism, from romantic idealism to sheer terror, and from self-pity to enduring devotion.[2]

Born and raised in Northampton, Brewster was a relatively unsuccessful, twenty-seven-year-old store clerk and a member of the local militia when he enlisted in Company C of the Tenth Massachusetts Volunteers in April 1861. Companies of the Tenth Massachusetts were formed from towns all over the western section of the state. The citizens of Northampton embraced the war fever that swept the land in the spring and summer of 1861. On April 18, only three days after the surrender of Fort Sumter, the first meeting of the Company C militia (an old unit chartered in 1801) turned into a large public rally where forty new men enlisted. By April 24, seventy-five Northampton women rallied and vowed their labor to sew the uniforms of the local company. As the cloth arrived, some women worked at home and others sewed publicly in the town hall. Local poets came to the armory to recite patriotic verses to the would-be soldiers. Yesterday farmers, clerks, and mechanics; today they were the local heroes who would "whip secesh." On May 9 Company C marched some seven miles for an overnight encampment in Haydenville, passing through the towns of Florence and Leeds on the way. In each village a brass band, an outdoor feast, and a large crowd cheered them. War was still a local festival in this first spring of the conflict. By June 10 the seventy or so members of the company attended a farewell ball, and four days later they strode down Main Street through a throng so large a corridor could hardly be formed. Flags waved everywhere, several brass bands competed, and Brewster and his comrades joined two other companies of the Tenth on a train for Springfield. En route the soldiers continued the joyous fervor of the day by singing "patriotic airs" to the accompaniment of a lone accordion.[3] Like most of his comrades, Brewster had enlisted for three years, never believing the war would last that long.

After a three-week encampment in Springfield, the Tenth Massachusetts again departed with great ceremony. As was the case in so many American towns that summer, the "ladies of Springfield" formally presented the regimental colors to Colonel Henry S. Briggs, commander of the regiment. It was a time, said the women's announcement, for "reverence" to flags, and they urged the men to "defend them to the death." The spokeswoman, a Mrs. James Barnes, assured these young warriors that "the heart of many a wife and mother and child and sister, will beat anxiously for your *safety*, but remember, no less anxiously for your *honor*." In Palmer, on the way to Boston, several hundred women gathered at the station to bid goodbye, some with bouquets of flowers. The regiment would camp ten more days in Medford, next to Charlestown, on the banks of the Mystic River. Before boarding transports for the voyage to Washington, D.C., the Tenth stood for one more ceremony, this time addressed by ex-Massachusetts Governor George N. Briggs, father of the commander. In a message fathers have for centuries passed to their sons, but rarely so explicitly, Briggs called upon farmboys and clerks to "show yourselves to be *men* and *New England men*." He urged them to be gallant and fierce, but always kind to their wounded or captured enemy. He then concluded with a flourish: "When the army of an ancient republic were going forth to battle a mother of one of the soldiers said to him: 'My son, return home *with* your shield or *on* your shield.' Adopting the sentiment of the noble mother, let me say . . . bring back those beautiful and rich colors presented you by the ladies of Springfield, the emblems of your country's power and glory, waving over your heads, unstained, or return wrapped in their gory folds."[4] One can never know how closely soldiers listened to such rhetoric in that romantic summer of 1861. The fathers' and mothers' call to war and manliness, in the war they were soon to fight, would indeed become for some men an exhilarating and ennobling challenge, while for others it would become disillusioning or unbearable. For Brewster, it became all of those things.

The Tenth Massachusetts spent the rest of 1861 and the winter of 1862 in Camp Brightwood, on the edge of the District of Columbia. There they joined the Seventh Massachusetts, the Thirty-sixth New York, and the Second Rhode Island as part of "Couch's Brigade." For three years, Brewster shared the same brigade and battle experiences as Second Rhode Island Private, ultimately Colonel, Elisha Hunt Rhodes, whose diary became famous as part of a 1990 PBS television documentary on the Civil War.[5] The Tenth participated in almost every major battle

fought by the Army of the Potomac, beginning with the Peninsula campaign through Antietam and Fredericksburg in 1862.
Chancellorsville, Gettysburg, Bristow Station, and Rappahan-
nock Station in 1863, and the Wilderness, Spotsylvania, and Cold
Harbor in 1864. By the time the survivors of the Tenth were
mustered out at the end of their three-year enlistment in June
1864, they had witnessed their summer outing be transformed
into the bloodiest war in history, seen thousands die of disease,
practiced war upon civilians and the southern landscape, loyally
served the cause as variously defined, and tried their best to
fulfill their communities' expectations. They returned in the
words of their last commander, Colonel Joseph B. Parsons, a
"shattered remnant" of "mourners."[6]

Brewster's father, Harvey Brewster, had died in 1839 when
Charles was only five years old, leaving Martha Russell Brewster
a widow with three small children, including two daughters,
four-year-old Martha and two-month-old Mary. Brewster's wartime letters, virtually all of which were written to his mother and
two sisters, clearly reflect a background of family financial distress, at the same time they exhibit deep affection. His wartime
adventures and sufferings would compel Brewster to expose his
self-estimation as a frustrated, if not failed provider in his capacity as the sole male member of his family. Nevertheless, for
Brewster, as has been sadly true for men throughout the ages,
war became an ordinary man's opportunity to escape from the
ordinary.[7]

Brewster came to loathe war itself; after imagined and romantic warfare gave way to real battle in 1862, he would describe it in
honest and realistic terms. Brewster came to understand that in
war, perhaps even more than in civilian life, fate was often indifferent to individual virtue, however much he wished it were
otherwise. Educated in the Northampton public schools, sensitive and remarkably literate, Brewster was no natural warrior.
But he aspired to leadership and craved recognition. The army,
and his incessant desire for status within its ranks, became for
Brewster the source of community and vocation that he had
never achieved.

Brewster survived more than three years of battle, hardship,
sickness, and boredom by a combination of devotion, diminished

alternatives, self-righteous ambition, and a sense of irony. Like literate soldiers in all ages, or like anyone undergoing loneliness and stress, letters became for Brewster both monologues of self-discovery and dialogues with home. Letters were a humanizing element in a dehumanizing environment, evidence that however foreign civilian life might come to appear, something called "home" still existed. Lying in a rifle pit in June 1862, having experienced his first major battle at Fair Oaks during the Peninsula campaign, Brewster scolded his mother for not writing more often. "It is the little common place incidents of everyday life at home which we like to read," Brewster declared. "It is nothing to the inhabitants of Northampton that the beans are up in the old garden at home, or that Mary has moved her Verbena bed into the garden, but to me, way off here in the swamps, and woods, frying in the sun, or soaking in the rain, it is a very important thing indeed. You do not realize how everything that savors of home relishes with us." Brewster wrote out of self-pity and as a means of feeling alive. In a volatile letter, where he wrote matter-of-factly about the prospect of his own death, he informed his mother that her letters were like "Angels' visits." But sleeping in the mud made even letters sometimes inadequate to the task of sustaining hope and self-respect. "I think it is too bad," said Brewster from the Peninsula, "when letters are the only thing that makes existence tolerable in this God forsaken country."[8]

Letters were a soldier's means of expressing and understanding the absurdity of war, as well as a way of reaffirming a man's commitment to the enterprise. But nothing threw this paradox into greater relief than letters to and from dead men. In the immediate aftermath of the battle of Gettysburg, Brewster lifted three letters from "a dead Rebel's cartridge box, written to his mother and sisters." He sent them to his sister Mary as a souvenir. "Poor fellow," Brewster remarked, "he lay upon the field with his entrails scattered all about by a cannon shot, I cannot help pity him although as you see he expresses no very kindly intentions towards poor us. . . ." Backhandedly, Brewster expressed a sense of kinship with his dead enemy. "The mother & sisters will look in vain in the far off Florida for his return," wrote the New Englander, "or even his grave among the green hills of Penn, where his body probably lies in a pit with lots of his comrades. . . ." Brewster maintained a certain emotional distance from his unnamed foe in an unmarked grave. But the symbol of the confiscated letters to "mother & sisters" could only have made him and his loved ones back home wonder about the "pit" beneath some "green hills" where Brewster might soon find oblivion.[9] Letters represented the continuity of life, even when they were to or from the dead.

To a significant degree Brewster's war was one man's effort to compensate for prior failure and to imagine a new career within the rigid and unpredictable strictures of the army. Brewster yearned for a "chance" to "better" himself, for the respect of his fellow soldiers, and for the symbols of authority and rank. He entered the service disappointingly as a non-commissioned First Sergeant and spent the first summer and autumn of the war pining for the status of a commission. Put simply, Brewster had a chip on his shoulder about the hand that life had dealt him. He frequently referred to a prewar pattern of bad luck as he gossiped about those who got promotions, resented perceived slights, desperately relished compliments about his performance, and moaned to his mother that it was "hope deferred that maketh the heart sick." Brewster constantly measured himself against his fellow soldiers and calculated his chances of promotion against their character and health. His relations with his comrades were a typical combination of male bonding and competition, and he was motivated by a workingman's sense of practical self-interest. "A fellow can sleep very warm in the woods," he told his mother in December 1861, "with a commission in his pocket."[10]

Brewster received his much-coveted commission and promotion to Second Lieutenant in December 1862. He sent a detailed description of the sword, sash, belt, and cap purchased for him as gifts at considerable cost by members of his company. His letter reads like a description of an impending graduation or a wedding night. "My heart is full to overflowing tonight," Brewster informed his sister. All pettiness and resentment vanished as he realized the "evidence of my standing in the affections of the men." His comrades pooled more than fifty dollars to buy the officer's accoutrements, and Brewster confessed to feeling "wicked" over his good fortune while his comrades in the ranks honored him. The army in winter quarters had become a society of men living together, developing their own rituals and conventions of domestic relations. On the eve of a ceremony that would recognize his new rank, Brewster prepared for a rite of passage and new living arrangements. "I am writing in *my* tent," he told his sister. "I have not slept in it yet but am going to tonight. Lieut. Weatherill and I have been arranging things all day." There were "new bunks" in his "future home" and he informed Mary that he would be ready to entertain her when she visited. Brewster made the most of this milestone in his life, and a certain tenderness crept into his language as he marveled at the "spontaneous outbreak of feeling" among the men.[11]

Brewster learned what war has often taught us: that men frequently find love and respect for each other more readily in warlike activities than in civilian pursuits. After first wearing his "new uniform," Brewster declared that he felt "quite like a free man once more, now that I am a commissioned officer, it is wonderful what a difference two little straps on the shoulder make. . . ." Once again, he recognized his own aims as practical and personal. "Before I had lots of work and very little pay," he wrote, "and now I have very little work and lots of pay."[12] To Brewster freedom meant increased wages, status, and independence in controlling his own labor. But Brewster's new status also represented some ideals in the relations among men that only the army seemed to provide: loyalty, respect, and the burdens and joys of leadership. Brewster would have been deeply heartened by a September 1861 letter written by Henry W. Parsons, a twenty-two-year-old private in his company. "In reguard to Charley Brewster," wrote Parsons to his aunt, "he improves every day   he is the best officer in the company that we have had with us yet   you will find a large heart beneth his coat." Within a month of writing this tribute to his favorite officer. Parsons died of disease at Camp Brightwood, but not before informing his aunt that Brewster was "a gentleman to all and will do all for the men that lays in his power—his friends may feel proud of him . . . let me tell you Aunt that this is the place to find out mens disposition   one can soon tell a man from a knave or coward. . . ." Deeply affected by the loss of such a friend so early in the war, Brewster told his mother that he could not "get over Henry Parsons' death. it came so sudden and he was a particular friend of mine, and he and myself had many a confidential talk together. . . ."[13] The quest for status, the love and respect of friends, and the sheer struggle for physical survival all became part of a young officer's daily existence.

As soldiers like Brewster developed their military identities, they were readily reminded of the radical disjuncture between their precarious existence and that of the community left behind. "How I wish some of the stay at homes could enjoy one winter campaign with us," Brewster complained in 1862, "I fancy we should hear less of 'onward to Richmond.'" Once fully initiated to war and to its psychological shocks, a soldier's misery found expression in his contempt for civilians. "People at the North do not realize at all what a soldier's life is. . . ." Brewster wrote in 1863, "a soldier has more misery in one day than occurs in a lifetime of a civilian ordinarily and their greatest comforts would be miseries to people at home." Brewster developed a veteran volunteer's increasing estrangement from civilians in a prolonged war. "It is the general feeling among the old regiments, the real *volunteers*," he said, "that the generality of the citizens loathe and hate them."[14]

By 1864 Brewster was disaffected from his hometown and homesick at the same time. Conscription laws exacerbated such ambivalence, drawing a greater distance between the original volunteers—who by 1863–64 had constructed a self-image as suffering victims—and the draftees from their hometowns. As Northampton strained to fill a draft quota in February 1864, Brewster declared that he did not "believe in drafted patriotism." Brewster worried about what would become of him once his war was over. "This military is a hard worrying and at the same time lazy miserable business," he wrote in April 1864, "but it pays better than anything else so I think I had better stick to it as long as I can." In words representative of Everyman's lament, Brewster declared that he had done his "share of campaigning but somebody must campaign and somebody else must have all the easy money making places and as the harder lot was always mine in civil life. I suppose I must expect the same in the military."[15]

Brewster's sentiments toward civilians, as well as his fears of making a living after the war, are reminiscent of dilemmas faced by veterans of other American wars. "I don't know what I am going to do for a living when I come home," Brewster wrote in his last letter from the front in June 1864. "As the end of my service grows near," he said, "I cannot but feel rather bad to leave it for all its hardships and horrors & dangers it is a fascinating kind of life, and much freer from slander jealousy & unkindness than civil life which I almost dread to come back to." Brewster groped to explain why the joy of going home should be so tarnished by fear of civilian livelihood. Suddenly, the army seemed an island of clarity, honesty, and genuineness in a laissez-faire sea of treachery. "The Veterans," he said, "wear long faces." He spoke for the veterans in warning that "those who will welcome them with such apparent joy" will be "ready to do them any injury for the sake of a dollar." His fears of civilian life and nostalgia for the comradeship of the army already made him a candidate for the cycles of selective memory that would both plague and inspire Civil War veterans.[16]

Brewster, like most men of his generation, was deeply imbued with the Victorian American values of "manhood" and "courage." He perceived war as the test of his courage, and he constantly sought reassurance that he could meet the challenge. He aspired to the individualized and exemplary conception of bravery, where officers especially had to exhibit their courage to the rank and file. "Courage was the cement of armies," writes historian Gerald Linderman, in the best study of this concept among Civil War soldiers.[17] Especially in the early stages of the war, there is no question that fear of personal dishonor, so rooted in social constructions of masculinity and in American culture, provided the motivation and much of the discipline of Civil War armies.

But the social expectations of manliness in the face of modern war and the degradation of disease almost overwhelmed Brewster, though he only guardedly admitted it. He was both a victim and a perpetrator of these values. His letters are full of observations about the endless struggle between courage and cowardice, his own and that of his comrades. Like most young men who went to war in the nineteenth century (and in our own more violent century as well), Brewster followed a destructive quest for manhood, fashioned a heroic self-image at every chance, and marveled at the capacity of war to subdue the environment. He also wrote of camp life and war itself as places strictly separating men from women, all the while imagining their scenes and horrors for his female correspondents. Such sentiments, of course, are not merely stored away in the nineteenth century, to be unpackaged for modern boyhood fantasies or the mythic uses of the vast Civil War literature. Readers of great memoirs from recent wars, like William Manchester's *Goodbye Darkness: A Memoir of the Pacific War*, may find certain echoes in Brewster's letters. When Manchester, the son and grandson of soldiers, writes of his withdrawal from Massachusetts State College and enlistment in the Marines in 1942, "guided by the compass that had been built into me," he represents a male tradition deeply ingrained in American society, and one that common and less literary-inclined men like Brewster had helped to cultivate.[18] Brewster's own manly compass sent him irresistibly off to war, however unprepared or ill-equipped for what it would do to his body or his imagination.

In May 1862, just before the battle of Fair Oaks, Brewster wrote daily, dramatic accounts of the impending battle; but even more so, he chronicled his desperate struggle with dysentery and "terrible exposure" while sleeping nightly in the mud. At one point he declares himself so sick that he will have to resign and go home; to fall back now to some makeshift hospital, he believed, would surely mean a hideous and ignoble death. Courage in this instance, Brewster learned, merely meant endurance and a little luck. He could "give up" and seek a furlough, he reasoned, but he feared that the "brave ones that staid at home would call me a coward and all that so I must stay here until after the fight at any rate." In a despairing letter two months later Brewster described "burying comrades who die of disease" as the "saddest thing in the service. . . ." Wondering what he would write to a dead comrade's parents, he took heart at how well the man had performed in battle: "thank the lord I can tell them he was brave."[19]

Unable to walk, and humiliated by his chronic diarrhea, Brewster spent the battle of Fredericksburg in December 1862, five miles behind the lines where he could only hear that desperate engagement. "I never felt so mean in my life . . . ," he wrote. "I lie here like a sculking coward and hear the din of battle but cannot get there   it is too bad." The situation is reminiscent of the scene in Stephen Crane's *The Red Badge of Courage*, where Henry Fleming, tormented by the sounds of battle—"the crackling shots which were to him like voices"—feels "frustrated by hateful circumstances." Henry and Brewster had different burdens to bear; the latter had not run from battle. But a week later Brewster demonstrated his ambivalence about the vexing concept of courage, hoping that the sickness would not seize him again "when there is a battle in prospect, for it lays me open to the imputation of cowardice, which I do not relish at all, although I don't claim to be very brave."[20] In the boredom, frustration, and danger of three years at the front, sometimes Brewster could manage to assert his own manhood only by attacking that of others. But with time he became a realist about the meaning of courage. On the eve of the Wilderness campaign in April 1864, Brewster hoped that his corps would be held in reserve in the impending fight. "I suppose you will call that a cowardly wish," he told Mary, "but although we see a great many in print, we see very few in reality of such desperate heroes that they had rather go into the heat of battle than not, when they can do their duty just as well by staying out. . . ." Having just lived through the worst combat of the war in late May 1864, he could write about courage without pretension. "You are mistaken about their being nothing cowardly about me," Brewster informed Martha. "I am scared most to death every battle we have, but I don't think you need be afraid of my sneaking away unhurt."[21] When introspection overtook the need for camaraderie and bravado, as it frequently did in the last months of his service, Brewster found the moral courage to speak honestly about physical courage.

Brewster kept his women correspondents informed but probably full of tension as he encountered real war. His letters allow us to follow a young man's romantic anticipation of battle through the experience of pitilessly realistic warfare. Upon seeing the aftermath of a battlefield for the first time at Williamsburg, he described it as a "fearful, fearful sight." "The ground was strew with dead men in every direction . . . ," he told his mother. "But language fails me and I cannot attempt to describe the scene. if ever I come home I can perhaps tell you but I cannot write it." Brewster would see much worse yet, and he would continue to write it into and out of his memory. But he was caught in that dilemma of literate soldiers in all modern wars: the gruesomeness of battlefields seemed, as Fussell put it, "an all-but-incommunicable reality" to the folks back home. Brewster's letters seem to have anticipated what Alexander Aitken wrote about his own rendering of the battle of the Somme in 1916: "I leave it to the sensitive imagination; I once wrote it all down, only to discover that horror, truthfully described, weakens to the merely clinical."[22] Brewster had a sensitive imagination, and he did try to write it all down; one wonders, though, if after the war, looking back at his letters, he might not have felt the same way Aitken did. In its own historical moment the obscenity of war, it seems, begs description; whereas, in retrospect, it often must be repressed from memory as people confront the tasks of living.

During Brewster's first major campaign (the Peninsula and the Seven Days, April to July 1862), he expressed virtually every emotion that battle could evoke. At the battle of Fair Oaks Brewster's regiment lost one of every four men engaged (killed, wounded, or missing), and, with good reason, the young officer wondered why he was still alive. He tried to describe the sounds and the stench of the battlefield, and the excitement and pulse of the fighting. He also began to demonize the enemy at every turn. In surviving such madness Brewster felt both manly exhilaration and dehumanization. The "life" the soldiers sustained, he said, "would kill wild beasts"; and the farmers of Northampton, he maintained, "would call it cruelty to animals to keep their hogs in as bad a place as we have to live and sleep. . . ." Most of all Brewster coped with fear and loaded up on opium to command his bowels. Anticipating the great battle for Richmond, he said he could only "dread it," as he had already "seen all I want to of battle and blood."[23] But he had two more years of this to endure; his demeanor and his language would both harden and expand with the experience.

While squatting in a field or brooding in a trench, Brewster sketched battle and its aftermath from a soldier's interior perspective, rather than from the sanitized vantage point of head-quarters. He rarely wrote about generals and grand strategy, providing an example, as John Keegan put it, of how very different the "face of battle" is from the "face of war."[24] Although he had no serious literary pretensions, Brewster's horror-struck depictions of battle scenes are sometimes similar to the agonizing ironies and relentless realism of Ambrose Bierce's short stories. After Gettysburg he described the endless corpses of dead men and horses as if they were macabre monuments. At Spotsylvania in 1864 the "terrors" he witnessed had become so common that he sometimes worried about his own lack of "feeling," and other times just lost himself in grim details. Describing one trench with dead and wounded Confederates piled "3 or 4 deap," he saw "one completely trodden in the mud so as to look like part of it and yet he was breathing and gasping." In the next letter came the vision of "the most terrible sight I ever saw," a breastwork fought over for twenty-four hours with the dead "piled in heaps upon heaps. . . ." As Brewster gazed over the parapet at dawn, "there was one Rebel sat up praying at the top of his voice and others were gibbering in insanity others were whining at the greatest rate. . . ." Stealing his nerves, preparing himself to continue this "terrible business," and ever the partisan, Brewster took an awkward solace that he had not, he claimed, heard any wounded Union soldiers "make any fuss."[25]

As he self-consciously became part of a machine of total war Brewster justified the pillaging of southern civilians, supported the execution of deserters, and in his harshest moments advocated the killing of Confederate prisoners. Yet, through nature's diversions and a healthy sense of irony, he preserved his humane sensibilities. Brewster nurtured a life-long interest in flowers, gardening, and the natural landscape, and he was an astute observer of the beauty and the strangeness of the Virginia countryside. Ever on the watch for the contrast of peace with war, many a "beautiful morning" in Brewster's letters provided a pastoral backdrop for the dullness of camp or the terror of battle. "I wish you could see what a splendid morning this is," he said to his mother while seated on an oak log on Chickahominy Creek in the spring of 1862. "The trees are in full foliage and the Birds are singing and the water ripples and sparkles at my feet with the sun shining gloriously over all, and if it were not for the Regt I see before me each with his deadly Enfield rifle on his shoulder I could hardly imagine that there was war in the land." Brewster savored opportunities to tell his womenfolk about wild roses and a host of other flower species he observed on the march. In a field near Cold Harbor in May 1864, "magnolias in full bloom" made him reverently grateful, for "their perfume is very refreshing," he said, "after the continued stench of the dead bodies of men and horses which we have endured for the last 19 days." Every war brings us these contrasts of ugliness with beauty, images of life next to death, a single poppy blooming in No Man's Land, visions of nature that somehow survive the worst of human nature. Sentimentalized blossoms so often outlast and even replace the stench of the dead and the vileness of war.[26]

One of the most intriguing themes revealed in Brewster's letters is his attitudes and actions regarding race and slavery. Brewster had voted for Abraham Lincoln in 1860, and embraced the Republican party's free labor and antislavery ideology. He had lived all his life in reform-minded Northampton, and believed from the first giddy days of the war that he was fighting to save the Union and free the slaves. But Brewster was no radical abolitionist (their ranks were very small in the Union army) and he enjoyed mocking the piety and earnestness of reformers. His racial views were those of a sardonic, white workingman who believed that blacks were a backward if not an inferior race. As historians Bell Wiley and Joseph Glatthaar have shown, use of such terms as "nigger" and "darky" were very common in the letters of Union soldiers, making Brewster's language typical rather than exceptional in this regard.[27] But at the same time Brewster believed that slavery was evil, that a war against secession was inherently a war against racial bondage, and that out of the bloodshed would come a different society. Moreover, he seemed to have held these views earlier than most Union troops. Although his estimations of black character did not change much, wartime experience forced an interesting evolution in Brewster's attitude toward blacks.

During the autumn and winter of 1861–62 the status of slaves who escaped into Union lines remained ambiguous. Contradictory policies toward fugitive slaves were the cause of considerable controversy in the Union ranks during 1861–62, and Brewster's regiment was no exception. The insistence of Generals George B. McClellan and Henry W. Halleck that fugitive slaves be returned to their owners, as well as President Lincoln's pragmatic ambiguity on the issue, were rendered unworkable with time. Very early in the war, at Fortress Monroe, Virginia, General Benjamin F. Butler declared the slaves who escaped to his lines "contraband of war," treating them as confiscated enemy property. The idea caught on as a moral and military imperative.[28]

Yet the slaves themselves were forcing a clearer settlement of this issue by their own courage and resolve. The Civil War was a conflict of such scale that its greatest lessons, collectively and individually, were being learned on the ground where abstractions must be converted into daily decisions. From Camp Brightwood on the outskirts of Washington, D.C., Brewster learned firsthand that many slaves were freeing themselves and converting the war's purpose. Slaves took "leg bail," Brewster wrote approvingly in November 1861, and in language that might have been fitting of a small-town, wartime abolitionist rally, he declared that "this war is playing the Dickens with slavery and if it lasts much longer will clear our Country's name of the vile stain and enable us to live in peace hereafter."[29] In such passages Brewster represented an attitude among white Northerners that, driven by the exigencies of war against the South, prompted Congress and Lincoln eventually to commit the nation to the reality of emancipation.

By December 1861, Lincoln administration policy toward blacks remained limited and conflicted. The President's annual message offered little hope to friends of the "contrabands"; he proposed only a plan to colonize escaped slaves and free blacks outside the country. From winter quarters, Brewster offered his own crude antislavery assessment of the situation. "We have got the President's message," he told his mother, "but I don't think it amounts to much he don't talk nigger enough, but its no use mincing the matter. Nigger has got to be talked and thoroughly talked to and I think niggers will come out of this scrape free."[30] In the common coin of camp and apparently back in Northampton as well, Brewster provides an example of the way in which racist language and antislavery ideology combined in the hearts and minds of Yankee soldiers. Brewster lacked eloquence, to say the least, when it came to the question of race; but in language which that great ironist in the White House would have fully understood, he argues unequivocally that the war should be prosecuted more vigorously against slavery.

Brewster spent his first winter at war intensely interested in the "contraband" issue. In January 1862, frustrated by how "slow" the war progressed, he complained that "it seems to be a war for the preservation of slavery more than anything else." Shortly after receiving his commission and setting up his new domestic quarters, Brewster took a seventeen-year-old runaway slave named David as his personal servant. Proud and possessive, he treated his "contraband" with a gushing paternalism. The young lieutenant took pride in relieving the Confederacy of this lone asset. "He was the only slave his master had," said Brewster, "and his master never will have him again if I can help it."[31] During the long winter months, the clandestine protection of his contraband from the former master's clutches became for Brewster the only war he had. But the contraband issue bitterly divided the Tenth Massachusetts, causing by March 1862 what Brewster called nearly "a state of mutiny" in the regiment. Brewster and his antislavery cohort (six contrabands were harbored in Company C alone) would lose this dispute to the pro-slavery officers in the regiment who determined to enforce a policy of exclusion. Some fugitives were tearfully returned to their waiting owners, while still others were spirited away toward Pennsylvania into an ambiguous fate. Brewster himself believed at one point that he would be charged and court-martialed for his resistance, and at another juncture claimed he was prepared to "resign." "I should hate to have to leave now just as the Regiment is going into active service," he wrote in March, "but I will never be instrumental in returning a slave to his master in any way shape or manner, I'll die first."[32] As Brewster describes this three-month-long dispute at Camp Brightwood it has both the quality of tragic farce and of high seriousness. This little war within a war reveals in microcosm the much larger social revolution American society was about to undergo, whether it was prepared to confront it or not.

A self-described "free man" with a commission, the recognition-starved Brewster now saw himself as a liberator of his fellow man. As a soldier he was well trained in tactical maneuvers and eager for a taste of battle. As a man he had a yearning to belong to some kind of community. In his contraband Brewster may also have found a need to give and a form of companionship he could truly control. But Brewster and his contraband may have mutually gained a sense of freedom from their short relationship. The same letter that begins with Brewster appearing in his "new uniform" for the first time ends with him asking his mother to help him outfit his servant. "I wish I could get some of my old clothes to put on him," Brewster wrote, "especially my old overcoat. I do not suppose you will have any chance to send them, but if you should I wish you would . . . make a bundle of coat Pants O Coat and vest . . . send them along, and then I could rig him up so his master would hardly know him." Rejoicing in his acquisition of the contraband in another letter, Brewster described David as "quite smart for a nigger though he is quite slow. . . ." But he "is willing," Brewster continued, "and I think has improved a good deal since I got him. I have not heard anything of his master, and if I do I shan't give him up without a struggle." Out of sheer self-interest as well as moral concern, Brewster objectified and coddled his contraband. But one is reminded here of the relationship between Huck and Jim in *Huckleberry Finn*. Like Huck, Brewster ultimately had a "sound heart" when it came to the right of a slave to his freedom, and he too decided to "go to hell" rather than return fugitive slaves to bondage. "Without the presence of blacks," Ralph Ellison aptly wrote, Mark Twain's classic "could never have been written." Without "Nigger Jim" Huck's commitment to freedom could never have developed into the "moral center" of that novel. On a simpler and hidden level, without his *"right smart nigger,"* Brewster might never have developed or even understood his own commitment to freedom. Brewster's struggle to free his "contraband" has the same ironic pattern as Huck's: acts of conscience mixed with adventure, moral revolt interrupting a life on a raft moving south. He never matched Huck's revelation that "you can't pray a lie," but Brewster's experience had forced him to clarify his beliefs and to understand much of what the war was

about. In his own crude way, Brewster would grasp the meaning
of Lincoln's haunting claim at the end of 1862, that "in *giving*
freedom to the slave, we *assure* freedom to the free."[33] Although
much of his prejudice would remain intact, the former store
clerk from Northampton had learned something valuable from
his "contraband."

After the Tenth Massachusetts returned home in June 1864,
Brewster, anxious about civilian life, re-enlisted under the auspices of the state of Massachusetts to be a recruiter of black
troops in Norfolk, Virginia. Away from the front, living in a
boarding house from July to November, Brewster could observe
the war and society from a new perspective. He was merely one
among a horde of recruiters who descended upon eastern Virginia and other parts of the upper South in 1864. Brewster
quipped in frustration that "there are two agents to every man
who will enlist." He frequently denigrated the very blacks he
sought to recruit, commenting on their alleged propensity to "lie
and steal" and their "shiftless" attitude toward work. But he
seemed delighted at the presence of a black cavalry regiment
that made the local "secesh" furious, and after holding back
judgment, he finally praised the black troops who had "fought
nobly" and filled the local hospitals with "their wounded and
mangled bodies."[34] In Brewster's mind, like that of most white
Americans, a full recognition of the dignity of blacks awaited
their battlefield sacrifice. Brewster had come to know the folly of
desperate heroism; but precisely such an expectation became the
test of manhood for the black men he helped to recruit in that
last anguished year of the war.

Unhappy and shiftless in his own way, feeling as though he
were "living among strangers," and deeply ambivalent about
what to do with the rest of his life, Brewster went about his
business with an element of greed and very little zeal.[35] He
boarded with a southern woman named Mrs. Mitchell, who had
just taken the oath of allegiance to the Union. Her husband and
one brother were in the Confederate army, while a second
brother served in the Union navy. All the servants at the house,
of course, were black and now "free." When Brewster, the Yankee conqueror and occupying officer, was not trying to find and
spirit black men into the army, he spent time playing with Mrs.

Mitchell's three small children, or going to the market with his landlady's mother and a "darky girl." Such bizarre domestic tranquility in the midst of catastrophic civil war makes an unforgettable image. Moreover, images of death and maiming frequently appear in Brewster's last letters from the war; he writes of street "murders" committed in Norfolk contrasted with the killing in war, and his only use of the concept of "courage" was applid either to black troops or to the surgeons who volunteered to go fight a yellow-fever epidemic in North Carolina.[36] Living among a subdued enemy, and quietly observing the revolution that Confederate defeat and black emancipation might bring, Brewster sat in a recruiting office reading and writing "love letters" for black women to and from their husbands at the front. This is what remained of his job and his war, and it was a remarkable vantage point.

Still patronizing toward the freedpeople, he nevertheless acknowledged their humanity and their influence. "We have to read thier letters from and write letters to thier husbands and friends at the front daily," Brewster observed, "so that I expect I shall be adept in writing love letters, when I have occasion to do so on my own account. they invariably commence (the married ones) with 'my dear loving husband,' and end with 'your ever loving wife until death.'" If we can imagine Brewster, sitting at a table with a lonely freedwoman, swallowing his prejudices toward blacks and women, and repeatedly writing or reciting the phrases "give my love to . . ." and "you Husband untall Death . . ." we can glimpse in this tiny corner of the war the enormous potential of the human transformations at work in 1864. Thousands of such quiet ironies—the Northampton store clerk turned soldier, recruiter, and clerical conduit for the abiding love among black folks that slavery could not destroy—helped produce what Lincoln referred to in his second Inaugural Address as the result so "fundamental and astounding."[37]

Brewster left the war for good in November 1864, and for a while he returned to working in a store. But by 1868, he must have written some love letters of his own, for he married Anna P. Williams, the sister of one of his friends in the Tenth. Charles and Anna would eventually have six children, some of whom achieved local prominence in western Massachusetts. By the mid-1870s, Brewster had turned his prewar sense of failure into a steady sash, door, and paint business. By 1880, he bought one of the finest residences in Northampton, built three green-houses, and opened a successful year-round florist business. Local friends remembered him as a man "of great independence of character." He remained an active Republican until the election of 1884 when, for reasons unknown, he supported the Democrat Grover Cleveland rather than James G. Blaine. Brewster became a financially successful, Gilded Age businessman. The disdainful, insecure, ambitious soldier of the war letters became the old veteran and family man who grew flowers, speculated in land and other property, made a comfortable living, and actively participated in the G.A.R. (the Grand Army of the Republic, the Union veterans' organization). The soldier of 1864 who so feared civilian life had married well, and done all right after all.[38]

By the 1880s, like most veterans, Brewster was ready for reconciliation with Confederate veterans. He seemed to love regimental reunions and other G.A.R. activities. In October 1886 he attended Blue-Gray reunions at Gettysburg and Fredericksburg, writing to his children that "papa has had the grandest time he ever had in his life." Of the Confederate veterans, he could only marvel at how they "seem as glad to see us as though we were brothers or cousins at least." The tour of the Gettysburg battlefield "brings the fearful old days so fresh . . . ," wrote the veteran, but it also left him full of a survivor's awe and pride. The visit to the slopes where he had endured the battle of Chancellorsville was the "most glorious time," he reported, marred only by the regret that he did not get to see the "old long breastwork" at Spotsylvania. Partly as tourists, partly as icons of a refurbished martial ideal, partly just as old men searching for their more active and noble youth, and partly as "symbols of changelessness" in a rapidly industrializing age, veterans like Brewster discovered a heroic nostalgia in these reunions.[39] The former soldier who had so fervently sought a sense of community in the army could now truly belong in a society building monuments, and rapidly forgetting the reality of combat and the deep racial and ideological roots of the war.

Brewster died in October 1893 aboard the clipper ship *Great*

Admiral in New York harbor, where his twenty-two-year-old daughter, Mary Katherine, was about to embark on an around-the-world voyage. Brewster had been the guest of the ship's Captain, James Rowell, himself a Civil War veteran. The grief-stricken Mary Kate decided to stay on the voyage as planned. Secure in her possession, and prominent in her plans for work at sea, were her father's original war letters, which she intended to transcribe for publication. A young woman with literary ambitions and considerable skill, Mary Kate cherished her father's letters which, of course, had all been written to her grandmother and aunts. To the end Brewster had an adoring female audience for his letters and his "war stories."[40]

As we imagine Mary Kate Brewster aboard ship somewhere in the Indian Ocean on her way to Australia, vicariously reliving her father's war experiences, we can also imagine American society distancing itself from and sentimentalizing the horror and the causes of the Civil War. By the 1890s, the next generation—daughters and sons—were following their parents' lead in constructing an idealized national memory of the war, rooted in a celebration of veterans' valor that rarely included Brewster's horrifying image of the screaming soldier in the trench at Spotsylvania, and instead preferred his descriptions of moonlit campgrounds and sun-drenched mornings on the march. Brewster had cursed and embraced war, hated and worshipped violence, condemned slavery and practiced racism. His interior struggle with his own values and with war itself was not the one best fitted to the emerging social memory of the Civil War, nor the imagination of a young Victorian woman. But today, Brewster's experiences serve as another reminder of the recurring power of war to attract and destroy individuals, and to draw and repel the human imagination.

Chapter 5

xxxxxxxxxxxxxxxxxxxxxxxxxxxx

"I's a Man Now":
Gender and African American Men

JIM CULLEN

At one point in the 1989 film *Glory,* a former slave named Rawlins who has enlisted in the Union army gets angry at a fellow soldier. A runaway South Carolinian private named Trip has just insulted Searles, an educated Bostonian, by telling him he acts like "the white man's dog." Offended by this remark, Rawlins gives Trip a piece of his mind, criticizing him for his insolent attitude toward whites, his fellow soldiers, and the war effort in general. "The time's comin' when we're goin' to have to ante up and kick in like men," Rawlins tells Trip. "Like men!" Trip is not instantly transformed by these remarks, and he will take some of his rebellious skepticism to a sandy grave off the coast of Charleston. But while he later tells his commanding officer that he does not wish to carry the regimental colors, he echoes Rawlins by saying he plans to "ante up and kick in." And on the eve of the battle, he tells his fellow black soldiers that whatever may happen, "we men, ain't we." (They affirm him in unison.)

Like so much popular culture, these fictionalized characters reveal—and conceal—a good deal about American history and culture. Cast in an unabashedly heroic light where even rebels like Trip ultimately carry the flag, *Glory* obscures the ambivalence, ambiguity, and disillusionment that military experi-

ence held for many African American men and women during
the Civil War. Indeed, the absence of black women in the film
belies their presence in many military encampments as civilians,
nurses, or, in the case of Harriet Tubman, crucial strategic combatants. On the other hand, *Glory* does suggest the diversity of
black life in the United States in its cast of characters, and does,
like many recent popular and academic histories, recognize the
role African Americans played in securing their own emancipation.

Glory is also illuminating in the way it deals with gender. As the
above example suggests, a concern with becoming and behaving
like a man is an important theme of the movie, as indeed it was
for many actual black soldiers. In newspaper articles, government affidavits, and letters to officials, families, and each other,
manhood surfaces again and again as an aspiration, a concern,
or a fact of life. But while it's one thing to note the recurring
reference to manhood in such documents, it's another to know
exactly what these people meant by it. Is one born (slave or free)
with manhood, or must one earn it? Is it derived by virtue of
one's sex, or is it the result of acting in a particular way? Did
manhood mean the same thing to black people as it did to white
people? Since many of these men were semi-literate—or had to
depend on others to write for them—they were not inclined to
elaborate on their terminology. Even those who were quite literate did not bother to explain what they assumed their readers
would understand.

However varied their understanding of the term, what's striking in looking over the records these men left behind is a widely
shared sense that the Civil War did indeed mark a watershed for
black manhood. As the *material* conditions of their lives
changed—as they joined the armed forces, were freed from slavery, or both—so too did their *ideological* conceptions of themselves as men. In some cases these new ideas were expressed
explicitly; other times implicitly. As historian Joan Scott has
noted, an awareness of sexual difference as fact or metaphor has
always been important, though the concept of gender as a separate analytic category is very much a late-twentieth-century invention.[1] This means any exploration of gender in historical
contexts should proceed with some caution. But proceed it

should, because the attempt, however imperfect, to understand
how other people understood themselves can perhaps still teach
us something about them—and ourselves.

The outbreak of war in 1861 led men all over the country to
volunteer for military service, and African Americans were no
exception. In Washington, Pittsburgh, Cleveland, Boston, and
many other cities and towns, black men offered their services
singly or in groups to recruiting officers. Almost without exception, they were turned down. Ironically, black men had some of
their best success in the Confederacy, though they were generally put to work building fortifications or other kinds of tasks
requiring heavy labor. In one sense, this is hardly surprising:
southern society had been organized for blacks to perform these
roles, which were probably accepted during wartime in the hope
of being looked upon with favor in the event of Confederate
victory. Except in emergencies, southern blacks were not permitted to fight, and organizations like New Orleans's Native Guards
(a part of the state militia composed of free African Americans)
found offers of their services declined. Rejections varied in tone,
but their content often echoed that of a Cincinnati man who said,
"We want you damn niggers to keep out of this; this is a white
man's war."[2]

Officially, he was right—at first it was a white man's war. The
efforts of abolitionists to the contrary, secession, not slavery, was
the pretext for the outbreak of hostilities, and the Lincoln administration assiduously courted slaveholding states still in the
Union by avoiding any appearance of restructuring existing race
relations. President Lincoln personally countermanded the orders of generals like John Fremont and David Hunter who attempted to free slaves in occupied Confederate territory, and
resisted Congressional efforts to punish rebellious slaveholders
by confiscating their "property."

Under such circumstances, one might wonder why African
Americans wanted to fight at all. And in fact some did question
getting involved. "We have nothing to gain, and everything to
lose, by entering the lists as combatants," wrote one man from
Troy, New York. Wrote another from Colorado: "I have observed with much indignation and shame, their [African Ameri-

cans'] willingness to take up arms in defence of this unholy, ill-begotten would-be Republican government." Many of those opposed to African American involvement were appalled by the prospect of fighting for a country that made no promise of redressing centuries of injustice. "I, as the Captain, in behalf of the company, am resolved never to offer or give service, except be it on equality with all other men," stated a prospective volunteer from Philadelphia.[3]

At the same time, however, many African Americans were eager to join the struggle even before the Emancipation Proclamation was issued, and cast their advocacy in gendered terms. On May 1, 1861, a group of freemen in New York City met and voted down a resolution offering to fight they knew would be rejected. Nevertheless, the *Anglo-African,* a weekly newspaper that circulated in the metropolitan area, urged its readers to remain in a state of readiness. Acknowledging the argument that the conflict was "a white man's war," the paper nevertheless asserted that the northern way of life offered privileges of free labor, education, and freedom from divided families that should be guarded, if not expanded. "Are these rights worth the having?" the *Anglo-African* asked. "If they are then they are worth defending with all our might and at any cost. It is illogical, unpatriotic, nay mean and unmanly in us to shrink from the defence of these rights and privileges." While some men challenged the *Anglo-African's* position in letters to the editor, still others wrote to support it. "The issue is here; let us prepare to meet it with manly spirit," wrote one Philadelphia man in rebuke to another who had argued for a more neutral approach to the war.[4]

In mid-nineteenth-century America, the word "manly" was rich with connotations of an acquired sense of civilization and duty.[5] For participants in the *Anglo-African* debate, the manly thing to do was defend, and perhaps expand, a way of life by fighting, a behavior considered the unique province of males. It also meant having the will to act on one's own behalf. "God will help no one that refuses to help himself," the Philadelphia writer said in his letter. "The prejudiced white man North or South never will respect us until they are forced to by deeds of our own."[6]

Yet a willingness to fight, and thus achieve manhood by waging a war for freedom, seemed moot if African Americans were barred from fighting. "Why does the Government reject the negro?" asked a frustrated Frederick Douglass in August of 1861. "Is he not a man? Can he not wield a sword, fire a gun, march and countermarch, and obey orders like any other?"[7] For Douglass, of course, the questions were rhetorical. All black men needed was the chance to demonstrate the important truth that they were the white man's equal in war as well as peace.

Actually, some men had been quietly getting the chance from the very beginning. Despite the official federal ban on black recruitment, unofficial African American units were organized in Kansas, South Carolina, and Louisiana, and saw action in the early years of the war (indeed, blacks had been participants in the guerrilla warfare over "Bloody Kansas" for years). Moreover, as readers of Herman Melville's fiction know, the American navy had long been a multiracial institution.[8] Some men also worked as spies. Many others weakened the Confederate war effort with acts of insubordination on plantations or by escaping from them, often finding refuge behind Union lines and working as cooks or laborers.

All these actions made official policy increasingly irrelevant. Meanwhile, intractable rebel resistance, military defeat, and growing difficulties in meeting manpower needs from white volunteers impelled the Lincoln administration to widen its war aims and turn the political screws on the Confederacy. It is in this context that the President issued the preliminary Emancipation Proclamation in September of 1862, which placed the war on new footing and placed the status of African Americans at the very center of national life.

Even as the political tide on slavery was turning in the summer of 1862, so was the U.S. position on arming African Americans. In July, Congress passed a confiscation act enabling the President "to employ as many persons of African descent as he may deem necessary and proper for the suppression of this rebellion." It also repealed a 1792 law that barred blacks from the military. Lincoln himself also made the case for black enlistments that month when discussing emancipation with the Cabinet, and gave the go-ahead even before the proclamation was issued in September or took effect in January of 1863.

Simultaneously, military considerations became even more urgent than political ones. In the spring of 1862, the Confederate-spurned Native Guards of New Orleans offered to join the Union effort after General Benjamin Butler occupied the city. Butler at first refused, but when threatened by a Confederate attack in August, he changed his mind and recruited three black regiments. At the same time, the need to withdraw cavalry forces from captured territory in the South Sea Islands off the coast of South Carolina led to the formation of the "Department of the South," under which freed slaves were permitted to become soldiers.

It was the Emancipation Proclamation, however, that opened the floodgates for black enlistment. Now possessing the means—and promised a worthy end—leaders of the black community enthusiastically joined the recruitment effort. John S. Rock, William Wells Brown, Sojourner Truth, and many other luminaries from the northern abolitionist community worked as recruitment agents. The first two northern regiments were formed in Massachusetts, though in fact they were comprised of men from all over the North and even Canada. Meanwhile, over 20,000 volunteers were raised in the Mississippi valley between April and December of 1863 alone. By the end of the war, approximately 180,000 African Americans served in the United States Armed Forces. Constituting less than 1 percent of the North's population, African American soldiers comprised roughly 10 percent of the army.[9]

One of the most tireless proponents of black enlistment was Frederick Douglass, whose own sons joined the fabled Massachusetts 54th Volunteer Infantry. "Let the black man get upon his person the brass letters 'U.S.'; let him get an eagle on his button, and a musket on his shoulder and bullets in his pocket, and there is no power on earth which can deny that he has earned the right to citizenship in the United States," he wrote in one widely quoted article.[10]

The editor of *Douglass's Monthly* was also fond of drawing on the manly rhetoric of action. In another piece, he asserted that African Americans were fighting "for principle, and not from passion," and that the black soldier secures "manhood and freedom" via civilized warfare. Douglass went on to make an unfortunate comparison between blacks and Native Americans, "who go forth as a savage with a tomahawk and scalping knife," but in doing so he revealed a definition of manhood as less the amoral use of brute force than the controlled application of power to achieve a just objective.[11]

It wasn't only Douglass—or the black leadership—who drew on the language of manhood. Enlisted soldiers often appeared as featured speakers during recruitment drives and made such appeals to their audience. The remarks of one soldier in Nashville in 1863 are highly revealing in this regard:

> Come boys, let's get some guns from Uncle Sam, and go coon hunting; shooting those gray back coons that go poking about the country nowadays (Laughter) . . . Don't ask your wife, for if she is worth having she will call you a coward for asking her. (Applause and waving of hankerchiefs by the ladies.)[12]

This passage is striking in two ways. First, it draws on the southern white habit of describing slaves as animals. Here, the blacks are the men and the rebels are the animals, rendered in a mode of male bravado that is still common in our own day. Second, these comments also suggest a definition of manhood derived from gender conventions understood—and endorsed— by women, of man as fighter who leaves the home in order to protect it.

Unfortunately, the story of the struggle for black enlistment is not an altogether happy one, and not only because these men fought for the right to kill and be killed. A variety of factors marred the effort. First among these was racism, which impeded the project in the North and checked it in the Confederacy until the very end of the war. "If you make [the African American] the instrument by which your victories are won," an Ohio congressman warned, "you must treat him as a victor is entitled to be treated, with all decent and becoming respect." Others supported black enlistment because they would rather have blacks die than whites. "But as for me, upon my soul!/So liberal are we here/I'll let Sambo be murthered instead of myself/On every day of the year" went a popular song attributed to Irish-Americans. Nor were such attitudes limited to the working classes. "When this war is over & we have summed up the entire loss of life it has imposed on the country I shall not have any regrets if it is found that a part of the dead are *niggers* and that *all* are not white men," wrote the Governor of Iowa to the general-in-chief of the army in 1862.[13]

Indeed, white eagerness to have blacks serve in the army reached vicious proportions. Civilians and government officials soon realized that enlisted blacks could be credited toward conscription quotas, and coercion and terror were often the result, as some black men were literally abducted from their homes and forced into the army. Northern states would send agents to enlist "underemployed" men of the occupied South for a fee, and they wandered the countryside in search of recruits, often impeding military operations and demanding food, forage, and transportation from their "hosts." In many cases, these men also bilked enlistees of their bounties.[14]

Even those who entered the army freely and enthusiastically quickly encountered situations making it clear that even if the Union was committed to freedom, it had no intention of offering equality. Once black enlistment became official policy, the government ordered that all black units should have only white commissioned officers, barring advancement to enlisted African Americans. Many blacks who were already officers, especially in New Orleans, were systematically hounded into resigning their commissions. The army did permit the commissioning of chaplains and surgeons, and there were some exceptions made to the rule, most notably Martin Delany, who was promoted to major at the very end of the war. Noncommissioned officers were also allowed, but these had much less prestige.[15]

Another source of frustration was pay. Despite the promise of receiving the same amount of money as whites, black soldiers were paid only about half of what their white counterparts were. Some black units refused their pay in protest, at great personal cost to themselves and their families, and still others threatened to lay down their arms. Some were shot or jailed for their protests. Some 80 percent of U.S. soldiers shot for mutiny were black.[16]

A letter to the Governor of Massachusetts by a commander of black troops suggests how central a place manhood—more specifically, a sense of manhood that insisted upon an equality previously limited to whites—occupied in such disputes:

They enlisted because *men* were called for, and because the Government signified its willingness to accept them as such not because of the money offered them. They would rather work and fight until they are mustered out of the Service, without any pay than accept from the Government less than it gives to other soldiers from Massachusetts, and by so accepting acknowledge that because they have African blood in their veins, they are less men, than those who have saxon.[17]

When, after much delay, Congress finally acted to correct the situation in June of 1864, it did so by making an invidious distinction between those who had been slaves before the war and those who were free. Such a policy impaired morale within these regiments, and exacerbated tensions between northern and southern blacks, and the previously slave and previously free.[18]

Finally, African Americans were often given a disproportionate amount of fatigue duty. Ordered to dig ditches, build fortifications, clean latrines, or other dirty work, they were often denied the opportunity to drill or perform the more esteemed tasks of soldiering. Such practices not only bred resentment but also contributed to the higher disease rate among blacks, many of whom shouldn't have been in the army in the first place or who were overworked by their officers. Whereas two white soldiers died of disease for every one who died in battle, for blacks the ratio was about ten to one. One in twelve whites in the Union army died of disease in the war; one in five blacks did.[19]

The flagrant abuses suffered by these men led many recruiters, including Douglass, to suspend their efforts, while those oppressed by these injustices sought the aid of sympathetic officers or government officials. Here, too, the language of manhood was used, not so much as an assertion that African Americans were entitled to the same challenges whites were, but as a request for decency for those whose identities could not be reduced to that of a mere worker, as was the case under slavery. "The black men has wives and Sweet harts Jest like the white men," stated an anonymous New Orleans black man in 1863:

. . . it is rettin that a man can not Serve two master But it Seems that the Collored population has got two a rebel master and a union master the both want our Servises one wants us to make

Cotton and Sugar and the Sell it and keep the money   the union masters wants us to fight the battles under white officers and the injoy both the money and the union.[20]

"Today the Anglo Saxon Mother, Wife, or Sister are not alone, in tears for departed Sons, Husbands, and Brothers," wrote another man to President Lincoln, describing the apathy and contempt with which blacks were treated, and the deprivations endured by the "needy Wives, and little ones" at home. "We have done a Soldiers Duty," he said. "Why cant we have a soldier's pay?"[21] Implicit in such writings was a belief that manhood meant responsibility not only to the nation or even one's race but to the "Sweet harts" and families whose pride—and, more pointedly, whose livelihoods—depended on those in the service. Indeed, it seems there were times when men affirmed their manhood by preferring family over the army. "I poor man, wid large famerly—my wife Rinah she can't work," said one husband, who had already served in the army, to a recruiter. "Dey took me an' kep me tree mont' an' nebber pay me, not one cent. My wife hav notting to eat—mus' starve."[22]

Despite the multiple setbacks these African American soldiers endured, some did find entrance into the armed forces to be an affirming experience. "Now we sogers are men—for the first time in our lives," a sergeant based in South Carolina told a meeting in Philadelphia. "Now we can look our old masters in de face. They used to sell and whip us, and we did not dare say one word. Now we ain't afraid, if they meet us, to run the bayonet through them." A former slave agreed with this assessment. "This was the biggest thing that ever happened in my life," he said. "I feel like a man with a uniform on and a gun in my hand." Even whites who worked with these men were struck by the transformation. "Put a United States uniform on his back and the *chattel* is a *man*," observed one white soldier. "You can see it in his look. Between the toiling slave and the soldier is nothing but a god could lift him over. He feels it, his looks show it."[23]

Becoming a "man" killed two racist conceptions of African Americans with one stone. In the years before the war, southern whites had defended their peculiar institution by describing blacks as children or animals, depending on which description made their "stewardship" more rhetorically defensible.[24] As armed soldiers, these people were neither. War has always been seen as a place where "boys" become men, but for African American men in the Civil War, this was particularly true, even poignant. Soldiering also endowed these men with a new power to prevent the capricious abuse of those who could no longer be considered property. "The fact is, when colored Soldiers are about they are afraid to kick colored people on the streets as they usually do," black minister Henry Turner told the secretary of war in February of 1866.[25]

Becoming a man also had sexual dimensions. Turner described an experience eight months before, when the men in his regiment stripped their clothes to cross a stream:

> I was much amused to see the secesh women watching with the utmost intensity, thousands of our soldiers, in a state of nudity. I suppose they desired to see whether these audacious Yankees were really men, made like other men, or if they were a set of varmints. So they thronged the windows, porticos, and yards, in the finest attire imaginable. Our brave boys would disrobe themselves, hang their garments upon their bayonets and through the water they would come, walk up on the street, and seem to say to the feminine gazers, "Yes, though naked, we are your masters."[26]

In this striking passage—and, one imagines, widely elsewhere—manhood becomes sexual power. In the antebellum South, intercourse (sexual and otherwise) was either taboo or cast African American men in a subordinate position. Now, however, these men have attained mastery over their bodies which they use for their own purposes, a mastery that compels white southerners to observe it in action. No force is used, no words are exchanged, but the effect of a new sexual order is unmistakable, symbolized by bayonets supporting (Yankee) uniforms.

For many men, black and white, the ultimate test of manhood was combat. As noted, African Americans participated in a number of land and sea battles in the first two years of the war, but three engagements in 1863 went far to validate—and valorize—the contributions of African Americans. The first of these was at Port Hudson in Louisiana, a key Confederate stronghold for the control of the Mississippi River. Black troops participated on an assault on the fort, which failed. But their performance impressed many observers. "It is no longer possible to doubt the bravery and steadiness of the colored race, when rightly led," the New York *Times* reported.[27] There is more than a little paternalism in this statement, as in Thomas Wentworth Higginson's remark that the men under his charge were "growing more like white men—less naive and less grotesque."[28] Yet just as much as the black soldiers it was white observers who were re-evaluating their perceptions in light of new developments.

This is true even of Confederates. Barely ten days after Port Hudson, at the battle of Milliken's Bend, African Americans played a crucial role in resisting a rebel attack designed to weaken the Federal grip around Port Hudson and Vicksburg. Perhaps the best explanation of what followed was offered by a southern general: "The charge was resisted by the negro portion of the enemy's force with considerable obstinacy, while the white or true Yankee portion ran like whipped curs almost as soon as the charge was ordered."[29] Even though "true" Yankees are white, this man allows that it was black soldiers who defeated the Confederates.

The most celebrated battle involving black troops was the struggle for Fort Wagner off the coast of Charleston in July of 1863. (This event forms the backdrop for *Glory*.) In part this stems from the participation of the Massachusetts 54th led by Robert Gould Shaw, the son of prominent abolitionists, who would die in the assault and be lionized for the next century. As in the case of Port Hudson, the assault on Wagner was a failure in military terms, but a resounding political and cultural victory for blacks. "It is not too much to say that if this Massachusetts 54th had faltered when its trial had come, two hundred thousand colored troops for whom it was a pioneer would never have been put into the field," according to the New York *Tribune*.[30] Black troops would later play an important role in the Virginia theater in 1864, and were the first to march into Charleston when the city finally fell in 1865.

As in so many other aspects of black life, these victories came at a price. First among these costs was death. At Milliken's Bend, one Louisiana regiment lost almost 45 percent of its men to death or casualties, one of the highest proportions of any battle in the whole war.[31] There is a cruel irony that black men did so much dying on the battlefield—considered the very zenith of manhood—even as they were still dismissed as less than men.

There was also a persistent concern that African Americans were used as cannon fodder. Seven months after the Fort Wagner attack, an attack all knew would be a bloodbath for the unit that led it, a correspondent from the New York *Tribune* testified before the American Freedmen's Inquiry Commission that a battle planner had said, "Well, I guess we will let [abolitionist general George] Strong lead and put those d----d niggers from Massachusetts in the advance; we may as well get rid of them, one time or another."[32] Ironically, even when white commanders had relatively good intentions, they could backfire. At the last minute, black units trained to lead the attack at the Battle of the Crater in 1864 were held back in favor of white units to avoid charges of treating black life casually. But when white units foundered in the assault, the blacks were sent to assist, got trapped, and the result was disaster for all.

Another problem was the enemy. The Confederacy refused to treat black soldiers as prisoners of war in exchange negotiations, which led the Union to stop exchanges altogether, with particularly tragic results for those in dangerously unhealthy prison camps. Threats to execute all black soldiers were never officially enacted, perhaps in fear of reprisals President Lincoln promised would follow. But rebel hatred for black troops led to widespread reports of brutal massacres, most notably at Fort Pillow, Tennessee, where future Ku Klux Klan founder Nathan Bedford Forrest allegedly allowed black soldiers who had surrendered to be executed and allegedly condoned the burning of a hospital. "Remember Fort Pillow!" became a rallying cry for black soldiers who subsequently fought with even greater ferocity, often flying a black flag that signified that they would not expect—or give—any mercy.

The most sincere form of flattery is imitation, and the Union's success in mobilizing black manpower led to proposals from leading Confederates to arm African Americans. To do so, however, would create difficult ideological contradictions for a would-be nation predicated on white supremacy and slavery, and such proposals were rejected. Still, as one proslavery theorist told Jefferson Davis in 1865, blacks could fight and be granted their freedom, but that's all—no voting, legal protection, or any form of equality. Indeed, such a suggestion seems prescient in suggesting the fate of African Americans before and after Reconstruction.[33] Even more persuasive than the force of such logic was the deteriorating military situation, and the support of General Robert E. Lee in enlisting blacks led the Confederate government to change its mind in the spring. By then, however, it was too late; within weeks, black Union troops would be among the first to march into Richmond. They would also be among the last to leave the army; the black proportion of the armed forces went from about one-tenth to over one-third by the fall of 1865, as earlier enlistees were mustered out first and some blacks were sent to remote outposts.[34]

The passage of the Thirteenth Amendment and Union victory in 1865 represented a watershed in African American history, one in which the actions of many blacks, North and South, slave and free, man and woman, had participated. The sense of pride of—and in—army veterans was especially strong, and many went on to become leaders in their communities. Some, like naval hero Robert Smalls and army officer Martin Delany, became important political leaders in state and national politics. For the rest of their lives, black men would relish their contributions. "If we hadn't become sojers, all might have gone back as it was before," former slave and army veteran Thomas Long wrote after the war. "But now tings can neber go back, because we have showed our energy and our courage and our naturally manhood."[35]

Perhaps the most important, and lasting, change freedom and fighting wrought was in African American families. For Long, demonstrating manhood was important not only for what it taught the outside world but also for the authority it would give him at home. "Suppose you had kept your freedom witout enlisting in dis army; your chilen might have grown up free and been well cultivated as to be equal to any business," he speculated. "But it would always have been flung in dere faces—'Your fader never fought for he own freedom'—and what could dey answer? Neber can say that to dis African Race any more."[36]

For some men, military experience provided a sense of empowerment even while they were away during the war. "Don't be

uneasy my children   I expect to have you," wrote Missouri soldier to his two enslaved daughters in September of 1864. To
their master, he wrote, "I want you to understand that mary is
my Child and she is a God given rite of my own and you may
hold on to hear as long as you can but I want you to remember
that the longor you keep my Child from me the longor you will
have to burn in hell."[37] (The man was hospitalized on this day
with chronic rheumatism and it's not known what happened;
one can only hope the girls were recovered—and that father and
daughters took solace from a sense of assertiveness that well
might have been unimaginable three years before.)

Before the war, the white gender conventions of separate
spheres and the cult of true womanhood were at best irrelevant
and at worst oppressive to African Americans. Unlike elite white
women, for example, black women were expected to work outside the home. Like some whites, black men performed physical
labor, but as historian James Horton argues, "slavery demanded
that black men forego the intellectual, emotional and tempera-
mental traits of manhood. The ideal slave recognized his inability to control his life." The coming of emancipation then offered
black women the possibility of returning to the home, and gave
black men a powerful sense of agency over their own lives and
responsibility for their families.[38]

In this regard, the war realigned gender conventions in the
black community; as a result, they more closely resembled those
of whites.[39] Indeed, at this point in their history, many African
Americans rejected any attempt to suggest racial difference.
Much to his frustration, Martin Delany, often considered a father of black nationalism, found it "dangerous to go into the
country and speak of color in any manner whatever, without the
angry rejoiner 'we don't want to hear that; we are all one color
now.'"[40] This rejection of racial difference would not remain in
place for all people and all times; by the end of the century, for
example, some black women were finding that white conceptions
of womanhood were still irrelevant or oppressive, and some
white men were arguing that true manhood was predicated on
whiteness.[41]

"How extraordinary, and what a tribute to ignorance and religious hypocrisy, is the fact that in the minds of most people, even

those of liberals, only murder makes men," W. E. B. Du Bois
would later write. "The slave pleaded, he was humble; he protected the women of the South, and the world ignored him. The
slave killed white men; and behold, he was a man."[42] Yet if
manhood was often conflated with the power to kill and destroy,
the documents explored here suggest that at least some black
men also saw it as a source of power to preserve and create. The
key to that power was a personal transformation, a fusion of
biological fact and social aspiration that allowed a man to help
change his world. "What are you, anyhow," a white man in-
sultingly asked a South Carolina soldier in the middle of the war.
"When God made me I wasn't much," came the answer, "but I's a
man now."[43]

PART III

xxxxxxxxxxxxxxxxxxxxxxxxxxxx

Women at War

*W*ar, explained the narrator in Gone with the Wind, "is men's business, not ladies'." *Perhaps Margaret Mitchell intended this as an ironic comment because, to a great extent, she structured her Civil War novel as a tribute to the indomitable will of at least one southern white woman in wartime. Yet, as the quote implies, war is seldom seen as women's work. Usually pictured in supportive roles on the homefront, knitting by the firesides and keeping the home fires burning, women are not usually included in the standard picture of battles, military maneuvers, and soldiering experiences. Certainly according to nineteenth-century notions of white womanhood, the grisly day-to-day experiences of the battlefront stood well outside the boundaries of woman's proper sphere.*

But the Civil War dramatically tested those boundaries of womanhood, forcing white and black women of both sections into new and unsettling circumstances. When women became the victims of wartime occupation, resettlement, or violence, war inevitably imposed a new set of tensions on them. But in other ways, when women became nurses or even combatants, they intentionally and self-consciously took on new roles. Indeed, so remarkable was women's participation in this conflict that one British journalist offered precisely the opposite assessment from that expressed in Gone with the Wind. No war in history, he explained, had ever seemed so much "a woman's war" as the Civil War.

Yet no war occurs in a vacuum, and so women at war, just like men, drew upon the social and cultural understandings of gender that were so much a part of their mid-nineteenth-century world. Southern white women, for example, purposefully struggled to be "ladylike" even when subjected to enemy occupation. Likewise, the men who drew women into the conflict were also aware of maintaining for themselves, and for at least some of the women involved, a sense of proper gender etiquette. Hence, the guerrilla fighters who engaged in some of the most brutal and horrifying acts of war consciously clung to some semblance of gentlemanly honor when they did not commit violence against white women.

Still, women at war inevitably found themselves both intentionally and unintentionally defying nineteenth-century norms. Even nursing, usually considered a refined and acceptable female position in wartime, forced women to challenge traditions and male authority. This may have been especially true for elite northern women who, perhaps more than their southern sisters, were able to gain admission into this profession. One of the best accounts of a Civil War nurse is the one by Susie King Taylor, a former slave; yet black women were almost universally excluded from this line of work. In her essay about nurses in the 1862 Peninsula campaign, Kristie Ross discusses elite northern women and the type of struggle they waged to define their new role. While at first many of the "lady volunteers" consciously sought to uphold their notions of refined womanhood, Ross notes that the experience of war gradually forced them to challenge the genteel and domestic framework imposed upon them by the male officials of the U.S. Sanitary Commission.

A more unusual wartime role for women was spying. The female spy situated herself at the heart of the conflict, sometimes even adopting a male disguise. Perhaps, as Lyde Cullen Sizer suggests in her essay on three Union women spies, this was one reason why some female agents pictured themselves not as warriors but as actresses. Sizer finds that many of the spy narratives, although implicitly challenging notions of women's sphere, tried to contain these unusual female experiences by justifying them with traditional notions of patriotism. The singular exception which Sizer discusses was Harriet Tubman, who, because of her race, apparently was freed from some of the gender constrictions imposed upon white female spies.

Within the Confederacy and in the border states, women experienced features of war that were unknown to most Union women. The boundary between homefront and battlefront blurred as women found themselves caught up directly in the military struggle. Gradually, the

*Union army invaded significant portions of Confederate territory,
placing both black and white inhabitants under Union occupation.
The ladies of occupied New Orleans, discussed in the essay by George
Rable, were among those who soon found that the war had come home.
Rable suggests that many of these embattled women applied a traditional understanding of masculine honor to their unsuccessful Confederate protectors. Their failure to be men, he implies, encouraged the
women to step beyond their prescribed role and engage in repeated
public showdowns with the enemy. These confrontations prompted
Union general Benjamin Butler to proclaim his famous order which
likened the abusive ladies of New Orleans to prostitutes. Butler's comparison was a significant one, reflecting as it did traditional notions of
the evil woman who took to the streets as opposed to the good woman
who kept herself at home. Moreover, he played upon wartime concerns
that affected many women who took up war work and who were told to
keep their distance from much of the battlefront experience for fear of
earning the notorious label of "camp follower."*

*Finally, whatever conventions and civilities Civil War participants
might have clung to, the greatest test of all came from the guerrilla
conflict. In a number of states, the war was waged not by the official
soldiers but by bands of armed guerrillas who carried out a much more
secretive fight with other guerrillas and against ordinary citizens. But,
as Michael Fellman explains in his essay on women and guerrilla
warfare in Missouri, even the guerrilla fighter sought to uphold some
notion of manly honor, perhaps as a way to justify his otherwise amoral
behavior. Significantly, Fellman notes that this often meant a certain
degree of restraint would be exercised with white women, but more
rarely with women of color. Perhaps the guerrilla war revealed the
most dramatic testing of gender proprieties—bringing about some of
the most unusual attempts to live up to notions of proper gender etiquette, as well as some of the most brutal violations of "manly" and
"womanly" behavior.*

Chapter 6

xxxxxxxxxxxxxxxxxxxxxxxxxx

Arranging a Doll's House:
Refined Women as Union Nurses

KRISTIE ROSS

At the end of July 1862, Katharine Wormeley wrote to a friend
from her home in Newport, Rhode Island, lamenting the end of
her twelve weeks as a nurse on the hospital ships sponsored by
the United States Sanitary Commission during the three months
of the Peninsular Campaign. She looked back on her experience
as a time when she and others aboard the transports had
"worked together under the deepest feelings, and to the extent
of our powers, shoulder to shoulder, helping each other to the
best of our ability, no one failing or hindering another." Wormeley was sad, she said, "to feel that it is all over."[1]

There is every reason to believe that Wormeley accurately attributed her melancholy mood to the conclusion of her work in
the 1862 Peninsular Campaign. However, her description of life
on board the Commission's transports as a successful experiment
in cooperation requires some qualification. Just three weeks earlier while still on the Peninsula, Wormeley wrote to a friend that
the women on the transports were not yet allowed to go ashore
and she was trying "to believe, as I am told, that it is impossible
we should." A few days later Wormeley contrived with Arabella
Barlow, wife of Colonel Francis Channing Barlow, to go ashore
"without orders and, indeed, without permission."[2] According to
Georgeanna Woolsey, also a nurse on board the Commission's

boats, Wormeley was by this date a "fascinating wreck."[3] Caught between her loyalty to the Commission and her growing competence and need to see for herself "the state of things," Wormeley reluctantly left the Peninsula not in the spirit of cooperation and unity she described to her friend but in a state of unresolved conflict.[4]

While exploring the alliance between the volunteer women nurses and the men of the United States Sanitary Commission, this paper will expose the subtle undermining of bourgeois gender distinctions by the evolving esprit de corps and experiences of privileged women like Katharine Wormeley on board the hospital transports.

In the weeks following the firing on Fort Sumter in April 1861, communities around the country were eager to organize soldiers' aid societies to funnel needed supplies to their local regiments. In New York City, a group of elite women came together at the instigation of Dr. Elizabeth Blackwell to found the Women's Central Relief Association (WCRA). Their objects were to coordinate women's relief work and to recruit and train female nurses. Inspired by the number and enthusiasm of civilian relief groups, a few influential and professional New York men subsequently formulated a plan to bring all the local aid societies under the control and direction of a national organization known as the United States Sanitary Commission (USSC). After securing official recognition in June 1861, the USSC undertook to construct a centrally organized relief network, to screen and train female nurses in cooperation with the WCRA, and to act as an advisory board to the Medical Bureau in the War Department. The WCRA formally agreed to become a branch of the Commission in September 1861.

Coinciding with these developments in New York, Dorothea Dix was commissioned Superintendent of Army Nurses by the administration in Washington. Blackwell and her associates in the WCRA were frustrated that they had not been officially recognized as the primary recruiting agency for female nurses. Dix, well known to politicians, physicians, and the public for her efforts to reform treatment of the insane, lacked professional credentials and according to Blackwell was "without system, or any practical knowledge of the business."[5] Though Dix was, in fact, quite knowledgeable in the area of hospital construction and management, she lacked experience in organizational structures and was not fully prepared to administer a controversial and potentially cumbersome bureau.

Despite their disappointment and misgivings, the women of he WCRA made sporadic efforts throughout the summer of 1861 to cooperate with Dix and sent thirty-two of their nurses for placement by the superintendent in hospitals around Washington. But they were concerned that their nurses were not being given the respect and authority that was their due. In October, the organization publicly announced its decision to send no more. The nurses had not, complained the WCRA, been placed as they "were fitted to be, in the position of head nurses," but had been "worn down with menial and purely mechanical duties, additional to the more responsible offices and duties of nursing." Moreover, they were "the objects of continual evil speaking among coarse subordinates, are looked at with a doubtful eye by all but the most enlightened surgeons, and have a very uncertain semi-legal position, with poor wages and little sympathy." In short these women had "been only *too refined* for their places." The WCRA would henceforth reserve its women nurses for positions in hospitals erected under the auspices of the United States Sanitary Commission.[6]

By the spring of 1862, the Commission had turned its attention to reforming the government's system of transportation of sick and wounded soldiers. The problems, including jurisdiction over the means of transportation as well as inadequate numbers of physicians and attendants, were not easily remedied. Throughout the war the Quartermaster's Department rather than the medical directors held complete authority over the boats, wagons, and railroads needed for medical transport. In the early months of 1862, at the battle of Fort Donelson and later at Shiloh, the Quartermaster's Department was overwhelmed with moving troops and supplies. The sick and wounded lay unattended and often unprotected for days on the battlefield or river's edge waiting for transportation down the Cumberland and Tennessee rivers to hospitals along the Ohio. The disorganization and wholly inadequate response of the government had stimulated civilian relief groups to charter, staff, and supply their own hospital steamers to help relieve the distress. The commissioners lobbied tirelessly in Washington to reform the system of transport to give medical directors and their subordinates the power to commandeer their own vehicles; and as the summer campaign began, they determined to enter the field to provide a model for needed reform.

As part of their agreement with the War Department to equip, supply, and manage hospital boats chartered by the government, the commissioners invited several women associated with the WCRA to join them as "nurses at large, or matrons" on the boats.[7] Allied by class and social status with the officers and physicians of the Commission, these women were assured the supervisory powers and social deference which had escaped their nurses in Washington's military hospitals. Included among this elite group of about fifteen women invited aboard by the Commission's leadership were Georgeanna Woolsey and her sister Eliza Howland, Caroline E. Lane, Christine Kean Griffin, Ellen Ruggles Strong, Harriet Douglas Whetten, and Katharine Prescott Wormeley. The commissioners, the women, and their oftentimes anxious families all shared the same assumptions about the proper role to be assigned to "lady volunteers" as well as the sort of regulations necessary for their physical and moral protection. The commissioners could be counted on to ensure that the women would be adequately supervised and not left unattended.[8]

The USSC's floating hospitals were under the overall direction of Frederick Law Olmsted, the Commission's general secretary in charge of the office in Washington. Olmsted, assisted by the Unitarian minister Frederick N. Knapp, had a strong penchant for tight organization. Aside from the actual crew, the boats were staffed by the USSC in New York, Boston, or Washington. The Commission employed or accepted as volunteers a wide range of personnel: physicians, female superintendents of nurses, male and female nurses, dressers (usually medical students), stewards, apothecaries, baggagemen, and servants. The boats were outfitted by the Commission and divided into wards. Ideally, each ward was assigned a surgeon, one or two wardmasters (often medical students), and a complement of nurses and their assistants—contrabands, servants, or convalescent soldiers. The medical director of the ship arranged the watches.[9]

The female superintendents were assigned to duty by Olmsted where he felt they were most needed and frequently arranged their own hours of rotation. They were expected to oversee the linen, the patients' clothing, the storeroom, and household supplies. In addition, they were in charge of all the cooking for the sick and had "a general superintendence" over all the wards and other nurses.[10] But they were not allowed to go ashore without the permission of either Olmsted or the physician in charge. This plan ingeniously gave the superintendents some independent authority while it accounted for their whereabouts and kept them at a distance from the more traditional hierarchy of hospital wards. Under these conditions, they were less likely to come into direct conflict with either the surgeons or the medical student dressers.

Two days after arriving on board the *Daniel Webster*, Eliza Howland described the arrangements in a letter to her husband:

> We four are the only women on board except a colored chambermaid, but there are 30 or 40 men nurses and hospital dressers, and several members of the Commission. . . . It is an old ocean steamship . . . now wretchedly dirty. A dozen stout contrabands are at work night and day scrubbing and cleaning, and as they finish, the whitewashers and carpenters succeed them, and by degrees it will be put in good condition.[11]

Gone in Howland's description were many of the social dangers discovered by the WCRA in other military hospitals. There were no insulting subordinates, unenlightened surgeons or purely mechanical duties. Everything was characterized by calm and order, each taking up where the other left off. Organized along class, gender, and racial lines, the Commission's hospital boats presented an opportunity for Howland and her associates to prove that refined women had something unique to contribute to hospital management.

Despite their lack of formal training, the women volunteers entered into hospital service with two important attributes: an eagerness to seize an occasion to escape the routine pattern of their lives and a familiarity with genteel standards of household organization. Far from experiencing any sense of deprivation, they seemed to thrive on the opportunity to be in the thick of unfolding events and to transcend the boundaries of everyday social intercourse. According to Harriet Whetten, life aboard the hospital boats was "without any varnish." It was raw, unpretentious, and lacking the formalities of her ordinary social interactions. Speaking for the whole group, Katharine Wormeley confidently noted that "we all know in our hearts that it is thorough enjoyment to be here,—it is life."[12]

The abandon with which these few elite women enlisted their service sprang not only from a liberating opportunity to broaden their experience and participate in a politically momentous event but also from the conviction that their superior education and powers of organization constituted an area of particular competence. Coming from rather large and elaborate households, these women drew on their backgrounds to oversee the arrangement of clothing, supplies, and equipment as well as supervise the work of the various other domestic workers on board. The women themselves recognized their organizing skills as their greatest asset. Katharine Wormeley said it well when she described their work early in May as "not the doing it, but the knowing how it should be done." Even those like Ellie Strong whom Harriet Whetten criticized as "touching things somewhat too much with the tips of her fingers," had, admitted her co-worker, "done very well in the way of ordering and arranging."[13] Olmsted credited Ellie Strong with saving the soldiers on board the *Elm City* from "the narrow incompetence of the surgeons— not as surgeons, but as hotel keepers." Mrs. Strong, asserted Olmsted "can keep a hotel." Apparently, there was a place for someone with Ellie Strong's managerial abilities within the hospital order.[14]

The recipients of Ellie Strong's organizational directives—the paid nurses, orderlies, and contrabands—were assigned much of the menial, physical labor involved in preparing and maintaining these floating hospitals. The commissioners and the superintendents believed that if left to themselves, the paid employees would remain disorganized, avoid their work, and perhaps do positive harm. Indeed, the notion that these "others" were simple, irresponsible, and "scatterbrained" justified the need for the volunteers in the first place. Georgeanna Woolsey confided to her journal on board the *Daniel Webster* that the staff had just refitted the staterooms because the male nurses had been "riot-

ing in boots in the nice clean beds" and pulling out the quilts to
be used as doors. Woolsey and her sister Eliza Howland reported
finding candle ends tucked away or stuck in cakes of soap "with
every facility for setting the ship on fire," an oversight they also
charged to the paid male nurses.[15] The contrabands too had to
be looked after and put to work. Woolsey complained to her
mother that she had a "daily struggle with the darkeys in the
kitchen, who protest against everything." Wormeley thought
their relations with the contrabands good until "it becomes a
question of work." For these women, here was a strong argument for their employment on the hospital boats. Without them,
they assumed that the Commission, like the government, would
have to rely on an ill-prepared, unmotivated, and inadequately
supervised labor force.[16]

To be sure, the female volunteers could never take their employment for granted, and many of their comments about other
workers can be read as part of an elaborate justification of their
precarious position. Close friends and relatives regularly communicated their concerns not only for the volunteers' health and
safety but also for their position as gentlewomen in a dirty, infected atmosphere among many classes of strange men.
Whatever their motivations, friends and relatives sensed the potentially transforming nature of life on the transports. Wormeley
reported that the mother of one of her companions wrote "dismal letters, which try her very much,—saying . . . that a lady
must put away all delicacy and refinement for this work." Many
of the volunteers responded to such threats to their status as
cultivated women in a way to maximize their usefulness and
minimize the dangers. Hired nurses, convalescent soldiers and
contrabands were an important part of this defense. Much like
household servants, they were always available to handle the
dirty work. As Harriet Whetten put it to a disapproving relative,
"You must understand that there are men nurses and orderlies
detailed so that we volunteer ladies have nothing disagreeable to
do. Administering medicines and food and caring for them in
every way as if they were our brothers is what we have to do." Of
course, this last sentence camouflaged a multitude of sins, but
whether Whetten was being entirely candid with her carping
relative is less important than the fact that the other workers

acted as a buffer between these volunteers and their anxious correspondents. Order, efficiency, foresight, and an appreciation of cleanliness, virtues they could claim as particular to their class and background, and not the actual physical labor were what these women brought to the project. "It is not too much to say that delicacy and refinement and the fact of being a gentlewoman could never tell more than they do here," wrote Katharine Wormeley. For those at home, outfitting a hospital transport was refined women's play. Experienced and educated household managers, they could do it with "as much ease as if they were arranging a doll's house."[17]

The lady volunteers' familiarity with genteel standards of housekeeping dovetailed nicely with the goals of the Sanitary Commission. Untutored as they were in the scientific and social intricacies of the nineteenth-century medical profession, they agreed with the men and physicians of the Commission that good management and attention to cleanliness and hygiene would go far in decreasing the amount of suffering and in preserving the Union Army.[18] "A good bath, seven days rest, and twenty-one good meals" were all most soldiers needed, wrote one of the volunteers. She thought that if the army could only provide such basics, then many of the men sent North could instead be sent back to their regiments.[19] Whether motivated by rules of good housekeeping or a professional reading of statistics, both the commissioners and the women enlisted in their service could agree on two things: first, that disorder, dirt, disease, and the general wasting of the army all went hand in hand; and, second, that the government and its officers were hopelessly remiss in providing for the hygienic needs of the army. "Without exception," wrote Georgeanna Woolsey to her mother, "the government boats so far have been inadequately provisioned, wretchedly officered, and in a general state of confusion." Similarly, Katharine Wormeley denounced the chaotic arrangements on the Peninsula. "You can't conceive what it is to stem the torrent of this disorder and utter want of organization."[20]

Although the commissioners and the female superintendents agreed on the domestic arrangements necessary to the successful operation of the transport service, the women's experience and growing self-reliance began to undermine the contract between the volunteers and the male commissioners. Though they had initially welcomed and, in fact, depended on the Commission's consideration and recognition of the attributes and privileges of refined women, some of the volunteers began to chafe under the restrictions imposed on them by their male colleagues. The commissioners remained intent on both directing and protecting the women enlisted in their service, while the women became increasingly independent in thought and deed. In the privacy of their letters and diaries the volunteers struggled to remain loyal to the policies and leadership of the Commission, while their growing self-confidence and mutual support pushed them to reconsider their subordinate and dependent position and to desire more information, greater freedom of movement, and some discretionary power. In their private comments about fellow workers and in their ongoing assessment of the Commission's leadership, the women began to expose the contradictions of gender distinctions and to suffer some of the psychological discomfort associated with their confusion.

Though Katharine Wormeley tried to reassure her friends and relatives that her work was perfectly consistent with her position at home, life aboard the hospital transports was hardly comparable to play in a doll's house. Amid the vicissitudes and accumulating horror of the Peninsular campaign, the staff on the Commission's boats, despite their attention to organization and system, was at times overwhelmed by the sudden arrival of hundreds of sick and wounded men, while at others they were unnerved by boredom. The unavoidable intimacy of life on the transports and the interdependency of the entire staff throughout alternating periods of crisis and idleness forced the female volunteers to reconsider the everyday forms and behavior of both men and women. For a few fleeting weeks, conditions on the transports highlighted the artificiality and socially contrived nature of the symbols and assigned attributes of gender, but neither the women nor their male colleagues were necessarily encouraged by the complexity of what they saw.

Katharine Wormeley's exposure to the Zouaves, a Union regiment serving as nurses on board the transports, prompted her to reassess her presumption of gender differences. Patterning their uniform after the Algerian Zouaves of the French colonial armies, these soldiers in their colorful costume of baggy trousers, gaiters, short open jacket, and fez initially repulsed Wormeley. "For an American citizen to rig himself as an Arab is demoralizing," she confessed. Struck by their flowing, more feminine garb, Wormeley realized that her mental picture and definition of white male citizenship did not fit these soldiers. Significantly, some two weeks later after the wounded from the Battle of Fair Oaks had expanded the dimensions of her work, Wormeley's opinion of the Zouaves had undergone a dramatic change. No longer did the Zouaves seem so foreign. In fact, their "efficiency, their good sense, their gentleness," according to Wormeley, were marked. Their dress which had so irritated her now took them "out of the usual manners and ways of men." They seemed to lack the "dull, obstinate ways of that sex." The Zouaves suggested the possibility that many distinctions between men and women depended only on the clothes they wore. In other words, these soldiers did not dress nor act like the men Wormeley knew, and they also made intelligent, gentle nurses. Wormeley could not help but see a reflection of herself and her companions in the Zouaves. She had, she admitted, become a "convert to them after a long struggle."[21]

But despite her change in attitude, Wormeley was unable to use her experience with the Zouaves to question gender distinctions in general. Threatened by the challenge to her own belief in gender differences, she relegated the Zouaves to a subordinate category all their own. In Wormeley's final analysis they were "unexceptional human beings of no sex, with the virtues of both." By denying their relevance to real men and women, Wormeley clung to her faith in gender distinctions and minimized any temptation to identify with these common soldiers as her peers. The Zouaves' transcendence of gender was for Wormeley a unique case, unrelated to the world Wormeley trusted and understood.[22]

Though Wormeley might dismiss the Zouaves as an exceptional "unexceptional" class of men, Olmsted could hardly be put in the same category. But he too seemed to exhibit sensitivities while on the Peninsula that might have been described as feminine. Driven, autocratic, and thorough, Olmsted had a face that, according to Wormeley, had "all the expressive delicacy of a

woman's." Georgeanna Woolsey confided to her journal her discovery of Olmsted's clandestine visits to the wards. "It was pleasant," she wrote, to see Olmsted come sit by a patient "with
his arm around his pillow as nearly around his neck as possible talking tenderly to him and slipping away again quietly."
Olmsted only came when "no one was round to look at him."
Though Olmsted may have been circumspect about his feelings
toward the sick and wounded, his softer, unofficial side was acknowledged and respected by the women volunteers.[23]

As the campaign began in earnest, Wormeley and her companions may have been encouraged by their intimate exposure
to men like Olmsted and the Zouaves to expand their own
gender-specific role in the Commission's scheme and to unleash
a wider range of sympathies and ambition. Experience with the
complexity of men may have allowed a fuller identification with
the masculine world surrounding them and a less inhibited exploration of their own personalities. As the casualties began arriving, these women moved away from housekeeping into nursing sick, maimed, and dying soldiers. At some point in the
process, they started to resist the guidance and protection due a
lady in favor of collaboration and collegiality.

Confronted with increasing numbers of suffering men, the
women were anxious to broaden their knowledge of nursing.
They went about their work with a purposefulness and spirit of
cooperation that surprised Olmsted. Returning to the *Ocean
Queen* on May 7, after hundreds of wet, half-starved, typhoid-
stricken soldiers had been put aboard, Olmsted described the
women's "untiring industry, self-possession and tranquil cheer-
fulness" as "incredible," far beyond anything he had imagined or
expected. In a letter to a friend, Wormeley introduced Mrs.
Reading, "an excellent surgical nurse trained in the Crimea under Miss Nightingale." Wormeley confessed to "pumping" Mrs.
Reading extensively. On another occasion after accompanying
ninety very sick fever patients out of the swamp, Wormeley was
relieved when one of the Commission's physicians finally arrived
to give her some general instructions concerning the use of mor-
phine. Harriet Whetten likewise embraced the work as "very real
and very hard and actual nursing, which includes more than
reading, writing and smoothing pillows," skills one assumes she

already had. So absorbed did Whetten become in her work that she apologized to her correspondents for boring them with her hospital stories. Whetten sensed that there was a gap opening between her life on the hospital boats and the life of her friends at home.[24]

Impatient to learn everything they could about the work they were sharing, the volunteers were soon differentiating between themselves and other women, even those of their same class. Like the Zouaves, a few of them discarded their conventional costume. Inspired by the dress of a physician, they substituted the comfort and practicality of flannel shirts for their soiled dresses. Wormeley admitted that she would "dread civilization" if she had to part with her new and, one might add, more masculine uniform.[25]

The female volunteers were acutely aware that, like soldiers, they too were changed by their sustained contact with such enormous destruction and loss of human life. Describing what she found while helping on board a government transport, one volunteer wrote:

> On the floor, our boys lay crowded, fever and wounds together. Eighty-five fever cases, some in collapse. some with black stiff tongues which could not move for want of moisture; others muttering in low delirium. Sixty-three of our brave wounded and fifteen dead waiting for embalment.[26]

Another volunteer tried to depict the wounded that arrived seven days after the Battle of Fair Oaks.

> That week they had lain upon the battlefield, exhausted—their wounds filled with maggots . . . one man dying of lock jaw, another of internal hemorrhage, and one raving in madness with the brain slowly oozing from his death wound.[27]

Some previously untapped resource allowed these women to move among hundreds of tortured and pain-wracked men without a loss of concentration or mental control. "We are changed by all this contact with terror," Georgeanna Woolsey reported to her·mother. "It seems a strange thing that the sight of such misery, such death in life, should have been accepted by us all so quietly as it was. We were simply eyes and hands for those three days." Whetten too realized while crouching down between two severely wounded soldiers that as little as a month earlier, she would never have believed herself capable of what she was now doing. A sort of stoicism, characterized by Olmsted as "granted for the occasion," was common to both men and women working in the human devastation of the Peninsular Campaign.[28]

Surprised by their reactions, the volunteer nurses began to doubt whether other women could muster the energy and self-control to succeed. Still others might bring disgrace to what had already been done. When the daughter of the medical director joined Harriet Whetten on board the *Spaulding*, Whetten worried that her frivolous behavior might compromise all the female nurses. About twenty years old, the lady appeared "in a pink muslin morning dress and embroidered petticoat and has never done anything since she came on board but flirt with one of the medical cadets. It is such people," declared Whetten, "that bring ridicule on the cause." Wormeley too was annoyed by four lady intruders who "if given a duty to do, . . . leave it." Through perseverance, hard work, and a willingness to discard the fastidiousness of bourgeiois society, these women had managed to carve out a respected place for themselves in a world usually reserved for men. Whetten's "cause" was, in fact, their cause. Comparing their flannel shirts with a pink muslin morning dress and the fickle behavior of the four lady intruders with their own steadfast purposes, the volunteers felt threatened by examples of womanhood that confounded such vain pursuits with the seriousness of their own.[29]

To avoid any confusion, the volunteers frequently discouraged untried women from joining them. By the end of July, Whetten confessed to being "afraid" of strange women, albeit well-connected ones, on board the transports. While visiting Philadelphia, Whetten was plagued by women desiring her favor in their quest to become nurses, but she withheld her patronage from such "patriotic females." Jane Newton Woolsey, the mother of Georgeanna Woolsey and Eliza Howland, reported to her daughters with some satisfaction that she had succeeded in turning away a lady with a "strong impulse to offer her services" as a lady nurse. Confronted with the trivial, constricted behavior of many women of their class, the volunteers were convinced that only a select few could actually succeed in fulfilling the role of an army nurse.[30]

The growth of a discriminating mentality enabled the volunteers both to support one another and to deflect criticism and threats to their position from the outside. They were indeed working "shoulder to shoulder" as Wormeley described.[31] As their confidence and nursing expertise matured, they relied less on social convention and more on their own judgment to define the boundaries of their work. With so much misery everywhere and the assurance that they were in fact saving lives, the women felt Olmsted's tight rein beginning to limit their possibilities for service and belittling their contribution.[32] Wormeley especially started to complain in her letters around the middle of June. The new surgeon at the shore hospital, she reported to her mother, "is very cordial to us women, and begs us to come and do what we can. . . . Mr. Olmsted frowns upon the idea,—frowns? No, but he remains impenetrably silent,—which is worse, for we can't rebel at it." Wormeley's mutinous language signaled her understanding of Olmsted's position at the top of the hierarchy, and underscored her frustration with his dictatorial rule. Two days later Wormeley confided in a letter to a friend that if given charge of a hospital she could "make it march" on the condition she "had hold of some of the administrative *power*." Shortly thereafter, Whetten too began gently to question Olmsted's authoritarian style. To her friend Hexie she explained, "we passed a week of restless idleness in the Pamunkey . . . expecting every hour to have the ship filled, and for that reason, I suppose, not allowed by the chief to do any duty on shore." Whetten did not really know why they were kept from helping on shore. Olmsted's "impenetrable silence" left the women guessing his thoughts and protected his sole decision-making power.[33]

Finally, at the time of Stuart's Raid (June 12–15), Wormeley's private grumbling burst forth in angry protest. Ordered out of an area vulnerable to Jeb Stuart's fast-moving cavalry, Wormeley reported that she and Georgy Woolsey were

> highly indignant at being sent away; we thought it shirking our duty, and very inglorious. At last our tongues got loose; we said all

we thought—at least I did. I said more than I thought, because I was in a passion; and all I got for it was the sense of having hurt Mr. Olmsted.[34]

Wormeley was left with the impression that her enthusiasm and longing to expand her role had personally offended Olmsted. She paid for her independence and ambition with feelings of guilt and shame that reminded her of her place and protected Olmsted from ever seriously considering her complaint. In early July, another period of enforced idleness drove Wormeley into a "weary and disconsolate condition."[35]

By this time Olmsted was convinced that the USSC ought to withdraw its hospital transports from the Peninsula altogether. He felt the Medical Bureau unappreciative and often openly hostile to the Commission's active participation in providing for the sick and wounded. He was encouraged as well by the legislative reorganization of the Medical Bureau and the appointment of Commission favorites William A. Hammond and Jonathan Letterman to positions of responsibility and control.[36] Regarding the ladies and female nurses, Olmsted was adamant in his communication to Henry Bellows, the USSC president, that no more be sent. The situation between the two armies was unstable and movement on the James River dangerous.[37] Olmsted on one level acknowledged the contributions of "our noble women," but he and the other commissioners never developed a framework that could accommodate female nurses working in the dangerous, dirty, and bloody crossfire between two opposing armies. As elite lady volunteers in need of male guidance and protection, they were simply part of the Commission's plan to demonstrate to the government the benefits of good management by the best people. Their shift from genteel housekeepers to skilled battlefield nurses was neither recognized nor desired by the officers of the USSC.

By this date, Katharine Wormeley was of two minds. She could sympathize with Olmsted's point of view that the USSC had fulfilled its mission and that the government could and should run its own operation. At the same time, as a seasoned army nurse, she was reluctant to leave her post if she was still needed. She refused to be seen as a passive observer, a lady out for a spin at the front. "To stay here doing nothing, is a sarcasm on the work we have already done," she complained to her mother. In the company of Arabella Barlow, a sympathetic female ally, Wormeley conspired to go ashore without Olmsted's knowledge and judge for herself whether or not she could be of use. Reassured by her foray, Wormeley reported to a friend that she was now "quite content to go home."[38]

Despite this last independent gesture, Wormeley was probably in no condition to pursue a real separation from the Commission's leadership. Perhaps more than her companions, Wormeley had wrestled with the contradictions and limitations of inclusion in the war based on the privileges and proscriptions of class and gender. Her experience had left her depressed and exhausted. She had been invited on board the transports because she was a lady, and yet the war and the work itself had begun to push and pull at the rules, preoccupations, and qualities which defined her as a member of that class. She had caught a glimpse of life beyond the boundaries of refined womanhood, and she was both intrigued and disturbed by the possibilities.

Wormeley watched as Olmsted parted for home dressed in the "fashionable garb of a gentleman." She too had changed for the occasion. Loathe to part with her flannel shirts, Wormeley gave up the "sweets of that easy garment" and left the Peninsula confined in a black lace tablespoon bonnet. It was "indeed all over."[39]

Some of Wormeley's associates on board the floating hospitals would use their experience in the transport service as a stepping-stone to continued participation in the war as relief workers and as army nurses. Indeed, Christine Griffin, Caroline E. Lane, Georgeanna Woolsey, and her sisters Jane and Abby Woolsey would all go on to lead the postwar movement to establish training schools for female nurses. Many of the same issues that left Wormeley confused on board the transports in the summer of 1862 would haunt the efforts of her colleagues to reform hospital nursing after the war. Was nursing a skilled occupation, perhaps even a profession, that required independent judgment and therefore some amount of authority, or was it simply a group of routine tasks to be ordered and delivered at the discretion of physicians and administrators? Was nursing naturally hierarchical? Could upper- and middle-class women retain their credentials as refined women and still get their hands dirty caring for the intimate needs of sick and infected strangers? Did women's "intuition" make them good nurses, as a writer for the Commission contended in 1862, or was it intelligence combined with sympathy as the women themselves privately asserted?[40] And, finally, were women better fitted to be nurses than men, or was gender irrelevant to good nursing? These issues lay unresolved at the end of July 1862, and would challenge these and other women as they tried to use nursing to gain an authoritative voice in public institutions after the war.[41]

Ironically, Katharine Wormeley could not bear the leftover turmoil from her weeks on the Peninsula and later became the leading female apologist for the USSC. Repressing her own grievances, Wormeley subsequently reproached women for the deep prejudice against them as nurses in the minds of army surgeons. Blaming other women for their resistance to male authority as she had blamed herself for her confrontation with Olmsted, she retreated from the open-mindedness, the personal stamina, the bonding, and sheer enthusiasm that had sustained the women volunteers through the summer of 1862. "It is hard to realize," she lectured in her 1863 book promoting the USSC, "that even benevolence must be obedient."[42] Wormeley's reentry into society was complete: nursing had become synonymous with benevolence; acquired skill and judgment had dissolved into obedience; and stress and conflict were buried beneath a blanket of cooperation.

Chapter 7

XXXXXXXXXXXXXXXXXXXXXXXXXXX

Acting Her Part:
Narratives of Union Women Spies

LYDE CULLEN SIZER

Raising her glass on stage in the middle of her performance in Union-controlled Louisville, Kentucky, Pauline Cushman toasted Jefferson Davis and earned hearty applause from Confederates in the audience. She thus made her debut, not into acting, but into spying for the Union army.

In her 1864 pamphlet *The Romance of the Great Rebellion*, Cushman described the incident that launched her new career. Just before the performance, two paroled Confederate officers waiting for an exchange had dared her to make a toast for Davis. Shocked by the proposition, she immediately went to a Union marshal. "That gentleman received me very kindly," she wrote, "and after an interview which satisfied him of my earnest loyalty to the Union, he suggested to me that my patriotism and nerve might be well employed as a 'detective' in the secret army service." The marshal told Cushman to take the dare and earn the confidence of the southern sympathizers, thus gaining a name for herself as one of them. Cushman agreed, stressing her satisfaction at being able to "serve my country perhaps importantly." In performing that night for a full house, she "never succeeded so well in any fictitious part as in this piece of serio-comic stage effect." Cushman was "greatly lionized by all the bitter enemies of our glorious Union" as a result, and was able "to render the Government essential service."[1]

Women spies were known to be circulating North and South during the Civil War and were widely discussed in the press. The two most famous of these were southern, captured and incarcerated in the Old Capital prison in Washington: Rose Greenhow, a Washington socialite, and Belle Boyd, a young Virginian belle. Some credit Greenhow with the Confederate victory at the First Battle of Bull Run for having channeled crucial information on timing, troop strength, and last-minute strategic decisions to Confederate generals. Belle Boyd plunged into public notice when she rushed across the battlefield to give Stonewall Jackson information on the Union troops he was about to attack. Before this incident she had smuggled quinine and carried notes back and forth across the border.[2]

One imagines that most women who acted as spies did not attract any notice. To do so, of course, meant some degree of failure: a good spy is never remarked upon, never makes the paper, indeed, never draws contemporary *or* historical attention. Those few who were caught, however, revealed some of the many ways in which a woman could assist in the war effort. Women crossing the lines, historian Oscar Kinchen notes, hid arms, medicine, and other crucial material in hoop skirts, reticles, parasols, and corsets. Messages were written on buttons, silk, tissue, and common-place letters in imperceptible ink. Diarist Mary Chesnut remarked upon Confederate women spies who coiled notes in their long hair.[3] Yet a woman's greatest advantage, Kinchen notes, was her gender. As women—one would add, white women—they were, at least in the first years of war, unlikely to be searched carefully by men.[4]

The narratives of women spies represented another kind of cultural work.[5] Just as much as spying itself, spy *stories*, fictional or factual, offered women an important avenue for revising or directly challenging gender convention. Whether narrated by the women spies themselves or by celebratory biographers, spy stories served differing political purposes revealed in the manner of their telling. Pauline Cushman was one among a few Union women, including S. Emma Edmonds and Harriet Tubman, who acted as spies and were known through their and others' writing to have done so. Unlike the heroines of the sensationalist pamphleteer Charles Wesley Alexander—in stories of

Pauline of the Potomac, Maud of the Mississippi, and Wenonah, an Indian Spy—Cushman has been accepted by modern historians as authentic.[6]

Stories about female spies and soldiers constituted a small but significant and revealing portion of wartime literature on women.[7] Much of this literature portrayed the world as dichotomized between women and men, blacks and whites, the middle class and working class, the North and South. This literature also focused primarily on the home, what nineteenth-century middle-class readers understood as woman's sphere. It was in the home that woman's influence was paramount and her position assured. What nineteenth-century writers—those writing on women spies among them—did not agree on were where the parameters of "home" ended or how they should define or limit their understanding of "influence."[8]

The narratives of two Unionist women spies examined in this essay, Pauline Cushman and S. Emma Edmonds, worked within two literary traditions. If these "thrilling" narratives belong to what historian Estelle Jelinek calls the "sensational/exotic" category in women's autobiographies, they also can be fit within the wider context of spy literature written by men.[9] Like sensationalist autobiographies, they described women who directly challenged gender roles by dressing or acting as men. Like men's spy narratives, they were full of peril and adventure, romance or flirtation, and adept heroines, and were "vaguely grand about dates."[10]

By contrast, Harriet Tubman's story, told in several different forms, spoke from different literary—and oral—traditions. In a short newspaper biography, and "as told to" narratives, Tubman fits into a larger genre of slave narratives, mostly told by or about African American men. These narratives were quintessential American success stories, chronicling the journey from slavery to freedom, often describing it as undertaken independently, and through the utmost ingenuity. Like spy stories, these narratives are full of peril, as the slave turned freedperson avoids treachery with his own agility.[11]

Whatever their literary frame of reference, these spy narratives were all the more thrilling precisely because they were about women, a point which many of the stories emphasized.

Whether the understanding of gender roles followed normative middle-class conventions with the man acting in a public sphere and the woman in the private sphere or represented a new reconstruction of African American womanhood, spying clearly was sensational behavior.[12] Requiring constant shifts in identity, and clearly requiring leaving home, these stories represented a rejection of any traditionally established set of values for women. Spy stories were thus clustered in one part of a larger spectrum of women's literature and thus women's politics.

But however categorized, they did not represent one position. At one extreme were "lady spies" who used their femininity to acquire power usually considered in the domain of men; at the other were women spies who cross-dressed, blurring the accepted dichotomies of gender (and those of class and race in some cases as well). Yet one can also detect some ambivalence within each position.[13] The white middle-class authors of these accounts sought to maintain a sense of traditional separate-sphere ideology even as they valorized the enhanced abilities of women. Though their wartime accounts stress the exceptional quality of their experiences or the experiences of their subject, they represent no sustained effort to extend the role of spying to women generally—just to represent their ability to adapt to and to excel at an unusual test of courage and patriotism.

Each of the women spy stories discussed below, then, represents a different point on the spectrum of the acceptable. Pauline Cushman's story, told in *The Romance of the Great Rebellion*, ostensibly by Cushman herself, and in the 1865 biography *Life of Pauline Cushman, the Celebrated Spy and Scout* by Ferdinand L. Sarmiento, situated Cushman among the more conventional in this unconventional group. If she was remarkably successful at first, she ended by making a crucial mistake, and ultimately had to be saved by men. Edmonds's narrative may have been more startling to the mid-nineteenth-century reader. In *Nurse and Spy*, or her title from a later edition, *The Unsexed*, Emma Edmonds described how she dressed as a man and participated in major Civil War battles, spying later in her career when the excitement of other roles wore thin. As she tells it, she never personally failed in her exploits, and deserted the army only when illness made discovery imminent. Yet Harriet Tubman, in an article in

the Boston *Commonwealth* by Frank Sanborn and more significantly in Sarah Bradford's two biographies, *Scenes in the Life of
Harriet Tubman* and *Harriet, the Moses of Her People,* did not need
to dress like a man to act like one—her race, ironically, freed her
from some limitations. Tubman's work as a leader in the Combahee River expedition and in undefined spying expeditions was
not, however, described with the same view to self-promotion as
the white spy narratives were. Her ability in this direction was
already established by the time the war began, and her services
were requested by a government well aware of it. Her story is
thus perhaps the most remarkable of all.[14]

Acting is an important metaphor within the narratives of Pauline Cushman and S. Emma Edmonds, and demonstrates a significant difference between themselves and Harriet Tubman.
Cushman and Edmonds acted what they were not, and in calling
it acting, suggested a sense of play and adventure missing from
the serious accounts of Tubman's actions. Cushman, who in taking on the career of an actress in mid-nineteenth-century
America was already challenging gender conventions, described
her acting career as preparing her to become a spy. Edmonds,
who dressed as a man, nursed, and fought on the battlefield, also
described her experiences as the "part" she was to "act" in the
great drama of war. Harriet Tubman, the most seasoned and
successful of the three, had been spying and fighting the insitu-
tion of slavery for twenty years before the war began; she, it is
clear, was not acting for drama's sake, nor for adventure's sake,
but in a deadly serious and longstanding battle for freedom. For
her, it seems from her quotes within the various texts, this struggle is more important than any kind of convention.

> Dashing, charming, fearless, yet lady-like, she combines in herself
> all the daring of the soldier with the tenderness and modesty of
> the woman.
>
> F. L. Sarmiento, *Life of Pauline Cushman, the Celebrated Union Spy and
> Scout*[15]

From the first, the story Cushman told about herself fits the mold
of sensational women's accounts: three times in the first three
pages the veracity of the story is asserted. The author felt, she
wrote, that it was her duty to write the account "in order to
properly satisfy the general interest that seems to have been thus

excited, and at the same time furnish a perfectly reliable narrative."[16]

Cushman's story was quite popular. Her narrative pamphlet was issued in two editions: *The Romance of the Great Rebellion* and *An Inside View of the Army Police,* apparently released at different times.[17] F. L. Sarmiento, a celebratory writer of war stories of different kinds, wrote an "as told to" biography of Cushman that related the entire story, and was published in three editions, one listed with no date, the others in 1865 and 1890.[18]

Although seemingly modest in claiming not to seek notoriety, Cushman cannot be accused of hiding her light under a bushel. Like other narrators of spy novels, she sought to establish herself as a heroic figure with particularly acute facilities. She passed quickly over her autobiography, confessing only that she was of French and Spanish descent and that she became an actress early in life, at fifteen. Cushman asserted that this was no challenge of social convention because she was "compelled, even in my girlhood, to seek some means of independent support." Acting could explain her later success as a spy, for although still a "sensitive, shrinking woman," "the quickness of perception, presence of mind on occasions of emergency, and self-reliance acquired in the training of the green-room, and the gaze of mingled audiences, aided me in the qualities demanded by my recent career."[19]

Cushman continues her Janus-faced approach in relating her story: she is a still "shrinking" woman even when changed to an adept spy through the force of circumstance. From Louisville, where Cushman made her famous toast, she went on to Nashville, Tennessee, to take another part. There she reported to Colonel W. Truesdail, the Chief of Army Police, who asked her to go behind the lines to search out the headquarters of General Braxton Bragg, and find out as much as she could about the conditions and locations of various other Confederate generals. In pointing out to the reader that Truesdail had sought her out for this particular duty she reinforced a claim to being reticent. "I was, indeed," she wrote,

> a little staggered at first by this startling hint, since the road suggested would undoubtedly prove to be a rough one, and there was

a lively prospect of bullets and hemp ahead for such a traveler; but being, as elsewhere stated, naturally prone to the perilous and picturesque, and recollecting that I had a plausible excuse for a visit to rebeldom, in the fact that a brother of mine, Colonel Asa A. Cushman, was then serving with the Confederates, I finally decided to make the attempt.[20]

If her task is described as rough and dangerous, her acceptance can thus be seen as even more courageous.

Cushman was coached in her new role by Truesdail, she related. He explained in great detail the particulars of her new role as a southern lady—ironically for her a very conventional one. Truesdail's "secret instructions" first stressed the danger of the assignment, and then the importance of maintaining appropriate behavior. She was to adopt a story—that she had been exiled to the South and was searching single-mindedly for her brother—and stick to it, never deviating in her answers to "all parties." After assuming "the sentiments and character of a rebel lady" she was to be "cautious against talking or saying too much, merely answering, in a modest and intelligent manner, the many questions" put to her. When she reached any camp she was to ask the commanding officer for "protection and aid" in finding her brother. Finally, she was told, "in consequence of your attractive personal appearance and modest demeanor, you will have many attentions paid to you by generals and staff officers, and will be invited to ride out through their camps, and visit their fortifications." These invitations she was to accept, but only after "some hesitancy and *seeming caution* as to the *propriety* of such excursions."[21] Under no circumstances was she to write anything down, but only to remember what she learned.

Again Cushman stressed her own modesty in accepting the role. "Qualms of sentiment," Cushman recalled, caused her some fear, but her "sense of the high duty I was called upon to perform for my country" quieted them and made her "impatient to be up and doing." On May 27, 1863, she set forward. Finding a house near the banks of the "Big Harpeth" she stopped to ask directions across and was invited to stay. This was the home of Benjamin Milam, a professed Union man engaged in smuggling across the river. He agreed to help her, and his partner took her over the ford the following day.[22]

Cushman describes herself as successful in her mission—initially. Officers displayed an interest, she recalled, one even going so far as lending her the uniform of a Confederate soldier so that she could dress as his aide-de-camp (she never admitted to any indiscretion that would lead him to this familiarity). Yet Cushman also broke her careful rules without an explanation, saying only that she sketched the rebel fortifications "notwithstanding my instructions to the contrary." She then worked her way back to Milam's house. The smuggler, suspicious that Cushman would want to go back to "enemy" territory, turned her in. The next morning, as she was preparing to leave, a rebel scout came to the house and arrested her.

The final chapter in the first short pamphlet described Cushman's travels deeper South, and her aborted attempt to flee. She no longer portrayed herself as modest, but simply able—and sympathetic. On one occasion she had the chance to kill her captor and decided against it. A friendly look from the scout saved his life, for she was a self-professed "cool, safe shot." On another occasion, as a bushwhacker jumped out at her, she frantically plunged her dagger "into the shoulder of my assailant, who, severely wounded, let go of me with a violent oath." This seemed to cause Cushman little consternation, nor does she feel the need to excuse herself for this unwomanly act, commenting only that the "perpetrator of this attempted outrage was arrested on the ensuing day, and may, if alive, still recall his brief acquaintance with the Union spy, Miss Cushman."[23] Despite the feats of great daring in an escape attempt, she was recaptured, and in the second pamphlet she described her imprisonment, her death sentence, and her ultimate rescue by the advancing Union forces.

If Cushman stressed both her modesty in accepting her task and her ability in carrying it through (despite her capture), F. L. Sarmiento's rendering of her tale focuses most of its attention on her unassailed womanhood—and by protesting too much suggests even more its unconventionality. Cushman, in Sarmiento's narrative, is dashing, virtuous, and able, and despite "the stern hardships of actual campaigning—entered into from a pure love of liberty—Miss Cushman is still the full possessor of all those accomplishments that characterize her sex."[24]

Within the drama of war, Sarmiento suggests, Cushman played a shrewd, courageous, and risk-taking—if careless—character. Only sickness and imprisonment return her to the proper role of woman: once in prison she described herself as well loved because of different kinds of qualities, those of dignity, compassion, and restraint. When imprisoned she shed the secret character of spy. When known and no longer acting, then, she placed herself within the comforting and limited boundaries of acceptable womanhood.

> I was not merely to go to Washington and remain there until a battle had been fought and the wounded brought in, and then in some comfortable hospital sit quietly and fan the patients, after the surgeon had dressed their wounds; but I was to go to the front and participate in all the excitement of the battle scenes, or in other words be a "FIELD NURSE."
>
> S. Emma E. Edmonds, *Nurse and Spy in the Union Army*[25]

At the start of her memoir, Emma Edmonds declared her desire to act in the drama of war, not merely to observe it. In the midst of the "sorrow and distress" of the first days of war, Edmonds recalled, she could not "seek [her] own ease and comfort." Rather, she asked herself, "what can I do? What part am *I* to take in this great drama?" Only after constructing her decision to participate in the war as a duty to her adopted country (like Cushman) does Edmonds reveal another motive for her actions. While watching the leave-taking of the men at the station in Michigan, she "could only thank God that [she] was free and could go forward and work, and was not obliged to stay at home and weep."[26] Her freedom was not only freedom from marriage, but freedom from the constraints of womanhood. Yet for Edmonds, this wasn't enough, and her desire to "act" can be seen another way as well. What she does not tell the reader—until midway through the text—is that she enlisted as a man.

"Frank Thompson," as Edmonds called herself, began her service in and around Washington, D.C., as a field nurse. If not a soldier at first, she described herself as a key player on the battlefield who risked her life to save and soothe the lives of the wounded. After arriving, she recalled, she immediately started work in the hospitals with a chaplain and his wife, whom she named B. and Mrs. B. The three were sent together to the battlefield at the first battle of Bull Run in July of 1861. There they assisted the wounded on the field even while the battle was in progress. Confederate sharpshooters fired a stream of minié balls at them, but they persisted until the stream was overrun. The Confederates drove the Union soldiers back toward Washington amid a heavy rainstorm. Edmonds was left behind the lines and had to walk undercover through the downpour to Alexandria where, after a rest, she returned to the Washington hospitals.

This dangerous and wearing work was not enough, Edmonds confessed. She wished to be even more involved in the war effort. After conferring with Chaplain B. and his wife she decided to apply to become a spy. The last spy had been caught in Richmond, and was to be executed. She was interviewed by several generals, and had her head tested in a phrenological exam for her "organs of secretiveness and combativeness."[27] From this point forward, she wrote,

> I was subject to all kind of orders. One moment I was ordered to the front with a musket in my hands; the next to mount a horse and carry an order to some general, and very often to take hold of a stretcher with some strong man and carry the wounded from the field.[28]

Throughout Edmonds's spying missions she put on and took off disguises with aplomb—adopting the characters and testing the limits of societal dichotomies. For her first mission, she impersonated not only a man but a slave. She cut her hair close to her head and covered herself with silver nitrate, which temporarily darkened her skin. She then donned appropriate clothes for a young male contraband, and returned to camp to test out her disguise. After being hired by a doctor she knew well, being questioned by Mrs. B., and helping to make biscuits with a black servant without detection, she deemed her mask effective and slipped through the lines.

She had good luck once there. She ran into a group of slaves going to work just over the line, and they welcomed her without curiosity, and shared their breakfast with her. When forced by a Confederate officer, she joined the others in heavy, taxing work building fortifications, pushing wheelbarrels of gravel up planks of wood. She found manual labor exhausting, but she "was often helped by some good natured darkie when [she] was just on the verge of tumbling off the plank."[29]

If Edmonds elsewhere reveals her understanding of the war as fought over both Union and emancipation, she does not here recognize her own prejudice even while for a few hours "experiencing" the life of a slave. As a slave Edmonds described herself as bonding with those of "her own color," responding to their generosity with her own—while ironically maintaining a sense of difference and intellectual superiority. Their manual superiority derived, she implied, not from their gender but from their race—just as did her intellectual superiority and physical inferiority. Indeed, they were "slaves" to her, not men.[30] With blistered hands, Edmonds drew maps of the fortifications and recorded conversations, hiding the papers in her shoe. When she was sent to the picket lines with food, she withheld some for the slaves she had worked with, who, she learned the day before, got little to eat. Later that night, when a Confederate soldier thrust a rifle into her hands, and told her to watch the picket line awake or die, she slipped away to Federal lines.

"Do my friends wish to know how I felt in such a position and in such a costume?" Edmonds asked. "I will tell them." She felt "as happy and comfortable," she recalled, as was possible under the circumstances. Duty overshadowed the shameful pangs that role reversal (and race reversal) might otherwise bring forth. Edmonds explained her actions in terms of her nature, which was

> naturally fond of adventure, a little ambitious and a good deal romantic, and this together with my devotion to the Federal cause and determination to assist to the utmost of my ability in crushing the rebellion, made me forget the unpleasant items, and not only endure, but really enjoy, the privations connected with my perilous positions. Perhaps a spirit of adventure was important—but *patriotism* was the grand secret of my success.[31]

The change in status in becoming an African American bondsman (or, later, an old Irish peddler woman), was simply a privation to be endured. Although Edmonds challenged the slave system elsewhere, she made no explicit criticism of it here. Rather, she presented her rationale for her behavior—and thus excused her actions—in the most explicit way she had done so far, by admitting her desire for adventure, even as she blended it with the duty of sacrificing for patriotism. Unlike Cushman's and to a greater extent Sarmiento's narratives, Edmonds related her experiences without constant references to her womanhood—or her emotions. She was, it seemed from the tone of her writing, just acting her part in the drama of war.

That part changed only when Edmonds was faced with an insuperable challenge: the prospect of detection. In her next adventure Edmonds became a woman again, with the particular attributes of "true" womanhood: fragility mixed with compassion for others, even enemies. She set out across the lines as an Irish peddler woman with cakes, pies, and a "considerable amount of brogue" which did much, she told her readers, "toward characterizing me as one of the "rale ould stock of bog-trotters."[32] Getting soaked while crossing a river on horseback, she caught a fever and spent two nights and days fighting it in a swamp. While sick she reflected on her reasons for being in that swamp, wondering why she had not let a man protect her rather than following her desire for adventure. When she recovered somewhat, she found a house nearby with a dying rebel officer inside.

The scene Edmonds related here as she aided and comforted the dying man mixed tenderness with stoicism. If she portrays herself as a traditional woman with her compassion and care, she also depicts herself as a stalwart soldier in her unflinching acceptance of death. Deathbed scenes, the prototype of which is Little Eva's in *Uncle Tom's Cabin,* are the particular province of women and a regularly occurring scene in women's literature. Edmonds fulfilled all of the dicta of gender convention in this instance by nurturing the dying soldier. She cooked him food, and waited until he finished before eating her own; she brought him water from nearby, and, most importantly, she discussed his faith with him. He seemed a pleasant man to Edmonds, despite the fact that he never quite answered her point-blank question: "Can you, as a disciple of Christ, consciously and consistently uphold the institution of slavery?"[33]

Yet Edmonds did not completely shed her role as the unflappable soldier. After the man died, and her labors for him were over, she tarried only to briefly ponder death and God before wrapping herself in a quilt near "the unconscious form of my late patient" and sleeping "soundly." She was well aware of the effect this might have on her readers, suggesting that perhaps they "will pronounce [her] a stoic, entirely devoid of feeling."[34]

The last chapters of Edmonds's work most explicitly confronted gender convention even while upholding it. It is when Edmonds described herself as beginning to feel and act like a woman again—when she was sick with malaria she caught in the swamp—that she left her post. Lying in her tent, after hearing a once dormant bomb suddenly explode outside, killing two men, she wrote, "All my soldierly qualities seemed to have fled, and I was again a poor, cowardly, nervous, whining woman. . . . And as if to make up for lost time," she continued, "and to give vent to my long pent up feelings, I could do nothing but weep hour after hour, until it would seem that my head was literally a fountain of tears and my heart one great burden of sorrow."[35] After leaving her post, she procured sick leave from a doctor, went to Cairo, Illinois, "procured female attire, and laid aside forever (perhaps) my military uniform."[36]

In her conclusion, Edmonds berated those who had not aided the war effort. She promised the reader that once recovered she would "return to the army to offer my services in any capacity which will best promote the interests of the Federal cause—no matter how perilous the position may be." Although the reader could scarcely know this, Edmonds did return to service, although this time dressed as a woman. At the Christian Commission at Harper's Ferry she worked among the wounded. She also distributed the proceeds of her earnings from her book, which sold over 175,000 copies, to soldiers' aid societies.[37]

Edmonds's abrupt return to womanhood—brought about by malaria—caused her to take up a new part in the wartime drama. Yet by revealing herself to her reader at the end, she only somewhat mutes the radically unconventional story she has told. Edmonds played with normative dichotomies central to the middle class's understanding of themselves. As a man for much of the text, a slave within a community of slaves, and an Irish peddler woman, she put on and took off many disguises, suggesting thereby both the titillating difference, and the underlying similarity between herself and what white Anglo middle-class society constructed as the "other."

> We saw the lightning and that was the guns; and then we heard the thunder and that was the big guns; and then we heard the rain falling and that was the blood falling; and when we came to get in the crops, it was dead men that we reaped.
>
> Harriet Tubman, from a postwar lecture in Charleston[38]

For Harriet Tubman, "acting" appeared less a matter of manipulating her image than an instrumental, unambiguous effort to do whatever was necessary to aid her people. Unlike Cushman and Edmonds, it was an effort that had occupied her for twenty years before the Civil War. Tubman had never accepted limits to her behavior, and her nineteenth-century white biographers, a man and a woman, never applied to Tubman conventions bound up in their minds with whiteness.

Tubman fought her civil war her entire life; the national conflict represented a climax in terms of the aid she got in her struggle. During the previous twenty years Tubman escaped from her Maryland master to Philadelphia, and successfully returned nineteen more times, bringing out of slavery an estimated 300 to 400 people. Perhaps her most daring trip involved rescuing her elderly parents in a self-made carriage. She brought them to New York State, where, with a loan from William Seward, she purchased a cabin and some property for them. She worked with a determination bordering on ruthlessness: if an escaped slave tarried, she pushed him on; if a baby cried, she muffled the sound. As she herself said later, according to her biographer Earl Conrad, "I was the conductor of the Underground Railroad for eight years, and I can say what most conductors can't say—I never ran my train off the track and I never lost a passenger."[39]

Over the course of those twenty years Tubman had achieved a good deal of fame through word of mouth in the abolitionist community. She was called "General" Tubman by an admiring John Brown. The Reverend Thomas Wentworth Higginson, with whom Tubman would later collaborate in a military expedition, told the gathered audience of the New York Anti-Slavery Society in 1858, "she is better known than the Bible, for she circulates more freely." Higginson considered her "Braver than

Florence Nightingale" (one of the most important woman icons of the war period), and noted how "that little quiet, elderly, coal-black woman" was known as Moses. "She leads them [slaves] out into the promised land, and, happier than the original Moses, she is permitted to go back again and again into Egypt, and lead her people again and again into freedom."[40] Charlotte Forten, who met Tubman on the South Sea Islands during the war and heard some of her stories directly from her, was also struck by her achievements. Forten wrote in her journal in 1863: "She is a wonderful woman—a real heroine."[41]

The literary basis for Tubman's legacy was laid during and after the war, revealing a persistent tension between these middle-class white writers and their black working-class subjects.[42] The two contemporary writers who chronicled her life seemed less concerned with Tubman's cause than in making Tubman an exception, a description she seems to contradict every time she actually gets the chance to speak for herself in their work. In the 1863 article by Frank Sanborn, as well as Sarah Bradford's 1869 *Scenes in the Life of Harriet Tubman* and the later, revised editions of her biography, *Harriet Tubman, Moses of Her People,* this tension is the defining characteristic of their work.

In both cases a strong voice emerged from Tubman herself, a voice of authority and self-confidence. Tubman's story-telling, captured in the long quotes of both editions of Bradford's books and to a lesser degree in an excerpted letter included in Sanborn's article, has a lyrical quality and shape redolent of an oral tradition.[43] She downplays her own role in the story; claiming no heroic stature, Tubman glories in the joy that her people express when freed.[44] Bradford, by contrast, constructs a heroic Tubman by elevating her above her people, in the celebratory biographical style redolent of a western literary tradition.

Abolitionist writer and editor Frank Sanborn, for his part, constructed Tubman as a paragon of self-sacrifice. Not only had Tubman been a conductor on the Underground Railroad of astounding success, Sanborn noted in his article, she was also at that time aiding the Union forces. Going immediately to Port Royal, South Carolina, after it was liberated, she at once "made herself useful in many ways" during a Federal military expedition. Tubman had dictated a letter to Sanborn asking for contributions to the cause, which Sanborn included with his piece. "We trust she will receive them," Sanborn wrote, "for none has better deserved it." Furthermore, he wrote, "she asks nothing for herself, except that her wardrobe may be replenished, and even this she will probably share with the first needy person she meets."[45]

Tubman's letter is businesslike and assertive, and offers a rare glimpse into her own objectives. She betrays no consciousness of breaking gender or racial conventions in her actions or the frank equality she claims through her tone. Her audience, she assumes, will appreciate the importance of what she is doing. Without reserve she asks for new clothes, for hers have been lost due to a quick retreat. "I want, among the rest," she dictated, "a *bloomer* dress, made of some coarse, strong material, to wear on *expeditions*." The italicized words in the article clearly delineate what Sanborn or the copy editor might have deemed controversial about Tubman's request—bloomers, a highly charged piece of clothing among women reformers, representing their attempt to escape the literal confines of womanhood; and expeditions, clearly a "male" activity. Tubman explains that as she was running for the ship with the two pigs of a freedwoman, she tripped on her dress. The need for bloomers thus served not an abstract political purpose for her, but a practical one.

If Tubman did not claim credit for what she herself did, she pushed for the recognition of the efforts of freedpeople generally. "We colored people," she asserted, should be included in the account of the successful Combahee River raid in South Carolina. "We weakened the rebels somewhat," the letter continued, ". . . by taking and bringing away *seven hundred and fifty-six* head of their most valuable livestock, known up in your region as "contrabands." No one was killed among the Union forces, but "a number of rebels bit the dust."[46]

To take on the work normally assigned to white men and African Americans generally, Tubman needed the garb suited to it. The letter does not suggest that taking on the job (or the garb) was anything less than the right thing to do. Although she hoped that her parents were well taken care of, she dictated, "I do not see how I am to leave at present the very important work to be done here." Hospitals filled with destitute contrabands, some nearly naked and ill, claimed her time. With some political savvy, perhaps, she stressed that it was important to "provide for them as best as I can, so as to lighten the burden on the Government as much as possible, while at the same time they learn to respect themselves by earning their own living."[47]

Like Sanborn, Bradford celebrates Tubman's startling achievements, but there is an implicit tension at work. Unlike Cushman or Edmonds, Tubman is never constructed as a demure woman taking on an unconventional role for patriotic reasons. Despite the widespread assumption that womanhood is universal, Tubman is somehow less than a woman in her uncompromised courage. "This fearless woman was often sent into the rebel lines as a spy," Bradford wrote,

> and brought back valuable information as to the position of armies and batteries; she has been in battle when the shot was falling like hail, and the bodies of dead and wounded men were dropping around her like leaves in autumn; but the thought of fear never seems to have had place for a moment in her mind. She had her duty to perform, and she expected to be taken care of till it was done.[48]

If less than a conventional white lady, then, Bradford offers her as a singular, African American woman.

The being who was "to take care of her," Bradford implies, was God. Tubman's religious faith was as remarkable as her lack of fear, and both were noted by the abolitionist friends of Tubman whose letters Bradford included in her text.[49] Abolitionist Thomas Garrett wrote that "certain it was that she had a guide within herself other than the written word, for she never had any education." Another, from Frank Sanborn, echoed Bradford's amazement. As "the most extraordinary person of her race" that he has ever met, Sanborn wrote, ". . . she has done what can scarcely be credited on the best authority, and she has accomplished her purposes with a coolness, foresight, patience and wisdom, which in a *white man* would have raised him to the highest pitch of reputation."[50]

Tubman's spying activities included convincing slaves to trust the Union invaders, Bradford explained. "It became quite important," she wrote, "that she should accompany expeditions going up the rivers, or into unexplored parts of the country, to control and get information from those whom they took with them as guides." This was the purpose of the expedition Tubman had described in her letter to the *Commonwealth*. On a mission up the Combahee River, gunboats took away 800 slaves who came to the shores, Bradford wrote (up from the 756 Tubman reported in her letter). The word of the coming of the boats "was passed along by the mysterious communication existing among these simple people," Bradford said.[51]

Tubman's description of this event emerges as an alternative to Bradford's in the text, one that contradicts her condescension and resists her brand of exceptionalism. In explaining the problems of communication Tubman constructs them as two-way; if she cannot understand, she also cannot always be understood: "Dey laughed when dey heard me talk, an' I could not understand dem, no how." Her portrayal of a night funeral and the spirituals sung there was respectful. "Der voices is so sweet," she told Bradford, "and dey can sing eberyting we sing, an' den dey can sing a great many hymns dat we can't nebber catch at all."[52] For Tubman, these are not "simple people" at all, but familiar people with a different language, and a real gift with song.

Tubman's story, told in a variety of ways—in speeches, by word-of-mouth and personal meeting, in newspaper accounts and two biographies—represents an important parallel tradition in American history. As the product of an oral and also a literary tradition, Tubman resists the grasp of her white biographers, giving her story a life of its own. Her spying incidents are not described in detail; they are merely the result of an ability honed and tried by her earlier experiences as a conductor on the Underground Railroad. What emerges from Tubman's story, however, is the vision of a strong, able, and determined woman, one of heroic stature. The Reverend Thomas Higginson remarked on this in an 1858 speech. "Now, I say," he told New Yorkers, "a race that has within its number one such woman as that has the right to hold up its head above the proudest Anglo-Saxon of us all, and say, 'I, too, can protect myself.'"[53] An interviewer, writing of Harriet Tubman in 1912, would agree. "Her life," he wrote, "has been one long word of consolation and inspiration to her people."[54]

The women discussed in this essay came from remarkably different backgrounds, and in some way represented an "other" to the presumed white middle-class Northern reader. This sense of difference—whether because of foreign birth or ex-slave status—may have made their unconventional actions more acceptable (or at least explicable). Pauline Cushman, of French and Spanish parents, was born in New Orleans but grew up in Michigan, and began her acting career early out of economic necessity.[55] Emma Edmonds, French-Canadian by birth, had dressed as a boy during her childhood, ostensibly to please her father, who had wanted sons.[56] Harriet Tubman, born a slave in Maryland, had successfully "stolen" 300 slaves from slaveholders there by 1861, including her seventy-year-old parents. Each spy fought in a different place: Cushman in Tennessee, or the western theater; Edmonds with the Army of the Potomac, in Virginia; and Tubman with Colonel James Montgomery and Colonel Thomas Higginson, primarily on the South Carolina coast.

For all their difference, however, all three shared an experience in having their achievements muted. Cushman, weakened by illness and imprisonment, and caught because of carelessness, is only made a major after her exploits are over, an authority she could never use. Edmonds, if later granted a pension by the government, got the same pay as other nurses rather than other soldiers.[57] She herself explained her change back into skirts as a failure of will. Tubman, if confident in her own abilities to the end, was not given a pension for her war work until over thirty years later.[58] Her part, especially in the successful Combahee River expedition, was not described in the newspaper accounts. Her white biographers, in addition, marketed her as an exception, rather than an inspiring representative.

Yet this muting did not erase the important messages that the lives of these women represented. As spies, scouts, and soldiers they were acting directly within the wartime drama, and their characters resonated with a revolutionary vision of womanhood. In taking on the roles of men, all three women directly challenged gender sphere ideology in the mid-nineteenth century. If Cushman and Edmonds eventually returned to a more acceptable role for middle-class white women—shedding their wartime disguise—that does not deny their radical questioning. Tubman's part is even more significant. If her biographers call her

"Moses," she herself makes no claims to gender reversal. Her actions are undertaken for an explicit purpose—to free her people—which she fulfills. Strong, adept, and self-confident, these women played an important part in the drama of women and war.

Chapter 8

"Missing in Action": Women of the Confederacy

GEORGE RABLE

It was bound to happen. Social historians are rapidly discovering the boundless riches of the American Civil War. What J. H. Hexter three decades ago termed "tunnel history" has become the dominant mode of historical discourse, but since Hexter coined the phrase, the tunnels have become much narrower and more numerous.[1] The forces of professionalization and specialization have isolated historians from each other as well as from the larger society.

More recently, the attention of professional historians to the social history of the Civil War in general and to women's lives in particular has suddenly blossomed even as the battle studies and biographies continue to roll off the presses. Yet both streams of literature remain nearly as isolated from each other as ever. Many Civil War buffs know little about or openly disdain women's history while social historians often treat narrative military history with haughty contempt.[2]

Despite this continuing cold war, the Civil War may well provide the badly needed common ground for a rapprochement between the so-called new and old histories. The sources are so rich and varied that the possibilities for striking combinations of fields and methods are nearly endless. "Tunnel history" is an especially wrong-headed approach to an era in which political and military activity constantly impinged on social and economic life, in which families and regiments became intertwined in complex networks of communication, anxiety, fear, and death.[3] More specifically, studying social definitions of gender and the ways in which real people embraced, lived up to, or rebelled against these ideal types should have a broadening rather than a narrowing effect on Civil War studies.

From the beginning, the war strained traditional definitions of gender by testing long-established customs in the fiery furnace of social revolution. A small but significant minority of Confederate women even participated in politics after a fashion. Besides sewing banners, cooking meals for campaign barbecues, or listening to stump speeches, few women in the Old South had played a public role in the political culture though better-educated women often discussed elections and candidates at home. As the Confederacy held its first national and state elections in the fall of 1861, a group of women drafted a tartly political letter to a Rome, Georgia, newspaper. In the pseudonymous fashion of the day, they chose to call themselves "many sewers."

Merely by writing to a newspaper, however, they had overstepped the boundaries of social custom. Worse, they poked fun at men for nominating so many candidates to represent the county in the state legislature. With barbed humor, they proposed that those who had so bravely declared their willingness to fight before the shooting started should now "represent us in some of the volunteer companies already in the field." Rather than canvassing for votes, these stay-at-homes could best serve their country in the army while other, older men held public office. To drive the point home, "many sewers" promised these laggards to "make their uniforms gratis."[4]

The designation "sewers" showed that these women sustained the war effort in a traditionally female endeavor, but in writing this letter they subtly challenged the notion that women should play no public role in political life beyond deferring to male judgments. Their statements implied that too many men were not living up to traditional standards of masculinity. Therefore women had to shame these cowards into doing their duty. And what better way to humiliate men in the nineteenth-century

South than to have women publicly pointing out their lack of courage?

"If only I was a man." This or similar phrases appear countless times in letters and diaries written by southern white women during the war. More often than not such laments had the paradoxical effect of reinforcing conventional gender roles while implicitly questioning the ability of men to act as southern men were supposed to act. Sarah Morgan Dawson of Baton Rouge, Louisiana, claimed that she would be in the thick of the fighting if she had been born a man but "as I was unfortunately born a woman, I stay home and pray with heart and soul." The striking counterpoint here between male activity and female passivity suggests discontent but also resignation in fulfilling an assigned social task. Writing to her husband from their home in Dyersburg, Tennessee, Mary Latta wished that they could somehow trade places so that she could face the hardships of camp life and the terrors of battle. Yet she quickly conceded that "I am only a woman and must enjoy the comforts with which your hand has so freely provided."[5]

Fantasies of action and revenge could all too easily become nightmares, and the bonds of social custom remained tight. Propriety inhibited action as Yankee armies approached and women re-examined their own and their society's core values. "What is the use of all these worthless women in war times?" Sarah Morgan exploded. Hoping in July 1862 that Confederate forces would soon move to recapture Baton Rouge, she decided she would "don the breeches, and join the assailants." But then came the hesitation: "How do breeches and coats feel, I wonder? I am actually afraid of them. . . . I have heard so many girls boast of having worn men's clothes; I wonder where they get the courage."[6] Reaching but then retracting, advancing but then retreating, asserting but then demurring, the war opened up possibilities while also leaving many barriers in tact.

In the old South, shooting was one of the most masculine of activities. Skill with a shotgun or pistol was part of a young boy's coming of age. At the beginning of the war, however, several Virginia women asked Governor John Letcher to send them pistols or other arms for self-defense. "I have practiced shooting and I would not be afraid to defend myself," Lucetta Clove added proudly.[7] When women formed their own military companies and even tried to follow the instructions for drill in William J. Hardee's *Rifle and Light Infantry Tactics*, were they merely playing at war? Perhaps, but the sight of women marching and shooting also appeared subversive to the gender hierarchy.

The question became, why did women need to strap on revolvers and parade in the hot sun? In early 1865, when teenage girls near Tallahassee, Florida, met for pistol practice, they vowed to shoot themselves rather than fall into enemy hands.[8] Women soon came to realize their defenselessness against an invading army, and although few said so explicitly, the truth was that Southern men could no longer protect their homes and families. In other words, they were no longer men.

This sense of emasculation also points to the potential for blending military and social history (including the history of gender) in Civil War studies. Even so familiar a tale as Benjamin F. Butler's confrontations with the women of New Orleans begs for broader and more imaginative treatment. Civil War historians have written many colorful accounts and delivered innumerable Civil War round table talks on "Beast Butler" and the feisty belles of the Crescent City without paying much attention to the larger significance of these sometimes comic-opera encounters. By the same token, scholars in women's history have generally ignored the topic.[9]

Like many others in the Confederacy, the white women of New Orleans spoke bravely of defying any Yankees who dared set foot in their city. A detached but not unsympathetic Union woman described New Orleans ladies as "almost hysterical" and evidently looking "forward to being blown up with shot and shell, finished with cold steel or whisked off to some Northern prison."[10] This stilted language conveys braggadocio but also indicates shifting definitions of proper female behavior in wartime. Women no longer saw themselves as passive victims, and however unrealistic their fantasies of resistance, they had begun to form new expectations for themselves while maintaining traditional expectations for their menfolk.

When Federal gunboats steamed past Forts Jackson and St. Philip on the Mississippi River below New Orleans, the city went into a panic. Confederate forces began to retire while their commander, General Mansfield Lovell, and Mayor John T. Monroe each refused to take responsibility for surrendering the city to Admiral David Farragut. By April 29, 1862, United States flags flew over the customs house and city hall.

Over fifty women, however, had petitioned the mayor and city council to hold out against Admiral Farragut's fleet. Others insisted that the Louisiana flag not be lowered, and one woman suggested that it simply be nailed to the flag staff.[11] However much the men may have admired this display of spirit they had no choice but to surrender the city. Lovell, Monroe, and other Confederate leaders could never adequately explain why the defense of New Orleans had been so badly bungled or why once the forts had been run, Confederate troops did not put up more of a fight.

Young Clara Solomon, whose father was serving with Wheat's Battalion in Virginia, could hardly believe that the forts had proved so useless and worse that there had been no true southern men left to defend the city once the Yankees arrived. Seeing the Federals idly lounging about in Lafayette Square, she hoped that yellow fever would strike the soldiers with such force that there would be no room in the city to bury all the dead. She could hardly stand to see the vile wretches on the streets parading about with a self-assured air of conquest.[12] She felt humiliated for her city, its vanished defenders, and herself.

What made such scenes even more disheartening was the striking contrast between male supineness and female defiance. "If the men had half the spunk which the women have," a fiery Creole woman informed an English visitor, "New Orleans would soon be ours again." For the time being she hoped to "trample on their [the Yankees'] dead bodies and spit on them." Such unladylike comments flew in the face of social convention but seemed more acceptable when the men had made no effort to recapture the city. Increasingly, women had to embody and preserve the ideals of Confederate patriotism. Longtime resident Julia Le Grand believed that *the women only do not seem afraid. They were all in favor of resistance, no matter how hopeless that resistance might be.* Yet Le Grand was no mere fire-breathing belle oblivious to military realities. When Farragut's fleet had first approached New Orleans, she had favored provoking the

Federals into shelling the city so Great Britain and France would intervene in the war.[13] Otherwise, the surrender of New Orleans brought with it a grim finality that threatened to plunge civilians and especially women into complete despair.

The ignominious capitulation of the Confederates naturally led women to search for scapegoats. Rumors that the northern-born Lovell had turned traitor or had been drunk the day the Yankees arrived spread rapidly. Women (and many men) in and outside the city soon concluded that Lovell had scandalously neglected to strengthen the forts. Over a week before the surrender, Elsie Bragg had already suggested that if New Orleans fell, Lovell "better look to his own life." Believing that few Confederate generals save her husband, Braxton Bragg, showed any talent, she reported that women were already threatening to have Lovell "swung as high as Hamman." After New Orleans had fallen, Elsie Bragg described the hapless Lovell as a "Benedict Arnold." Other women blamed Jefferson Davis or former Secretary of War Judah P. Benjamin or Secretary of the Navy Stephen R. Mallory for losing the city.[14] The Confederate government and the Confederate army had left the people of New Orleans to their own devices.

The city's defenders had either fled or now cowered before the enemy, though in many ways acquiescence seemed worse than flight. Women had to vent their pent-up wrath on the occupiers, and especially on General Benjamin F. Butler of Massachusetts. The squint-eyed, owl-faced Butler looked the villain's part, and given his penchant for invective and histrionics was bound to ruffle the feathers of New Orleans's female population. Yet Butler also served as an outlet for displaced frustration. After the general forbade citizens to observe any days of fasting and public prayer proclaimed by Jefferson Davis, Clara Solomon railed not so much against Butler as against the New Orleans male population: "I do not understand how men can endure, but in this they accommodate themselves to circumstances, *too readily*."[15] For women who accepted traditional definitions of masculine honor, their menfolk had thoroughly disgraced themselves, first by surrendering the city and then by fitting their necks to the despot's yoke.

If their fathers, husbands, and sons were not willing or able to battle tyranny, many women felt obliged to take up the cudgels. Defying Butler's men struck blows at northern brutes while presumably humiliating southern cowards. Well-dressed women hiked up their skirts and crossed to the other side of streets rather than pass a Yankee on the sidewalk; they stormed out of churches and streetcars whenever they spotted blue uniforms. The less refined made faces, spat, or dumped slops on the soldiers from second-story windows (on one occasion a chamber pot was emptied on Admiral Farragut's head). One female toddler shouted "Hurrah for Depp Dabis and Beaudegard."[16]

The more genteel stayed indoors (the southern social hierarchy in part dictated varying class responses to the Yankee presence), continued to sew Confederate flags, and refused to attend operas or concerts for fear of unpleasant confrontations.[17] At first Butler took such actions with good humor. When some women on a balcony turned their backs and "threw out skirts in a regular circle like the pirouette of a dancer," he loudly remarked, "These women evidently know which end of them looks best."[18] The coarse behavior of both Butler and his female antagonists indicates how much the war had altered conventional gender relations, at least in occupied territory.

Finally deciding that enough was enough, Butler issued the notorious General Order No. 28, which declared that "when any female shall, by word, gesture, or movement, insult or show contempt for any officer or soldier of the United States, she shall be regarded and held liable to be treated as a woman of the town plying her avocation."[19] This raised the hackles of Confederates from Virginia to Texas. Always sensitive about feminine purity while hypocritically tolerating miscegenation, southerners fulminated against "Beast Butler" in language considerably more salty than the general's.

Editors and politicians might denounce the woman order and Confederate generals might even send their troops into battle with cries of "Butler and New Orleans" ringing in their ears, but the very intensity of their fury was also a confession of impotence. What many women in New Orleans already realized, many women in other parts of the Confederacy were beginning to learn: southern men could not protect them against the Yankees. Outrage and fear tugged at emotions as the war had seemingly reached a new level of barbarity.[20]

In New Orleans, the reactions ranged from fantasies of vengeance to quiet indignation to creative defiance. Teenager Clara Solomon dreamed of having ropes tied about Butler with all the New Orleans ladies tugging at the Beast. Or better yet fry him up in a great pan. Or force him to eat salty food and have water before him but not allow him to drink a single drop. Such daydreams, and writing them down, might temporarily allay anxiety. But Solomon also observed that Butler's order greatly "exasperated" the men because it was also aimed at them. For Butler had simply driven home the point that Confederate men in abandoning the city had left the women defenseless against a merciless foe. Other women quietly pinned small Confederate flags to their dresses or occasionally waved them from second-story windows. In an act of comic protest, the city's real prostitutes pasted pictures of their balding nemesis to the bottoms of chamber pots.[21] This crude revenge, whether widely known at the time or not, may not have offered much comfort to most women in the city but seemed more effective than the windy protests by Mayor Monroe or bombastic denunciations of Butler by Jefferson Davis and various state governors.

Yet the public outcry in New Orleans quickly subsided. After all the press was under military censorship, and women soon learned that Butler would, unlike certain Confederate generals they knew, do more than bluster. During the spring and summer, Union soldiers arrested several women on charges ranging from the display of secession flags to possession of a Federal musket to threats against the life of a United States officer to general sedition. Butler took special delight in confiscating Confederate flags that had been hand-sewn by rebel belles and sent one to some Massachusetts schoolchildren as a souvenir of war.[22] Yet all these activities showed how women had to break or at least bend a bit the gender conventions of their society. With unquestioned propriety women could sew flags, but to display them in occupied New Orleans was a distinctly political act in a society where women's political opinions, to the extent they should be expressed at all, belonged in the home. The possession of a

Union musket seemed still more anomalous. Threatening the life of a Federal officer was simply unladylike. And since women were not full-fledged citizens how could they be guilty of sedition?

Regardless of these problems, few of the arrests attracted much attention. Perhaps it was simply embarrassing that a handful of women seemed to be carrying the burden of resistance against the Yankee occupiers and the less said on that subject the better. The exception to this general silence came in the case of Eugenia Phillips, wife of former Alabama congressman Philip Phillips. Early in the war she had been briefly detained in Washington on charges of espionage. Federal officials had sent her through the lines, and the family eventually settled in New Orleans. A sharp-tongued and intensely patriotic Confederate, she refused to bend a knee to such a man as Butler. When a funeral procession for a Union soldier passed near a balcony of the Phillipses' house, she laughed heartily and ostentatiously. Apparently several other women on that same day entered streetcars sporting secession flags and broad smiles. Butler again took swift action. Denouncing Phillips as a "bad and dangerous woman, stirring up strife and inciting to riot," on June 30 he ordered her arrest. She admitted being in "high spirits" on the day in question but denied mocking the dead or teaching her children to spit on Union soldiers. After a tumultuous interview with Phillips and her husband (who could only weakly protest against the "string of invectives" aimed at his wife), Butler exiled Eugenia Phillips to Ship Island where she could communicate with no one except her maid.[23]

There she lived in an abandoned railroad car, plagued by mosquitoes, bad water, and musty food. Despite the restrictions, she managed to send out a few letters about the gruesome conditions that made her imprisonment a cause célèbre. Butler evidently regretted turning an irksome rebel into a martyr and ordered her release after two and half months of confinement.[24] She had shown considerable public relations acumen, and her prison journal reveals an ironic sense of humor, especially in her wry proposal to use a steam device to pump moisture into the rock-hard bread. Though not exactly besting Butler, she had played the wily Massachusetts politician to a draw.

And so perhaps had the other women of the Crescent City. When Yankee officers looked for diversion with irascible rebel belles, they met with cold rebuffs—or at least no contemporaries admitted that any Confederate females would consort with the enemy. Butler's men therefore invited black ladies to their dances, but that only raised angry cries about "miscegenation balls." Butler threatened to expel from the city anyone who would not take an oath of allegiance to the United States government, though, after badgering much of the business community into compliance, he relented for the rest of the civilian population. Attempting to maintain their society's traditional obsession with honor, women found the notion of swearing such an oath particularly insulting.[25] The fact that local political and business leaders had less trouble adopting a more pragmatic stance must have especially galled them.

The "woman order" and the harsh treatment of Eugenia Phillips had tempered public hostility. Woman began confining their invective to vivid and revealing comments in their diaries. Ann Wilkinson Penrose, an invalid widow with a son in the Confederate army, declared that the "most despotic sovereign of Russia or Austria could not be more tyrannical or merciless than the U.S. Govt. and its myrmidions." Dreading that soldiers were about to search her house or worse, one night she slept with guns strapped around her thighs and a knife by her bed. For orthodox Christians familiar with the strong Biblical admonitions on caring for widows, Penrose's condition suggested that something had gone terribly awry in the Confederacy. Even Butler recognized the unsettling implications of occupation for the southern social order. When a Mrs. Semmes requested a passport to visit a sick daughter, Butler sharply refused, claiming he had been too often taken in by such pleas in the past. He then tellingly remarked that he never could subdue the rebellious women but could more easily manage the cowardly men.[26]

Butler was obviously twitting his petitioner and indulging in a bit of his usual blow, but he had also touched a raw nerve. Women's hatred of the enemy exacerbated frustration about the limits of the female sphere. "I am like a pent-up volcano," Julia Le Grand complained. "I wish I had a field for my energies. I hate common life, a life of visiting, dressing, and tattling, which seems to devolve on women, and now that there is better work to do . . . I suffer, suffer, leading the life I do."[27] Cut off from the rest of the Confederacy, public expressions of discontent forbidden, such women naturally felt isolated and more powerless than ever.

The removal of Butler and the arrival of the new Union commander, General Nathaniel P. Banks, in December 1862 brought some psychological relief, though Ann Penrose could not understand why anyone would put much faith in another New Englander. Banks tried to flatter local belles with invitations to balls and concerts, but the social gulf generally remained unbridgeable. Clashes between soldiers and civilians continued. Several teachers at a fashionable girls' school were arrested for either allowing or encouraging their pupils to draw Confederate flags. Women still waved secession banners. They occasionally spat at soldiers and more regularly berated the occupiers as "Lincoln hirelings" and "nigger thieves." One exasperated bluecoat wondered "if these Southern girls can love as they hate? If they can, it would be well worth one's while trying to get one of them."[28] Thus a touch of sexuality was also added to the already volatile mixture of war, politics, and gender.

Besides the chronic tension and various small incidents, there was one final, dramatic clash between Federal troops and their female antagonists. On February 20, 1863, as a group of Confederate officers was being shipped to Baton Rouge as part of a prisoner exchange, several thousand people jammed the levee to cheer their departing heroes. Women carried flowers, waved handkerchiefs, and hurrahed for Jeff Davis. Nervous Union officers called for troops, who with bayonets fixed drove the crowd back for two blocks while women shook their handkerchiefs and parasols at the advancing Federals. In the scuffle, a few women suffered minor injuries.[29] The so-called "Battle of the Handkerchiefs" made Banks look more ridiculous than tyrannical. For a brief time, several hundred women had reveled in expressing their Confederate sympathies, but regardless of its public character, this event recalled an earlier time. Waving handkerchiefs at revered heroes bespoke a musty tradition, of women playing older, more auxiliary roles in a great national crisis.

Such an appearance might be deceiving because women's experiences under both Butler and Banks had shattered at least for the time being the myth of the male as protector. Not only had the Federal troops wickedly persecuted innocent women and children—at least according to Confederate propaganda—but southern men had signally failed to defend their families—a point that good Confederates were loath to admit. The furor in New Orleans and elsewhere over Butler and the behavior of the Federal troops masked the real problems: the near collapse of Confederate defenses in the western theater and the inability of the Confederate, state, or local governments to protect families. For Ann Wilkinson Penrose and other disillusioned women, the implications were clear: "We cannot help feeling sometimes very bitter towards our Govt. that so utterly neglected us, and now seems to take no heed, or care of us, leaving us entirely in the power of our direst foes." However proudly women might stand up to the Yankee occupation troops, they could not help but feel abandoned and betrayed by their own menfolk.[30] And speeches lauding the devotion of Confederate women could no longer conceal these plain truths.

As a way to more fully integrate gender into traditional Civil War topics, the story of Butler, Banks, and the women of New Orleans has some usefulness but can only suggest wider and more ambitious possibilities. Opportunities abound for breaking down barriers of topic and method that have impoverished historical writing on the Civil War. A creative scholar might fashion a "total history" of a southern community at war by dealing with both the home front and battlefield, by exploring family life and camp life, by examining domestic shortages and regimental logistics. Such a study might weave together evidence from military correspondence and family papers while also incorporating neglected sources such as newspaper advertising.

Alternatively, an imaginative synthesis of military and social history could unravel the strands of battle as they affected both armies and communities, both commanders and female heads of household, both public figures and obscure individuals. Through the intersection of events, social patterns, and biography, such a project could transcend limitations of more traditional approaches in both Civil War and women's history. Such a work also might break down some of the artificial boundaries between intellectual, cultural, social, political, and military history. The result would be not a gender history of the Civil War but rather a rich and complex Civil War history interested not only in matters of gender but also in a full range of familiar and not-so-familiar questions. And historians' tunnels might grow wider and on occasion even intersect.

Chapter 9

Women and Guerrilla Warfare

MICHAEL FELLMAN

Through its special quality of erasing many of the crucial distinctions between soldiers and civilians, guerrilla warfare during the Civil War blurred gender boundaries and gender decorum in often horrifying ways. In Missouri, which saw the most intense guerrilla fighting of the war, where pro-Confederate guerrillas roamed far behind Union lines, and where Union guerrilla hunters behaved just as abysmally as their enemies, women from both camps often became both victims and participants in the heart of the conflict. Amid the pillage, burning, and slaughter, such warfare also spawned a gender crisis. In both attitudes and actions, women and men frequently violated peacetime moral boundaries, which they had to revise drastically in order to survive; men and women alike also clung desperately to shreds of their prewar values—based on the sanctity of Christian forbearance, honor, and private property—in order to prevent themselves from collapsing, in their most intimate relationships and in their self-conceptions, from acceptable humanity into amoral monstrosity.

Defined by the Union forces as criminals, cut off from the Confederacy for which they were fighting, roaming in unformed bands, living by a combination of pleading and force off the citizenry, guerrillas had a desperate need to believe that they were gentlemen to the ladies. This need was functional, as guerrillas depended upon women allies for supplies and information, but it was also a psychological necessity—a reinforcement of their belief that they were defenders of the local virtues against alien invaders. At the center of their notion of community was family, with inviolate women in the very middle. Elevation of women in times of social catastrophe was also a means of keeping alive positive views of morality and self-esteem to counter that endemic destructiveness the guerrillas knew they must employ.

One October Sunday in 1863, four guerrillas, pistols in hand, burst into the house of Lucy Jane McManus of Andrew County. They said they had come to search for arms. McManus "told them to search ahead," she later reported to the local Union Provost Marshal. "They asked her if she was a widow woman. She said she was not but was alone. They said if that be the case they would not interrupt anything but would like to get some supper." While dining they told her they were looking for her husband Richard, and that when they found him "they would soon put him under the sod."[1] They treated the wife of this man they hunted with what they considered all due respect. They were showing McManus and themselves that they distinguished between guilty men and innocent women. She should understand they meant her no personal harm, as they were good men compelled to ruthless action by military necessity. They sought to deny they were directly intimidating a woman even while breaking into her house and threatening her husband, by behaving like gentlemen when they learned that she was alone and undefended by a man, and of course no threat to them.

Such a combination of gentility and brute force lies behind the legends of outlaws who would leave thousand-dollar bills under their plates after being served by just such defenseless women. Missouri guerrillas certainly partook of the belief in the noble outlaw, the better to convince themselves that though called lawbreakers, they were indeed serving nature's law. Sam Hildebrand, who bragged of killing over one hundred Union men single-handedly in the Ozarks during the war, wrote later of his chivalry toward one German woman, noting that when he had seized her husband, her horse, and her mule, he had refused to take her side-saddle: "I told her I could not rob a lady; to keep the saddle and that I was sorry from my heart to be compelled to give her uneasiness or trouble; the war had no mercy; and that through it all I hoped she would be protected from harm." He then took the husband about a mile down the road and hanged him. Then he returned the man's pocket money, horse, and mule to the poor widow.[2] What is especially striking about this story is that Hildebrand later published it, clearly to put himself in a good light. Killing this man had been acceptable because it was war and not the soldier which had been merciless, something he demonstrated by being gallant to the new widow he had just made.

Guerrillas wished to believe they were the protectors, not the despoilers of home and family, and honoring this code was a daily demonstration of their ideals. In his open letter to Union General Egbert B. Brown in 1864, the notorious Bill Anderson made the demand for the release from prison of his women sympathizers the demonstration of his claims to social respectability and power." I do not like the idea of warring with women and children, but if you do not release all the women you have captured in LaFayette County, I will hold the Union Ladies in the county as hostages for them. I will tie them in the brush and starve them. . . . I will have to resort to abusing your ladies if you do not quit imprisoning ours."[3] Defending "their" women was the chief function of masculinity. Honor demanded vengeance if they were injured. Indeed the massacre at Lawrence in August 1863 of 150 unarmed civilian males was justified at the time and after the war by William C. Quantrill's men in large part because several of the guerrilla's sisters, including two of Bill Anderson's, had died when a rickety Union prison had collapsed on them in Kansas City.[4] In response, guerrillas sought to kill only the male perpetrators of such deeds, and always spared the women and children on the other side. Thus they claimed moral superiority to Union soldiers; they were the true upholders and enforcers of the natural law enjoining honorable conduct toward women. Customary deference to women had become twisted, making them pawns to be kept upright while the knights and rooks knocked over each other. All the while, the warriors could proclaim that the slaughter of men was done in service to their righteous worship of women.

Strikingly, there are only infrequent reports of rape of white women, and all of those second-hand. To give an example, N. F. Carter had heard that "Ned Ellis was shot at [one recent] night; his wife and Mrs. Stevens were raped by the Militia and everything they had taken from them."[5] It is hard to analyze this report, and the absence of others. It is possible that rape did occur with some frequency and was such a badge of shame as to go undisclosed. But in that case rape was the only violation to remain unmentioned, as everything else was told to the authorities and broadcast as propaganda against the enemy. It is possible as well that rape was infrequent.

If rape was unusual, extreme brutality toward women was common, including what one might call near rape or symbolic rape, often combined with looting and the killing of men. One southern sympathizer reported several cases of harassment of pro-southern women in his neighborhood. "Union militiamen forced Mrs. Trigg to play for them while they danced . . . one of the men remarked to Mrs. Thos. Shields (who is quite a fine looking young woman) that he liked her looks and would come back that night and stay with her. At Col. Bellis's they . . . abused his wife shamefully, felt of her person, and used insulting language."[6] These might be considered very nasty pranks, ones unlikely to have occurred during peacetime, though there was some political discrimination and hence intent concerning which women were chosen to be violated.

More often attacks on women took place in the context of looting, and sometimes of killing of civilian men. For example, M. G. Singleton, a wealthy farmer who lived near Centralia, and who lived under oath and bond after having served in the secessionist state militia at the start of the war, reported the attack of twenty Union militiamen who came calling for dinner. His wife, who had her two nieces as company, refused to serve the men. The militia commander flew into a rage and demanded to be fed. The troops then commenced ransacking the house, "all the time using the most profane and vulgar language," in order to offend the women. "One fellow danced with the heels of his boots on the carpet in my wife's chamber till he cut it through. They had thrown their overcoats and a gun on her bed, which she quietly removed—placing the coats on a chair and set the gun up by the side of the bed—when one of them threw them on again and

called on the rest to pile on their guns—and then jumped on the
bed and rolled over it—took the pillows threw them down on the
floor, sat and then stamped them under his feet." After they had
dined, two armed Negroes who accompanied them ate "the family dinner," and then took a pan of bread dough and threw it on
the kitchen floor.[7]

Mrs. Singleton enraged the troopers, who doubtless would
have looted the house of a known southern sympathizer in any
event, by correcting the soldiers' etiquette, first refusing them
dinner, then taking their coats and guns off her bed. They further violated her domestic space by having Negroes eat off the
family china (albeit after they had eaten, thus preserving their
Caucasian superiority while violating hers), and encouraging
them to desecrate her kitchen. In front of her, they also assaulted
her bedroom, her most private space, piling guns on her bed and
tearing apart her bed clothes. One need not be a Freudian to
sense the intense violence of this scene. The soldiers attacked the
setting of Mrs. Singleton's femaleness, yet they did not actually
rape her or her nieces. Symbolic rape such as this was frequent.
The impulse to rape, which was certainly present, was projected
onto this woman's most intimate objects in place of her body.

There was also an additional element here of bad boys acting
out against a nagging, smothering mother. Mrs. Singleton put
their coats and guns in the proper place; they heaped them on
the improper place, as part of the destruction of her bed and her
rules. Some of these young men may have been vandals during
peacetime, but here they could be rule breakers openly and defi-
antly. Uniformed, officially empowered, they were not forced to
run off after breaking a window, but could stay on, encouraging
one another in competitive destructiveness until they reached
some mutually understood implicit limit, one which would vary
from instance to instance and group to group. They pushed at
the limits of a code they did not violate entirely.

On the night of May 6, 1865, Mrs. Mary Hall was awakened in
her bed by a group of guerrillas. They demanded she light a
candle, and then took it and set light to her children's clothes,
shoving them under the bed where the three children were
sleeping. "I caught the clothes they were burning" she recounted, "and threw them in the fire place. One of them says

God damn you let them; if you don't I will burn up the house. I answered they will burn just as well where they are and will give more light." They then went to the bed of her eighteen-year-old son and demanded his pistol. He said he had traded it for a watch and added, "its hanging by the glass though some of you have it—as I do not see it. One of the guerrillas said God damn him. Shoot him. I thought they would shoot him and knocked up the pistol several times, injuring my shoulder by so doing," Hall reported. "They finally succeeded in shooting him in the head killing him instantly. I was screaming and entreating them all the time to spare his life. After they had killed him one of them says shut your God Damn mouth or I will blow a hole through your head. . . . All this time my niece, 16 years of age was lying in bed. One of the guerrillas stood by the bedside and as she made an effort to rise ordered her to lie still saying one woman was enough at a time. After they had killed my son and plundered the house one of the guerrillas ordered me out of the house and shut the door. The door had scarcely closed before I heard my niece scream and say Lord Aunt Mary run here to me. I started and as I reached the door my niece who had succeeded in effecting her escape from the men came rushing out. I says let the poor girl alone you have done enough . . . I do not think they effected their designs on the girl." As they had destroyed all her son's clothing, Hall had to buy a suit in which to bury him.[8]

Mary Hall could not protect her son from slaughter, but she could aid in preventing her niece's rape. The assault went up to the edge of rape and murder of women. Breaking into a house in the middle of the night, destroying and burning property out of pure malevolence, killing a man right in front of his mother, simply because he was grown and probably sympathetic to the other side, and threatening women in the grossest manner, were all characteristic guerrilla invasions of the realm of women. This passion for destruction, which had little to do with military necessity, stopping just short of rape and murder of women, lay on the dark side of the code of protecting women.

Some inviolable positive value—the protection of women—was necessary psychologically to these guerrilla fighters. The attacks on women described above were indeed assaults on those traditional values, but there was usually some mitigation of violence. It seems that these warriors did *not* make fundamental distinctions between the images of the angel and the whore. "Bad," abusive, or duplicitous women departed from the general code of nice ladies, but they were rarely re-conceptualized as completely debased. However perversely, the fighters were eager to maintain ideals of honor in their relations with women.

This moral framework applied to white women only: black women and Indian women were beyond the pale for fighters on both sides. Indeed one might argue that all white women were treated with respect in part because other nonwhite women were available to be trampled. One can find evidence of behavior toward blacks and Indians which was never accorded whites. Racism, tied to the license to destroy, was the deadliest combination. However, the liberation of blacks during the war which led to white resentment also tended to mitigate brutal treatment of black women.

Raping and beating black women, sometimes beating them to death, were intrinsic parts of slavery, an institution which gave superhuman powers to the owners. Good owners avoided random and excessive brutality, and decried the viciousness of harsh masters. Yet few good masters refrained from whipping, and many used their enormous power over slave women to coerce them sexually, with varying degrees of explicitness. White men were not punished for raping black women.

There were many allusions to the rape and abuse of black women during the war, particularly of those "contrabands" who followed the army. There are few direct reports, however, of actual rape. One concrete example came in the court-martial of guerrilla James Johnson of Platte County. Frances Kean testified that Johnson, John Nichols, and another bushwhacker seized her eighteen-year-old slave girl. Kean reported what the girl had told her. "They rode on a piece and said to her, 'God damn you we will punish you' . . . Nichols then got off his horse and said now boys ride and she told me they all done with her what they wanted to—she said they violated her person."[9]

In March 1864, a slave owner named Tapley, of Pike County, recaptured his escaping slave woman. As she would not tell him where she had hidden her three children, she was, according to an unsigned letter in the Chicago *Tribune,* "stripped and beaten on the bare back with a band saw until large blisters formed, and then the wretch sawed them open, under which treatment the poor woman died." Mrs. J. R. Roberts, secretary of the Freedman's Relief Society of Quincy, Illinois, clipped this newspaper story and sent it in a letter to the provost marshal of Missouri. The story went on to say that Missouri slaveholders in general were enraged with Lincoln's proclamation freeing the wives and children of black soldiers: this woman had been running off to join her soldier husband when her owner caught her.[10] While Tapley's fate is unknown, James Johnson was sentenced to death, in part for his crime against a black woman.

The Civil War led many whites to re-work at least in part their attitudes toward blacks, including black women. Physical punishment of blacks, formerly a disciplinary norm, and murder of them, were in the process of becoming crimes in white eyes. This was in large part due to the reliability of black information given Union troops concerning secessionist activities and, later in the war, to the appearance of black regiments fighting for the Union. White Union soldiers had some sense of camaraderie with black soldiers; therefore, they came to understand that black soldiers sought to protect their women in the same way they wished to shelter their own.

In February 1863, the First Iowa Infantry was foraging on the farm of a noted northern Arkansas rebel. They asked a slave woman if there was a gun hidden away. "She denied knowing anything about it but being threatened she owned that it would be death to her if she told anything," Private Timothy Phillips recorded in his diary. "Our boys promised to rescue her and take her along with them," Phillips wrote. Perhaps this was the *quid pro quo* the woman was bargaining for all along; perhaps she wished vengeance against her owner; perhaps she was terribly frightened. In any event, the Iowa troops found the gun where she had said they would, and she was placed on a horse in the baggage train. Later, the owner caught up with the column and offered twenty dollars in gold to anyone who would return his slave. She was returned and the $20 paid. "The whole thing was got up so quick that few in the train knew anything about it," Phillips wrote in his diary that evening. Lieutenant Dunham, the head of Phillips's squad, was blamed, and forced to turn the money over to the Colonel. Phillips concluded, "There is considerable excitement in the regiment about this matter and if the boys had it in their power they would make short work of Lieut. Dunham."[11]

The most obvious conclusion one might draw is that Lieutenant Dunham was glad to turn over a "nigger wench" for $20. Phillips's moral was more complex. The exchange took place so quickly he had not responded at the time, he wrote later, perhaps in expiation for what he realized—between the act and the pen—had been a terrible betrayal by omission of his own. Unlike his lieutenant, he believed that breaking an official word given a black woman was criminal. Also, he reasoned, other slaves, hearing of this incident, might be less forthcoming in the future. It was just plain wrong to him.

For many Kansas regiments, freeing slaves was central to their agenda, less out of racial sympathy than because of their desire for revenge against their longtime enemies, the Missouri slaveholders. Surgeon Joseph H. Trego reported that two captains had resigned their commissions in his Fifth Kansas cavalry regiment when Colonel Clayton ordered the return of a group of fugitive slaves. "This case was particularly agrivating because the fugitives were wenches and one of them was whipped severely when her master got her home." Although Trego used racist language and shared the obsession for punishing Missourians, he empathized with the female victims of his enemies, and sought to free and protect them.[12]

Ambivalence toward convention, which in any event had been largely undermined by cultural chaos, led women as well as men into contexts where they were compelled at least to consider dangerously new conceptions of self and of others. The ability to function within traditional roles and values was weakened, altered, and at times reversed during the guerrilla war. Under great stress and novel opportunity, women sometimes impersonated men (and occasionally men impersonated women), and in general, sexual mores became more fluid as the boundaries between male and female roles weakened. If men and women struggled to retain many of their received notions of proper roles and behavior, they also entered situations where the old values were challenged by dramatically disorienting experiences which could not be explained in ordinary terms.

During such a war, where a guerrilla could be defined, at minimum, as a mounted, armed troublemaker, there were openings for at least a few adventurous women to join in. There are a few first-hand reports of women bushwhackers. In June 1864, Major Jeremiah Hackett reported the arrest of Mrs. Gibson and her daughter, caught while tearing down telegraph wires. Iowa Private Henry Dysart wrote in his diary in April 1862, "A few days since a party, several of whom were women, plundered the hospital at Ketesville robbing the wounded of their arms, clothing, money and the women taking the lead, the latter whose presence in the hospitals should rather be to cheer the wounded than to terrify and rob them are now here prisoners with several of the men." Dysart was struck by the symbolism of women, who should be nurturing wounded men in the hospital, instead attacking them like "inhuman savages," as he called all guerrillas.[13] To him, it was bad enough that men behaved this way, but nearly inconceivable that women should do so.

Each time a man would comment on women warriors, he would remark, as had Dysart, on the departure from those conventional womanly roles he expected and valued. Private Sardius Smith wrote in his diary, "The gentler sex are anything but gentle and I am told that some of them have went so far as to dress in mens clothes and go to a union mans house and demand his property." Unlike Dysart, Smith had not actually seen such women who disguised themselves as men and behaved as did the worst bushwhackers, but he reported a popular rumor which indicated male soldiers' fears that women were no longer unarmed and gentle. Wanting to maintain a monopoly of violence, soldiers like Smith especially feared armed women. Even if a woman picked up the gun in defense of home and family, and even if she were on the right side of the conflict, this actively aggressive version of women was troubling to many soldiers. Smith wrote, "If [southern guerrilla women] are warlike, union women are about equally so, and the old lady with whom I supped once stood between her husband and a Secesh with a loaded gun who was trying to shoot her husband and actually kept him out." For Smith, it should have been the husband defending the wife. Although he rather admired the ferociousness of this Union woman, who after all was on his side and who still served him a nice supper when she was not being Judith of the Holofernes, Smith did not expect or like to see a woman acting as soldier of the hearth. Smith also reported with wonder about the organization of two militia companies in southern Missouri: "I have seen at an early hour they began to assemble in squads women as well as men and the place was soon full of men and women of all ages and descriptions."[14]

Such changes disturbed women as well as men. It was important for them to attempt to maintain "normal" sex roles. Women dressing and acting like men upset other women; this possibility contained complex and threatening implications for women too when they defined gender. Take for example a story told by Private James H. Guthrie of the First Iowa Infantry, as his regiment was traveling south on board a Mississippi River steamboat. "We have a boy on board with very long hair and the most feminine appearance I ever saw. It was an easy job to make the women on board believe it was a woman in soldier's clothes. It created quite a sensation and lots of fun. One of the women got so high that in distributing pocket handkerchiefs she gave all but our supposed woman one and would not even speak to her. I slipped the boy one and posted him where he played the joke finely. The women went to the Doctor to get him [to] make an examination and if a woman to put her overboard. One of the women said 'look at the shape of her ankles, legs and hipps which proves her to be a female.' "[15] Guthrie did not seem anything but amused about an effeminate soldier, and the soldier himself enjoyed confusing women about his sexual identity, but the women were furious about the possibility of a woman impersonating a male soldier. They wanted to discover and maintain the "truth," to maintain clear gender distinctions.

War also meant that men had contact with women a long way from the security and the limitations of home, and that these women met armed strangers from what often might have seemed an alien planet. Distances were most keenly felt when northern soldiers from more modern and tidy locales encountered poor backcountry Missouri farm women. Such soldiers were often shocked by what to them were female emblems of cultural backwardness. These appeared to be less than ladies, proof that Missouri was a foreign and inferior culture where proper values hardly existed. If not rendered as completely laughable, such women could be objects toward whom northerners could allow themselves to express a more general cultural contempt for backcountry secessionists. Sardius Smith wrote of those women he observed one day drilling in militia companies that they "are generally an ignorant set dressed in old fashioned costumes of divers colors and appearing awkward and bashful in presence of so many Strangers."[16] Smith proudly reported that his regiment carefully refrained from openly ridiculing such female yokels, who had the virtue of being pro-Union hicks.

As well as ignorant and uncivilized, such women were frequently believed to be unclean, a notion always applied by those who believe themselves to be culturally superior. In the best of circumstances it was difficult for poor rural women to keep their homes and clothes clean, and this was made harder by the absence of men to help out and the other dislocations caused by war. However, for northern soldiers such dirtiness was an indication of cultural slovenliness. Charles W. Falker wrote to his "darling wife" in Wisconsin from camp near Warrensburg in 1865, "I have not seen a barn on the road not one church and but one or two school houses. The women are the homeliest dirtiest specimens of the feminine gender I ever saw. I cant conceive how a white man could be induced to live with one. Niggers are quite plenty."[17] The lack of schools and churches, the proximity of dirty white women to blacks, whom he described as livestock rather than humans, all formed a package to be rejected totally by this agent of northern enlightenment.

Some soldiers who carried the same preconceptions about southern rural women into the war learned to look beyond first appearances and gained at least some sense of their humanity and essential femininity. When he saw women performing traditional male tasks in southern Missouri in 1864, Ohio-born Corporal Seth Kelly placed this unsexing in wartime context. "Saw two women each with a yoke of oxen plowing a field by the roadside," he wrote in his diary. "War and the Rebellion has taken away the male population." Most people had fled the guerrilla-devastated countryside and had crowded into garrison towns. In Berryville, Arkansas, Kelly observed, "The women are better looking and more tidy than I expected to see them." His preconception was that they should be homely slatterns, but they seemed quite all right on a closer look. In fact if a bit strange, they could even be appropriate sex objects. Thus Kelly wrote of a particularly successful foraging expedition in northern Arkansas, "Several pretty women, secesh, bewitching. Good circumstances, no men. Got plenty of corn, also honey. Ladies chew tobacco—it's a fact—I saw it. Widow Carter."[18] This unpromising country could be land of feasts, honey, and the Widow Carter after all. She might chew tobacco—imagine that—but she sure was a lot of fun.

The familial dislocations particularly true in a guerrilla war, added to the ready cash and plunder in soldier's hands, doubtless multiplied the number of prostitutes who entered army camps. Such women made themselves available, in exchange for money and some security, and carried on with elements of women's work, albeit in an untraditional context. A semi-literate Illinois infantryman of German descent described such women at the big Union base, Benton Barracks, in St. Louis. "There is a lot of women that have some friends in camp and they furnish them with whiskey. They pedle fruit and do washing. They with a pass are allowed to go in and out but they was caught last night. They searcht two or three of them and got about 40 bottles of the clear stuff. They had secreted them under there dress strung on there hoop skirts, they marched them to the gard house."[19]

Sometimes prostitutes would march with an army column, and some of these women would attempt to maintain respectability, often portraying themselves as widows in need, which doubtless many were. Surgeon Joseph H. Trego recorded in his diary his contemptuous response to one heavily veiled self-proclaimed widow, "Capt Miller has a woman with him . . . represented as a widow returning to her friends in Missouri, her husband having been killed when they were making their exodus from Dixie. . . . She has proven to be the commonest kind of 'Army Woman' . . . she is called Capt Miller's 'masked battery.'"[20]

Often treated as objects of derision, at other times at least some soldiers analyzed the wartime pressure on women and felt sympathy for army whores. Kansas Cavalry Sargeant W. W. Moses wrote in his diary about the fall of sixteen-year-old Mary French, "a very respectable young girl," who had been seduced "by promises of marriage (although indirectly promised)" by Lieutenant William Henry. "For about a month [he] slept with her every night while William Sheldon slept with her mother." Her father, a Union soldier, when on leave took Mary back home to St. Louis and left his wife behind, "a public whore," but Mary returned "to see her intended husband Lieut. Henry. Alas she is unaware that disgrace and disappointment are in store. She fondly hopes some day to be his wife. She does not know that Henry has a family at home. She will soon be added to the no. of prostitutes that throng our cities and towns and hang around the camps of our soldiers." Moses blamed the Lieutenant, though he evidently failed to do anything to warn Mary of her danger. He seemed to wish to let the drama take its course. To Moses, she was the victim of a scoundrel, but she had fallen. Moses then drew a conclusion about his own threatened probity. "Alas how has this war corrupted the morals, destroyed the health and blighted the fond hopes and joys of our land. Virtue is indeed scarce. A wonder few have passed through the army without yielding to the tempter. God help me to still live right and shield me from all sin."[21] Moses should never be party to debasing virtuous women, lest he himself fall from grace.

Some soldiers dealt with problems of sexual etiquette and honor with humor. This was one means of defusing those temptations and threats offered by war. Colonel Basel F. Lazear of Callaway County, for example, wrote long letters to his wife, both funny and nasty, which illustrate some of the ways he managed his strong erotic love for his wife and his interest in those women war pushed toward his lap. He both threatened and reassured his wife with his letters, which gave a clear notion of peacetime sexual norms under wartime pressure, particularly for such a handsome colonel, who cut a grand figure as his regiment marched into town after town.

When at an inactive post, pining for his wife, Lazear repeatedly begged her to come, disregarding any danger she might undergo on the voyage, and asking her to leave behind her household duties. "I am very tired and lonesome here. I have so

little to do. You being with me last winter has spoiled me." Two
weeks later, moved to a livelier town, Lazear wrote to his wife,
"When I wrote you last I was very anxious for you to come and
see me but you need not come now for I had dinner yesterday
with a dozen of the prettiest girls in the town and that aint
all . . . there is a nice young widow here . . . who I expect
will steal your old man so you need not come." Lazear let his wife
know that he could have the choice of the seraglio of ladies left
manless by war. Nor were these the only potential bedmates. "I
now have two very pretty rebel girls on my hands as prisoners
and what the devil to do with I dont know, as I dont like to put
them in the guard house. I expect I will have to take them into
my room and let them sleep with me."

One should note the defensive passivity of that last barb—
Colonel Lazear would have to let the saucy rebel girls have their
way with him, so how could he be to blame? Also, in a vein of
humor probably central to their relationship, he wrote his wife
frequently, and always unfurtively and openly about his erotic
fantasies. Yet there was a significant element of threat and abuse
involved as well. Whatever jostling had occurred during ordinary times in this household was clearly highlighted by the pecu-
liarities of this extraordinary set of circumstances. We do not
have Mrs. Lazear's replies, so we cannot know whether she just
absorbed such banter, or dished it back to him. She was not so
annoyed as to destroy the letters either during the war or later.
In any event, after the war Lazear went back home to Auxvasse,
where he was a mere postal clerk and dutiful husband, as he had
promised he would in his usual manner in a letter written from
Jefferson City in 1864: "I have been trying to find me a nice
widow here but I can't come across one yet and I reckon I will
have to come home to that old black snaggle tooth again don't
you think so too but we will make this all right when I come."[22]

The women who dined with Colonel Lazear would not in
peacetime have entertained roaming military officers without
their husbands present. Other women frequently made negative
comments about such loose socializing. Even this much role reor-
ientation opened doors to incorrectly altered behavior. Clearly,
however, sexual relations with men were more diverse than in
peacetime.

In other respects as well, women acted in ways which cut against ordinary expectations. This included treatment women accorded one another. A brutal, almost Dickensian example concerned Mrs. William J. Dixon, wife of the keeper of the St. Charles Street prison for women in St. Louis. Prisoner Mary Pitman testified to a Union Board of Enquiry concerning the prison, about the terrible food, lack of heat, sale of "dainties" sent to prisoners, burning of letters of protest to the Union command, and continual demands for bribes made by Mrs. Dixon. Poor women, without the means to bribe, were especially mistreated. Dixon forced Mrs. Carney, who was pregnant, to sew for the Dixon family, to sleep in filthy rags, and to be segregated as supposedly "lousy." On one occasion, Dixon demanded prisoner White's new comforter in exchange for an old one, which White refused, saying "it was too dirty for a white person or a negro to sleep under." Dixon then threw the old comforter in her face. White said, "if you throw those into my face again I will knock you down," to which Dixon replied, jerking the new comforter away, "[you] had better try it—[you are] a lousy, dirty hussy and ought not to have anything to sleep on." Dixon then locked White in her room on half-rations and without toilet facilities so "she had to do the best she could." Dixon allowed her to clean herself and her room only when the Union colonel who employed the Dixons came for one of his inspections. Dixon also arranged evenings alone in the parlor for one prisoner, Miss Warren, and Captain J. B. Keyser, a defense lawyer. One evening, Pitman "saw her lying in his arms. The Captain had his arms around her and his hands on her bosom. Then I saw him get up and turn the light lower down and [I] went upstairs."[23] Despite all of the evils which were normal for life in this prison, Pitman maintained a sense of outrage, and appealed to authorities, believing that women should not so abuse one another and that some greater justice still could be served. Dixon's behavior was not accpetable to Pitman, who herself may have felt compromised as a trustee running favors for Dixon.

Guerrilla war undermined the peaceful settings in which good—that is to say, conventional—conduct could be maintained. When conditions grew even worse, widespread guerrilla warfare uprooted women and children from their homes and sent them fleeing for security. The chaotic lives of Union troops and bushwhackers torn from their homes, roaming from fire-fight to firefight, was matched by wandering, fatherless, destitute families. Frequently family members lost contact with one another for many years, and lost the sense of a safe and stable family home to which to return. Timothy Phillips, an Iowa infan-tryman, noted in the refugee camp in Forseyth, "We have now here some two dozen women and not less than a hundred children—more or les varying in age from two weeks to 15 years." He then went on to tell what was to him a touching tale of the reunion of a wandering soldier with his war-displaced wife. "One soldier belonging to the 1st Ark (Union) having business in our camp found his wife here which he had not seen for twelve months. The meeting was a joyful one and was brought about by singular circumstances. His wife fleeing from starvation seeking protection from us."[24] Phillips told of many other refugees but not about any other reunions.

Many women and children had the better fortune of being able to return to safe havens with family in other states, though they too had the anxiety of not knowing what was happening back home. Mollie McRoberts returned to her parents' home in Circleville, Ohio. Yet she found little peace of mind since her husband, A. J., remained back on their Missouri farm. She wrote to him at one point that she had just received his first letter in two weeks, and "that when I don't get a letter it makes me almost sick. I was so troubled last night that I could not sleep." She told him to simply abandon their farm, "for I feel sure you will be killed and dear, your life is far more precious than all the wealth on earth. I would much rather go out and wash by the day than have you expose yourself the way you have been doing." She was willing to lose the family assets, and to do the the most demean-ing labor if that would reunite her family. Survival outweighed conventional respectability. He should get away from those guer-rilla "bloodhounds." "I know we won't starve. We have a kind father in heaven who is willing to help those who help them-selves."[25]

If Mollie McRoberts was a Union exile gone north, Mrs. Edwin H. Harris of St. Clair was a secessionist exile gone south to Paris, Texas. She hated Texas, with its bleakness and sandstorms, and was filled with anxiety and homesickness. "So many rumors" of events in Missouri circulating among the exiled Missourians filled her with a "constant dread . . . . I sometimes feel that I cannot stand so much uneasiness and think I will start to Missouri to see if I can find you," she wrote her husband Edwin. She heard from him about Union troops ransacking their house. "I was indeed sorry to hear of our dear home being so much torn up. Oh how I long for the time to come we can again be together and live in peace in our dear old home." At one point Edwin wrote his wife to scotch rumors of his having turned Unionist. "That Devil's dam, Aunt Polly Fewell, is at the bottom of all the damned villainy here, and I suppose she would like to cover up the short-comings of her own foul brood by bringing odium upon others. . . . Say to one and all that when I cease being a Southern man to all intents and purposes there will not be many left."[26]

Aunt Polly Fewell doubtless had spread malicious gossip before the war, but now she could be answered only with difficulty. Hundreds of miles away from home, Mrs. Harris could only gnash her teeth in the face of rumors and bad news, some of which might well prove to be true. Her war in exile was lived in a necessarily passive and lonely fearfulness.

All this dislocation and destruction caused by guerrilla war made more urgent than ever the need for a compensatory sense of love and connection, with God, among kin, and between men and women, with that most cherished loved one. Quite frequently, often late at night, fighters would write to their mothers and sisters, and most especially to their sweethearts and wives. To take but one example, writing by lantern light near midnight one night, when all his tentmates were asleep, George Avery told his wife, "It is now that I can talk to my Lizzie with emotions of pleasure; but much sweeter would be the interview could I but sit by your side with your fair form reclining upon my bosom."[27] To write this was to enter a kind of trance where writing was conversation and "talk" triggered a palpable feeling of physical presence, both as memory and as promise. In the quiet of the night George Avery could find an escape by reaffirming his ties with his wife.

Even shreds of loving memory for men behaving unlovingly

were crucial when the world of normal expectations had come undone. For women, too, such desire made survival possible. It reminded them of times of comfort, security, and even joy, of times when life consisted of more than just grimly holding on. Love was distant from an everyday wartime life that was filled with brutality and lying and running, but that one had loved meant one might love again, and this sustained people even as they terrorized other people. Perhaps guerrilla war had so altered values that the capacity for love was a mechanism by which the wicked could think well enough of themselves to carry on destruction without feeling empty. But more generally, even destroyers sought to be human, and loving humans also could be destroyers.

PART IV
XXXXXXXXXXXXXXXXXXXXXXXXX

The Southern Homefront

*I*n a world of idealized gender behavior, men march off to war and
*women stay at home, sending support and encouragement to the
boys at the front. Although hardly a world of ideals, the Civil War
South did witness much of this partitioned patriotism as the Confederate government celebrated and exalted the special homefront role of
white women. Indeed, lacking any real centralized support system,
especially a northern-style Sanitary Commission, the Confederate administration often required women to undertake a wide range of activities which, in more recent times, have been performed by government
bureaucracies. Both white and black women sewed uniforms. Confederate women made battle flags and other emblems of war. And women
everywhere outfitted fathers, sons, brothers, and lovers with a variety
of necessities and personal comforts.*

*Even more, white women were often expected to keep farms, planta-
tions, and businesses running smoothly while husbands were away.
Suddenly women were not just sewers or knitters—tasks which conformed to traditional roles. Now, they were managers and accoun-
tants, perhaps even overseers—tasks which went well beyond accepted
boundaries. These demands posed special problems for southern ladies,
perhaps even more so than for northern women, because of the extremely rigid sexual boundaries which had grown up in the South's
plantation society.*

*Southern women confronted the new demands of the homefront in a
variety of ways. In her analysis of a southern marriage during the war,
Joan Cashin observes how one woman gradually took on greater authority in the management of slaves and the plantation. In subtle ways*

she challenged the domination of both her husband and the white overseer. Other white women gained a new sense of confidence in their ability to manage and make decisions, a confidence which many historians believe extended into the postwar period.

Yet the question of just how willingly Confederate women shouldered new responsibilities and coped with the problems of war remains unsettled. As the war dragged on and as Confederate losses mounted, life on the southern homefront became almost intolerable. Food shortages, inflation, the break-up of slavery, and the appearance of the enemy in many southern communities imposed severe strains and burdens on families of all classes. In April 1863, Richmond women, many of whom were wives of workers at the local iron works, led the largest riot in antebellum southern history. The Richmond bread riot revealed the frustration and desperation of many southern women who found it impossible to cope with extensive wartime shortages. In her essay on Confederate women, Drew Faust discusses the Richmond riot as well as a number of other episodes that suggest an increasing alienation on the part of many white women from the Confederate cause. Promised the paternal protection of male honor, southern white women began to balk at the Confederacy's failure to live up to time-honored agreements. Faust suggests that historians who ponder the reasons for southern defeat might well consider the role played by this increasingly defiant female population.

If white women began to weaken the foundation of the Confederate homefront, southern slaves certainly did their part to undermine the support system that was crucial for keeping the war machine running. Throughout the Confederacy, especially as the Union army approached, southern slaves found various ways to weaken the ties of bondage. Estimates are that as many as one-seventh of the slave population came within Union lines, and thus within the bounds of freedom, in the course of the war. In addition, many of those who stayed behind refused to conform to the rigid prewar discipline.

One component of emancipation that has received little attention is the way in which slave children confronted the transformations of war. Peter Bardaglio explores this component of life on the homefront. He examines how children responded to the breakdown of planter rule, familial dislocations, and the experience of freedom, and how gender, among other factors, influenced their actions and behavior.

As slavery crumbled, African Americans, men and women, children as well as adults, began to explore the wide range of options and possibilities which freedom opened up. In a variety of ways, they gained a voice which they had previously been denied. As Martha Hodes explains, the new discourse could be explosive. In her essay on inter-racial sex in the Civil War South, Hodes reveals how black men's words concerning their sexual relations with white women gained, for the first time, a public hearing. Although northern Democrats raised up a myth of miscegenation for political purposes and southern whites did the same during Reconstruction, Hodes shows how white anti-slavery northerners in the Civil War South gained, albeit for a brief moment, a fascinating insight into the sexual coercion of black men by white women. Clearly, as this essay suggests, the realities of the southern homefront bore little resemblance to the idealized pictures of manly heroism and feminine sacrifice which were so dearly cherished by the leaders of the Confederacy.

Chapter 10

XXXXXXXXXXXXXXXXXXXXXXX

Altars of Sacrifice: Confederate Women and the Narratives of War

DREW GILPIN FAUST

It is the men, Hector tells Andromache in the sixth book of the *Iliad,* who "must see to the fighting." From ancient history to our own time, war has centered on men, for they have controlled and populated its battlefields. Even in our era of shifting gender definitions, perhaps the most assertive—and successful—defense of traditional roles has been the effort to bar women from combat. Yet war has often introduced women to unaccustomed responsibilities and unprecedented, even if temporary, enhancements of power. War has been a preeminently "gendering" activity, casting thought about sex differences into sharp relief as it has both underlined and realigned gender boundaries.[1]

Like every war before and since, the American Civil War served as an occasion for both reassertion and reconsideration of gender assumptions. Early in the conflict, Louisianian Julia Le Grand observed that "we are leading the lives which women have led since Troy fell." Yet because the Civil War was fundamentally different from those that had preceded it, the place of women in that conflict stimulated especially significant examination and discussion of women's appropriate relationship to war—and thus to society in general. Often designated the first "modern" or total war because of the involvement of entire pop-

ulations in its terrible work of death, the Civil War required an
extraordinary level of female participation. This was a conflict in
which the "home front" had a newly important role in generating mass armies and keeping them in the field. Particularly in the
South, where human and material resources were stretched to
the utmost, the conflict demanded the mobilization of women,
not for battle, but for civilian support services such as nursing,
textile and clothing production, munitions and government office work, slave management, and even agriculture. Yet white
southern women, unlike their men, were not conscripted by law.
They had to be enlisted by persuasion. The resulting discourse
about woman's place in Confederate society represented the rhetorical attempt to create a hegemonic ideology of female patriotism and sacrifice.[2]

Articulate southerners, male and female, crafted an exemplary narrative about the Confederate woman's Civil War, a
story designed to ensure her loyalty and service. As in the tales of
war enshrined in Western literature from Homer to Sir Walter
Scott, its plot recounted woman's heroic self-sacrifice, casting it
as indispensable to the moral, political, and military triumph of
her men and her country. The historian John Keegan has com-
pellingly described the way in which the "battle piece," the highly
conventionalized and heroic account of combat, has shaped
men's expectations and experiences of war. But women have
been no less influenced by a genre of female "war stories," intended to socialize them through accounts of their foremother's
deeds. The conventional designation of all women as noncom-
batants inevitably enhances the wartime significance of gender as
a social category, as well as a structure of self-definition. The
focus of Confederate public discourse on a "classless" white
woman reinforced the privileging of female identity. Usually cast
in the homogeneous singular, the "woman" who shared with her
sisters rich and poor the experience of sacrificing men to battle
represented a useful rhetorical convention within a Confederate
ideology struggling to minimize the class divisions that might
threaten national survival. At the same time that Confederate
discourse appealed to a new and recognizable commonality
widely shared by white southern women—whose husbands or
sons were nearly three times as likely to die as were their northern counterparts—it promoted the notion of an archetypal

"Confederate woman" as a form of false consciousness obscuring social and economic differences among the new nation's female citizens. Ultimately, the focus of Confederate ideology on female self-abnegation and sacrifice as ends in themselves would alienate many women from that rendition of their interests, from the war, and in many cases, from the Confederacy itself. Ideology and its failures played a critical role in shaping the relationship of women to the Southern Cause and in defining Confederate viability. In recent years scholars have answered the historiographical perennial, "why the South lost the Civil War," by emphasizing deficiencies in southern morale. Almost all such arguments stress the importance of class conflict, especially growing yeoman dissent, in undermining the Southern Cause. Yet with a white civilian population that was overwhelmingly female and that bore an unprecedented responsibility for the war's outcome, we must not ignore gender as a factor in explaining Confederate defeat.[3]

To suggest that southern women in any way subverted the Confederate effort is to challenge a more than century-old legend of female sacrifice. The story of Confederate women's unflinching loyalty originated during the war and first found official expression in legislative resolutions offered by Confederate leaders to mark the contributions of female citizens. The Confederate Congress established the model in a declaration of gratitude passed in April 1862; the gesture was replicated in proclamations like that of the Mississippi legislature in 1863 thanking the "mothers, wives, sisters and daughters of this State" for their "ardent devotion . . . unremitting labors and sacrifices."[4] After Appomattox this hortatory narrative of female dedication was physically realized in monuments to wives and mothers of the Confederacy and incorporated into scholarly literature on women and the war as conventional historical truth. Even the titles of scholarly works, such as Mary Elizabeth Massey's *Bonnet Brigades*, published in 1966 as part of the Civil War centennial, or H. E. Sterkx's more recent *Partners in Rebellion: Alabama Women in the Civil War*, communicate the image of Southern women fighting alongside their men. The same vision had a century earlier inspired Henry Timrod, poet laureate of the Confederacy, to entitle his wartime ode to Confederate ladies "Two Armies." Praising women's contributions in caring for the sick, plying the "needle and the loom," and "by a thousand peaceful deeds" supplying "a struggling nation's needs," Timrod promised women equal glory with the war's military heroes.

> When Heaven shall blow the trump of peace,
> And bid this weary warfare cease,
> Their several missions nobly done,
> The triumph grasped, the freedom won,
> Both armies, from their toils at rest,
> Alike may claim the victor's crest.[5]

The tenacity of such a rendition of southern women's wartime role—its survival from Confederate myth into twentieth-century historiography—is less curious than at first it seems. Confederate versions originated so early in the conflict as to have been necessarily prescriptive rather than descriptive. This was not simply a story, but an ideology intended to direct southern women, to outline appropriate behavior in the abruptly altered wartime situation. The flattery, the honorific nature of this discourse, was central to its rhetorical force. And the deference to women's importance ensured the survival of the narrative and its evolution into historical interpretation. Ironically, it fit neatly with an emergent twentieth-century feminist historiography eager to explore women's contributions to past events previously portrayed from an exclusively male point of view. Yet the passage of women's history beyond its earlier celebratory phase and the adoption of more critical and analytic approaches to female experience may enable us at last to see the story as the fiction it largely is, to explore its development, political origins, and rhetorical purposes and thus to understand how it shaped Confederate women's wartime lives.[6]

With the outbreak of hostilities in early 1861, public discourse in the Confederacy quickly acknowledged that war had a special meaning for white females. The earliest discussions of the Confederate woman in newspapers and periodicals sought to engage her in the war effort by stressing the relevance of her accustomed spiritual role. The defense of moral order, conventionally allocated to females by nineteenth-century bourgeois ideology, took on increased importance as war's social disruptions threatened ethical and spiritual dislocations as well. "Can you imagine," asked the magazine *Southern Field and Fireside*, "what would be the moral condition of the Confederate army in six months" without women's influence? What but a woman "makes the Confederate soldier a gentleman of honor, courage, virtue and truth, instead of a cut-throat and vagabond?" "Great indeed," confirmed the *Augusta Weekly Constitutionalist* in July 1861, "is the task assigned to woman. Who can elevate its dignity? Not," the paper observed pointedly, "to make laws, not to lead armies, not to govern empires; but to form those by whom laws are made, armies led . . . to soften firmness into mercy, and chasten honor into refinement."[7]

But many southern women, especially those from the slaveowning classes most instrumental in bringing about secession, were to find that a meager and unsatisfactory allotment of responsibility. As one woman remarked while watching the men of her community march off to battle, "We who stay behind may find it harder than they who go. They will have new scenes and constant excitement to buoy them up and the consciousness of duty done." Another felt herself "like a pent-up volcano. I wish I had a field for my energies . . . now that there is . . . real tragedy, real romance and history weaving every day, I suffer, suffer, leading the life I do." Events once confined to books now seemed to be taking place all around them, and they were eager to act out their designated part. "The war is certainly ours as well as that of the men," one woman jealously proclaimed.[8]

In the spring and summer of 1861, many articulate middle- and upper-class women sought active means of expressing their commitment, ones that placed less emphasis than had the *Augusta Constitutionalist* on what they might not do but instead drew them into the frenzy of military preparation. As recruits drilled and bivouacked, women found outlet for their energies sewing countless flags, uniforms, and even underwear for departing units; penning patriotic songs and verse; submitting dozens of designs for the national flag to the Confederate Congress; raising money as Ladies Gunboat Societies, forming more than a thousand relief associations across the new nation; and sponsoring dramatic performances to benefit soldiers, particularly tableaux representing historic and literary themes. "I feel quite important," one lady observed with some amazement after an evening of such scenes raised a substantial amount of money for Virginia troops.[9]

That declaration of importance was in marked and self-conscious contrast to the feelings of purposelessness that appeared frequently in letters and diaries written by women of the master class. "Useless" was a dread epithet, repeatedly directed by Confederate women against themselves as they contemplated the very clear and honored role war offered men. "We young ladies are all so . . . useless," bewailed Sarah Wadley of Louisiana. "There are none so . . . useless as I," complained Amanda Chappelear of Virginia. "If only I could be of some use to our poor stricken country," wrote a young Louisiana girl to a friend in Tennessee, while Emma Holmes of Charleston sought escape from her "aimless existence." "What is the use of all these worthless women, in war times?" demanded Sarah Dawson. "I don't know how to be useful," another Virgina woman worried.[10]

Some women translated these feelings into a related, yet more striking expression of discontent. Without directly challenging women's prescribed roles, they nevertheless longed for a magical personal deliverance from gender constraints by imagining themselves men. Some few actually disguised themselves and fought in the Confederate army, but far more widespread was the wish that preceded such dramatic and atypical action. "Would God I were a man," exclaimed Elizabeth Collier. "How I wish I was a man!" seconded Emma Walton. "I do sometimes long to be a man," confessed Sallie Munford. Such speculation represented a recognition of discontent new to most Confederate women. Directed into the world of fantasy rather than toward any specific reform program, such desires affirmed the status quo, yet at the same time, they represented a potential threat to existing gender assumptions.[11]

Without directly acknowledging such frustrations, Confederate public discussion of women's roles sought to deal with this incipient dissatisfaction by specifying active contributions women might make to the Southern Cause and by valorizing their passive waiting and sacrifice as highly purposeful. Confederate ideology construed women's suffering, not as an incidental by-product of men's wartime activities, but as an important and honored undertaking. In a popular Confederate novel aptly entitled *The Trials of a Soldier's Wife,* the heroine explained to her husband, "Woman can only show her devotion by suffering, and though I cannot struggle with you on the battle-field, in suffering as I have done, I feel it has been for our holy cause."[12]

Public treatments of woman's patriotism soon broadened her accepted spiritual responsibilities to encompass wartime morale. "The time has come," Leila W. wrote in the *Southern Monthly* of October 1861, "when woman should direct into the right channel the greater power which she possesses in giving tone to public sentiment and morals, and shaping national character and national destiny." Moral service to God would now be paralleled by morale service to the state. Southern women, the *Mobile Evening News* concluded, held the "principal creation and direction" of Confederate public opinion "in their hands." The *Natchez Weekly Courier* assured the "Women of the South," that "the destinies of the Southern Confederacy" rested "in your control."[13]

Women thus became acknowledged creators and custodians of public as well as domestic culture in the wartime South, exercising their power over communal sentiment in a variety of ways. They filled the pages of newspapers and periodicals with patriotic stories and verse and, perhaps even more important, composed many of the songs that served as the central medium of public wartime expression and constituted the most substantial publishing effort of the war. With men preoccupied by military affairs, magazines such as the *Southern Literary Messenger* eagerly sought contributions from women writers and struggled to evaluate the torrents of unsolicited poetry with which patriotic ladies flooded their offices.[14]

But the escalating demand for troops after the bloody battle of Manassas in July 1861 offered women a new role to play. Here their patriotism and moral influence began to assume a more personal dimension, foreshadowing demands to be made of them as the conflict intensified. And this contribution involved women from a much wider social spectrum than had many of the earlier, largely middle- to upper-class efforts of ladies' societies and lady authors. Military manpower needs from the fall of 1861 onward required a rationalization of female sacrifice and a silencing of women's direct interest in protecting husbands and sons. The nineteenth-century creed of domesticity had long urged self-denial and service to others as central to woman's mission. But war necessitated significant alterations, even perversions, of this system of meaning; women's self-sacrifice for personally significant others—husbands, brothers, sons, family—was transformed into sacrifice *of* those individuals to an abstract and intangible "Cause."

The effective redefinition of women's sacrifice from an emphasis on protection of family to a requirement for relinquishment of family was problematic enough to occupy a significant portion of Confederate discourse on gender. Songs, plays, poems, even official presidential pronouncements sought to enlist women of all classes in the work of filling the ranks. One popular theme inverted *Lysistrata,* urging young women to bestow their favors only on men in uniform. In a much-reprinted song, a male songwriter assumed a female voice to proclaim, "I want to change my name." This fictionalized heroine was searching for a husband,

> But he must be a soldier
> A veteran from the wars,
> One who has fought for "Southern Rights"
> Beneath the Bars and Stars.[15]

"None but the brave deserve the fair," a letter from "MANY LADIES" to the *Charleston Daily Courier* warned cowards and slackers in August 1861. Even Jefferson Davis addressed the question of ladies' appropriate marital choice, declaring the empty sleeve of the mutilated veteran preferable to the "muscular arm" of "him who staid at home and grew fat."[16]

One song published early in the war acknowledged the conflict between woman's traditional role and the new demands on her. From "stately hall" to "cottage fair," every woman, rich or poor, was confronted by her own "stormy battle," raging within her breast.

> There Love, the true, the brave,
> The beautiful, the strong,
> Wrestles with Duty, gaunt and stern—
> Wrestles and struggles long.[17]

But, like male songwriters who addressed that theme, the "Soldier's Wife" who had penned the lyrics was certain that women would win their own "heart victories" over themselves and in their "proudest triumphs" send their menfolk off to war. Stirring popular marches captured the very scene of parting, with men striding nobly into the horizon, while women just as nobly waved handkerchiefs and cheered their departure. "Go fight for us, we'll pray for you. / Our mothers did so before us." Popular songs and poems urged women to abandon not just interest but also sentiment, repressing their feelings lest they weaken soldiers' necessary resolve. One graphic, even gruesome, ballad entitled "The Dead" portrayed a boy "oozing blood" on the battlefield as in his dying breath he insisted,

> Tell my sister and my mother
> Not to weep, but learn to smother
> · Each sigh and loving tear.[18]

A poem published in the *Richmond Record* in September 1863 elevated such repression of emotion into woman's highest duty. "The maid who binds her warrior's sash / And smiling, all her pain dissembles," "The mother who conceals her grief" had "shed as sacred blood as e'er / was poured upon the plain of battle." Not only was she to sacrifice husband, brother, or son, woman was to give up feeling as well. As a Virginia woman diarist remarked, "we must learn the lesson which so many have to endure—to struggle against our feelings." But "tis a hard struggle for me sometimes," she admitted.[19]

Much of Confederate discourse negated the legitimacy of that emotional struggle by denying its reality altogether. Women, one newspaper proclaimed, had been offered a "glorious privilege" in the opportunity to contribute to the Cause by offering up their men. Any lingering resistance, the logic of the essay implied, should be overcome by the far greater—because transcendent— satisfaction of participation in the birth of a new nation.[20]

Yet popular expressions often acknowledged women's doubts in an effort to dispel them. A newspaper poem, "I've Kissed Him and Let Him Go," was among the frankest of such treatments.

> There is some, I know, who feel a strange pride
> In giving their country their all,

> Who count it a glory that boys from their side
> In the strife are ready to fall,
> But I sitting here have no pride in my heart;
> (God forgive that this should be so!)
> For the boy that I love the tears will start.
> Yet I've kissed him, and let him go.[21]

Best was to feel right, so dedicated to the Cause that personal interest all but disappeared. Next best was to stifle lingering personal feeling. But the minimal requirement was to silence doubt and behave properly, even if right feeling proved unattainable.

There is considerable evidence that women of all social levels acted in accordance with these principles in the early months of conflict. Wartime gender prescriptions were so clear to a group of young ladies in Texas that they sent hoopskirts and bonnets to all the young men who remained at home. Other women comprehended the message well enough but, even early in the conflict, embraced it reluctantly. "Oh, how I do hate to give him up," a Louisiana woman sighed, but "I suppose I have to be a martyr during this war."[22]

And propelling men into the army was only the beginning. Once soldiers had enlisted, women were to help keep them in the ranks. The silencing of feeling and self-interest was to continue. "DON'T WRITE GLOOMY LETTERS," warned the *Huntsville Democrat*. Some women, noted an 1862 correspondent to the Georgia *Countryman*, seemed to be giving "up too easily. Some of them write very desponding letters to the soldiers. This is wrong. I am not surprised at their feeling badly; but they should not write gloomy letters," which would cause soldiers to "lose confidence in themselves."[23]

From the outset, the home front was acknowledged to exert significant control over military morale. And as the conflict wore on and desertions and disaffection increased, the connection became clearer. Women must do more than send their men to battle. When men deserted, women were to demonstrate that devotion to the Cause had primacy over personal commitments to husbands or sons. The *Richmond Enquirer* appealed directly "to the women to aid us in this crisis. None have so momentous an interest; and none, as we firmly believe, wield so much power. . . . They know those stragglers, one by one, and where they are to be found. They, the mothers and sisters, may, if they will, be a conscript guard impossible to be evaded. They know whose furloughs are out, whose wounds are healed, who are lingering idly about . . . philandering and making love. . . . Will not the women help us, then?"[24]

As the character of the war changed, so did public considerations of woman's place in it. Early discussions struggled to define some positive contribution women might make, some outlet for the patriotism that especially characterized women of the slave-owning classes. But the growing scale of the conflict transformed a rhetoric that tended to patronize women into one that implored them to make essential and increasing sacrifices for the Cause. As the Reverend R. W. Barnwell emphasized in an address to the Ladies Clothing Association of Charleston, "WITHOUT YOU, THIS WAR COULD NOT HAVE BEEN CARRIED ON, FOR THE GOVERNMENT WAS NOT PREPARED TO MEET ALL THAT WAS THROWN UPON IT." Beginning with the rising toll of battle deaths, the reality of the demands on women—the reality of war itself—intruded unremittingly not just on women's lives but on the stylized narrative created about them. Experience began to challenge the assumptions sustaining their early sacrifices.[25]

From the perspective of 1865, the first months of the conflict would come to seem an age of innocence, a time, as one Virginia matron put it, "when we were playing at war." Stories of military history and romance began to pall in the face of the unrelenting pressures of real war. In mid-1862 a Virginia girl answered in verse her cousin's inquiry, "If I had found enough romance in this War":

> Yes, wild and thrilling scenes have held
> A joyous sway upon my heart,
> But what a dread romance is this,
>   To fill in life so sad a part.
>
> Slighter changes oft have thrilled
> My Spirit's gay and gladening song.
> But this plaug'd [plagued], horrid, awful War
>   Has *proved* to *me romance too long*.[26]

Much of the shift in women's perceptions of the war arose from the ever-expanding dimensions of required sacrifice. The need for military manpower was unrelenting, until by the end of the war, three-fourths of white southern men of military age had served in the army and at least half of those soldiers had been wounded, captured, or killed, or had died of disease. This left almost every white woman in the South with a close relative injured, missing, or dead. But women had to sacrifice more than just their men. First luxuries, then necessities were to be relinquished for the Cause. "Fold away all your bright tinted dresses. . . . No more delicate gloves, no more laces," one poem urged. Women "take their diamonds from their breast/ And their rubies from the finger, oh!" a song proclaimed. A Virginia lady later reminisced that in the summer of 1861 she felt "intensely patriotic and self-sacrificing" when she resolved to give up ice creams and cakes. This, she remarked with some irony, "we called putting our tables on a war footing." By the next year, meat and grain had begun to disappear from many plates, and by 1864 one Confederate official informed Jefferson Davis that in Alabama, at least, civilian "deaths from starvation have absolutely occurred." In the face of such realities, a Richmond periodical struggled to reassure the region's women and revalidate the notion of sacrifice:

> But e'en if you drop down unheeded,
> What matter? God's ways are the best:
> You have poured out your life where 'twas needed,
> And He will take care of the rest.[27]

An initial conception of wartime self-denial as an enforced separation from loved ones and the absence of cakes and ice cream had been transformed even for the most privileged women of the South into the possibility of starvation for themselves and their families and the likelihood of death or injury for a husband or child.

For women of the slave-owning classes, the departure of husbands and sons and the continuing pressures of war took on additional significance. The burden of slave management, the designated responsibility of male planters and overseers before the conflict, now often devolved on women. The isolation of many plantation women in rural areas populated overwhelmingly by blacks exacerbated white women's dismay. Unsupervised slaves began to seem an insupportable threat. "I lay down at night," Addie Harris of Alabama complained, "& do not know what hour . . . my house may [be] broken open & myself & children murdered. . . . My negroes very often get to fighting."[28]

The slave system of the American South rested upon the realities of paternalistic domination—upon the power of white males over both women and black slaves. But the ideology of paternalism always presumed reciprocal obligations between the supposedly powerful and the powerless. Both the rhetoric and the practice of white gender relations had assigned political and social control to males in return for their assumption of the duty to maintain social order, to exert effective dominance over potentially rebellious bondsmen. Protecting white women from threats posed by the slave system upon which white male power rested was an inextricable part of planters' paternalistic responsibility. Yet when masters departed for military service, the Confederate government, as collective representation of slaveholders' power, failed to provide adequate means to control plantation slaves. Under such circumstances, many Confederate mistresses felt not only terrified but also abandoned and betrayed. Slave management was a duty for which most women believed themselves unsuited; they had not understood it to be in the domain allocated them by the paternalistic social order they had long accepted as natural and right. As one woman explained, she was simply not a "fit and proper person" to supervise bondsmen; another insisted she had not the "moral courage" to govern slaves. "The idea of a lady" exercising the required corporal dominance over slaves, Alice Palmer of South Carolina noted, "has always been repugnant to me."[29]

The absence of white men accustomed to managing slaves and the disintegration of slavery under the pressures of growing black assertiveness thus placed an unanticipated and unwanted burden on plantation mistresses, most of whom had never questioned the moral or political legitimacy of the South's peculiar institution. But in the new war-born situation, Confederate women could not indulge in the luxury of considering slavery's merits "in the abstract," as its prewar defenders had urged, nor unthinkingly reap its material rewards. Slavery's meaning could not rest primarily in the detached realms of economics or politics, nor could white women any longer accept it as an unexamined personal convenience. The emotional and physical cost of the system to slaveholding white women had dramatically changed. Women now confronted all but overwhelming day-to-day responsibilities that they regarded as not rightfully theirs, as well as fears that often came to outweigh any tangible benefits they were receiving from the labor of increasingly recalcitrant and rebellious slaves.

The war's mounting death toll dictated the emergence of yet another dimension of female responsibility. While men at the front hurried their slain comrades into shallow graves, women at home endeavored to claim the bodies of dead relatives and to accord them proper ceremonies of burial. Woman's role was not simply to make sacrifices herself but also to celebrate and sanctify the martyrdom of others. In the Confederacy mourning became a significant social, cultural, and spiritual duty. Through rituals of public grief, personal loss could be redefined as transcendent communal gain. Women's tears consecrated the deaths of their men, ensuring their immortality—in southern memory as in the arms of God—and ratifying soldiers' individual martyrdom. Such deaths not only contributed to Confederate victory but also exemplified the sacred conception of Christian sacrifice with which the South had identified its nationalist effort. And in honoring men's supreme offering, women reminded themselves of the comparative insignificance of their own sacrifices. Loss of life of a beloved could not compare with loss of one's own; civilian anxiety and deprivation were as nothing in face of soldiers' contributions. "Even when a woman does her best," Kate Cumming observed of her efforts to nurse wounded soldiers, "it is a mite compared with what our men have to endure."[30]

Whatever doubts about the value of her contributions Cumming held, her labor, like that of thousands of other southern women, was essential to the Confederate social and economic order. The size of Civil War armies and the unforeseen dimensions of the conflict required civilian productivity of an unprecedented scale. And since women constituted such a large proportion of white southern civilians, the production of goods and services became in large measure their responsibility. "We must go to work, too," as a DAUGHTER OF "OLD VIRGINIA" wrote in the *Richmond Enquirer*. The exigencies of war thus weakened the role prescriptions that had denied white women remunerative labor outside the home and had directed that only black women should work the land. Public ideology now needed to redefine such activities as valued, while limiting the potential shift in gender expectations implicit in the altered behavior.

The debate within the Confederacy about nursing exemplifies the complexity of such wartime attitudes toward change. From the earliest months of the conflict, many journalists and editors urged that women be permitted—in fact, encouraged—to nurse wounded soldiers in military hospitals. Yet even these advocates of nursing reform were well aware of the dangers implicit in their proposals. Women, the *Confederate Baptist* observed, might prove "most valuable auxiliaries" within the hospital, as long as they remained "in their proper sphere" and did not seek to "direct or control the physician." Nursing would be acceptable as another dimension of women's service and sacrifice, but it must not be transformed into female empowerment.[31]

Many women showed themselves eager to make such contributions regardless of the ideological terms in which their actions were construed: they volunteered to help overworked army physicians and began to establish "wayside hospitals" to care for traveling soldiers at depot towns throughout the South. But the entry of women volunteers into hospital settings provoked outbursts of protest from those who believed nursing "would be injurious to the delicacy and refinement of a lady." In the eyes of many Southerners, both male and female, hospital work was simply "not considered respectable."[32]

By the fall of 1862, however, the Confederacy's need for nurses had yielded legislation providing that women be recruited and remunerated for hospital labor. Yet resistance lingered, especially among male physicians. Phoebe Pember, a matron at Chimborazo Hospital in Richmond, encountered widespread resentment from doctors that greatly increased the difficulty of her job, and Cumming transferred from one hospital because of a senior physician's opposition to female nurses.

There was, she summarized, a "good deal of trouble about the ladies in some of the hospitals of this department."[33]

Many women shared the aversion to female nursing. Ladies who dedicated themselves to ward work, such as Pember, Cumming, and Louisa McCord, were subjects of gossip and speculation. Women working in hospitals seemed in the eyes of many southerners to display curiously masculine strengths and abilities. Clara MacLean confided to her diary that her neighbor Eliza McKee, recently departed for Virginia as a nurse, had always possessed such strength as to seem "almost masculine—Indeed I used to tell her I never felt easy in her society if discussing *delicate* subjects; I could scarcely persuade myself she was not in disguise." And Mary Chesnut, the famed South Carolina diarist, felt much the same about the intimidating strength of her friend McCord, who seemed to possess "the intellect of a man." Nurses were not truly women, but in some sense men in drag.[34]

Such attitudes enabled southerners to blunt the impact and significance of women's changed behavior by framing it within existing ideological categories. These beliefs permitted some women to become nurses, excused others—who lacked the requisite "masculine" traits—from doing so, and at the same time discouraged any permanent expansion in the boundaries of the female role: nursing continued to be regarded as deviant, requiring behaviors inconsistent with prevailing class and gender expectations.

Public discussion of women's wartime entry into teaching demonstrates a similar effort to employ ideology to limit the impact of war-born behavioral change. Although a feminization of teaching had occurred in the North in the antebellum era, southerners had not encouraged women's assumption of classroom responsibilities. But, as the *Augusta Daily Constitutionalist* remarked in May 1863, the war had "swallow[ed] up" the men preparing to be teachers. "We are left no resource then but to have female teachers. . . . Women are peculiarly fitted, naturally and morally, for teachers of the young."[35] The report of the superintendent of common schools of North Carolina for 1862 reminded the people of his state that there was no employment in which ladies rendered needy by circumstances of war might labor more usefully than "in the business of forming the hearts and minds of the young." The State Education Association of North Carolina offered a prize in November 1861 for the best essay on the subject of the "propriety and importance of employing more female teachers in our common schools," thus inviting the general public to help redefine the ideological consensus the association hoped to foster.[36]

Confederate educators gave significant attention to training women as teachers. To some degree the shift was self-interested, for in the absence of young men, professors' livelihoods depended on recruiting other minds for instruction. Trinity College in North Carolina began in 1864 to fill its depleted classrooms with women, and many women's colleges thrived during the war. Wytheville Female College in Virginia reported its population "but very slightly diminished"; Baptist Female College of Southwest Georgia grew steadily, even though it had to move into the president's house and relinquish its main building to a soldiers' hospital. Hollins College in Virginia worked to establish a system of scholarships for future teachers, and the Statesville North Carolina Female College created a new teaching department.[37]

But Southerners by no means uniformly embraced this new departure. Emma Holmes of South Carolina reported in 1862 the opposition a friend confronted from her family when she took over the village school, and Holmes herself faced stubborn family resistance to her desire to become a schoolmistress. Elizabeth Grimball's mother was "terribly mortified" by her daughter's insistence on teaching, and as late as mid-1863, the Convention of Teachers of the Confederate States pointedly restricted membership to "any male citizen" of the new nation. Yet, as the president of Davidson College in North Carolina baldly declared to a 1864 graduating class of women, *"Our females must engage in the work of teaching;* for there is no other alternative."[38]

Discussions of gender appeared in almost every public mode of communication within the Confederacy—in sermons, newspapers, poetry, song, the new Confederate drama, even painting—and in personal documents such as diaries and letters.[39] But the comprehensive narrative of Confederate women and the war evolved in the course of the conflict and, while comprising a largely coherent whole, usually appeared piecemeal rather than as a complete story. In 1864, however, an Alabamian named Augusta Jane Evans published a novel that might justly be regarded as the most systematic elaboration, and in many ways the culmination, of the discussion that had preceded it. As a novel, it was quite literally a narrative, a story of woman and the war entitled *Macaria; or, Altars of Sacrifice.* Evans had written it as she sat at the bedsides of wounded soldiers, and she dedicated it to the Confederate army. *Macaria* became a wartime best-seller, read widely not just by women, for whom novel reading had become such an important and pleasurable pastime, but by men in the intervals between battles or during periods of hospital convalescence.[40]

Like the mythological figure in her title, who sacrificed herself on the altar of the gods in order to save Athens in time of war, Evans's heroine Irene is "ambitious of martydom." The novel is structured as her pilgrimage toward "Womanly Usefulness," which she ultimately realizes in the Confederate war effort. Here, at last, after the long struggles that constitute the bulk of the story, Irene finds her lifework, giving her father and her beloved beau Russell up to die on the battlefield and dedicating herself to the highest possible existence, laboring in "God's great vineyard." Married women, she admits, may be happier, but life was not made for happiness. It is the blessing—and *macaria* also means blessing in Greek—of the single woman to be more useful "because she belongs exclusively to no one, her heart expands to all her suffering fellow creatures." For Irene, sacrifice becomes a vocation, not unlike that of the nun. And, indeed, Evans describes Irene abandoning fashionable garments for robes of black or white, tied at the waist by a tassel, suggesting that the analogy with the female religious is entirely self-conscious—for Evans as well as Irene. To her childhood friend, similarly bereaved by war, Irene declares, very much in the language of prevailing Confederate ideology,

> You and I have much to do during these days of gloom and national trial—for upon the purity, the devotion, and the patriotism of the women of our land, not less than upon the heroism of our armies, depends our national salvation.[41]

In the context of Irene's persistent cry, "I want to be useful," the war comes as something, not to be endured, but to be celebrated, for it offers her the possibility for self-fulfillment she has been seeking. Stunningly beautiful, Irene is nevertheless no docile, subservient lady. She is in many ways what the nineteenth century would have seen as a "modern" woman, fiercely independent, for example even as a young child declining to permit a slave to carry her school books. "I don't choose," she declares, "to be petted like a baby or made a wax-doll of . . . I am strong enough to carry my own books." She refuses to marry at her father's behest, engages in abstruse astronomical researches, which she publishes in scientific journals—although under a pseudonym. She speaks of herself in the language of bourgeois individualism, stressing her rights of self-ownership and self-determination. To her suitor Hugh who insists "you belong to me and you know it," Irene responds, "No! I belong to God and myself." Yet with the coming of war, Irene, like so many actual southern women, only briefly laments "if I were only a man" before dedicating herself to the difficult work of sacrifice. Self-realization, toward which she has been striving in the first two-thirds of the novel, is now defined as finding its fullest expression in self-denial. Irene is rendered semidivine by her martyrdom to service and sacrifice and repeatedly echoes Christ's words at the time of his crucifixion: "Not my will, oh, God! but thine!"[42]

Macaria appealed directly and calculatedly to sentiments prevailing within its potential audience of southern women readers—acknowledging their fears of uselessness, of widowhood or spinsterhood, as well as their attraction to a new language of self-determination. These notions were rhetorically conjoined in the novel with the ideology of feminine nationalism and Christian sacrifice that Evans offered as her solution to the dilemmas of both the Confederate woman and her country. Irene and her friend Electra busily devote themselves to nursing the wounded, caring for the war's orphans, and, in artist Electra's case, creating cultural forms for the new nation. Feminine fashion and extravagance are roundly attacked. Even women's most basic economic needs are dismissed: a poor woman declares she "would rather live on acorns" than keep her husband out of the army to support her. And by titling her story *Macaria*, Evans situates it within the long tradition of war narratives of female silence and sacrifice:

> all the stern resolution and self-abnegation of Rome and Lacedaemon had entered the souls of Southern women. Mothers closed their lips firmly to repress a wail of sorrow as they buckled on the swords of their first-born, and sent them forth . . . to battle for the right.[43]

But in the effort to establish a resonance with her readers, to address themes that would secure their emotional and intellectual participation in her narrative, Evans undermines the very ideology of martyrdom she hoped to valorize. Affirming the values of individualism by associating them with her beloved Irene, Evans only with difficulty resolves their implicit challenge to the ideology of personal sacrifice. And she manages it largely through the invocation of an analogy with Christ, a literal *deus ex machina*. The tensions inevitably remain, as they certainly did in the minds of women throughout the South increasingly unable to reconcile themselves to the demands war placed on them.

Even as Augusta Evans wrote, even as thousands of southern women eagerly read her paean to self-sacrifice, they had begun emphatically to dissent from the roles and scenarios composed for them. A pseudonymous woman wrote revealingly to the *Montgomery Daily Advertiser* in June 1864. At first, she observed, women had rivaled "the other sex in patriotic devotion," but

> Oh what a falling off is there! . . . a change and such a change, has come over the spirit of their dream. The Aid Societies have died away; they are a name and nothing more. The self-sacrifice has vanished; wives and maidens now labor only to exempt husbands and lovers from the perils of service. . . . Never were parties more numerous. . . . Never were the theatres and places of public amusement so resorted to. . . . The love of dress, the display of jewelry and costly attire, the extravagance and folly are all the greater for the brief abstinence which has been observed.[44]

The effort to define sacrifice as purposeful was failing. As a New Orleans Creole woman wrote her soldier son, "je ne vois que des sacrifices, des victimes, la ruine, la misère, rien de gagné." Women's willingness to be disinterested, to embrace the needs of the nation as prior to their own, had begun to disappear. As one woman facing the conscription of her last son explained, "I know my country needs all her children and I had thought I could submit to her requisitions. I have given her cause my prayers, my time, my means and my children but now the last lamb of the fold is to be taken, the mother and helpless woman triumph over the patriot."[45]

White southern women, socialized from an early age in the doctrines of paternalism with their implicit promises of reciprocal obligation, expected that their sacrifices would be recompensed. At all class levels, women had retained the sense of a moral economy of gender in which they traded female self-abnegation for care and protection. The "helpless woman" held an implicit power of requisition within her very assumption of helplessness. By the later years of the war, however, the ability of southern men to meet requirements for care and protection, to ensure the physical safety—and even the subsistence—of the civilian population had broken down. In response, many women began to demonstrate the conditional nature of their patriotism; there were clear limits to their willingness to sacrifice. Concerns about personal loss and personal survival—both physical and psychological—had eroded commitment to the Cause. The romance of the "battle piece" had disappeared before the pressing realities of war. Unable any longer to imagine herself one of the legendary "Spartan women," Lizzie Hardin confided to her diary, "Perhaps there are few of us who in reading stories of ancient heroism or the romance of modern war have not had some idle thoughts of the role we might have played in similar circumstances. How often have I dropped the book while my fancy kept time to the warlike trumpet or languished in some prison cell or sent up Te Deums from the bloody field of victory. But how different the picture when you view it in a nearer light." On a tour of the battlefield at Seven Pines in search of her wounded cousin, Constance Cary (later Harrison) reported seeing men "in every stage of mutilation" and proclaimed herself "permanently convinced that nothing is worth war!" Margaret Junkin Preston greeted the news of the death of her stepson and several of his friends by protesting, "Who thinks or cares for victory now!" Sarah Jane Sams proclaimed herself "sick and tired of trying to endure these privations to which we are all subjected," and as early as 1862, Julia Le Grand had come to feel that "nothing is worth such sacrifice." For the most part, women's satiety with war remained personal. Yet even if growing dissatisfaction with the day-to-day management of Confederate affairs did not shade over into explicit criticisms of southern war aims, women were becoming increasingly alienated from the new nation and resentful of its demands on them. "What do I care for patriotism," one woman pointedly demanded. "My husband is my country. What is country to me if he be killed?" "The Confederacy!" Emily Harris complained to her diary late in 1864, "I almost hate the word."[46]

Wartime experiences rendered some women almost incapable of functioning. Modern psychology might define such women as in the grip of traumatic stress reactions or severe depression, but Confederates used quite effective descriptive language of their own. Lila Chunn explained to her soldier husband in the spring of 1863, "I experience such constant dread and anxiety that I feel all the time weary and depressed." Another woman described many wives and mothers she knew as "stunned and stupefied . . . forever" by grief, and a resident of Lynchburg, Virginia, believed that her poverty and suffering had driven her "almost upon the borders of crazziness." Cornelia McDonald, struggling to care for a family of seven children in embattled Winchester, Virginia, clearly understood the relationship between her debilitated physical condition and her emotions. Emaciated and weakened by hunger, she found that by 1863 she had become "faint-hearted" as well. "My feelings were beyond control . . . I had lost the power of resistance and all my self-command." Her depression was so intense she felt she "could willingly say 'good night' to the world and all in it." A mother writing to a son captured by the Yankees and imprisoned in the North may perhaps have put it most simply and eloquently: "I would wrote before now but I was Clean out of hart."[47]

But many Confederate women retained hope that their sufferings would be relieved. Within the framework of paternalistic assumptions to which they clung, hardships were defined as injustices worthy of attention and intervention by rulers of the Confederate state. As an "unassuming girl" from Alabama explained to the secretary of war in requesting a furlough for her brother, "I feel there is yet justice & *mercy* in the land, to *you* therefore I present my humble petition." Women thus began to regard their difficulties as a test of the moral as well as the bureaucratic and military effectiveness of the new nation and tied their patriotism to the competency of the state's performance in these matters of personal concern. Women penned anguished letters to President Jefferson Davis and a succession of secretaries of war seeking assistance in return for their sacrifices. Miranda Sutton of North Carolina was unable to sign her name, but she dictated a petition asking that one of her sons be released from the military to help provide her with food. Six of her sons had served in the army; two, in addition to her husband, had died. She professed certainty that the moral economy of sacrifice would bring favorable attention to her request. "Your petitioner humbly concieves that having made such sacrifices for the southern cause her claims humble though she be will not be overlooked." Sixty-year-old Harriet Stephenson of North Carolina was perhaps even more direct. With five sons in the army, she informed Secretary of War James Seddon, "I think I have did enough to you for you to take sum intrust in what I so mutch desrie of You"—the discharge of one of her sons to provide her support. Nancy Williams of Mississippi made a similar request of Davis: "I think I have done well for our cause, give up all of my sons, one of which was only fifteen. . . . please answer my letter immediately." When he did not, she wrote again, still expressing faith that her expectations would be fulfilled. "I ask this favor from the government, hoping and believeing that it will be granted." Frances Brightwell of Louisa County, Virginia, appealed directly to Davis's paternalism in asking the discharge of her husband after her father's death had left her an "orfrint child." "My heart is broken I have no one to take care of me oh I think it will kill me Please try and doo sumthing for me. . . . I know a good gentlemond like youself feals for a tinder female."[48]

Some bolder—or perhaps only less calculating—women seemed less to implore Confederate officials than to threaten them. "One of the anxious widowed mothers of Alabama" was unwilling to sign her letter of complaint to the president. But she promised him that the unjustified conscription of her son guaranteed that "a day of retribution will surely come" to the South. Another female correspondent who believed her son had been unfairly taken by the army informed Davis, "I suspect that our confederacy must fall where such injustice reigns." Almira Acors wrote Davis, describing her desperate poverty and the failure of her neighbors to aid her, a failure suggestive of a more general breakdown of paternalism throughout southern society: "it is folly for a poor mother to call on the rich people about here there [sic] hearts are of steel they would sooner throw what they have to spare to their dogs than give it to a starving child . . . I do not see how God can give the South a victory when the cries of so many suffering mothers and little children are constantly ascending up to him. . . . if I and my little children . . . die while there Father is in service I invoke God Almighty that our blood rest upon the South." A War Department official marked the outside of the letter "File"; Almira Acors did not even receive a reply.[49]

For all their intended audacity, these women offered only a limited challenge to Confederate power and legitimacy. They threatened Davis and his government by invoking a higher, divine paternalism, rather than by assaulting the larger assumptions of paternalism itself. God, they warned, would punish the Confederacy because it had not lived up to its own ideals—particularly its obligations to the women and children that its social assumptions had defined as powerless and dependent. Within such a framework of criticism, women still regarded themselves as largely passive—even if increasingly angry. God, not they themselves, would avenge their wrongs. If Davis and his secretary of war would not protect them, they would summon a yet more powerful father figure to the task.[50]

But by 1863, at least some Confederate women had become more aggressive in their expressions of discontent. In the case of women from yeoman families particularly, oppressions of class and gender reinforced one another, impelling numbers of the aggrieved toward overt action against the war effort. Destitute female petitioners warned Confederate officials that they would urge their husbands and sons to desert if their basic needs for family subsistence were not met. As Nancy Mangum explained to Governor Zebulon Vance of North Carolina, prices must be

lowered or "we wimen will write for our husbans to come
. . . home and help us we cant stand it." Other wives and
mothers did not bother with warnings. Martha Revis informed
her husband after news reached her of southern defeats at Gettysburg and Vicksburg, "I want you to come home as soon as you
can after you get this letter." One mother, whose willingness to
sacrifice had reached its limit, wrote her son, a Confederate captain and prisoner of war, "I hope, when you get exchanged, you
will think, the time past has sufficed for *public* service, & that
your own family require yr protection & help—as others are
deciding." As the desertion rate rose steadily in the southern
army throughout 1864, Confederate officials acknowledged the
significant role needy wives and mothers played in encouraging
soldiers to abandon their posts. As one North Carolinian bluntly
explained, "Desertion takes place because desertion is encouraged. . . . And though the ladies may not be willing to concede
the fact, they are nevertheless responsible . . . for the desertion in the army and the dissipation in the country."[51] And
women undertook a kind of desertion of their own, many from
the northern tier of Confederate states fleeing to friends and
relatives in the North because of what a Confederate provost
marshal described as their inability "to support themselves
here."[52]

As the emotional and physical deprivation of southern white
women escalated, the Confederate ideology of sacrifice began to
lose its meaning and efficacy. Hardship and loss were no longer
sacred, no longer to be celebrated, but instead came to seem
causes for grievance. Late in 1862 an article in the *Children's
Friend*, a religious periodical for boys and girls, found in what
might earlier have been labeled a dedicated wartime "sacrifice"
only deplorable "Oppression." "Many women," the paper reported, "especially in large cities, have to work hard, and receive
very little for it. Many of them sew with their needles all day long,
making garments for others, and get so little for it that they have
neither food enough, nor clothes, nor fire to make their children
comfortable and warm. There are many such now in Richmond
working hard, and almost for nothing."[53] Southerners had defined the purpose of secession as the guarantee of personal independence and republican liberty to the citizens and households

of the South. Yet the women of the Confederacy found themselves by the late years of the war presiding over the disintegration of those households and the destruction of that vaunted
independence. Most white southern women had long accepted
female subordination as natural and just, but growing hardships
and women's changed perception of their situation transformed
subordination, understood as a justifiable structural reality, into
oppression, defined as a relationship of illegitimate power.

The erosion of the sacredness of sacrifice was also evident in
the changed attitudes toward death that appeared among Confederate civilians by the last months of the war. As one Virginia
woman explained, "I hear now of acres of dead and . . .
wounded with less sensibility than was at first occasioned by hearing of the loss of half a dozen men in a skirmish." This shift in
perception was reflected in altered mourning customs. As Kate
Stone explained in the spring of 1864, "People do not mourn
their dead as they used to." Constance Cary was shocked by the
seemingly cavalier and uncaring manner in which military hospitals treated the deceased, dropping six or seven coffins in "one
yawning pit . . . hurriedly covered in, all that a grateful country could render in return for precious lives."[54] The immediate
and tangible needs of the living had become more pressing than
any abstract notion of obligation to the dead.

The urgency of those needs yielded a sense of grievance that
by 1863 became sufficiently compelling and widespread to erupt
into bread riots in communities across the South. In Savannah,
Georgia; Mobile, Alabama; High Point, North Carolina; Petersburg, Virginia; Milledgeville, Georgia; Columbus, Georgia;
and in the capital city of Richmond itself, crowds of women
banded together to seize bread and other provisions they believed their due. Their actions so controverted prevailing ideology about women that Confederate officials in Richmond
requested the press not to report the disturbance at all, thus
silencing this expression of female dissent. In the newspapers, at
least, reality would not be permitted to subvert the woman's war
story that editors had worked so assiduously to develop and
propagate. A Savannah police court charged with disciplining
that city's offenders similarly demonstrated the incompatibility
of such female behavior with the accepted fiction about southern

women's wartime lives. "When women become rioters," the judge declared baldly, "they cease to be women." Yet in resorting to violence, these women were in a sense insisting on telling—and acting—their own war story. One Savannah rioter cared enough about the meaning of her narrative to print up and distribute cards explaining her participation in the disturbance. "Necessity has no law & poverty is the mother of invention. These shall be the principles on which we will stand. If fair words will not do, we will try to see what virtue there is in stones."[55]

Upper-class women did not usually take to the streets, but they too expressed their objections to the prescriptions of wartime ideology. And, like their lower-class counterparts, they focused much of their protest on issues of consumption and deprivation. The combination of symbolism and instrumentalism in the bread riots was paralleled in the extravagance to which many Confederate ladies turned. In important ways, reckless indulgence represented resistance to the ideology of sacrifice. Mary Chesnut's husband James found her "dissipated" and repeatedly criticized her refusal to abandon parties and frivolity. In February 1864 the *Richmond Enquirer* declared the city to be a "carnival of unhallowed pleasure" and assailed the "shameful displays of indifference to national calamity." Richmond's preeminent hostess was reported to have spent more than thirty thousand dollars on food and entertainment during the last winter of the war. Even a council of Presbyterian elders in Alabama felt compelled in 1865 to "deplore the presence, and we fear, the growing prevalence of a spirit of gaity, especially among the female members of some of our congregations." And instead of resorting to riots, numbers of more respectable Richmond ladies subverted ideals of wartime sacrifice and female virtue by turning to shoplifting, which a Richmond paper reported to be "epidemick" in the city, especially among women of the better sort. Women, one observer noted in 1865, seemed to be "seeking nothing but their own pleasure while others are baring their bosoms to the storms of war."[56]

The traditional narrative of war had come to seem meaningless to many women; the Confederacy offered them no acceptable terms in which to cast their experience. Women had consented to subordination and had embraced the attendant ideology of sacrifice as part of a larger scheme of paternalistic assumptions. But the system of reciprocity central to this understanding of social power had been violated by the wartime failure of white southern males to provide the services and support understood as requisite to their dominance. And in a world in which Augusta Evans's independent and assertive Irene could become the war's most popular literary heroine, women would not assent indefinitely to the increasing sacrifice and self-denial the Civil War came to require. Although the fictional Irene was able to bear the tension between self-abnegation and self-realization in her own life, many southern women found themselves unable or unwilling to construct their own experiences within a similar narrative. By the late years of the conflict, sacrifice no longer sufficed as a purpose. By early 1865, countless women of all classes had in effect deserted the ranks. Refusing to accept the economic deprivation further military struggle would have required, resisting additional military service by their husbands and sons, no longer consecrating the dead, but dancing while ambulances rolled by, southern women undermined both objective and ideological foundations for the Confederate effort; they directly subverted the South's military and economic effectiveness as well as civilian morale. "I have said many a time," wrote Kate Cumming in her diary, "that, if we did not succeed, the women of the South would be responsible." In ways she did not even realize, Cumming was all too right. It seems not insignificant that in wording his statement of surrender, Robert E. Lee chose terms central to women's perceptions of themselves and the war. The Confederate effort, he stated at Appomattox, had become "useless sacrifice." Confederate ideology about women had been structured to keep those terms separated by interpreting sacrifice as a means of overcoming uselessness, by rendering sacrifice itself supremely purposeful. But the war story offered Confederate women at the outset of conflict had been internally flawed and contradictory and finally proved too much at odds with external circumstance; it was an ideology designed to silence, rather than address, the fundamental interests of women in preservation of self and family. As Julia Le Grand explained, it was an ideology that left women with "no language, but a cry," with no means of self-expression but subversion. In gradually refusing to accept this war story as relevant to their own lives, women undermined both the narrative presented to them and the Confederate cause itself. And without the logistical and ideological support of the home front, the southern military effort was doomed to fail.[57]

Historians have wondered in recent years why the Confederacy did not endure longer. In considerable measure, I would suggest, it was because so many women did not want it to. The way in which their interests in the war were publicly defined—in a very real sense denied—gave women little reason to sustain the commitment modern war required. It may well have been because of its women that the South lost the Civil War.

Chapter 11

"Since the War Broke Out": The Marriage of Kate and William McLure

JOAN CASHIN

Scholars are just beginning to examine how the upheavals of the Civil War affected sex roles and married life among white southerners. Thus far two schools of thought have emerged on the impact the war may have had on the ways that men and women related to each other. Some historians argue that women's lives were essentially unchanged by the war, as women continued to adhere to traditional sex roles, while another scholar contends that the war opened up opportunities for more women to go to school and participate in voluntary activities outside the home. We know very little about how the war may have affected men's personal lives or about how relationships between men and women may have begun to shift during the war itself. A close examination of one couple's experiences can begin to answer these questions, and it may suggest the ways that other Southern marriages were being transformed.[1]

The marriage of William and Kate McLure of South Carolina changed profoundly during the war years. While William McLure served in the Confederate Army, his wife lived on the couple's upcountry plantation, and she was soon thrust into a struggle for power involving her white male relatives, her husband's white overseers, and one of the McLure slaves. At issue was who would wield the decision-making power on the plantation.

By 1865 Kate McLure had begun to disregard the advice of the overseers and her male relatives, including her husband, and make decisions herself. She came to rely on a slave named Jeff for assistance in running the place, and she did a good deal of hard work herself.

Her husband's life, except for his absence from home, was not marked by such wrenching changes. William McLure served in the Palmetto Sharpshooters, a unit of South Carolina volunteers who fought under Generals James Longstreet and Robert E. Lee, but he saw no combat after he became quartermaster in 1862, and for the rest of the war had the pick of the unit's available supplies. Perhaps because his life was comparatively easy, William McLure did not grasp at first how much his wife's circumstances had changed, and when she started to make decisions on her own he did not accept it gracefully. It was hard for him to give up his assumption that white men must make decisions for white women and slaves, even when he was hundreds of miles from home and it was impossible for him to supervise his plantation personally.

The couple met in Union County, South Carolina, where William McLure was working as a merchant in the early 1850s. Christened John William, he was the son of William McLure, a merchant of Scotch-Irish descent who lived in upcountry South Carolina in the early nineteenth century. William McLure *père* did well as a merchant, but he did not own slaves. He and his wife Amelia Stringfellow McLure had four surviving children; his second son, William, was born on March 31, 1831. William McLure, Sr., did not live to see his children reach adulthood, however, as he died in 1837 of stomach disease. Soon afterward his widow married a physician, Samuel Rainey of York County, South Carolina, who owned several dozen slaves. Young William McLure went away to boarding schools in the South and then enrolled at the University of Virginia when he was seventeen years old.[2]

While he was at Virginia, William McLure's personality and political views began to emerge. He was a gregarious, somewhat reckless young man who liked to drink, and he was not a serious student. According to a descendant, he never had much "liking for culture." As an undergraduate, he poured his energies into campus politics. He was a precocious secessionist, and in the

1848–49 school year he organized a society to advocate immediate southern independence. He was so obstreperous, in fact, that
the University asked him to leave at the end of his first year.[3]

He then went to work with his uncle John McLure, a successful
merchant in Unionville, South Carolina, the seat of Union
County with a population of about five hundred people. He stuck
to his radical political views, and he remained a hard drinker,
ignoring his mother's pleas that he give up alcohol. He then
alarmed his family by falling in love with one of his stepsisters, but
his uncle John quickly stopped the romance. In the early 1850s,
William began to think seriously of marriage. His courtship of a
local woman ended in disappointment in the spring of 1852, but
shortly thereafter he fell in love with Jane Catherine (Kate)
Poulton and announced his engagement to her that summer.[4]

Kate Poulton had also lost her father at an early age, and she
had had a rough passage in life. Born in Exeter, England, on
October 31, 1829, she came to the United States with her parents
in 1833. Her father Thomas Poulton, a clergyman and minor
bureaucrat in the London government, migrated both to revive
his failing health and to claim land he owned in Canada, but he
died in 1834 on a packet boat in the Erie Canal before he ever
reached Canada. His family then dispersed. While his widow
Mary Allen Poulton soon remarried and settled in Ontario, his
oldest daughter, Mary, aged thirteen, enrolled at Emma Willard's
female academy in Troy. His four younger daughters were
informally adopted by several American families. (Why they did
not join their mother in Canada is not explained.) Kate was taken
in by a family in Lockport, New York, but she was not happy
there, and she later revealed that the family had forced her to
work as a servant. Several years later she joined her sister Mary at
Miss Willard's and then followed her to South Carolina when
Mary took a teaching job in Laurens County in the early 1840s.
When Mary Poulton married planter Thomas Dawkins in 1845,
she brought Kate along to her new home. They all lived in Union
County in a big, comfortable house—her brother-in-law was
wealthy, the owner of thirty-one slaves in 1850—but it was not a
peaceful place. Thomas Dawkins was a heavy drinker, and he
once disappeared on a binge for two weeks without telling his wife
where he was going. His younger brother James, who lived with
him, was also a notorious drinker and gambler.[5]

Kate Poulton was a rather passive young woman, shy and often ill with "neuralgia" or heart "palpitations." She loved animals and had numerous pets, including several dogs and canaries. When Kate was in her late teens, she daydreamed about becoming a missionary for the Episcopalian church. Mary Dawkins tried to match her up with several local swains, and she may have been relieved when McLure proposed to her sister. For her part, Kate does not seem to have been in love with William McLure, whom she had known for several years. She assented to the match with little enthusiasm. The couple wed on July 27, 1852, at Niagara Falls, and came back to Unionville where William went into the mercantile business. There is considerable evidence, however, that Kate McLure gradually grew to love her husband, and they both doted on their children: Mary Amelia, the first of their eight offspring, was born in 1853. Their antebellum correspondence, as sparse as it is, suggests that the McLures played the traditional roles foreshadowed in their courtship: he made choices, and she acquiesced.[6]

William McLure's political views continued to be that of the most extreme pro-slavery expansionist. In 1853, when he was married and a father, he apparently took part in a secret filibustering expedition to South America. So it was natural when he inherited some slaves and ten thousand dollars in cash from his uncle John in 1855 that he became a planter. He bought more slaves and a cotton plantation called Oakwood in northern Union County near the Pacolet River several miles from the Dawkins plantation, where Kate's sister and brother-in-law still lived. In the 1850s McLure purchased a large house called Oak Hall for his family, and in 1860 he owned forty-five slaves and sixteen thousand dollars' worth of land. He ran the plantation himself while his wife cared for their young children.[7]

When South Carolina seceded in December 1860, William McLure did not hesitate to throw in his lot with his state. He enlisted in a local volunteer company in January 1861, and he was in Charleston when the shelling commenced at Fort Sumter in April. (He took a slave named Tom along with him as his personal servant). He expressed great contempt for "Yankees" and thought they would be easily beaten. In the only surviving letter she wrote during the secession crisis, Kate McLure agreed with her husband's views, calling the southern cause "our cause" and a "just" one, and she believed that it "must triumph," although she feared that southern independence would require a great loss of life. Her views were indistinguishable from those of thousands of white southern women. Although she might be perceived as a British or Northern figure, she had spent her formative years in the South; in the twenty-odd years since she had moved to South Carolina, she had accepted slaveowners' values, and she married a committed secessionist. Throughout the War she never wavered in her support for the Confederacy. Her racial views at this time were apparently just as conventional. She taught Bible classes to the McLure slaves and knew all of them by name, as her husband did not, but there is no hint in any of her antebellum letters that she ever questioned prevailing views of the racial inferiority of blacks.[8]

During the first half of 1861, the McLure's Oakwood plantation operated much as it had before Fort Sumter. William McLure arranged for Elijah Dawkins, a relation of his brother-in-law Thomas Dawkins, to deliver extra food to the plantation if necessary, and he marketed his cotton crop himself when he was in Charleston in the spring of 1861. Then he left everything in the hands of a new overseer, B. F. Holmes. After McLure's unit was dispatched to Virginia, he corresponded directly with Holmes about the details of running the plantation. But McLure's absence inevitably began to alter his relationship with his overseer; in fact, several key relationships on the plantation shifted during the summer and fall of 1861. Whenever McLure forgot to tell Holmes something, he put it in his next letter to his wife, who either passed the instructions on to Holmes or carried them out herself. For instance, Kate McLure, not the overseer, purchased many of the plantation's supplies in September. William McLure was so surprised at her ingenuity at this task, which she had never done before, that he joked that he would leave this to her in the future—a prophecy that came true before the war was over.[9]

William McLure sometimes confused the situation by sending contradictory directions. He once told his wife to instruct a slave named Jeff to look after the food crops, while simultaneously asking her to tell Holmes to sow a field of fall wheat. In another letter he urged her to "hurry" Holmes through the cotton harvest. By the end of 1861, Holmes's authority on the plantation was being divided in ad hoc manner between Kate McLure and the slave named Jeff. William McLure does not seem to have understood how he was dividing his authority, perhaps because he still saw himself as the ultimate authority. Holmes may have been uncomfortable with the situation; in November 1861 he still had not decided if he would stay on for the next year. He finally chose to stay, and the power triangle of overseer, mistress, and slave continued in uneasy balance.[10]

It is frustrating that little can be discovered about Jeff, the slave who figures prominently in the McLure family's life during the war. The McLures had owned Jeff since 1856 at least, but their letters give no information on his age or marital status. He probably worked as a field laborer or stable hand rather than as a house servant, since in the past William McLure had put him in charge of caring for the horses. Kate McLure did not elaborate on her opinion of Jeff, but it is clear that she respected and trusted him. The overseer Holmes, the other actor in the triangle, was probably Benjamin "Homes," age twenty-five, listed in the county's 1860 census a few households away from the McLure residence. Married and the father of two children, he was the owner of almost a thousand dollars' worth of real estate, and he had been a farmer, not an overseer, before the war. His motives for taking the job, as well as anything else about his personality, remain obscure.[11]

In the meantime, William McLure found army life congenial. He enjoyed the camaraderie and air of "pleasant excitement" in his camp in northern Virginia. His brigade took part for a few hours in the battle of First Manassas on July 21, 1861, and he exulted in the rout of the northern forces, but it is not clear whether McLure actually fired a weapon during the engagement. In the summer and fall of 1861, he remained in camp in northern Virginia, "not drilling much" and visiting friends in other units. By November he had gained five pounds. Although he became bored with camp life during the winter and missed his wife's "loved face," he re-enlisted in January 1862 and was appointed assistant quartermaster for the Palmetto Sharpshooters, a South Carolina unit. He called the appointment "rather a pleasant one," and he did not even have to participate in drills. In May 1862 he was promoted to regimental quartermaster. McLure never fought in another battle, and he spent the rest of the war following supply trains through Virginia, Tennessee, and North Carolina, living in tents well behind the lines, issuing supplies, and shuffling paper. He occasionally rode through the countryside to requisition supplies from civilians, the only aspect of his job that put him in any serious danger. It was not much of a challenge for the fiery secessionist of antebellum days, but McLure never complained about his job.[12]

The McLure marriage still conformed to its antebellum patterns in some ways. William McLure perceived his wife as weak and delicate, and he sometimes treated her as if she were a child. When he was camped near Richmond, he vetoed a possible visit because he thought she could not stand the "excitement" of the city. This mild disagreement soon passed, but a major conflict arose when William hired a free black woman to work as his cook and laundress. (His slave Tom died of the measles in 1862.) Kate McLure must have suspected that her husband was having sexual relations with his servant—whom neither of the McLures referred to by name—or that other people would think it was the case. She became "annoyed," even angry, and told her husband that his reputation as a "Christian" and a "Gentleman" would be compromised. He quickly dismissed her objections, asserting that he could commit "even more questionable acts" before his reputation would be damaged. Besides, he said, the black woman was the best servant he had ever had.

We do not know if this woman continued to work for William McLure or if he simply concealed the relationship from his wife after this point. We do know that several years later William McLure brought one of his male slaves from South Carolina to work as his servant, and the free black woman did not appear again in the McLure correspondence. But the exchange between husband and wife gives us pause and hints at sexual tensions in the McLure marriage. It also reveals an unattractive side of William McLure's character and suggests that he thought he could do as he wished.[13]

Back at home, Kate McLure had to grapple with more immediate problems. The overseer Holmes did not plant enough food crops to feed everyone on the plantation, he raised too much cotton, and he did not care for the livestock properly. Although he was usually polite to her, Holmes took direction only from other white men, either William McLure or Doctor John A. Reidy, the husband of McLure's sister Frances who came over from neighboring Chester County to treat an outbreak of measles among the McLure slaves. Kate McLure was so worried about the general situation that she was plagued with chronic insomnia and tried to persuade her husband that Holmes had to go. By the summer of 1862, William McLure allowed that the plantation seemed to be in an "unsettled, unsatisfactory" condition. The fall harvests were paltry, and Kate McLure was finding it hard to obtain shoes for the slaves.

Subsequently, William McLure stopped writing directly to Holmes and instead conveyed his wishes through his wife, which no doubt increased the difficulties between overseer and mistress. She took to riding through the fields herself to see if Holmes was following instructions, something she had not done before the war, and only her strict economy with the food supply permitted everyone to get something to eat, as her husband now admitted. He finally agreed that Holmes was a "sorry fellow." William McLure was genuinely concerned about his wife and children, but he seemed incapable of imagining that his wife could run the plantation unassisted. He promised to return to Oakwood at the first opportunity to straighten everything out, but he was able to come home only three times during the entire war—once in 1862 and twice in 1863. During his brief visits home he was preoccupied and did not seem to perceive how life on the plantation was being transformed.[14]

At the end of 1862, William McLure fired Holmes, but he followed traditional lines of authority to do it. He told his brother-in-law Reidy, not his wife, that he decided to fire Holmes, and he asked Reidy, not his wife, to carry it out. Perhaps his method reflected the fact that Holmes would accept only these lines of authority, as William's mother implied that Holmes would not leave if Kate McLure alone tried to fire him. As a consequence, the other actors in the triangle, the slave Jeff and the mistress McLure, expanded their responsibilities. Jeff was now entirely in charge of the food crops and the livestock, and his mistress sent him out alone on errands across the countryside. Kate McLure set up a small, experimental salt works on the plantation to maintain her own salt supply. Her husband nonetheless directed her to ask her in-laws, Thomas Dawkins and John Reidy, for advice in order to relieve her of all "care and annoyance" regarding the plantation. He was glad to be able to "leave you in the care of such kind friends."[15]

These impractical, not to say preposterous, suggestions reveal how badly William McLure misread the situation at home, or, perhaps, how much he wanted to have a white man in charge. Thomas Dawkins was a drunkard, and John Reidy resided in another county over twenty miles away, scarcely within handy reach of Oakwood plantation for daily consultation. By early January 1863, it was clear that Kate McLure did not want to ask either one of them for advice, especially Reidy. Her husband had given him "carte blanche," asking only that he "consult" Kate McLure, but Reidy irritated her by neglecting even to discuss arrangements with her. Elijah Dawkins, a wealthy bachelor, often forgot his earlier promise to send over food for Kate McLure and her four small children. But William still could not imagine his wife running the plantation alone, so in early 1863 another overseer arrived at Oakwood, a man named Mabery, hired by Thomas Dawkins. The overseer's first name does not appear in the correspondence, but his motives for taking the job were crystal-clear: he very much wanted to avoid service in the Confederate Army.[16]

Another power triangle of mistress, overseer, and slave was set up on the plantation. This time, however, the mistress McLure and the slave Jeff had had two years of experience behind them, while the newcomer had taken the job as a last resort. His work was unsatisfactory almost from the beginning. By March 1863, William McLure was exhorting his wife to get Mabery to *"take care"* and "use every exertion to make enough [food] to live on," and he wanted frequent reports from her about Mabery's behavior. Kate McLure also became displeased with the overseer. That spring she returned from visiting her mother-in-law to say that "I find everything needing my attention here" and that the crop was "very much behind hand." Her responsibilities continued to increase: she began to work in the garden herself, and when two of the McLure slaves fell ill with pneumonia, she nursed them under the supervision of a local doctor (not Doctor Reidy). Her relationship with Mabery came to resemble her relationship with

Holmes, but this one soured at an accelerated pace, quickened no doubt by her growing confidence in her own abilities and her personal dislike for Mabery. By the fall of 1863, mistress and overseer were on such bad terms that she communicated with him only in writing, leaving notes for him indicating her orders. Perhaps in retaliation, Mabery neglected to reply to William McLure's requests for information about the plantation. As the winter closed in, many of the slaves had inadequate clothing and shoes. Things were not working out.[17]

Kate McLure wanted and expected Mabery to be fired at the end of 1863, and when her husband told her brother-in-law Dawkins to renew Mabery's contract anyway, she exploded in anger. The overseer did not carry out her instructions, she wrote to William, and she said it was "useless" to try to work with him. She reminded her husband that Mabery was a "low" and "profligate" man, the sort he should be protecting her from, not forcing her to work with, but, she observed with cutting sarcasm, "I suppose he suits you." Thomas Dawkins was unavailable to help her because he had suffered a bad fall and could not walk unassisted. The slave Jeff, she pointed out, gave her accurate information about the health of the other slaves. The implication was clear: Jeff alone could be relied on. Although it was in her interest to develop a good working relationship with Jeff, if only to keep the plantation operating, evidence of this kind of relationship between mistress and slave is rare. By the end of January 1864, she had deputized him to help her run the plantation so that "I am quite independent of Mabery." She announced that matters would run smoothly "if I can have Jeff when I want him." As if to underscore the point, she permitted Jeff to enter her house but not Mabery. By the spring of 1864, her husband began to agree with his wife on some points, at least in his letters; when a fence needed to be repaired he decided to "leave the matter to your judgment." Later that year, she decided to begin dyeing cloth herself, another task she had never done before. But, as she pointedly reminded her husband, "I am learning a good many things since the War broke out."[18]

William McLure, however, had had a much less dramatic experience since the war began. He lived a comparatively tranquil life, one of the safest available to a soldier in uniform, and his duties as quartermaster were arguably less demanding than the responsibilities devolving on his wife at home. Yet he proved to have little imagination, and he could not seem to comprehend the new kinds of relationships developing on his plantation. Perhaps his seclusion in a virtually all-male community like the Confederate Army, in which a few elite white men still commanded everyone else, made it difficult for him to imagine anyone else exercising power. He still believed that only a white man could be in charge, as his surreptitious correspondence with one of his brothers-in-law in the summer of 1864 demonstrates. Unbeknownst to his wife, he wrote to John Reidy and asked him to help her run Oakwood, and if he could not, he asked James Dawkins, Thomas's unsavory younger brother, to do it. Any white man would do, it seems.[19]

Kate McLure resisted the advice of Reidy and Dawkins, however, and she refused to follow her husband's express wishes on another point: that she should sell her corn that summer at the exorbitant price of sixty dollars a bushel. She wished to market it for the price recommended by the Confederate government—fifteen dollars a bushel—because it was "right," and she wished to give some of it away to her hungry neighbors. (Kate McLure had already shared some flour and corn with another family earlier that summer.) She also wanted to keep some corn in reserve to barter for other goods, especially iron. Her husband made no reply to this battery of arguments, and she seems to have prevailed.[20]

In December 1864, the tension between Kate McLure, Mabery, and the McLure slaves reached its peak. She first reported a "disturbance" among the slaves regarding Mabery and a slave woman named Susan. She did not give the details, but it seems that the two had become involved in a sexual relationship. Mabery refused to explain the situation to Kate McLure, and she was not completely sure at first that the story was true, but she was inclined to believe the slaves, especially Susan's brothers and sisters who came to her about the matter. Mabery realized that he might lose his job at last, and he hoped that the master would come home for Christmas so he could make a last-ditch appeal to protest his innocence. (William McLure did not come home for Christmas.) Then one night in early December Kate McLure was awakened by the screams of a slave named Dane, Susan's husband. He had been the first to reveal the scandal, and now, in a moment of fury, Mabery "fell on him" and started whipping him. Dane broke away and ran toward the McLure's house, pursued by the overseer. When he found it locked up, he called out Kate McLure's name "like some one being murdered." In his terror, he broke a pane of glass in the door, and when she appeared and saw the two men through the jagged window, she immediately understood what had happened.

This was a turning point in the "civil war" on Oakwood plantation. Dane's appeal to his mistress suggests that he realized who had the power on the plantation; Mabery's resort to beating a slave in the middle of the night also indicates how much his authority had diminished. Furthermore, Kate McLure had made it clear that she took sides with the slaves against her overseer. Sometime in January 1865, Mabery disappeared. Thomas Dawkins, incredibly, wanted him to stay on as the McLure's overseer; it is not clear if Mabery quit or was fired, or if he was fired, who let him go. But Kate McLure ran the plantation with the assistance of Jeff for what remained of the war. Another white man, a disabled Confederate veteran, approached her several times about the job, but she would not hire him. In her letters she never discussed race, slavery, or emancipation, but on her own plantation she had broken the ranks of racial solidarity and allied herself with her slaves against her white overseers, her white male relatives, and, when necessary, against her husband.[21]

To the very end of the war, however, William McLure proved unable to relate to his wife as a person who was in charge of a working plantation and several dozen slaves. He did not write about Susan, Dane's beating, or Mabery's behavior, but he sent his wife a patronizing letter in January 1865 about a horseback ride of several dozen miles she had taken alone to carry one of her daughters to visit her sister. He exclaimed that it was "quite a ride" for her and that she was returning to the vigorous "days of your girlhood." This was hardly an impressive feat, especially in light of the other problems with which she had dealt recently. And Kate McLure was no longer a girl; she was a mature and capable thirty-six-year-old. But her husband may have wished to see her as the passive young woman he had married in 1852, or the dependent wife he had left in 1861. The war had wrought substantial changes in Kate McLure's vision of herself but not in William McLure's perception of their roles.[22]

Whether the war effected permanent changes in the inner
dynamics of the McLure marriage remains a mystery. William
McLure was detailed with Joseph E. Johnston's army in North
Carolina when the war ended in April 1865, and he came directly
home. There is little postwar correspondence between the couple
and none that reveals the texture of the relationship as fully as the
wartime letters. Nevertheless they had four more children, and
remained together for the rest of their long lives. William McLure
continued to raise cotton on his plantation for several years,
presumably by hiring black workers, but he eventually sold the
land and went back to the mercantile business in Unionville. Kate
McLure died in 1912 and William in 1916, and both were buried
in Unionville. None of their correspondence after 1865 mentions
the people who were so important in their lives during the war:
Jeff Holmes, Mabery, Susan, or Dane.[23]

The wartime experiences of the McLures nonetheless demonstrate some of the many paradoxes of the Civil War. In this
marriage, the husband in the army had to face fewer challenges
than the wife at home. William McLure clung to traditional power
arrangements and tried repeatedly to keep authority firmly in the
hands of a white man, even as the antebellum world collapsed.
Kate McLure, however, proved to be much more adaptable in
meeting the challenges of wartime society and creating new kinds
of working relationships on the plantation. The struggles on
Oakwood plantation were dramatic, as dramatic as the military
events of the war itself. Historians may yet find that similar
changes swept other plantations during the turbulent years between 1861 and 1865.

Chapter 12

xxxxxxxxxxxxxxxxxxxxxxxxx

The Children of Jubilee: African American Childhood in Wartime

PETER BARDAGLIO

> Now praise and tank de Lord, he come
> To set de people free;
> Ole massa tink it day ob doom,
> But we ob jubilee.
>
> [John Greenleaf] Whittier's Song[1]

Private Spotswood Rice, hospitalized in St. Louis for chronic rheumatism, took his pen in hand on September 3, 1864, to write to his enslaved children. A Missouri ex-slave who enlisted in the Union army in February, Rice had learned that the woman who owned his daughter Mary prohibited her from visiting him and, even more insulting, Mary's mistress accused the father of trying to "steal" the child. Rice's fury pulsated throughout the letter to his offspring as he sought to assure them that he intended to gain possession of "his own flesh and blood." He informed the girls that he would take part in a Union military operation moving through the area later in the month, and that if the mistress didn't "give you up this Government will and I feel confident that I will get you." "You tell her from me," Rice directed his daughters, "that She is the frist Christian that I ever hard say that aman could Steal his own child especially out of human bondage."

Just to make sure that "Miss Kaitty" got the message, the former slave dispatched another letter directly to her that same

day. "now I want you to understand that mary is my Child and she
is a God given rite of my own and you may hold on to hear as long
as you can," he warned, "but I want you to remembor this one
thing that the longor you keep my Child from me the longor you
will have to burn in hell and the qwicer youll get their." Not
mincing any words, Rice added, "where ever you and I meets we
are enmays to each orthere. . . . my children is my own and I
expect to get them and when I get ready to come after mary I will
have bout a pwrer and autherity to bring hear away and to
exacute vengencens on them that holds my Child."[2]

We can imagine the astonishment of Kitty Diggs as she cast her
eyes down the page of Spotswood Rice's letter. But just as interesting to consider is the reaction of the enslaved daughters to their
father's message of hope and to the remarkable developments
that put him in a position to send it. Despite the thousands of
volumes that have been written on the Civil War, we know all too
little about the black and white children who became entangled in
this tumultuous struggle, and about how their early encounter
with the tides of history influenced their outlook and behavior as
adults.[3]

We cannot assume unquestioningly that events in the past
resonated at the same pitch for children as they did for adults.[4]
We must try to comprehend what young southerners felt and
experienced during the Civil War, and the distinctive meaning
that these experiences and feelings held for them. In particular,
how did the boys and girls born into bondage during its final years
see the war, and what impressions did they take away from their
passage through this fiery crucible? Looking at the war through
the eyes of these children, what can we learn about how it
transformed their lives?[5]

A number of scholars have investigated the experience of slave
children before the firing on Fort Sumter in April 1861 and,
consequently, we have a fairly clear understanding of the main
currents that shaped this experience. Perhaps the key characteristic of growing up in the shadow of the peculiar institution was
the inability of black parents to protect their children from the
cruelties and violence of slavery. Caroline Hunter, for example,
lived with her slave mother and three brothers on a small farm
near Suffolk, Virginia, on the eve of the war. She recollected the

profound sense of frustration that slave parents felt in response
to the intrusion of white authority in the lives of their children:

> During slavery it seemed lak ya' chillun b'long to ev'body but you.
> Many a day my ole mamma has stood by an' watched massa beat
> her chillun 'till dey bled an' she couldn' open her mouf. Dey didn'
> only beat us, but dey useta strap my mamma to a bench or box an'
> beat her wid a wooden paddle while she was naked.[6]

Such demonstrations of control did not necessarily shatter the
bond between parent and child or undermine the respect that
children had for their parents. But learning to endure the abuse
and punishment of family members was one of the most agonizing lessons a slave child had to master. William Wells Brown never
forgot the day that he heard his mother crying out as the overseer
whipped her. Brown remained in his cabin, "not daring to
venture any further"; distraught at his inability to assist his
mother, he retreated to his bed "and wept aloud." These sorts of
experiences drove home to young slaves not only the powerless-
ness of their parents but also their own subordinate position.[7]

Slave parents took on an extraordinarily complex task in trying
to teach their children how to handle the treacherous dynamics of
bondage, and they had to engage in a fierce tug-of-war with
slaveholders and other whites on the plantation to acquire the
requisite authority to socialize their children appropriately. The
slave child saw his or her parents presenting a divided self to the
world: performing the role of provider and protector in the slave
quarters and assuming an obedient, deferential posture in the
fields or the big house. An important parental strategy for coping
with this contradiction was to impose a strict discipline on the
offspring, whipping them for numerous offenses. This expression of control aimed at impressing the children with the parents'
capacity to exercise some measure of power over their behavior
and, by extension, communicating to the slaveowners the parents'
determination to claim their right to chastise their own children
despite their lack of legal guardianship.[8]

Both mothers and fathers of slaves usually participated in the
process of socializing their children, but fathers exerted less
influence than mothers on the development of the child's personality. Masters consciously sought to undercut the black father's

position, and slave trading also disrupted the ties between bonds-men and their children. The absence of slave fathers was partic-ularly noticeable in areas of the Upper South such as Virginia that exported male slaves out of state.[9] Still, for many slave offspring, their father proved to be a significant presence in their upbring-ing. One ex-slave spoke forcefully of his boyhood on the planta-tion: "I loved my father. He was such a good man. He was a good carpenter and could do anything. My mother just rejoiced in him."[10]

Although the nuclear family represented the ideal in the slave community, it was intricately woven into a larger pattern of associations and obligations. A wide range of relatives and fictive kin in the slave quarters shared the responsibility for child rearing; especially in the absence of a parent, individuals from outside the nuclear family assumed a major role in bringing up the children.[11] On the larger plantations, when the slave mother returned to full-time work after a month or so of lying in, the newborn was placed in a nursery during the day. Often an elderly slave, sometimes assisted by the older children, took charge of the youngsters. Whether a nurse too old to labor in the fields, the grandparents, or one of the older siblings cared for the child, the mother would be released from her toil to breastfeed her infant three or four times a day. Given the harsh routine of plantation life, however, the slave mother had little time to nurture the new addition to her family in a sustained way.[12]

Despite the plantation legend of the carefree slave child, young blacks in the antebellum South led a precarious existence. Slave infants suffered extremely high mortality rates, and fewer than two out of three African American children reached the age of ten in the years between 1850 and 1860. But if the child survived infancy, it was not uncommon for him or her to realize some semblance of what we recognize as childhood, at least during the early stages. One of the most striking features of these years was the extent to which children lived in an age-segregated commu-nity. Girls and boys had little contact with adult slaves, who were away working most of the day. The aged nurses who supervised the children more often than not left them to their own devices. While the younger boys and girls spent their time playing among themselves in the nursery, the older ones explored the fields and woods, sometimes visiting friends on neighboring plantations and farms. With the end of the work day, the children would return to their cabins for the evening meal with their parents and other family members.[13]

However isolated from the adults, the world of slave children was not strictly differentiated in terms of gender. Girls and boys dressed much the same, wearing smocklike shirts until puberty, and they played the same games. Favorite activities pursued by both sexes included marbles, jump rope, and various ring games. Slave children played not only among themselves but also with white youngsters on the plantation or farm, interacting with a rough degree of equality. Although this sort of companionship across racial lines may have obscured the view of bondage held by African American children, some of the games they played—for example, whipping each other with switches and holding mock auctions—reflected a clear awareness of their condition as slaves. Like all such imitative play, this was serious business, for it helped to relieve slave youth of their anxieties and fears, and created an environment in which they could practice adaptation and survival skills.[14]

Anticipating the fact that both sexes became field hands and frequently did similar work as adults, slave children performed many of the same chores. Assigned few duties before the age of five or six, over the next several years they carried out light tasks such as collecting kindling, cleaning up the grounds, or gathering eggs in the barnyard. The plantation mistress also set them to work making beds, washing and ironing clothes, helping to prepare and serve meals, and taking care of the white infants, among other jobs. In only a few areas did a sexual division of labor exist among the slave children. Masters invariably selected boys to escort them on hunting trips and to serve as body servants, while girls took up sewing, churning butter, milking cows, and ministering to the personal needs of their mistresses.[15]

If they hadn't already done so, slave youngsters grasped the full significance of bondage when they entered the fields around the age of ten or twelve years old. About this same time the young slaves received adult clothing—dresses for the girls and pants for the boys—and the onset of sexual maturity led to a growing divergence in the life experiences of males and females. Those slave girls who were enlisted for service in the big house, in particular, increasingly found their lives delineated by the same norms regarding separate spheres that governed the lives of slaveholding women. The heightened exposure of the adolescent female slave to the threat of sexual exploitation, whether in the big house or the field, was a special cause of worry to her parents.[16]

For both genders, however, initiation into the labor force was a traumatic event, and many former slaves recalled the pain with which they confronted the stark reality of bondage at this point in their lives. Not only the discipline of the lash, but also the inevitable break in their friendships with white children came as a shock, leading many black youth to raise troubling questions about the nature of slavery.[17] As James Curry observed of his master's children, even though "we loved one another like brothers," "the love of power is cultivated in their hearts by their parents, the whip is put into their hands, and they soon regard the negro in no other light than as a slave."[18]

The whirlwind of the Civil War stirred up even more such realizations among slave children about the arbitrary character of bondage. The resort to arms cracked open the confines of the plantation and farm, exposing thousands of African American youngsters to the outside world and giving them an unprecedented glimpse of the potential for change in their lives. Booker T. Washington, who was only nine years old in 1865, first became aware that he and his family were slaves and that freedom was a possibility "early one morning before day, when I was awakened by my mother kneeling over her children and fervently praying that Lincoln and his armies might be successful, and that one day she and her children might be free." Ignited by the outbreak of war, this powerful moment of revelation for Washington altered irretrievably his way of looking at himself and the people around him.[19]

Once the Civil War erupted, southern slaves tried to learn all they could about the conflict, and children became proficient at gleaning information from conversations they overheard among the adults, black and white. This was not always an easy task. Lizzie Davis, a former slave from South Carolina, reported that she found out about the attack on Fort Sumter because "my parents en de olden people speak bout dat right dere fore we chillun." Normally, however, "de olden people never didn' allow dey chillun to set en hear dem talk no time." A Tennessee ex-slave recalled how during the war she and the other children "would go round to the windows and listen to what the white folks would say when they was reading their papers and talking after supper."[20]

Washington was more fortunate; he found it unnecessary to engage in this kind of subterfuge to gain news of the war's progress. Sitting up late at night with his mother and the other slaves, he listened attentively to the "whispered discussions" about the progress of the fighting, which they followed through the "'grape-vine' telegraph." "Every success of the Federal armies and every defeat of the Confederate forces was watched with the keenest and most intense interest," he recounted.[21] For most slave boys and girls, though, the desire to know more about how the war was going ran into previously existing barriers between adults and children on the plantation, although the children did what they could to penetrate these barriers.

With a growing wave of southern whites enlisting, drilling, and marching off to battle, of course, it became preposterous to think that knowledge of the conflict could be kept from the younger members of the slave quarters. Most slaveholders sought to keep their human property as ignorant as possible about the world beyond the limits of the plantation, but after 1861 the world came to the plantation, generating an equal measure of fear and excitement among the black children, who became more and more cognizant of the war and its repercussions. Rachel Harris, a teen-aged slave in Mississippi at the time, recollected, "I went with the white chillun and watched the soldiers marchin'. The drums was playin' and the next thing I heerd, the war was gwine on. You could hear the guns just as plain. The soldiers went by just in droves from soon of a mornin' till sundown." Even the youngest children were aware of the seriousness of what was taking place. "Dey was sad times, honey; all de people was goin' to war wid de drums beatin' all aroun' and de fifes blowin'," remarked Hattie Anne Nettles, a former slave in Georgia who was no more than four years old at the outset of the Civil War.[22]

Although traditional games such as marbles and horseshoes remained favorites among the slave children, their play activities inevitably mirrored the coming of war, becoming increasingly differentiated by gender as a result. The boys, not surprisingly, seemed fascinated with the military aspects of the conflict. A South Carolina ex-slave who was five years old when the Civil War began remembered watching his master drill with the local Confederate unit, known as the Spartanburg Sharp Shooters. "When I got home," he commented, "I tried to do like him and everybody laughed at me." Play between the white and black youngsters also took on new dimensions. Candis Goodwin of Virginia reported that in the first months of the war the black and white children would "play Yankee an 'Federates, 'course de whites was always the 'Federates. They'd make us black boys prisoners an' make b'lieve dey was gonna cut our necks off; guess dey got dat idea f'om dere fathers."[23]

For many young slaves, among the most memorable incidents early in the military struggle was the departure of the master or one of his sons to the battlefield as a member of the Confederate army. Mary Williams, who lived on a Georgia plantation and was ten years old at the end of the war, recalled "the day young master Henry Lee went off to war. . . . Young master Henry (he was just eighteen) say he goin' to take old Lincoln the first thing and swing him to a limb and let him play around awhile and then shoot his head off." Things did not go according to plan for the self-confident youth, however, who was obviously used to having his own way. One morning his mother received a letter that told how Henry had been "in a pit with the soldiers and they begged him not to stick his head up but he did anyway and they shot it off." In Williams's words, "Old mistress just cry so."[24]

Such sudden twists in the course of events must have proved illuminating for black children conditioned to seeing white men as masters of their fate. The war had kicked into gear forces that could not be controlled, and slave girls and boys on the plantations and farms across the South sensed that their world had a fluidity, an unpredictability, previously unknown to most of them. "When de war broke out everything was changed," observed William Curtis, a former slave who was approximately sixteen years old at the beginning of the conflict.[25]

One of the most immediate changes experienced by slave children was the expansion of their workload as the white men went off to fight and growing numbers of slave men left the plantation, either impressed into service by the Confederate and Federal governments or recruited by the Union army. "You know chillun them days, they made em do a man's work," declared James Henry Nelson, an ex-slave who was ten years old at most when the Civil War concluded. James Gill fondly remembered antebellum summers spent fishing and swimming as a slave child in Arkansas; according to him, "all dem good times ceasted atter a while when de war come and de Yankees started all dere debbilment."[26]

Memories of the constant labor that they performed loomed especially large in the recollections of former slaves who were adolescents during the conflict. Lee Guidon's summary of his wartime experience is typical: "Yes maam I sho was in the Cibil War. I plowed all day and me and my sister helped take care of the baby at night. It would cry and me bumpin' it." Eliza Scantling, fifteen years old in 1865, recalled how in the early months of that year she "plowed a mule an' a wild un at dat. Sometimes me hands get so cold I jes' cry."[27]

With the advance of Union soldiers, many planters fled into the interior of the state or beyond, taking their slaves with them to safer grounds. This practice became particularly widespread in the Mississippi Valley and in lowcountry Georgia and South Carolina as slaveholders moved thousands of slaves deeper into the state and to Texas. "About that time it look like everybody in the world was going to Texas," recounted Allen Manning, who was born in Mississippi in 1850 and whose master tried to evade the northern army during the war. "When we would be going down the road we would have to walk along the side all the time to let the wagons go past, all loaded with folks going to Texas." "Running" slaves in this manner had a devastating impact on the slave family, accelerating the process of dislocation and separation brought on by the war. Since adult male slaves were more valuable and moved faster, a disproportionate share of them went with the planters, and frequently women and children were left to fend for themselves, although several former slaves younger than Manning—all of them male—remembered having to leave their homes during the Civil War.[28]

For those young slaves who stayed behind, the arrival of the

Union army produced sharply etched memories which they readily recollected years later. Anticipating the northern advance, white southerners tried to frighten the children with stories about the demonic appearance of the Yankees and the awful atrocities they would commit if the slaves did not escape their clutches. "Us was skeered of dem Yankees," noted an Arkansas ex-slave who was around ten years old at the beginning of hostilities. No wonder: the overseer had told the black children that "a Yankee was somepin what had one great big horn on he haid and just one eye and dat right in de middle of the breast." Mittie Freeman, who was the same age, hid in a tree when the northern troops arrived. She refused to climb down until the Union soldier who found her removed his hat and revealed whether he did indeed have horns.[29]

Despite whatever initial fear they felt, the children were fascinated with the brass buttons and blue coats of the soldiers. Fanny Johnson, about five years old when "the war started rushing," remarked, "When the Yankees came thru, I wasn't scared. I was too busy looking at the bright buttons on their coats." "Yes sir, I seed de Yankees and I remember de clothes dey wore," recounted Zeb Crowder, a former slave from North Carolina who was seven years old at the time. "Dey were blue and dere coats had capes on 'em and large brass buttons."[30]

Although the black youngsters clearly admired the uniforms of the Yankee soldiers, their arrival on some plantations and farms led to looting and destruction, and for slave children this was usually an upsetting experience. "I member when the Yankees come and took things I just fussed at em," related Cyntha Jones. "I thought what was my white folks' things was mine too." Sam Word, an Arkansas ex-slave born in 1859, recollected that the Union troops "wanted to hang old master cause he wouldn't tell where the money was. They tied his hands behind him and had a rope around his neck. Now this is the straight goods, I was just a boy and I was cryin' cause I didn't want em to hang old master." While many of the adult slaves viewed the coming of the Yankees as the visitation of God's wrath, the children perceived the sudden violence that accompanied their arrival as a collapse of all that was familiar and predictable. Many of the boys and girls were too young to understand the character of bondage, and the

Union disruption of what they regarded as their home angered them.[31]

Even more startling for these children was their confrontation with the horrors of battle. Lizzie Dunn recalled, "The sound was like eternity had turned loose. Everything shook like terrible earthquakes day and night. The light was bright and red and smoke terrible." "During the war all the children had fear," observed La San Mire, a former slave from Louisiana who drove an ox-cart in which he helped load the dead soldiers to take them to the burial grounds. Raised in bondage, most black children had experienced violence before, but during the war they came face to face with killing on an unprecedented scale. "De dead wuz laying all long de road an' dey stayed dere, too," remembered James Goings, who was ten years old when the Confederates surrendered at Appomattox. "In dem days it wuzn't nuthin' to fin' a dead man in de woods." Surely, the exposure of these youngsters to this sort of mass slaughter made them serious beyond their years.[32]

As the war and destruction of slavery swept through the South, African American families encountered new burdens and opportunities, both of which had profound consequences for the lives of children. The negative repercussions of the war at times must have outweighed the positive ones in the eyes of black youngsters. Relocating slaves often disrupted African American families, as previously noted, and the overall rise in slave mobility led to many other separations. In addition, the impressment of adult male slaves by Confederate and Federal authorities to work on military construction projects and in armies, factories, and hospitals had a destabilizing effect on black family life.[33]

Probably the most dramatic changes in slave families during the Civil War, both constructive and corrosive, stemmed from the military service of fathers in the Union army. Like Private Rice, those slave fathers who served in the Union army took on the role of liberators and defenders of black women and children. Colonel Thomas Wentworth Higginson believed that this role gave black troops a special motive for fighting, and made them "the key to the successful prosecution" of the war against the Confederacy.[34]

This is not to say that black women were passive during the

Civil War. On the contrary, they shouldered an even greater share of the day-to-day responsibility for the care of children than they had during the antebellum period. The combined impact of wartime relocation, impressment, and military recruitment and conscription policies tended to separate slave men from the women and children. As the primary caregivers, slave women sought to provide for the safety of their children while striking blows against the slaveholding South. Fulfilling both goals was a difficult task, but it could be done. One extraordinary wartime incident involved a seventy-year-old slave woman who led her twenty-two children and grandchildren to freedom in Georgia, floating forty miles down the Savannah River on a flatboat until they encountered a Federal vessel.[35]

Although slave women like this courageous grandmother made a critical contribution to the downfall of bondage, the formal endorsement of African American men as liberators by the Union army reshaped gender roles in the black community, bringing them into closer alignment with the Victorian ideal of protector and protected.[36] The increased stature of the slave father that accompanied his enlistment made a lasting impression on his children. "When my father went to the army old Master told us he was gone to fight for us niggers freedom," related George Conrad, Jr., in 1937. Conrad's father had escaped as a slave and returned a liberator, and in his son's judgment he was a hero. Service in the Union army countered the degradation of bondage and heightened the self-esteem not only of black soldiers but also of their children. This may have been particularly true for African American boys, who looked to their fathers as role models. In the case of Conrad, his father's stint in the military apparently inspired him in 1883 to enlist in the U. S. Army, where ironically he joined the effort in the West to drive the Plains Indians onto reservations.[37]

Soldiering during the Civil War provided black men with the opportunity to protect their families, but it also generated tremendous stresses. The act of separation itself was a wrenching experience for the women and children left behind. A witness to one such scene on the Sea Islands in 1862 described how the "Women and children gathered around the men to say 'farewell.' Fathers took the little children in their arms, while the Women gave way to the wildest expressions of grief." The sense of loss did not necessarily abate with the passage of time, especially for those children whose parents died during the war. Amie Lumpkin, a former slave from South Carolina, remembered years later the scars left by the fighting on her family: "My daddy go 'way to de war 'bout this time, and my mammy and me stay in our cabin alone. She cry and wonder where he be, if he is well, or he be killed, and one day we hear he is dead. My mammy, too, pass in a short time."[38]

To discourage slave men from enlisting in the Union army and to punish those who did, slaveholders harassed the families of black soldiers. Planters forced women and children from these families off plantations when the fathers left to join the northern army, denied them food and clothing, or physically mistreated them.[39] As one slave woman wrote to her soldier husband in 1863, "I have had nothing but trouble since you left . . . they abuse me because you went & say they will not take care of our children & do nothing but quarrel with me all the time and beat me scandalously the day before yesterday—Oh I never thought you would give me so much trouble as I have got to bear now." Dispatches like this compelled black soldiers and some of their concerned officers to demand that the Federal government provide protection to those remaining behind. "If the Government calls on the negro to fight her battles—in Gods name protect their wives and children while they are in the army," pleaded Lieutenant Jeff Mayall in a report to General William Pile in 1864.[40]

To escape vengeful owners, slave women and children frequently went along with the men to the recruitment centers or fled on their own at some later point, settling near army camps where their husbands, fathers, and sons were stationed. The living conditions in these camps were miserable; lacking proper food, shelter, and medicine, the residents suffered high disease and mortality rates. Union army officers, moreover, believed that the women and children who flocked to the army outposts undercut the military efficiency of their husbands and fathers. Viewing these families as a nuisance, military officials launched repeated attempts to remove them from the makeshift settlements. At Camp Nelson, Kentucky, white soldiers evicted hundreds of women and children in November 1864, leaving them with no shelter from the bitterly cold weather. In the wake of the suffering caused by this brutal expulsion, northern missionaries and sympathetic officers criticized the army treatment of black dependents, and eventually won a reversal of Federal policy. The generally shabby handling of women and children in the military camps, however, led to a downturn in black volunteering. To provide further inducements for southern blacks to take up arms, Congress passed a joint resolution in March 1865 that offered freedom to the wives and offspring of African American soldiers and any future volunteers.[41]

The social upheaval and uncertainty generated by the Civil War made the family all the more important as the foundation of the black community in the South. Even though the rigors of war put African American families to the test, crucial new possibilities emerged for placing domestic relations on a firmer footing. With the death of slavery, hundreds of black couples rushed to legalize their marriages, and northern missionaries and Union army clergy conducted mass wedding ceremonies to accommodate the flood of requests.[42] Former slaves, young and old, fanned out across the post-emancipation South, determined to reunite families separated by sale or some other cause. "They had a passion, not for wandering, as for getting together," a Freedmen's Bureau agent in South Carolina pointed out, "and every mother's son among them seemed to be in search of his mother; every mother in search of her children. In their eyes the work of emancipation was incomplete until the families which had been dispersed by slavery were reunited."[43]

During the chaotic transition from bondage to freedom, slave and freed parents made every effort to protect their children and the integrity of their families. The reconstitution of black families following emancipation underscored the strength of kinship ties forged during slavery.[44] African American parents in the South, furthermore, demonstrated their concern for the future of their offspring by vigorously seeking to provide them with an education. Schoolhouses for black children sprang up throughout the wartorn region, despite financial difficulties and southern white resistance.[45] Postwar efforts in the southern black community to care for orphans also spoke powerfully to the broad sense of kin obligation among former slaves. "I find the colored people themselves taking into their families the orphaned children of their former friends and neighbors thus saving us the necessity of bearing large expenses in caring for them," observed Thomas Conway, the head of the Department of the Gulf's Bureau of Free Labor in 1865.[46]

Freedom had many meanings for African Americans, but certainly a central component was the effort to remove their families from the control of whites. Black youth, in particular, perceived the coming of freedom primarily in terms of its impact on their family life. Charlie Barbour, who was fourteen years old when the war ended, exclaimed, "Yes 'um, i reckon I wuz glad ter git free, case I knows den dat I won't wake up some mornin' ter fin' dat my mammy or some ob de rest of my family am done sold." According to William Curtis, whose father had been sold to a Virginia slaveholder, "dat was de best thing about de war setting us free, he could come back to us."[47]

Not all young blacks, however, greeted the possibility of escaping white authority with an outpouring of joy. Those children who had been separated at an early age from their slave parents, and had little or no contact with them before emancipation, experienced sharply conflicting emotions when their mother or father suddenly showed up at the end of the war to take them away. For these children the destruction of slavery led to the shattering of a life that represented protection and stability, and some found this life difficult to leave behind, especially if they had been well cared for. Lou Turner, for example, grew up on a Texas plantation, forging a close attachment to the mistress, who provided her with plenty of food and pretty clothes. She vividly remembered her mother "gettin' me 'way from there when freedom come." In her words, "Old missy have seven li'l nigger chillen what belong to her slaves, but dey mammies and daddys come git 'em. I didn't own my own mammy. I own my old missy and call her 'mama.' Us cry and cry when us have to go with mammy."[48]

The tragic story of Lou Turner reminds us that children viewed the momentous events of the Civil War from a unique angle of vision, and that boys and girls each had their own way of looking at the conflict. Searching for security and affection, Lou Turner saw emancipation as a dangerous threat to the fragile web of caring that she had woven for herself. As Carol Gilligan suggests in her perceptive study of female moral development, girls see "a world of relationships and psychological truths where an awareness of the connection between people gives rise to a recognition of responsibility for one another."[49] It would not be surprising, then, if Lou Turner and other young female slaves were more ambivalent than the boys about the war. Despite significant commonalities in their lives, particularly in the area of work, slave girls and boys encountered well-entrenched notions of gender in their interactions with adults and with each other. The Victorian culture in which they were at least partial participants regarded males in terms of categories that treated them as individual actors, while females were defined almost entirely in relational terms.[50] It may be that, as a result of these vital differences in gender socialization in the nineteenth-century South, male youngsters tended to perceive the Civil War as an adventure that opened up their access to the world as autonomous individuals, while girls were more concerned about the impact of the war on the network of relationships in which they found themselves. We simply do not know enough at this point about the different responses of southern children to the war to say for certain, but the matter bears further investigation.

There is no disputing the fact that the war turned the world of Lou Turner and other young slaves upside down; this upheaval clearly left them with feelings of both loss and gain regardless of their gender. In all likelihood, though, most African American children shared the excitement of Sam Mitchell, who was a young slave living near Beaufort, South Carolina, in November 1861 when the United States Navy appeared off the coast of the Sea Islands. As the Union guns began firing, he told an interviewer from the Federal Writers' Project in the late 1930s, "I t'ought it been t'under rolling, but dey ain't no cloud. My mother say, 'son, dart ain't no t'under, dat Yankee come to gib you Freedom.' I been so glad, I jump up and down and run."[51]

It turned out, of course, that the arrival of United States Navy did not bring about the immediate collapse of the peculiar institution on the Sea Islands. Not until President Lincoln's Emancipation Proclamation of 1863 did Sam Mitchell, his mother, and the other blacks living on the sandy islands of South

Carolina acquire the legal status of free persons. But the entrance of Union vessels into Port Royal Sound in 1861 set in motion a chain of events that led to their liberation. After more than two hundred years of bondage, the tides of history shifted at last that autumn, eventually sweeping out to sea a social system that had denied African American children the opportunity to wade in the blue waters of freedom.

Chapter 13

XXXXXXXXXXXXXXXXXXXXXXXXXXXX

Wartime Dialogues on Illicit Sex:
White Women and Black Men

MARTHA HODES

In the wartime and Reconstruction climate of social upheaval in
the American South, sex between white women and black men
became a highly charged political issue, spurring whites to a level
of public violence unknown under slavery. The subject of sex
between white women and black men entered the national political arena during the Civil War in the presidential election campaign of 1864. It was then that the Democratic party coined the
pejorative term "miscegenation" (from the Latin *miscere*, "to
mix"; and *genus*, race) and asserted that Lincoln's Republican
party advocated sex and marriage across the color line. Posing as
Republicans, a group of Democrats distributed an anonymous
booklet advocating political and social equality, and specifically
the mixture of black and white.[1] The authors wrote that although
the "frenzy of love in the white Southern woman for the negro"
was rarely acted upon, plantation mistresses had a stake in slavery
because it permitted them sexual access to black men. Yet until
racial prejudice was overcome, the authors maintained, the "full
mystery of sex—the sweet, wild dream of a perfect love—can
never be generally known," and thus should white women be
entitled to black husbands.[2] The Democratic posers also wrote
about the desire of black men for white women, contending:
"Our police courts give painful evidence that the passion of the

colored race for the white is often so uncontrollable as to over come the terror of the law."[3] Although the publication was ignored or renounced by most Republicans, and viewed with suspicion by most American readers,[4] the fears upon which its authors played were very shortly to be expressed with seriousness by white southerners.

Democratic politicians also brought the specter of sex between white women and black men into wartime and Reconstruction congressional debates about such issues as integrated transportation and schools and black suffrage. In an 1864 Senate exchange about the exclusion of blacks from Washington, D.C., railroad cars, for example, one Maryland Democrat introduced the point that a white woman marrying a black man would provoke a "trembling, anxious, depressing, harassing, crushing fear" on the part of the woman's male family members.[5] Republicans commonly countered such Democratic offensives by presuming the absurdity of the conflation of black suffrage with sexual transgressions across the color line. A Pennsylvania Republican, for example, wondered in 1866 how anyone could believe that marriage with a white woman would result "because a colored man is allowed to drop a little bit of paper in a box."[6] Thus did white southern politicians begin to conflate the newly won political power of black men with the issue of black male sexuality. With the advent of emancipation, southern whites who sought to maintain a racial hierarchy began systematically to invoke the idea that black men posed a grave sexual threat to white women.

White communities in the antebellum South that had been forced to contend with sexual liaisons between white women and black men (in the forms of bastardy or adultery, for example) had rarely given the black men a chance to tell their own stories. The men were not always named in legal documents and, if named, were rarely consulted for the public record.[7] During the tremendous social chaos of the Civil War years, however, the voices of black men on the subject of sex with white women entered the historical record in the chronicles of the national government.

"I will tell you a fact that I have never seen alluded to publicly, and I suppose a man would be scouted who should allude to it publicly; but my relations with colored people have led me to believe that there is a large amount of intercourse between white women and colored men." So Captain Richard J. Hinton, an ardent white abolitionist who commanded black troops during the Civil War, testified in Washington, D.C., in 1863.[8] Captain Hinton spoke before the American Freedmen's Inquiry Commission (AFIC) which had been formed under the War Department of Congress to address the incorporation of emancipated slaves into American society. The AFIC, composed of three white anti-slavery men, would ultimately propose the establishment of the Freedmen's Bureau to assist former slaves in the transition to free labor.[9]

Captain Hinton was not the only witness to tell the wartime commission that white women and black men in the South had sex. The indexer for the commission, in fact, saw fit to make entries under the letter "I" for "Intercourse between white women and colored men common—Instances of," and "Illicit intercourse between white women & black men not uncommon."[10] James Redpath, another white abolitionist and a self-described revolutionary, had traveled through the South during the 1850s to talk with black residents.[11] While Redpath told the commission about sexual liaisons between white women and black men in considerable detail, he had withheld this knowledge from the public just a few significant years earlier. In his collection of dispatches from the South, published in 1859, Redpath "most solemnly" declared "that in no one instance have I sought either to darken or embellish the truth—to add to, subtract from, or pervert a single statement of the slaves." Yet Redpath had in fact omitted information about sexual liaisons between white women and black men from the book, at one point extolling the chastity of southern white women, and sympathizing with them for the immoral sexual conduct of their white husbands, fathers, and brothers.[12] Perhaps Redpath had understood (along with his publisher) how dangerous to the cause of abolition would be any disclosure of sexual liaisons between white women and black men. Four years later, in the middle of the Civil War, James Redpath, Richard Hinton, and others seized upon the historical moment of social and political change to speak up. As it turned out, in deference to their own political agenda, the officers of the AFIC would suppress the testimony they had heard about sex between white women and black men. Thus, it was only in the brief moment of wartime disruption that the voices of black men were given credence in a public, political arena. The narratives offered in these wartime dialogues (mostly, though not entirely, mediated through the words of white northerners) allow us to move a little bit closer to the truth about sexual liaisons between white women and black men in the antebellum South.

Testifying before the AFIC, James Redpath first elaborated on the depravity of white men who sexually exploited slave women, prompting one of the commissioners to ask: "Well sir, among such a universal system of libertinage what is the effect upon white women?" Of his black informants, Redpath said: "I have often heard them talking and laughing about the numerous cases that have occurred in which white women have had colored children." One black man told Redpath that "it was just as common for colored men to have connection with white women, as for white men to have to do with colored women." Another said that "it was an extremely common thing among all the handsome mulattoes at the South to have connection with the white women." Redpath relayed an episode of a white woman "of good family" in Mobile, Alabama, who carried on an affair with a slave, had sex with him on the morning of her wedding, and bore his child nine months later. Redpath concluded: "[T]here is a great deal more of this than the public suspect."[13]

Another white man, Major George Stearnes, told the commissioners: "I have often been amused that the planters here in Tennessee have sometimes to watch their daughters to keep them from intercourse with the negroes. This, though of course exceptional, is yet common enough to be a source of uneasiness to parents."[14] And Samuel Lucille, also white, told the commissioners that in Mississippi the "cross between a white woman and a black man" was "not uncommon," adding: "I knew well a ferry man on the Wachita river, whose mother was a white woman and his father a black man. He was a free voter, but it was notorious in the neighborhood that he was a half-blooded negro."[15]

Richard Hinton told the AFIC in no uncertain terms that white women in the South sought out sex with black men. A black Mississippi River steamboat steward named Patrick H. Miner (he was the son of a white plantation owner in New Orleans, and a graduate of Oberlin College[16]) told Hinton about the women of a particular white family. According to Miner, "the colored men on that river knew that the women of the Ward family of Louisville, Kentucky, were in the habit of having the stewards, or other fine looking fellows, sleep with them when they were on the boats." Miner also relayed a personal anecdote about a Ward woman who, when on Miner's boat, had offered him five dollars and "told him to come to her house at Louisville on a certain day, giving him particular directions as to the door at which he was to knock." Upon arrival, Miner was "shown to the room adjoining her bedroom," where he waited until he had to return to work. Although the rendezvous never took place, Miner "had no doubt that she wanted him to have connection with her."[17] Another story offered by Hinton concerned the Missouri frontier where white settlers from North Carolina and Tennessee had grown richer; the daughters in these families were envious of their brothers who "got a flashy education, which they completed in the slave quarters and the bar-room." As Hinton understood it: "The girls knew that their brothers were sleeping with the chambermaids, or other servants, and I don't see how it could be otherwise than that they too should give loose to their passions."[18] Redpath had heard similar stories. When pressed on how liaisons with white women came to pass, one black man had told Redpath: "'I will tell you how it is here. I will go up with the towels, and when I go into the room the woman will keep following me with her eyes, until I take notice of it, and one thing leads to another. Others will take hold of me and pull me on to the sofa, and others will stick out their foot and ask one to tie their boot, and I will take hold of their foot, and say "what a pretty foot!"'"[19]

Most antebellum documents regarding liaisons between white women and black men concern women from the servant or yeoman classes, women whose families did not command the social authority to stay out of court for transgressions such as bastardy or adultery.[20] The narratives of the black men as recorded in the wartime testimony, on the other hand, also concern illicit liaisons with planters' daughters or plantation mistresses, and specifically illuminate the phenomenon of the sexual coercion of black men by white women. Again in no uncertain terms, Hinton informed the commission that white women of the planter classes could force black men into having sex with them.

In southern slave society, men of the planter classes ruled, but white women of slaveholding families also commanded power over slaves, both female and male.[21] While scholars have documented the sexual exploitation of black women by white men,[22] the voices of black men, recorded during the Civil War years, point to a consequence of slave society that has remained unexplored.

"I have never yet found a bright looking colored man, whose confidence I have won," Hinton said, "who has not told me of instances where he has been compelled, either by his mistress, or by white women of the same class, to have connection with them." Hinton recounted a conversation with a white Kansas doctor who knew "from his experience in Virginia and Missouri, that a very large number of white women, especially the daughters of the smaller planters, who were brought into more direct relations with the negro, had compelled some one of the men to have something to do with them."[23] A former slave likewise told Hinton about his experiences with his forty-year-old widowed mistress. The man, who had been "brought up in the family," said he had "never had anything to do with his mistress until after her husband died," but that almost a year into her widowhood, the woman "ordered him to sleep with her, and he did regularly."[24]

A black underground railroad agent named Captain Matthews told Hinton about another black man who relayed that "a young girl got him out in the woods and told him she would declare he attempted to force her, if he didn't have connection with her." The black steward, Patrick Miner, told Hinton "several cases of the same kind."[25] Although the class status of the women in these last incidents remained unspecified, poorer white women might not have attempted such a threat. Those who held authority in antebellum southern communities were likely to consider white women outside the planter classes to be the depraved agents of their illicit liaisons with black men.[26] White women of the planter classes, however, were protected by an ideology of white female virtue. Redpath asked one black man who had spoken of sexual liaisons with planter-class women: "'Do you dare to make advances?'" to which the man answered, "'No, we know too much for that.'" Of the white daughters on the Missouri frontier, Hinton said: "It was a great deal safer for them to have one of these colored fellows than a white man."[27] This point was corroborated by one of Redpath's informants, who pointed out: "'If I have connection with a white girl she knows that if she takes precautions she is safe, for if I should tell I should be murdered by her father, her brother, or herself.'"[28]

During Hinton's testimony, one of the commissioners prompted him: "But the consequences are terrible to the negro if found out?" When Hinton agreed, the commissioner asked: "What are the consequences to the woman if found out?" to which Hinton replied: "They generally brush it up."[29] This testimony is supported by an antebellum North Carolina case in which a white woman had local justices of the peace record an oath that the father of her bastard child was white, when many people knew that the father had been one of the family's slaves.[30] Planter-class white women were also more likely to have access to effective birth control, as indicated by the words of Redpath's informant about taking precautions. The black man who had been ordered to sleep with his widowed mistress told Hinton that the woman had "procured some of those French articles, that are used to prevent the consequences of sexual intercourse," a reference to condoms.[31] Another black man had told Redpath that white women (of more well-to-do families) and black men had sex "because the thing can be so easily concealed. The woman has only to avoid being impregnated, and it is all safe."[32] While dominant ideas about the depravity of poorer white women could in fact serve to override blame for black men with whom those women entered into sexual liaisons, it was both more dangerous for black men to consort with planter-class white women and more dangerous for them to resist sexual coercion by those women.

Questions about agency and consent are difficult to untangle in a slave society. If a coerced slave man complied with a white woman, that compliance was in some measure strategic; and just as some black women chose to risk fending off white men, some black men who were propositioned also chose to risk refusal.[33] At the same time, the wartime testimony before the AFIC points to well-guarded circles of black men, both free and slave, as one arena in which black men expressed defiance about sex with white women. Recall the words of the steamboat steward Patrick Miner, who said that black men who worked on the Mississippi River shared information among themselves about the desires of certain white women to "sleep with them." Recall Redpath's words about his informants, who were slaves in the 1850s: "I have often heard them talking and laughing about the numerous cases that have occurred in which white women have had colored children." Even if Hinton and Redpath were exaggerating their roles as insiders, there is no reason to doubt that black men traded information and laughed together about their defiance of law and taboo.

Moreover, the possibility of men like Hinton and Redpath having fabricated their testimony before the AFIC is contradicted by more direct, if rarer, records of black voices. In her 1861 autobiography, for example, fugitive slave Harriet Jacobs wrote of planters' daughters: "They know that the women slaves are subject to their father's authority in all things; and in some cases they exercise the same authority over the men slaves. I have myself seen the master of such a household whose head was bowed down in shame; for it was known in the neighborhood that his daughter had selected one of the meanest slaves on his plantation to be the father of his first grandchild." Jacobs pointed out that this white woman "did not make her advances to her equals, nor even to her father's more intelligent servants." Rather, this woman "selected the most brutalized, over whom her authority could be exercised with less fear of exposure."[34] Just after the war, the black press in the South made reference to coercion by white women. An 1866 essay in the Augusta, Georgia, *Colored American* noted that white men feared that white women would marry newly freed black men, and added that the white man "seems to be afraid that some of his daughters may do what a good many of his sons and himself have done time and again."[35] If there were such a thing as a consensual sexual relationship between a black man, either slave or free, and a white woman, black men talking to white abolitionists like Hinton and Redpath may have crafted their narratives as stories of coercion in order to present themselves as innocent participants in such legal and social transgressions. Yet stories of reluctance and resistance, even if crafted for white ears, would not have been fabricated out of imagination alone; rather, their tellers would be drawing upon dynamics that they knew to exist between white women and black men.[36] Although we have no way of knowing how common or uncommon were scenarios such as those the black men described to Hinton and Redpath, their words uncover a ground of coercion in the slave South that lurked as a possibility regardless of how often it was acted upon.

While dominant white southern ideology about female sexuality exempted planter-class women from convictions of depravity, northerners were less convinced of this distinction among the white women of the South. The theme of profligacy among white southerners of all classes was common in northern anti-slavery thought, and Hinton and other witnesses before the AFIC unmistakably drew upon this tradition in their wartime testimony.[37] Hinton's portrayal of all southern white women was one of total licentiousness. "The complete demoralization of the South is astonishing," he told the commissioners. "I have seen white women who call themselves ladies, stand on the street and call minor officers, as they were passing by, 'sons of bitches,' 'God damn' them, and use all such phrases; and I have never been to any locality where the officers and men, who were so disposed, did not sleep with all the women around."[38]

Another white northern man described the white men and women of the Gulf States, saying that "a more degraded, profligate, ignorant and sinful race cannot easily be imagined."[39] In one printed report, commissioner Samuel Howe wrote: "[I]t is certain that the inevitable tendency of American slavery is not only to bring about promiscuous intercourse among the blacks, and between black women and white men, but also to involve white women in the general depravity, and to lower the standard of female purity." Howe continued: "The subject is repulsive, but whoever examines critically the evidence of the social conditions of the Slave States, sees that the vaunted superior virtue of the Southern women is mere boast and sham."[40] (White southerners, for their part, counter-accused northern white women of promiscuity, fastening particularly upon those who came South to teach in the freedpeople's schools. One southern white man wrote in 1864 about "Yankee 'School marms' who philanthropically miscegenate as well as teach," noting sarcastically "the prolific birth of mongrel babies by these worthy school mistresses."[41])

The wartime testimony also indicates that black convictions about the sexuality of southern white women were in accord with those of white northerners. The sentiments of a black man who had fled the South for Canada were likely shared by others; the town's white mayor reported to the wartime commission: "A colored man ran away with a white girl, and a colored man, speaking of the affair, said 'I always looked upon him as a respectable man. I didn't think he would fall so low as to marry a white girl.'"[42] Even approval on the part of black communities indicates black convictions of the depraved nature of white women. A black bishop from the British Methodist Episcopal Church, who had also left the South for Canada, told the commissioners that when a white woman and a black man got married, "If the man is an upright man, and the woman an upright woman, they treat them as if they were both colored." This man also mentioned two white women married to black men who were both accorded as much respect as "any black woman."[43]

White ideologies about black male sexuality in the slave South were far from straightforward. Black men had been accused and convicted of raping white women, in the context of a racist legal system, since the colonial era, and the castration and lynching of black men for the alleged sexual assault of white women was not unknown in either the antebellum or wartime South.[44] On the other hand, while whites feared slave uprisings during the Civil War, no great tide of sexual alarm engulfed white southerners as white men left white women at home with slave men. One white schoolteacher, for example, wrote in her Tennessee diary about a group of armed black men who were being mustered out of service. "If these corrupted negroes are to be turned loose among us," she commented in a manner that can hardly be characterized as terrified, "I do not know what will follow, but evidently no great amount of good."[45] If anything, white women left alone were inclined to see white Yankee soldiers as sexually threatening.[46]

The wartime testimony indicates as well that white northerners were ambivalent about black male sexuality. Richard Hinton both invoked and contradicted the idea of black men as especially sexual; at the same time that he accepted the idea of black male sexual ardor, Hinton also presented black men as reluctant to comply with the sexual aggressions of white women. When Hinton spoke about the white woman who took a black man into the

woods and threatened to cry rape if he didn't have sex with her,
one of the commissioners commented: "He didn't need much
persuasion, did he?" Hinton answered: "I have generally found
that, unless the woman has treated them kindly, and won their
confidence, they have to be threatened, or have their passions
roused by actual contact, which a woman who goes as far as that
would not hesitate to give." Elsewhere, however, Hinton sustained white ideas about black male potency. For example, he
concluded the story of the Missouri frontier daughters who
wished to "give loose to their passions" by saying, "and I suppose,
as the negro is very strongly amative, that the gratification of
passion would be greater with them than with a white man."[47]

In the end, the American Freedmen's Inquiry Commission
kept the testimony they had heard about sex between white
women and black men a secret from the Secretary of War and
from Congress. Hinton's testimony had covered thirty-two pages,
with the information on white women and black men occupying
the last six of those pages. On the cover sheet, someone had
penciled: "This paper can be printed as far as this mark x on page
27. The remaining portion should be suppressed." The "x"
marked Hinton's disclosure about sex between white women and
black men.[48] Neither of the two major reports printed by the
AFIC addressed the subject of sex between white women and
black men. The commission clearly judged it too detrimental to
let the Secretary of War and Congress, or any other readers,
believe that emancipation would bring sex between white women
and black men in its wake, especially if such liaisons could not be
written off as the province of the poorer classes of white women.

Ultimately, it was the conflation of politics and sex in the minds
of white southerners that would generate so much of the
Reconstruction-era violence in the South. With the demise of
slavery, the separation of black and white became essential to
white southerners who wished to retain racial supremacy. Thus
did sex across the color line become a much more severe taboo
than it had ever been before. Because it was the men among the
former slave population who gained political power, and therefore had the potential to destroy the racial caste system, southern
whites focused on the taboo of sex between white women and
black men with a new urgency. Sexual transgressions in the form

of liaisons between white women and black men that had previously been the province of local communities and courts took on national political dimensions after the war.[49] In testimony about the Ku Klux Klan taken before Congress in 1871, white southerners often charged black men with illicit sexual conduct toward or with white women alongside charges of Republican activism or successful crops, that is for political or economic independence.[50]

To separate politics and sexuality at this moment in the history of the American South would be to define politics far too narrowly. When a congressional investigating committee asked a North Carolina Klansman about the purpose of his organization, the man said: "It was to keep down the colored un's from mixing with the whites." And by what means would this be accomplished? "To keep them from marrying, and to keep them from voting," he answered.[51] Another white North Carolina man said: "[T]he common white people of the country are at times very much enraged against the negro population. They think that this universal political and civil equality will finally bring about social equality." He added: "[T]here are already instances . . . in which poor white girls are having negro children."[52] After the war, then, with the determination of white southerners to retain dominance through the construction of a rigid color line, whites conflated the new political power of black men with sexual transgressions against white women.

While white ideology about the hypersexuality of all black men developed swiftly from emancipation forward, the twin ideology about the purity of all white women never took on the same ironclad quality. Rather, class distinctions in white ideology about white female sexuality remained.[53] The reputation and character of white women was constantly assessed by white southerners in the 1871 congressional testimony about the Klan, and the investigating committee participated in this discourse, with both sides identifying white female transgressors as "low-down," as "tramps," and as women of "bad character."[54] The sexual coercion of black men by white women was in fact still understood to be a possibility. In the narrative of freedman Henry Lowther, who survived castration by Klansmen, one white witness said that the white woman with whom Lowther was accused of consorting had followed Lowther into the woods and "solicited him to have intercourse with her." Of this woman, a white judge remarked, "the inference I drew was that she was a very bad, abandoned character."[55] White women judged by Klansmen to be lacking in virtue were, like black women, also subject to abuse ranging from insulting language to rape and sexual mutilation.[56]

The wartime dialogues on sex between white women and black men got no farther than a government commission composed of three white, northern, abolitionist men. Yet the voices of black men recorded therein now serve to better illuminate both the nature of sexual liaisons between white women and black men in the slave South, and white ideologies of sexuality in the crucial transitional period of war and emancipation. At the same time, the wartime suppression of the testimony, along with southern whites' conflation of black male political power and black male sexuality, indicate how sex between white women and black men came to be a deeply political issue connected directly to the maintenance of racial hierarchy from emancipation forward.

PART V

xxxxxxxxxxxxxxxxxxxxxxxx

The Northern Homefront

*T*he Confederacy had no monopoly on patriotism as the outpouring of Union support demonstrated in the weeks and months following Fort Sumter. Even though their construction of war's necessity may have been a fiction, secessionists portrayed their military mobilization as a means of defending their homeland against Yankee invasion. Making the protection of family and household the cause of war rather than slavery was a brilliant tactical stroke.

Yankee invaders, meanwhile, took the high ground of claiming they were only protecting their "home"—the Union divided by Confederate spoilers. Preserving the Union became a noble, exalted role which could be shared by both men and women in their appropriate spheres.

Following the celebratory glorification of the separation of spheres—while manly men marched off to war and womanly women tended the home fires—was the breakdown of rigid gender categories and sexual barriers brought about by wartime necessity. Women patriots in both regions, but especially northern females, seized the moment by challenging and even temporarily suspending gender privilege which excluded women's labor from calculations of productivity. Warwork, as Jeanie Attie demonstrates, was a key component of women's strategy to reconfigure their roles within society, and perhaps the restored Union. She focuses on the small but significant group of northern women who exploited this opportunity. However, the vast majority of northern women—even women participating in mobilization—took a more traditional view.

Hundreds of thousands of women, in sewing circles, wrapping bandages, or selling homemade goods at local sanitary fairs, contrib-

*uted to the Union cause with their sex-segregated labor. Their patrio-
tism was vibrant and valuable, yet provided little challenge to women's
confinement to the domestic sphere. Certainly, many wives and mothers
saw their duties to be like those of Penelope—waiting at home for
wandering heroes to return, patiently tending the hearth. They were
willing helpmeets, but they also believed their greatest influence might
be that of restraint: Clara Barton, the founder of the American Red
Cross, characterized her role as the "bit in the mouth, the curb on the
neck of the war horse."*

*The majority of female kin, deprived of sons and husbands, fathers
and brothers, viewed war as a personal crucible. Families were not only
denied income and supplies, but threatened with permanent destruction
by the black-bordered notice sent home to loved ones to announce a
soldier's death. As battles dragged on and losses mounted, families
required some better explanation, to help cope with the relentless ordeal
of burying sons rather than harvesting crops. Maintaining morale was
crucial to the Union cause. Women should not see themselves merely as
instruments of restraint, but as active partners in the cause of saving
the Union.*

*So, again like Penelope, they used their personal resources and wove
and unwove conventional views into a patchwork ideology which
refashioned notions of gender and the Union. Many female patriots
cleverly outwitted males confining them to their sphere. Women transformed personal deprivations into acts of political sacrifice: tributes to
the state which must be acknowledged and, as Jeanie Attie demonstrates, repaid. Their roles on the homefront were not token in their
significance, but crucial to supplying the war machine with necessary
goods and services. These domestic talents translated into public good
and women sought recognition.*

*The impact of these changes can be decoded from a variety of sources.
None has been more richly mined in the antebellum era than northern
writers and their works, especially those berated by Hawthorne as
"damned scribbling women." Literary themes reflected a decline of
sentimental values as the reality of war engulfed the nation. As a result,
northerners' dwindling support undermined the Union government's
efforts.*

*There was no more visible and violent evidence of public disaffection
than the New York City draft riots in July 1863. Journalists noted the
large number of women participating in the rampage which left over a*

hundred dead and more than three hundred injured during the several days of urban unrest. Women joined male rioters to protest the exploitation of those at the bottom of the economic ladder: those without resources to buy a substitute when drafted. By 1863 even the moral imperative of emancipation seemed a feeble rationale for many whites—measured against the prolonged loss of life and economic deprivation suffered in northern towns, especially by the immigrant poor.

Circumstances had forced President Lincoln to declare a preliminary Emancipation Proclamation in September 1862. Urged on by abolitionists such as Harriet Beecher Stowe, Lincoln hoped to turn the war into a battle against slavery as well as a means to preserve the crumbling Union. Stowe saw the war not only as a battle over the status of slaves, which it had become, but also as a vehicle for transforming her literary reputation and career. Patricia Hill chronicles the more problematic questions of the antislavery elites in wartime as well as Stowe's personal relationship to the crisis of Union.

Men and women shared burdens in wartime, but on the homefront females found themselves disproportionately burdened. Soldiers marched off to war—and it has been estimated all but 400 were male, this small number representing wives and sweethearts disguised as men, as well as solo female cross-dressers. Women were expected to stay at home. If found at the front, they were assumed to be the cooks and laundresses who made up the servant class—or worse, treated as prostitutes. Male kin fought and died—more in camps than battle as two out of three soldiers were felled by disease—while women tended to morale, supplies, and survival behind the lines.

Women's tasks were crucial to victory, but their roles have been minimized by scholars. Reassessment of the critical role played by those on the homefront will lay the foundation for a new ideological interpretation, one that incorporates women's complex roles and central contributions that led to Union victory.

Chapter 14

XXXXXXXXXXXXXXXXXXXXXXXX

Warwork and the Crisis of Domesticity in the North

JEANIE ATTIE

Wars appear naturally gendered. Nationalist discourse invariably extolls masculine attributes of aggressiveness, courage, and strength while it lauds female qualities of forbearance, generosity, and sacrifice. Feuding nations frequently draw on ideal categories of masculinity and femininity to bolster their own self-image and denigrate their opponents; gender imagery provides a means for emphasizing dominant and subordinate positions. Gendered military discourse also permeates relations within a nation, demarcating warfronts as masculine and homefronts as feminine. Patriotic propaganda sanctions existing patterns of gender relations, calling on men and women to assume gender-appropriate roles to further nationalist objectives.[1]

Yet in the process of constructing a unified position, nationalistic movements often reveal tensions inherent in established divisions of power. Such was the case during the American Civil War. Northern war mobilization, which depended so heavily on voluntary participation of citizens and markets,[2] exposed the power inequities created by the reorganization of labor under capitalism, among them the division between labor and capital. The transformation of production was also accompanied by a new ideology for the sexual division of labor, one which separated women and men into arenas of home and work, of sentiment and value. The antebellum ideology of domesticity, a construction that obscured the economic significance of unpaid household labor as it also romanticized women's lives, provided a means of mystifying the real nature of the creation of value.[3] Both before and during the war the rhetoric of Unionism masked a gender system that divided a supposedly unified political community between male citizens and female dependents. But just as class divisions were exacerbated by inequitable demands for military manpower,[4] so the gender polarization of northern society was aggravated under the pressure of defining the sacrifices required to support a war.

In the course of *warwork*—the voluntary contribution of homemade goods to the Union Army—northern women undermined assumptions about female household labor and challenged the gendered nature of Civil War nationalism. In an attempt to clarify their relationship both to the market and to the state, they raised the issue of accountability; if they were to produce household and hospital goods for the war effort, they would require assurance that their labor was not wasted or squandered. As the war progressed, women voiced increasing concerns about the legitimacy of the demands being placed upon them. They made clear that they would not assume the welfare demands of an army if the responsibilities were deemed excessive, if they overlapped with those of the federal government, or if they were removed from local control. As unpaid household labor became politicized and public, thousands of women grasped the opportunity to elucidate the nature of their work.

The escalation of military demands and the length of the war even constrained some of those in power to acknowledge that women's work was of more than emotional importance, that it constituted more than a leisure activity and filled real economic and political needs. The war chipped away at the ideology of domesticity. Though the critique of the economic devaluation of women's unpaid household labor would be muffled by war's end, the antebellum ideology of gender spheres faced one of its first crises.

Homefront support of the army was founded on a broad-based voluntary mobilization of local resources. At the outbreak of the military conflict the federal government possessed neither the fiscal ability nor the administrative manpower required to raise and outfit a national army.[5] Before the Lincoln administration had sufficiently expanded to meet the demands of coordinating money, men, and supplies, the task of recruiting and supplying Union troops fell to local governments and private citizens.[6] As men hastened to volunteer for the military, women organized spontaneously and in response to public demands to redirect their household skills toward outfitting departing troops.

As northerners hastened to raise a citizen army and revel in displays of patriotism, many northeastern elites viewed popular mobilization with a combination of awe and concern. In dismay, they watched an ill-prepared federal government stand by as Americans rushed to organize themselves in a haphazard, autonomous fashion. Such behavior not only accentuated the fragmented political structure they lamented, it risked damaging the war effort. At the same time, however, they viewed in civilian mobilization a chance to redirect a groundswell of patriotic sentiments into something more enduring.

In the spring of 1861 a group of New York-based ministers, physicians, and professionals founded the United States Sanitary Commission (USSC), a private war-relief agency dedicated to offering advice to the government and systematizing homefront benevolence on behalf of the Union army.[7] Ostensibly created to meet the medical and supply needs of the Army, the Commission represented a novel challenge to established patterns of social welfare. In its ambitious scheme for mobilizing the female homefront into a disciplined entity, ready to answer any and all demands for hospital supplies, the USSC did not repudiate voluntarism; indeed, it called for greater discretionary efforts on the part of the public. But it proposed to remove from donors control over the destination and uses of their gifts.[8]

Apart from the belief that the war emergency demanded social coordination on an entirely new level, the Commission leadership viewed conventional patterns of community organization as symptomatic of the decentralized polity which impeded their vision of national progress. Along with other Republican leaders, liberal Protestants, professionals, and merchants, Sanitary officers espoused a novel version of nationalist thought. Their nationalism formed part of an urban ideology which, at midcentury, was in the process of reconceptualizing class relationships and political power. They understood the requirements of a "viable" nation to include not only elements of unity and size, issues clearly at stake in the war, but also the capacity for economic growth and cultural cohesion.[9] In galvanizing public support for the Union, this self-conscious nationalist vanguard glimpsed the possibility of building both a powerful state and an abiding patriotism.

By harnessing the voluntary relief efforts of northern women to effect major changes in military conditions, the Commissioners hoped to guide the public in the peaceful and voluntary transfer of loyalties from local to national institutions. The key, as they so often stated, was to provide a political education to the people. "I have had the impression," Commission president Henry Bellows confided to Frederick Law Olmsted, its general secretary, "that the telling of the History of the Sanitary Commission would afford one of the best themes for political instruction to the people, ever afforded anyone."[10]

Indeed, it was possible that the Commissioners considered the actual donations of homefront women as insignificant in the winning of the war; those contributions would pale against the supplies ultimately acquired from war contractors. In a public letter to women in 1862, Olmsted explained that the purpose of organizing aid societies was for "keeping love of the Union alive through healthy, social contact, expression, and labor."[11] For Sanitary leaders, the crucial component supplied by the women was the *process* of their participation in what Bellows termed "the national life." It was only after the war that Bellows admitted the agenda which propelled the organization. "The Sanitary Commission was not from its inception a merely humanitarian or beneficient association," he acknowledged.

> It necessarily took on that appearance, and its life depended upon its effective work as an almoner of the homes of the land to fathers, brothers and sons in the field. But its projectors were men with strong political purpose, induced to take this means of giving expression to their solicitude for the national life, by discovering that the people of the country had a very much higher sense of the value of the Union . . . than most of the politicians of the States . . . seemed to recognize; that the women of America had at least half of its patriotism in their keeping.[12]

Bellows's remark about the fractured nature of Civil War patriotism pointed to the way in which most northern elites approached the question of women's patriotic duties. The massive voluntary mobilization of resources and manpower reinforced the cultural definition of femininity shaped in antebellum society. Throughout the war, women encountered the dominant version of female patriotism from politicians, newspapers, pulpits, and Sanitary publications. An elaboration on the ideology of bourgeois womanhood, female patriotism placed economic voluntarism at the heart of women's participation in defense of the nation.

Despite the extensive character of antebellum female charitable work, midcentury Americans approached the issue of female voluntarism as a question of sentiment rather than exertion.[13] Jeanne Boydston has persuasively argued that the nineteenth-century ideology of separate spheres provided the rationale for a process that differentiated labor and the household, equating the former with wages and the latter with leisure. Unpaid household work was the antithesis of real labor, embodying "natural" capacities of women rather than productive work. In a society increasingly oriented to the market, wage labor, and the cash nexus, the economic value of women's household work was all but invisible.[14]

The Civil War version of female patriotism proved to be another means for mystifying women's labor, bathing it in an aura of sentiment, calling it love and not work. War reconstituted household labor as non-labor, natural and emotional. Employing the essentialist concepts of the domesticity ideology, the gendered construction of nationalism considered female war benevolence a natural extension of their prescribed status, even of their femaleness. In time of national crisis, it provided a place for women in public life while at the same time safeguarding the gender hierarchy of northern society.

Just as the war and the language of nationalism temporarily obscured the problems raised by the spread of wage labor, subordinating them to the struggle against slavery, so they also escalated the capacity of men to exercise authority and economic control over female labor, moving from simply claiming ownership of such labor in the home to claiming hegemony over it for the nation. While men were never expected to support the Union for free, either as soldiers or as Sanitary Commission officers and agents, women, whether the upper-class leaders of Sanitary branches or the poor and middle-class members of the vast female public, were expected to demonstrate their loyalty through sacrifices of labor.

Women's inclination for voluntary labor was deemed so natural that the extent of their wartime involvement surprised no one. Writing the official history of the Commission, Charles Stillè remarked that the "earliest movement that was made for army relief began, as it is hardly necessary to say, by the women of the country." Assuming women's entrance into wartime activities reflected their heightened moral empathy more than a real political sentiment, Henry Bellows explained their achievements in 1867 by noting: "The women were clearer and more united than the men, because their moral feelings and political instincts were not so much affected by selfishness and business, or party considerations."[15]

When, in the middle of the war, nationalist activists worried that northern women might be losing heart in the face of growing demands for their labor, they stepped up a propaganda campaign that reiterated the assumptions inherent in female patriotism. A pamphlet, published by the New York Loyal Publication Society and written by an anonymous woman, tackled the question of gender and patriotism by defending the ladylike sacrifices performed by northern women against the cruder actions of their southern counterparts. Cataloguing rumors about Confederate women who were said to torment wounded Union soldiers, poison food and water, and even engage in acts of torture, the author reminded her audience that, "According to our Northern creed when a woman ceases to be a woman, she becomes nothing, or worse than nothing." Underscoring the notion that women's voluntarism was a product of their leisured status, she admonished them to continue to labor for soldiers in need: "Let us abridge our luxuries for their sakes; let us give them of our leisure."[16]

While women received a consistent message about the differences between male and female patriotism, many failed to concur. The war provoked fervent interest in political and military issues and led many women to articulate a sharper consciousness of national affairs. Maria Lydig Daly, an upper-class New Yorker, observed that the firing on Fort Sumter "united all the North. . . . All feel that our very nationality is at stake."[17] Explaining to a friend living abroad the mood in New York in May of 1861, Jane Stuart Woolsey declined to offer her own political viewpoints but added, "Not, in passing, that I haven't any! We all have views now, men, women and little boys."[18] After receiving numerous letters from New York State women during the first weeks of the war, the feminist paper *The Mayflower* commented that "nearly every letter we receive breathes a spirit of deep feeling upon the war question." The editorial added that among women, "There seems to be little disposition to think, speak, read or write of anything else."[19] Even the corresponding secretary of the Commission, Alfred Bloor, observed about women that, "They can not fight, but nevertheless they like to feel that they, as well as the men, are of some importance to the State."[20]

Women's passionate interest in the course of the war and the politics that drove it left many of them skeptical and resentful about the representations of their distinct nationalism and weak political consciousness. Some insisted on equality with male patriotism by defining their own in decidedly "masculine" terms. Given the limitations imposed by the reigning definition of female patriotism, it is not surprising that some women wished they could be men. At the outbreak of the war, Louisa May Alcott confided in her diary: "I long to be a man; but as I can't fight, I will content myself with working for those who can."[21] Others appropriated masculine forms of expression, such as the group of women from Skowhegan, Maine, who used local artillery to stage "a salute of thirty-four guns." Maria Daly was surprised to hear elite women "admiring swords, pistols, etc., and seeming to wish to hear of the death of Southerners." Finally, there were the famous cases—estimated at a minimum of four hundred—of women who disguised themselves as men and joined the Union army.[22]

In an almost pointed rejection of the dominant version of female patriotism, women who published wartime memoirs frequently stressed the parity between their loyalties and those of

men. Sarah Henshaw remembered that as men from the North-
west went to the front, the women remained "filled with a like
patriotism." Explaining her decision to volunteer as a nurse in
military hospitals, Sophronia Bucklin drew the inevitable comparison to male and female behavior: "The same patriotism
which took the young and brave from workshop and plow, from
counting-rooms, and college halls . . . lent also to our hearts its
thrilling measure."[23]

Denied masculine means of political expression, women everywhere turned to public, symbolic ways of demonstrating their
nationalism. Through homemade products, military rallies, village parades, flag raisings, and fairs, women devised a visible
national identity. In the process, they expressed a sense of difference, basing it explicitly on the sexual division of labor, while
dramatizing the distinctiveness of women's labor. In voluntary
acts women demonstrated a willingness to contribute labor for
political purposes when those purposes were akin to their own,
and the labor remained under their control.

Beyond the autonomous patriotic culture created by women,
however, was the patriotic work which they were expected to
supply. Here the conflict would develop. Among the Sanitary
Commission's first directives to the female homefront was a call to
form a soldiers' aid society, answerable to the Commission, in
every village and city in the North. To justify such a sweeping
strategy, the Commission propagated the story that countless
local aid societies, organized immediately after the outbreak of
the conflict, were creating chaos by shipping immense quantities
of army goods whenever and wherever they pleased.[24] Expecting
to be able to draw on female voluntary labor at will, Bellows
expressed confidence that "the good women of the country would
need only to see with their own eyes what is called comfort in the
camp, to have their tender hearts moved to increased generosity."[25] The Commissioners proclaimed "entire confidence in
the good sense, the patriotism and the charitable instincts of their
fellow-citizens."[26]

Yet from the moment the Commission undertook supply work,
news from the homefront poured into both national headquarters and branch offices detailing the limits of female voluntarism.

Women wrote unsolicited letters as well as answers to personal inquiries and, later, formal questionnaires. The extensive correspondence revealed major difficulties in fostering sustained, voluntary labor for national purposes, and challenged assumptions about the instinctiveness of household and charitable labors. Correspondents complained about the lack of economic resources, conflicting personal and family responsibilities, and skepticism about the Commission's promise to provide fair distribution of homefront gifts. Sarah Bradford of Geneva, New York, wrote that she had to resign as secretary of her local aid society "having many other cares & duties claiming my attention."[27] Women like Miss Denroche used the opportunity of corresponding with the Commission to delineate the realities of household labor, possibly to acquire recognition for the otherwise invisible efforts that defined their lives:

> I am shut in school from 8 1/2 untill 4 P.M. every day. I have all my own housekeeping to do and we have no baker here. . . . I have an acre and three quarters of land to take care of out of school and in winter all my wood to saw and split at least I had to do it until a week since I found it was injuring my health. . . . you must see I have not much leisure.[28]

Responding to continuous appeals to contribute to the war effort, women demanded acknowledgment of the hard realities of domestic labor.

Through warwork it became possible for many women to articulate a resistance to their secondary status and to expose, if only for a moment, the erroneous beliefs about female voluntarism. Throughout the war, women tried to make public the nature of their real economic contributions not only to the nation but to their families and local economies as well. They struggled to have their political aspirations included in public discourse and valued with those of men. In short, they resisted the male construction of a distinct and inferior female patriotism.

Those who led the organization could not fail to hear the message. Despite their patronizing testimony to women's instinctual patriotic feelings, it was clear that warwork was anything but innate or instinctual. Commissioner Bloor could write of women's "natural disposition to follow a lead," and yet his own experience of corresponding with regional representatives was fraught with problems. As he complained to his colleagues:

> I do not know whether you and others recognize how hard it is to carry on this correspondence, from week to week and month to month, and year to year with women—the good and the bad in them, always the more intense and unmanageable because they are women; how hard it is to smooth over difficulties—to hear over and over again the same complaints—to repeat over and over again the same thing made to look different in each case. . . .[29]

By early 1863, women's resistance to the Commission's centralized welfare plan, rooted in opposition to presumptions about their patriotism and their voluntarism, generated problems that were serious enough to threaten the entire undertaking. Opposition from the female public—evident by its growing criticism of the Commission plan, continued support of local regiments, and the shifting of its donations to the rival Christian Commission—produced a crisis from which the organization never fully recovered.

Evidence that prewar notions about social authority and the gendered definition of labor had weakened under the pressures of war were abundant. The persistent theme on the homefront was the fear of fraud. Throughout the North, women recounted stories of soldiers being forced to pay for donated supplies, of Sanitary agents lining their own pockets with the value of voluntary labor, and of Commissioners running a welfare agency for private gain. In the day-to-day experience of working with the organization, women questioned the legitimacy of urban elites' claims over their labor and over the welfare of a national army.

Charges of corruption and profiteering invariably targeted the Commission for misappropriating homemade donations. One woman related, "[A] return soldier says that *every thing* is *sold* by the Commission to the patients," and, as a result, the people in her town "positively *refuse* to contribute the least delicacy." Ophelia Wait reported that "the common people have the impression that every thing is converted into money, *even the lint and bandages are sold for paper rags.*" To some, these stories revealed the true purpose of the Commission. "Some think the Commission a speculation," disclosed Mrs. Dales of Bloomville, New York. People in Depeyester were "asserting it is a speculation," while those in Churchville called it "a swindling concern."[30]

By accusing the Commission of corruption, the female public articulated an opposing construction of political obligation that included an adherence to a rural-based version of Unionism. These women interpreted the behavior of the Commission as part of the larger centralizing—at times antidemocratic—actions of the federal government. The wartime acceleration of New York's role as the center of finance capital no doubt accentuated fears about the city as the source of economic lawlessness in the "age of shoddy." As Bloor reported back to his colleagues after canvassing the Northeast: "[T]he patriotic purposes of the Sanitary Commission were in reality an objection to it among these people."[31]

The experience of organizing supply work and observing the patriotic work which women accomplished nevertheless impressed the men who created the Commission. After the war many of them offered recognition of the value of household contributions and even interpreted female war participation as a step toward claiming rights to full citizenship. In 1867, Bellows argued that during the war women had learned to "despise frivolity, gossip, fashion and idleness" and, "thus, did more to advance the rights of woman by proving her gifts and her fitness for public duties, than a whole library of arguments and protests."[32]

A year after the war ended, Alfred Bloor, who had complained so melodramatically about his dealings with the female homefront, publicly concluded that women were instrumental in the organization's accomplishments. He wrote:

> The supplies, amounting in aggregate value to many millions of dollars—some fifteen millions I should name as a rough estimate . . . .—were almost univerally collected, assorted, despatched, and re-collected, re-assorted, and re-despatched, by women, representing with great impartiality, every grade of society in the Republic.[33]

The $15 million figure, repeated in numerous Commission documents, provides an interesting way of highlighting the paradox inherent in the Civil War ideology of female patriotism. The Sanitary Commission, having sought support from the female public, found itself accountable to that public and, in response to charges of corruption, was forced to demonstrate its integrity through careful bookkeeping. In order to quantify its presence at the homefront and its impact on the war front, the Commission had to equate women's household labor with monetary values. By noting the cash equivalent of female donations, the organization implicitly accepted the superior valuation of labor expressed in money terms; at the same time it acknowledged the ease with which society could place a cash value on women's household products.

Summoning women's labor by stressing its naturalness and invoking women's patriotism by alluding to its simplicity led Sanitary leaders into an intractable contradiction. They created a giant philanthropic operation, the very size of which stirred deep-rooted, republican fears about the inevitable corruption bred by concentrations of power. Assuming that domestic labor was not quantifiable and that women had little interest in accountability, the Commissioners set themselves up for accusations of fraud and embezzlement. When compelled to give a cash equivalent to homefront donations, they found themselves not only recognizing the value of unpaid labor, but even reversing established verities about women's political capacities. Based on the notion that women's nationalistic feelings were inexhaustible and naïve, the Commission experiment triggered a far-ranging critique of the centralizing impulses brought on by the war as well as the radical nationalism of urban elites.

For northern women, the process of fashioning an acceptable philosophy of political obligation led them to glimpse the possibilities of a more balanced gender system and the rudiments of female citizenship. Those individual women who found in war-work a desire for continued public service demonstrated an enduring resistance to ideas about separate spheres in the postwar years. As they carved out positions for themselves as leaders of charity organizations, these war-trained women discarded the language of sentimentality and disinterestedness in favor of a discourse that stressed social prerogative and organization.[34]

Though some postwar feminists would employ arguments

about women's natural moral superiority to advance their cause, the source of feminist strength after the Civil War came from the development of new social theories to justify equality between the sexes. A number of postwar feminists questioned not only the precepts of the domesticity ideology but belief in the idea that the state was a source of protection or justice. These women chose "science," not political theory, to construct a degendered alternative to liberal versions of political and economic authority, an alternative that stressed symmetry, cooperation, and what they termed "universal humanity."[35]

In their conflict with the Sanitary Commission, thousands of women crystallized their political sentiments for the Union and an alternative version of female patriotism. Their nationalistic feelings were equal to those of men, inspired by identical political concerns for the future of the nation. Their labor obligations to the state must be recognized as donations of labor—labor that created real value and constituted authentic assistance to the national cause. In the end, northern women implicitly challenged the tenets of the domesticity ideology by stripping away some of its sentimental veneer and rendering clearer its fictitious underpinnings.

Chapter 15

Writing Out the War:
Harriet Beecher Stowe's Averted Gaze

PATRICIA R. HILL

Harriet Beecher Stowe confided, in a letter to her family, that a stiff dose of brandy taken to quell a raging toothache caused her to sleep through the cannonade and bell ringing with which Boston greeted the end of slavery. "Strange," she commented, "that when the consummation of my life's desires was announced I should be lying vanquished by toothache."[1] Strange perhaps, but strangely consistent with her deliberate attempts to distract herself and her audience from the horrors of civil warfare by writing romantic fictions and by focusing upon the details of domesticity. The setting of this scene is also symbolically appropriate to my narrative of Stowe's war years. The home in which Stowe was ensconced (and passed out) was the residence of James T. Fields, editor of the *Atlantic Monthly* and husband to Harriet's beautiful young friend Annie, who served as the reigning muse of Boston's premier literary salon. Stowe then was literally positioned at the heart of New England's literary world while she slept through the official frenzy celebrating the demise of slavery. Her status as a privileged guest in this home reflects the changed sense of herself that was signaled by her abandoning the Congregationalist *Independent* as a political platform, and producing herself in the pages of the *Atlantic* as a leading light among America's literati and as a cultural critic.[2] Stowe, as a cultural critic, politicized the home when she argued her need to write (and her readers' need to read) material that would serve as an anodyne to war and would strengthen the home as the locus of "the things that remain."[3] The war, of course, stubbornly intruded, making its invasive presence felt at the domestic hearth. When that happened, Stowe disclaimed political intent, telling her editor that "an irresistible impulse *wrote for me*. . . . Many causes united at once to force on me this vision, from which generally I shrink."[4]

But if Stowe consciously strove to avert her gaze from the war, we must nevertheless refuse to accept this construction of her self as a shrinking violet. Stowe did, in the early months and years of the war, employ her public voice and presence to rebuke England's failure to support the Union and to pressure Lincoln into emancipating; privately she outfitted a son to do battle for her glorious cause. If she also spent those early days of the struggle finishing an Italian romance, we must look carefully at the ways her conception of fifteenth-century Italian politics comments on civil war. And if she simultaneously completed the nostalgic novel of Maine that can be said to have inaugurated the local color school, we must examine its comparison of family life North and South. However, the ideological content of those things that remain, as signifiers of the cultural and moral values that Stowe hoped would shape the future of the nation, can be found most fully articulated in the "House and Home Papers" and "The Chimney Corner" series which appeared in the *Atlantic* in the last years of the war. In these sketches Stowe spoke through a domesticated male narrator, thus positioning a man symbolically in the role she herself occupied literally as she oversaw the construction and decoration of a new family home and offered her troubled children moral, medical, and vocational advice in the midst of war. The vision from which Stowe tells us she shrank can be "read" as the subtext in both the private life and the public voice that insisted on the centrality of a politics of sentiment applying private feelings, "home" emotions, to public issues. This politics of sentiment required Stowe to re-present gender in her programme for transforming America into a genteel republic, and to re-present herself as a man of letters. Stowe's progress from antislavery crusader to cultural arbiter—her production of herself as an artist, encapsulated in her essay, "Sojourner Truth, the Libyan Sybil"—displays the mechanisms that operated to differentiate high culture from low. My "reading" in this essay of Stowe's separation of herself from "the folk" supplies a context for understanding the emergence of genteel reform during and after Reconstruction.

The outline of Stowe's wartime career hints at the nature of the transformations this essay explores. When war broke out in April 1861, Stowe was writing two novels. *The Pearl of Orr's Island* was being serialized in the *Independent*. The other, *Agnes of Sorrento,* promised to the *Atlantic* and to the English journal *Cornhill,* was begun in Italy the previous year. The difference between these forums is significant. The *Independent* was a Congregationalist antislavery newspaper which had served Stowe as a primary platform throughout the 1850s. The *Atlantic,* which Stowe had helped found, was aimed at an elite, "high culture" audience; indeed, it was instrumental in the process of differentiation between high and low, or mass, culture that was occurring in American society.[5] *Cornhill,* catering to the intellectual fashion for things Italian, was also scheduled to publish George Eliot's Italian novel, *Romola.* Stowe, recently returned from a European tour on which she had hobnobbed with expatriate Anglo-American artists and literati, preferred her Italian story to the New England novel that she had offered to the *Independent.* It is therefore not surprising that with the arrival of war, she decided to suspend writing *The Pearl of Orr's Island,* but to continue with *Agnes of Sorrento.* She substituted for weekly installments of the Maine novel some front-page columns commenting on political developments and urging a policy of emancipation. By late fall, she felt ready to resume writing her New England tale. From December through April of 1862 she devoted her professional energies to completing the two novels. The final installments of both appeared in April, and were produced as books in June.

In August she was writing again for the *Independent.* She had also purchased land in Hartford and embarked on the project of building a Gothic mansion to provide a suitable home in which to reciprocate the hospitality of her well-to-do friends. In November, she traveled to Washington to assure herself that Lincoln meant to go through with the Emancipation Proclamation; apparently reassured by her conference with the President, she produced for January publication in the *Atlantic* her major wartime statement, "A Reply to 'The Affectionate and Christian Address of Many Thousands of Women of Great Britain and Ireland to Their Sisters, the Women of the United States of America.'" Although saddened by her father's death that winter and preoccupied with house plans, Stowe found the energy to write a sketch of Sojourner Truth for the April *Atlantic*. Summer brought the trauma of having her son Fred wounded at Gettysburg. In the fall, while overseeing construction of the Hartford house, Stowe began writing her "House and Home Papers" for the *Atlantic*. She also arranged Fred's discharge from the army, and brought him home a confirmed alcoholic. Stowe initially comtemplated supplying a new novel to the *Atlantic* in 1865, but instead extended her series of domestic essays under the rubric "The Chimney Corner." Her New Year's piece for 1865 was an anomaly in that it focused directly on the war—or seemed to until it turned to a discussion of religious sisterhoods devoted to rescuing prostitutes. With the war's end and Lincoln's assassination, Stowe was stirred to write for the *Atlantic* one other overtly political piece, "The Noble Army of Martyrs."

In this welter of wartime activity two patterns of change emerge: in her private life Stowe is negotiating a move up the social ladder, and professionally she is engaged in producing her self as artist and arbiter of taste rather than as antislavery advocate and preacher manqué. Because she—like many other abolitionists—chose to interpret the Emancipation Proclamation as signaling an inevitable end to slavery, she was freed from her commitment to antislavery activity.[6] Yet she retained her posture as a public moralist in the *Atlantic* series that made her family's private life public property—or at least a commodity marketed to an elite audience. The genteel bourgeois family in these essays becomes an end rather than a rhetorical means for indicting the slave system. *Uncle Tom's Cabin* depended upon a maternal ideology that decried the destruction of families and located salvation in feminine values if not always in a mother-savior figure.[7] This maternal politics was reconstituted in the war years as an ideology of sentiment that came to depend upon drawing men into the family circle. As Stowe engaged upon this project of defining the emerging culture of gentility, she simultaneously displayed a self-consciousness in claiming for herself the role of artist and man of letters—a role that had been much less apparent, if not entirely absent, in her antislavery fictions.

The transition was already emerging in *The Pearl of Orr's Island,* which subtly responds to the war but also clearly reflects the cultural sophistication that Stowe was wont to claim after her European tours. The novel offers a heroine who is an artist as well as a female savior, although her art is limited to flower paintings. The first half, completed before the war, is pure local color and is focused on childhood. The second half offers a distanced comment on the war by attributing the wildness in the hero's character to his antecedents in slaveholding Florida and Spanish Cuba. His salvation lies in his having been shipwrecked and orphaned on the coast of Maine where a proper family life and true religion are available. More significant, Stowe's use of Shakespeare's *Tempest* as a model shows Stowe's estimation of herself as an artist. *The Pearl of Orr's Island* deliberately plays off *The Tempest,* incorporating it into the text as a fundamental element in the child Mara's imaginative world. Mara thinks of her relationship to the shipwrecked Moses as duplicating that between Miranda and Ferdinand. The magical effects Stowe so much admired in Shakespeare are ones she tries to replicate in this novel. She clearly hopes her own shrewd analysis of human nature will match Shakespeare's searching exploration of the human soul. She has finally the temerity to hint that her fiction is superior to Shakespeare's. In one respect at least, she felt her story surpassed Shakespeare's tale; she had replaced the romance plot with a Christian plot. To drive home her message, Stowe interrupts the narrative just after Mara has reconciled herself to approaching death to argue for the superiority of her narrative to the ordinary romance.

> There are no doubt many, who have followed this history so long as it danced like a gay little boat over sunny waters, and who would have followed it gayly to the end, had it closed with ringing of marriage-bells, who turn from it indignantly, when they see that its course runs through the dark valley. This, they say, is an imposition—a trick upon our feelings. We want to read only stories which end in joy and prosperity.

But have we then settled it in our own mind that there is no such
thing as a fortunate issue in a history which does not terminate in
the way of earthly success and good fortune? Are we Christian or
heathen?[8]

Stowe's effort to resist the desires of the reader of sentimental
narratives, to impose her own theological reading that insisted
that Mara's death did not transform a comedy into a tragedy but
rather moved the narrative to a transcendent plane, may strike us
as futile when we remember that the novel's literary legacy has
been understood as the inauguration of a new school of regional
writing rather than as an effective religious polemic. It reveals,
nevertheless, in its deliberate confrontation of the Shakespearian
plot, just how seriously Stowe took herself as an artist. And *The
Tempest* is, not coincidentally, a play that explores the aftermath
of civil war, and produces a happy resolution of lingering hostilities. Stowe's own ending, suitable for a novel written in the midst
of the Civil War, urges the reader to become reconciled to salvific
death.

A similar salvific martyrdom figures in her Italian novel. If
Agnes of Sorrento was begun as a romantic Italian idyll featuring
an orphaned heroine who is revealed to be the legitimate daughter of a prince, it took on darker tones of menace as the war
deepened. The corruption wrought by the Borgias in Rome
forms a central theme in the narrative. Savonarola emerges as a
northern (and proto-Protestant) reformer. The threat of civil war
to topple the Borgias is rendered in dark hints of exiled armies
assembling in France. The scenes of anguish among his followers
and the details of Savonarola's execution form a significant
portion of the tale. The happy ending, with banished families
restored, was no doubt reassuring to Stowe's northern audience
at a time when the war seemed to be going badly for the North.
True order and religion are restored. The final pages picture
Agnes as a sanctified princess of the house of Sarelli. Savonarola
emerges as a martyr triumphant whose lineaments Raphael has
placed in a grand salon in the Vatican, among the apostles and
saints, and whose "memory lingered long in Italy, so that it was
even claimed that miracles were wrought in his name and by his
intercession."[9] In this novel the romance plot is allowed to flour-

ish, because history had supplied Stowe with a martyr suitable to her theological and political ends.

When the war did intrude upon her consciousness, an assertion of the efficacy of martyrdom was Stowe's consistent response. It is the explicit "reading" of the war and its sacrifice of blood that she offered the women of England in her "Reply" when she wrote:

> Better a generation should die on the battle-field, that their children may grow up in liberty and justice. Yes, our sons must die, their sons must die. . . . [T]hey give their blood in expiation of this great sin, begun by you in England, perpetuated by us in America, and for which God in this great day of judgment is making inquisition in blood.[10]

The "Reply" constitutes a bitter rebuke of England for the inconstancy of its antislavery commitment.[11] It was a brilliant polemic; Nathaniel Hawthorne tendered his congratulations, saying, "If anything could make John Bull blush, I should think it might be that."[12] The argument designed to make England blush depended upon advancing the claim that the Emancipation Proclamation proved irrefutably that eliminating slavery was the fundamental issue in the conflict. Stowe's ingenious logic establishes this point, allowing her to proceed to express her disappointment in the half-million women of England who had signed an antislavery address to the women of America that had been delivered to Stowe in 1853. She cleverly quotes from their address, indicting them with their own words. But her greatest disappointment was not in the half-million but in the distinguished few, members of the evangelical aristocracy, with whom she had so eagerly cemented friendships during her trips abroad in the 1850s. These friendships played an important role in supplying Stowe with the social confidence necessary to participate fully in the definition of manners and morals for the maturing bourgeoisie in America. They were props she had depended upon not only in her antislavery crusade but in her campaign to play the part of a sophisticated woman of letters.

With the novels finished, and the matter of slavery settled in her mind, Stowe turned her attention to private matters. And these private matters became grist for her professional mill, supplanting the political columns she had earlier written for the

Independent. Stowe drew on her family affairs to supply a picture of the regenerated culture of evangelical gentility that her theology argued would characterize postwar America. The "House and Home Papers" supplied to the Atlantic offer advice on consumption; they delineate the material culture of genteel domesticity. And the narrative strategy she adopted produced her as a man of letters instructing his household circle. Christopher Crowfield, the middle-aged narrator of these sketches, was clearly understood by readers to be Stowe herself. The self-reflexive nature of Stowe's use of this thinly disguised persona was reinforced by the conceit of the sketches: Crowfield reads aloud to his family circle the sketch, drawn from their family life, that he proposes to submit to the *Atlantic*. Assuming the role of father to the Crowfield family also positioned Stowe as advisor to the rising generation (of girls—and their beaus). It allows her to negotiate between old and new manners and mores; for Stowe this means praising some aspects of life in New England in earlier generations while admitting the impossibility of returning to that mode. Similarly, as a sophisticated American traveler, s/he comments on European customs, differentiating between those that can be adapted to the American setting and those that are either impractical or positively inappropriate in a democracy. The voice Stowe modulates throughout the essays is one of moderation and common sense.

Since the primary subject of "House and Home Papers" is how to consume, it seems appropriate to offer a shopping list of topics covered: the moral economy of consumption (living within one's income); patriotic consumption (buying American); the display of taste and erudition rather than wealth (how to avoid the sins of the *nouveaux riches*); how to ensure health through domestic architecture (the importance of sunshine, fresh air, plants, and modern plumbing); how to entertain (a plea for familial warmth, simplicity in hospitality, rather than elaborate culinary productions beyond the skills of servants); solutions to the SERVANT PROBLEM in a democracy (homes without servants, cooperative laundries, bakeries and cookshops); and the moral uses of art in the home. Cumulatively the essays elaborate, for those who would live a life of cultivated gentility, a moral aesthetic of acquisition.[13]

In discussing such topics, what is the effect of having the authorial presence in drag? At one level, Stowe is using gender conventions to clothe herself with authority. Simultaneously, she implicates the bourgeois male in the domestic plot. The maternal ideology that informs *Uncle Tom's Cabin* has been abandoned for a familial paradise where marriage is a partnership, even though husband and wife retain gender-specific roles. The apparent conventionality of this vision makes possible the efforts at redefining gender in which Stowe engages. In the course of Crowfield family conversations, Stowe argues that women should vote, that they should be trained for and permitted to undertake any work for which they have a vocation. (She recommends especially medicine and architecture as fields to be thrown open to women.) Men, the essays suggest, should make their home life central to their existence. And while not all men could, like Crowfield, work in the home, the illustrative examples Crowfield employs of good and bad practices in domestic consumption show males only at home; their "work" is mentioned merely to indicate their income.

Stowe continued the Crowfield family circle in "The Chimney Corner" series. Having told her readers how to build and furnish their homes, how to entertain, and how to dress themselves, she devoted the new series to telling them how to live, pointing out common faults to be corrected in the interests of familial harmony. The war intruded on this second series once, as I have noted, when Stowe was writing the first number of 1865. The New Year's Day article shows her more insulated from the war than she had been when she still had a son on the battlefield. She is a spectator who gazes upon the grief war brought. Stowe, in her persona as a man of letters, considers herself a spectator authorized to hold out the consolations of martyrdom, the spiritual treasures—"peaceable fruits of righteousness"—that come from suffering and sorrow. With the military outcome no longer in doubt, Stowe's concerns focused on the future: "We, as individuals, as a nation, need to have faith in that AFTERWARDS."[14] Far from advocating faith without works, Stowe cites examples of work to be done, from service in hospitals to the education of freed slaves. But these are not all; she argues that

[W]ar shatters everything, and it is hard to say what in society will not need rebuilding and binding up and strengthening anew. Not the least of the evils of war are the vices which a great army engenders wherever it moves,—vices peculiar to military life, as others are peculiar to peace.[15]

The peculiar vice that preys on Stowe's mind is clearly prostitution. Lone women, forced to support themselves by selling their bodies, must be rescued. Shifting her reforming energies from slavery to prostitution was not such an anomalous move as it might appear. Sexual violation was the haunting specter that had made maternal ideology so effective in evoking the horrors of slavery. The threatened violation of the innocent female body is also a central dynamic in Stowe's novelistic condemnation of the Borgia regime in *Agnes of Sorrento*. Nor is Stowe alone in this shift to a focus upon prostitution. The pages of the *Atlantic* in the war years contain other fictions that urge the redemption of prostitutes and sympathetically consider the claims of free-love ideologues who compared loveless marriages to the degradation of prostitution and urged divorce reform.[16] In this they foreshadow the obsession with prostitution that preoccupied purity crusaders later in the century. Genteel domesticity required the affirmation of a new form of conjugal partnership, a reconfigured heterosexuality. Stowe, like other evangelical moral reformers (as well as, ironically, free-love advocates), focused on saving the unfortunate woman and firmly resisted the construction of male sexuality that classified prostitution as a necessary evil.[17] The politics of sentiment that condemned slavery and evoked pity for the prostitute depended upon an attitude toward the female body that draped it in the sanctity of potential motherhood and required of men a reverence for all women.

Swerving back to the main theme of her essay, Stowe closes by urging that her readers understand the war as a great affliction visited upon the nation by a chastening Father. It will call forth, she argues, a higher national life:

The prophetic visions of Nat Turner, who saw the leaves drop blood and the land darkened, have been fulfilled. The work of justice which he predicted is being executed to the uttermost. But when this strange work of judgment and justice is consummated, when our country, through a thousand battles and ten thousands of precious deaths, shall have come forth from this long agony, redeemed and regenerated, then God himself shall return and dwell with us, and the Lord God shall wipe away all tears from all faces, and the rebuke of his people shall he utterly take away.[18]

The Biblical cadence of these lines, appropriate to a theological interpretation of the war's meaning, indicates how much Stowe had invested in this analysis.

Once more in 1865, this time suspending the Crowfield fiction entirely, Stowe responded to events with her old political fire. Writing on "The Noble Army of Martyrs," she expressed her rage at Lincoln's assassination and more fiercely at the treatment of prisoners of war in Confederate prisons. Her polemic was directed against those who advocated leniency toward Robert E. Lee and Jefferson Davis, but it shifted at the end to a suggestion that those inclined to feel pity should direct that pity toward the victims and their survivors. The "return" she argues that the nation can make them is to erect monuments inscribed with their names—a cultural practice that did prevail as her policy of bloody retribution to be visited upon Confederate leaders did not.[19]

But if most of Stowe's writing in the later years of the war was not "political" in a direct sense, what "political work" does her familial ideology do? Family is explicitly a metaphor for the state. One Crowfield sketch of 1864 that responds directly to the exigencies of war develops the following rationale for buying American:

But our country is now in the situation of a private family whose means are absorbed by an expensive sickness, involving the life of its head: just now it is all we can do to keep the family together; all our means are swallowed up by our own domestic wants; we have nothing to give for the encouragement of other families, we must exist ourselves; we must get through this crisis and hold our own, and, that we may do it, all the family expenses must be kept within ourselves as far as possible.[20]

Family as a metaphor for the state figures civil war as fratricide, but also enables reunion and reconstitution of familial bonds. As a conservative metaphor for the state, it masks the transgressive portions of Stowe's vision of a postwar paradise of families. As a constitutive element of the culture of gentility, the bourgeois family is construed in the Crowfield sketches as the natural form of human society in a way that disguises the class-specific features of Stowe's vision. The family circle has replaced the "folks at home" as Stowe has negotiated her own class move, yet this circle is produced in ways that can include and contain the "folk."

This transition is conveniently embodied in a piece that Stowe published in the *Atlantic* in April 1863. Entitled "Sojourner Truth, the Libyan Sibyl," this article begins with an account of Stowe's first meeting with Truth, a meeting that had occurred nearly a decade earlier in Stowe's own home when Truth arrived unexpectedly. Truth no doubt hoped to gain Stowe's endorsement as well as make her acquaintance; it was her practice to call upon the famous and influential and ask them to inscribe her Book of Life. With Stowe she was more successful than she could possibly have imagined. The *Atlantic* sketch spread Truth's fame far beyond the abolitionist and radical reform circles in which she had previously traveled. The entire piece was included in the expanded *Narrative of Sojourner Truth* compiled for her in 1875, and its extensive "transcript" of Truth's sermon remains an important source for scholars attempting to recover the words of the illiterate itinerant orator. Stowe's initial comments focus on her visitor's physical presence that she tells her readers "gave the impression of a physical development which in early youth must have been as fine a specimen of the torrid zone as Cumberworth's celebrated statuette of the Negro Woman at the Fountain." Stowe claims that "when I recall the events of her life, as she narrated them to me, I imagine her as a living breathing impersonation of that work of art." The heightened diction that Stowe employs and her reference to an image she assumes will be familiar to *Atlantic* readers situate Stowe as a cultivated connoisseur, ready to display a choice specimen from her private collection and able to "read" the meaning of this *objet d'art*. Stowe's description of Truth is admiring and appreciative; she acknowledges the power of her presence and her self-possession. She even notes that "there was almost an unconscious superiority, not unmixed with a solemn twinkle of humor, in the odd, composed manner in which she looked down on me." The encounter, recorded in dialogue for

the *Atlantic* readers, allowed Stowe to produce Truth's voice in
dialect.

> "So, this is *you*," she said.
> "Yes," I answered.
> "Well, honey, de Lord bless ye! I jes' thought I'd like to come an'
> have a look at ye. You's heerd o'me, I reckon?" she added.

Dialect speech marks Truth as socially inferior, as does—para-
doxically—her naïve assumption that her fame matches that of
the writer of *Uncle Tom's Cabin*. Stowe, finding Truth's manner
original, summons her friends. Truth, she reports, was pleased to
have her do so. "An audience was what she wanted,—it mattered
not whether high or low, learned or ignorant." In suggesting the
dichotomies that did not matter to Truth, Stowe reveals their
importance in the way she structured her own perceptions of the
world. Yet her purpose here is not to denigrate Truth, but to
manage her translation from one sphere to the other, and to
intimate that Truth in a more perfectly ordered world would
have naturally inhabited the higher realms. "No princess," Stowe
writes, "could have received a drawing-room with more composed dignity than Sojourner her audience." In the space of a few
paragraphs, Stowe has transformed Truth from a "full-blooded
African" wearing a Madras turban into a princess. And yet, as the
text makes clear, this natural aristocrat is illiterate and speaks
substandard English.[21]

Having established her subject as an object of interest precisely
because of the discrepancy between Truth's natural gifts and her
social condition, Stowe then reproduces Truth's narrative of her
life and conversion. Curiously, she makes no comment on the
narrative, except to note the approval with which the assembled
clergymen received the "sermon." Truth's own construction of
her life resists Stowe's interpretive powers. However, Stowe includes in the transcript all nine stanzas of the hymn Truth sang
for the assembled company. She prefaces the hymn with the
parenthetical comment that Truth "sang in a strange, cracked
voice, but evidently with all her soul and might, mispronouncing
the English, but seeming to derive as much elevation and comfort
from bad English as from good." After quoting the hymn, Stowe
continues her interruption of Truth's narrative with observations

on the "wild, peculiar power of negro singing" with its "indescribable upward turns and those deep gutturals." And Stowe argues that Truth sang with "such an overwhelming energy of personal appropriation that the hymn seemed to be fused in the furnace of her feelings and come out recrystallized as a production of her own." This phenomenon of artistic appropriation is in fact an apt description of Stowe's own "production" of Truth, for she proceeds to compare Truth's hymn singing with Rachel's chanting of the "Marseillaise" in a manner that made her the impersonation of the mob rising against aristocratic oppression. Truth, she claims, "seemed to impersonate the fervor of Ethiopia, wild, savage, hunted of all nations, but burning after God in her tropic heart, and stretching her scarred hands towards the glory to be revealed."

This impersonation of Ethiopia was invited to stay several days with the Stowes—providing entertainment of an evening. Her conversation, Stowe tells her readers, had a "droll flavoring of humor" that Calvin Stowe enjoyed eliciting when he was feeling dull. Stowe's descriptions of the evenings at home highlight the contrast between the gentility of the Stowe parlor and the shrewd originality of Truth as the embodiment of the folk. Truth

> would come up into the parlor, and sit among pictures and ornaments, in her simple stuff gown, with her heavy travelling shoes, the central object of attention both to parents and children, always ready to talk or to sing, and putting into the common flow of conversation the keen edge of some shrewd remark.

By placing Truth as an object among the *objets* that adorn the parlor, Stowe subtly reinforces her earlier description of Truth as the breathing impersonation of a work of art. The Stowe family is resituated in the role of connoisseurs relishing this specimen of folk art. As a sample of Truth's wit and wisdom, Stowe reproduces her remarks on women's rights and uses Truth as a medium for expressing her own moderate endorsement of expanded rights for women. The comic vein in which the remarks are made also allows Stowe to join in the popular ridicule of radical women's rights advocates. But Truth is not only an entertainer and a curiosity as Stowe produces her for the *Atlantic* readers; she is a figure of great power and sweetness whose authority in a sickroom is practical as well as spiritual. She is a work of art that, in accordance with the imperatives of Victorian aesthetics, embodies moral truths.

Having established Truth as an admirable figure, Stowe then, in an anecdote borrowed from Wendell Phillips, uses her to contain the rage of African Americans. The anecdote she retells features Frederick Douglass predicting publicly that the only hope of justice lay in blood, in blacks fighting for themselves. The prophecy of blood that Stowe herself had derived from Nat Turner and offered as her own in *Dred,* her second antislavery novel, and that she believed was being fulfilled in the war, she apparently considered too dangerous a concept for a freed slave to espouse. Stowe, although a firm supporter of arming black soldiers in the war, one who believed that their performance in battle would prove their fitness for citizenship, limits the empowerment she wants freed slaves to feel by insisting that any bloodletting be, contained in a religious frame. She does so by describing the "electrical" effect of Truth's response to Douglass's speech. Stowe italicizes Truth's question, "'Frederick, *is God dead?'*" And she writes that "[n]ot another word she said or needed to say; it was enough." It was enough, that is, to discredit any advocacy of violence not ordained by God, as Stowe believed the war had been. And that war was, of course, initiated and conducted by white men on their terms; while Stowe was persuaded that it would mean a final end to slavery, freedom would come not through a slave revolt, but through "legitimate" political and military struggles.

This anecodote establishes Truth's spiritual authority—and aligns it with Stowe's own theological interpretation of the war and her racial politics. In the succeeding paragraphs, where she fantasizes about what Truth might have been with an education, those racial politics become clear. Stowe adheres to theories both of inherent racial characteristics and of cultural influences on development. Her views on race are remarkably liberal for one whose own cultural environment was permeated with invidious assumptions about racial difference. Truth is for Stowe an example of a gifted person who had been "cramped, scarred, maimed" by the institution of slavery. Stowe speculates that "Sojourner with the same culture might have spoken words as eloquent and

undying as those of the African Saint Augustine or Tertullian."
As this speculation reveals, Stowe imagined the cultural development of Truth's potential always in the context of her identity as
an African; so to understand Stowe's racial assumptions, it is
crucial to examine what meaning she associated with Africanness.
She cites specifically—and with approbation—

> the theory of some writers, that to the African is reserved, in the
> later and palmier days of the earth, the full and harmonious
> development of the religious element in man. The African seems
> to seize on the tropical fervor and luxuriance of Scripture imagery
> as something native; he appears to feel himself to be of the same
> blood with those old burning, simple souls, the patriarchs,
> prophets, and seers, whose impassioned words seem only grafted
> as foreign plants on the cooler stock of the Occidental mind.

From Stowe's deeply evangelical perspective, this imputation of
religious and Christian empathy to the African race represents a
high valuation of its merit. This valuation is reinforced by the
suggestion that the African race was to play a central role in the
millennial future in which Stowe so firmly believed. For Stowe,
however, Truth was not only African but, as important, female,
and so Stowe dilates on Truth's qualities as a type of African
woman:

> How grand and queenly a woman she might have been, with her
> wonderful physical vigor, her great heaving sea of emotion,
> her power of spiritual conception, her quick penetration, and her
> boundless energy! We might conceive an African type of woman so
> largely made and moulded, so much fuller in all the elements of
> life, physical and spiritual, that the dark hue of the skin should
> seem only to add an appropriate charm,—as Milton says of his
> Penseroso. . . .

This remarkable passage endows Truth with the qualities of
Stowe's ideal woman, and confronts directly the color prejudice
so nearly universal among white Americans. On one level Stowe's
entire piece functions as a persuasive polemic in the debate over
the post-Emancipation future of African Americans. Stowe is
certainly refuting claims that Africans are inherently inferior to
Europeans, although her view of the damage done by slavery and
the need for compensatory education is compatible with a gradu-

alist approach to the granting of political and social equality. Yet
her suggestion that black might be perceived as beautiful, with
the sexual overtones heightened by the quotation from Milton
that she cites, hints at possibilities of amalgamation that Stowe
probably did not consciously entertain. Rhetorically the reference to Milton, as it displays Stowe's erudition, also serves as a
transition to Stowe's closing discussion of the Libyan Sibyl.

Whisking Truth herself abruptly away from center stage,
Stowe informs her readers that

> though Sojourner Truth has passed away from among us as a wave
> of the sea, her memory still lives in one of the loftiest and most
> original works of modern art, the Libyan Sibyl, by Mr. Story, which
> attracted so much attention in the Late World's Exhibition.

This passage shows precisely how Stowe's attention has shifted.
She speaks of Truth as if she were dead when she was in fact still
very much alive. But in a sense she is dead to Stowe; it is only
Stowe's memory that matters. In calling on that memory and
reproducing Truth's history over breakfast for the benefit of her
fellow guests at William Wetmore Story's home in Rome, Stowe
claims to have inspired Story to sculpt the Libyan Sibyl as a
companion to his Cleopatra. Whether Stowe's claim is entirely
justified, Story did call this statue his "anti-slavery sermon in
stone," and he later proposed an enlarged version in bronze as a
suitable monument to Emancipation.[22] But, as Stowe confesses,
Story had already turned with his Cleopatra to Egypt in search of
alternatives to classical Greek models. The political significance of
Story's expansion of ideal sculpture beyond the confines of
European traditions was apparent to Stowe; she concludes her
essay with the hope that copies of both "the Cleopatra and the
Libyan Sibyl shall adorn the Capitol at Washington." For the
contemporary reader of Stowe's essay to grasp the significance of
this hope, one must recall that in the mid-Victorian era the
narrative content of art and its moral message were highly valued.
Ideal sculptures, depicting historical, Biblical, and mythic figures,
were held to embody meanings that could be interpreted by the
cultivated viewer, and to evoke feelings in less-educated specta-
tors as well. Art then could be conceived of as a powerful
educational tool, containing meanings that cultivated viewers or
guidebooks could convey to the uninitiated and evoking moral

William Wetmore Story's statue, the Libyan Sibyl, which Stowe claimed to have inspired by recounting Sojourner Truth's history. Stowe's Atlantic sketch firmly identified Truth as the Libyan Sybil; the identification persists in virtually everything written about Truth since the Civil War. Stowe succeeded in imprisoning Truth in a wildly inappropriate marble image, but one that served to elevate Truth's status in Victorian eyes. (The Metropolitan Museum of Art, gift of the Erving Wolf Foundation, 1979. (1979, 266) All rights reserved, the Metropolitan Museum of Art.)

feelings in every spectator's breast. The politics of sentiment that informed this view of art had endowed the female form with particular significance; from this perspective, Story's pair of statues possessed a moral authority and a power of political representation greater than any likenesses of representative men that might adorn the seat of government.[23] Story's sculptures were also appropriate for the Capitol because they represented in Stowe's view "a new manner of art" for the New World, and because an "anti-slavery sermon in stone" would be an object lesson for the Republic.[24] Their placement would also link the United States to "that burning continent whose life-history is yet to be," that is, in the millennial future. And there is certainly a proto-feminist impulse at work in inserting an African queen and an African prophetess (who is really an African American seer) into the heart of Washington. But these statues are also suitable for display because they are examples of American art that has received international (European) acclaim, and it is for this reason, too, that Stowe wants to associate herself with them.

In this small narrative then Stowe has contained Truth as the representative of the African folk, first in the domestic space of her parlor and finally by imprisoning her in marble and placing her on display for the State. In doing so, Stowe also presents herself first as the celebrated authoress of *Uncle Tom's Cabin* and therefore as a heroine to the African folk embodied in Truth, and as a cultured observer able to interpret Truth by analogy to a celebrated statuette and to Milton's Penseroso, as well as to Augustine and Tertullian. Stowe then portrays herself as a powerful storyteller, retelling Truth's history to an international coterie of artists and in so doing inspiring a statue now receiving European acclaim. She remains explicitly a champion of freedom for the enslaved, but she has used that advocacy in ways that empower her as an artist.

Professionally it would seem that Stowe managed both to write and to ride out the war rather successfully. And yet, wherever her averted gaze fell—on the Italian *quattrocento*, on coastal Maine of more recent memory, on her domestic affairs, on reviews of the London Exposition—the war framed her every response. Even a toothache had to be discussed in relation to Emancipation.

PART VI

XXXXXXXXXXXXXXXXXXXXXXXX

The War Comes Home

*W*hen the Civil War ended in April 1865 the national "house" was, on one level, reunified. The Confederacy, as well as the cause of secession, passed away as Lee and Grant hammered out the formal terms of the South's surrender. North and south, soldiers returned home to jobs and farms, and a long and difficult process of rebuilding and reconstruction was under way.

But in many ways, the postwar scene perpetuated the image, and the reality, of the "house divided." Northerners and southerners continued to view each other suspiciously, with both sides uncertain as to how political power would ultimately be reconfigured in the new nation. To a great extent, both regions experienced the war's conclusion influenced by considerations of gender. Southern white men returned home after Appomattox, conscious of their defeats and failures and very much aware of the influence which southern women had exercised in their absence. In many ways, they were anxious to reassert some measure of influence and authority.

At the same time, as Nina Silber points out, northern men were equally conscious of stressing their manly superiority over their southern foes. The war's finale, many northerners believed, offered an opportunity to demonstrate the South's manly and womanly inadequacies and the clear predominance of Yankee manhood. The rumors of Jefferson Davis's attempted escape in women's clothing further fueled *the northern notion that the superior man had triumphed and would be needed to play the leading role in reordering the postwar society.*

In this way, the politics of Reconstruction became entwined with issues of gender. This became most apparent as the full range of postwar measures were unfolded. As the program of Radical Reconstruction gradually reworked the legal and political foundations of the nation, it opened up questions of citizenship and political participation for both African Americans and women. Women failed to gain the vote in these years but, at least among northern women, the campaign for women's rights took off in new directions in the 1860s and 1870s.

In the South, the Reconstruction period witnessed a revolutionary transformation in the condition of four million former slaves. Freedom opened up new possibilities for black men and black women, not the least of which was the opportunity to re-cement marital and familial bonds. Moreover, African American men and women made new choices regarding their labor—both within and outside their own newly reconstituted households.

Yet, as freed men and women explored their freedom, they also continually faced resistance from much of the old southern ruling class, a class that anxiously sought ways to reassert power and authority. Catherine Clinton, in her essay on African American women in the Reconstruction period, shows how much of this postwar power struggle revolved around gender and sexual control. Black women in the Reconstruction period, she argues, were often the victims of sexual violence committed by southern white men who waged a brutal campaign for both political and sexual domination.

The omnipotent rule of the southern slave master had been broken. But, in a variety of ways, paternalism was reconstituted throughout the postwar South. Victoria Bynum explores how patriarchal authority was re-established through the southern courts, specifically in terms of divorce proceedings. She finds that a growing number of men, both black and white, sought divorces in the postwar years and that divorce was increasingly used as a vehicle to control women's behavior.

The era of the Civil War and Reconstruction witnessed a number of startling disruptions and transformations regarding relationships and ideals of gender. By the time the war ended, women in both the North and the South had taken on new roles and had, in certain ways, challenged some of the most sacred features of male authority. In the South, both black men and women gained a degree of control over their

*lives. The new possibilities which had been stirred up by war lingered
into the postwar period. Yet as women and African Americans showed a
determination to follow through on gains that had been won, a new
war, or perhaps a series of wars, sprung up on the homefronts across the
nation. At every step, they encountered resistance—from northern men
who sought to curtail the women's rights movement and from southern
men who sought to reassert a level of prewar authority over both women
and blacks. To a great extent, these would be the struggles that would
define the American scene for many years to come.*

Chapter 16

XXXXXXXXXXXXXXXXXXXXXXXXXXXX

Intemperate Men, Spiteful Women, and Jefferson Davis

NINA SILBER

In April 1865 the American Civil War concluded in much the same way that it had begun—in a flurry of chaos and confusion in which the emotions of the participants swung between dramatic highs and lows. For the people of the North, it was a thrilling, but ultimately unsettling, victory. The fall of the Confederate capital in Richmond, Virginia, on April 3 signaled an intense joy and optimism among northerners that would be surpassed only by the excitement of April 10—the day that most Americans learned of Lee's surrender to Grant at Appomattox. But the northerners' initial euphoria was soon shattered. With the news of Appomattox only five days old, they awoke to the news of the assassination of President Abraham Lincoln. Reeling from the heights of joy to the depths of grief, northerners re-ignited long-standing hatreds of the Confederacy and its leaders.

As northerners rekindled their anger against the Confederacy, they gave vent to a very specific set of complaints. Northern men, especially of the middle and upper classes, attacked the manhood of southern leaders, chiding the "chivalry" for their dissipative, idle, and intemperate ways and suggesting that southern masculinity lacked that quality of restraint which was one hallmark of northern manliness. Despite the unkind comments made against southern men, many of these same northerners saved their sharpest rebukes for southern women. Prominent speakers and journalists in the North frequently savaged southern ladies for what was seen as their excessive support of the Confederacy. Indeed, according to some northerners, the very foundation of the Confederacy rested on southern womanhood, making the entire Confederate system little more than a government in petticoats. These abuses were not simply a blanket condemnation of all southern men and women, but a specific assault against the southern class system, which identified the southern aristocracy with these corruptions of proper gender codes.

For a brief moment, the threads of this abusive rhetoric were tied together during the uproar surrounding the capture of Jefferson Davis in May 1865. According to the embellished tale of the arrest, the former Confederate president had attempted to evade his pursuers disguised in the petticoated garb of a woman. Dozens of songs, poems, cartoons, and newspaper accounts presented Davis in any and every form of womanly attire, as a feminized and feckless fugitive who, in his ignoble flight, affirmed the southern system's violation of appropriate gender standards. Within a few years, however, Davis's bizarre departure had been overshadowed by the dramatic events of Reconstruction and received only occasional notice in the annals of nineteenth-century culture. Yet echoes of the broader discourse on gender lingered for some time as northern journalists, novelists, and dramatists, men and even some women, returned to the themes of weakened southern manhood and southern female intransigence throughout the late nineteenth century. Ultimately, then, through their general discussions and through their depictions of Davis, northerners painted a picture of emasculated southern men, spiteful and unruly southern women, and a southern system that had been thoroughly and utterly feminized.

This article examines the preoccupation with southern gender which was frequently voiced by many socially and politically prominent men of the North in the immediate postwar period and the early years of Reconstruction, touching on the gendered images presented in the Jefferson Davis incident. This examination helps to illuminate the ways in which a gendered discourse has shaped American political culture.

Working with the ideas of such scholars as Carroll Smith-

Rosenberg, Michael Rogin, and Joan Scott, I have found that sexual anxieties have often pervaded American and European political dialogues, frequently presenting bourgeois men with a way to voice their concerns about the social and political disruptions of their era. The post–Civil War depictions of weakened southern men and volatile southern women played a similar role, giving northern men a language with which to address their anxieties arising from the wartime and postwar crises. Moreover, as historian Joan Scott has suggested, such gendered metaphors have often been used in modern political discourse as a way to signify "natural" and "legitimate" relations of public power. In this regard, northern men drew on the images of impetuous southern men, disorderly southern women, and a former Confederate president in women's clothes to establish ideas of northern control over a weakened and submissive South. And, ultimately, the notion of the feminized South offered a vehicle of reconciliation, revealed most graphically in the image of marital reunion between heroic northern men and subdued southern women.[1]

These images of gender not only shaped ideas of political power but also contributed to northern men's understanding of their distinctive, regional identity. By contrasting restrained northern masculinity with southern effeminacy, northern men relied on gender to understand the full range of moral, social, and political factors which divided North from South. Northerners derided the southern slave system, and its accompanying code of honor, for counseling idleness and dissipation of its menfolk, especially in the southern aristocracy. In contrast, northern men stressed their superior masculinity which rested on hard work and self-improvement. In effect, within the prewar and postwar sectional debate, northern men projected an image of two competing notions of masculinity and suggested that their Civil War victory had settled this contest once and for all.

Not all northerners were so preoccupied by this postwar gender discourse. The ideas examined in this essay were primarily the creation of northern men, mainly Republicans, of the middle and upper classes, who were acutely aware of competing understandings of masculinity and of power relations in the war-torn nation. Yet, though these ideas sprang from the northern male elite, I suspect that they occasionally entered the province of northern women and northern workers, especially in the immediate postwar years when a hatred of the Confederacy permeated much of northern society. In this regard, the depictions of the captured Jefferson Davis suggest one way in which a male-dominated, middle-class ideology may have been channeled to a broader audience through the forms of popular culture.

As the Civil War drew to a close, northern men discovered in their victory a confirmation of their moral righteousness and superior civilization. They also found that winning offered an affirmation of their manhood and a way to assault southern claims of courage and strength. New York lawyer George Templeton Strong, for example, noted the stories that circulated through the North in June 1865 concerning the Confederates' military ineptitude. Referring to a Major Nichols of General Sherman's staff, Strong wrote in his diary, "He confirms the story told by all Sherman's officers that the braggarts of South Carolina were the slowest fighters, and are the most abjectly whipped rebels in all Rebeldom. They did nothing but whine, he says, as Sherman's column marched over their plantations." Whitelaw Reid, a northern journalist who toured the South in May 1865, also portrayed the Confederates as less-than-adequate soldiers. Concerned primarily with social pretensions, "with feasting, and dancing, and love making, with music improvised from the ball room," Reid claimed that these light-headed socialites had "dashed into revolution as they would into a waltz"—thus taking an impetuous, even feminine, approach to war.[2]

Yet the postwar questioning of southern manhood involved much more than turning the rebels into whining and whimpering cowards. Rather, this discussion reflected and extended northern society's critique, formulated in the antebellum period, of the southern social and economic system. Under the influence of a unique plantation system and social structure, a strong tradition of chivalric and heroic behavior had taken root in the antebellum South, propagating a code of masculinity that affected the lives of all southern white men. In many ways, this southern code of honor became the standard by which southern manhood, especially the aristocracy, was judged. Yet although the social institutions had been different, until the early nineteenth century, northerners had been steeped in a similar tradition of honorable commitment to family and community. But precisely when the economic distinctions between North and South became most pronounced, in the early nineteenth century, the North and South parted company on the questions of honor and manhood. Masculinity in the North no longer rested on a code of "usefulness" for the community but on the ideas of self-improvement and self-cultivation. "Respectability" became the new watchword for northern men, demanding a condemnation of vices that had formerly been considered honorable. Behind this notion of respectability lay a host of religious and moral values, especially an emphasis on restraint and self-control. And, increasingly, respectability denoted economic status and the possibility of class mobility.[3]

This northern reassessment of manliness dovetailed with the developing free-labor ideology of the early nineteenth century. Just as the new code of masculinity focused on the individual as opposed to the community, so the free-labor outlook stressed the individual laborer's ability to improve his economic and social status. Viewing themselves as economic individuals striving in an uncertain and unpredictable market, northern men became increasingly concerned with tempering and restraining their individual passions and feelings, with exercising physical and emotional control in order to better assure their advancement and success. In short, economic self-improvement demanded and encouraged moral and religious self-cultivation, counseling the antebellum northern man to restrain his social and sexual vices. In this regard, northern free-labor ideologues often explained economic success or failure in terms of self-control. The Republican press, for example, attributed the economic panic of 1856 not to the forces of the market but to "ruinous habits" and "luxurious living," personal failings which exemplified a lack of moral restraint.[4]

The distinct economic world views of the North and South, and their corresponding notions of masculinity, shaped the sectional debate of the 1850s. Southern men emphasized their highly touted fighting abilities which they contrasted to northern men's apparent lack of virility. Northern abolitionists, portrayed as men of talk and not of action, were especially subjected to this gen-

dered ridicule. Antislavery lecturers, the *Baltimore Patriot* declared, had to be escorted by "a life-guard of elderly ladies, and
protected by a rampart of whale-bones and cotton-padding." To
counter this abuse, northern antislavery men welcomed John
Brown's attack on Harper's Ferry for reinvigorating their cause
with a spirit of manly vitality. Even anti-abolitionists like *New
York Herald* editor James Gordon Bennett recognized what
Brown had accomplished and hoped that southern men would
now recognize northern masculine energy. "Truly," Bennett
explained in an attempt to anoint the beleaguered abolitionist
with the scepter of masculinity, "there is as much difference
between the manly heart and the politician's gizzard, as physically
between the massive form of the Abolitionist and the insignificant
figure [of the average politician]. Would not a Southern gentleman respect the former far more than the latter?"[5]

Certainly, as Bennett's anxious plea to the southern gentleman
suggests, some antebellum northerners remained ambivalent as
to which section, ultimately, had produced a superior strain of
manhood. According to William Taylor, some northerners' ap-
prehensions about the expansive acquisitiveness of their growing
market economy made them look with kindness and sympathy on
the image of the southern gentleman, respecting his disdain for
materialistic enterprise. Yet, as Eric Foner has countered, most
northerners did not readily accept the image of a superior
southern society, certainly not as the sectional crisis gathered
steam in the 1850s. In this regard, northern publicists and
politicians frequently relied on the free-labor ideology to delineate the qualities which marked the free-laboring northerner as a
man and the idle, slaveholding southerner as a corrupted version
of manhood. The southern aristocrat, whose slaves relieved him
of all economic responsibilities, was assumed to have little interest
in hard work and self-control. He was assailed for his laziness and
licentiousness, qualities which placed him at the opposite pole
from the industrious and restrained northerner. Even the southern man's supposed physical vitality only affirmed his failure to
adhere to the new masculine ethos of self-control. The southern
slave system, explained one northerner, promoted "pride, indo-
lence, luxury, and licentiousness. . . . Manners are fantastic
and fierce; brute force supplants moral principle . . . a sensi-

tive vanity is called honor, and cowardly swagger, chivalry."
Indeed, both ante- and postbellum northerners were keenly
aware that the southern man laid claim to a certain aura of
manliness, but by using the rhetoric of the free-labor ideology,
northern men attempted to uncover the fallacy of those claims. In
short, many northern men suggested that the southern gentleman, hiding behind the pretenses of honor and chivalry, and
behind the labor of his slaves, lacked the purposeful and sustained self-control which allowed a northern man to do honorable work and keep his anger and his temper in check.[6]

The war's conclusion saw a resurgence of northern men's
attack on southern masculinity, a diatribe which continued and
extended many of the North's critiques from the antebellum
period. The northern victory, many claimed, proved that the
assertions of antebellum southern men had been a sham, that all
the talk about the southern gentleman's strength and chivalry
had been mere bravado. Hence, Whitelaw Reid and George
Strong focused their attacks on the pretenses of southern men,
seeking to reveal the truth about the "braggarts" of the South.
According to Union soldier John Phelps, southern men knew
nothing of true masculinity and "the Southern idea of manhood"
was little more than "a self-assumed superiority and arrogance
over the people of the South." Oliver Wendell Holmes likewise
believed that the notion of southern manliness rested on false-
hoods and fakeries, on their arrogant notions of superiority. "I
hope that time will explode," wrote Holmes in a letter to Senator
Albert Beveridge, "the humbug of the Southern Gentleman in
your mind. . . . the Southern gentlemen generally were an
arrogant crew who knew nothing of the ideas that make the life of
the few thousands that may be called civilized." And the *Chicago
Tribune* emphasized how the war revealed the true conditions of
northern and southern masculinity, despite the pretenses of the
plantation aristocracy. Before the war, the paper observed, the
southern "'chivalry' did not respect the Northern 'mudsills.' The
Northern man did not come up to the Southern gentleman in his
essential ideas of manhood. . . . [I]n manly courage, a noble
sense of honor, and statesmanlike qualities a Northern man had
no claims in the estimation of the South which the oligarchy were
bound to respect." But now, as the *Tribune* explained, this gen-

dered hierarchy had been turned on its head. Northern "cour-age," claimed this editorial, "has commanded respectful consid-eration."[7]

Even in the postwar period, northern men suggested that the still intransigent South must be met by a continual show of northern masculine force. In this regard, George Strong sug-gested that the North must prove its masculine superiority in crushing the rebellious spirit behind Lincoln's assassination. Strong confidently noted the pervasive aura of manliness that enveloped New York City on the day after the assassination; he found the tone of the meeting outside the Custom House to be "healthy and virile" and, later, he approved of the resolutions passed that day in Trinity Church, condemning the southern leadership, as "masculine and good." Moreover, in reasserting their own manhood, northern men were loathe to acknowledge any degree of southern masculinity. In this regard, John Phelps fumed at President Johnson's attempt in 1866 to allow the south-ern states to return to the Union "with all their manhood." And a transplanted southerner living in Boston during the years of Reconstruction found that many northerners could not bring themselves to notice southern manliness. This former resident of Tennessee thus was enormously pleased upon hearing a lecture by northern editor Josiah Holland who "paid several compli-ments to Southern manhood." Much to this southerner's chagrin, however, Holland's remarks were "the first . . . true manly avowal that there was such a thing as manhood in the South" that the Tennessee refugee had seen or heard since moving to the North.[8]

But despite the suspicions of this southerner, northerners did not ignore southern manhood; they merely redefined it in terms that made it obnoxious and offensive to the northern under-standing of respectability and self-control. And, in so doing, northern men touted not only their masculine superiority over the South but their political superiority as well. According to the *New York Tribune*, the chief criterion by which southern men should be judged was their ability to take up honest labor, an activity which the *Tribune* editors suggested might be unknown in the southern code of honor. "If there be any manhood among the ex-slaveholders," this paper editorialized, "we shall soon find it out. We mean the manhood which cheerfully attacks the difficulties of peace and wins victories not less renowned than those of war. . . . The sooner all Southern employers, whether 'gentlemen' or not, understand 'the new organization' [of labor], the better for Southern production and prosperity." And even when southern men had demonstrated courage in battle, northern men reinterpreted that valor as a product of southern men's unrestrained nature. "The pugnacious customs of Southern society," explained Union officer and Reconstruction novelist John DeForest, "explain in part the extraordinary courage which the Confederate troops displayed during the Rebellion." Somewhat kinder to southern men than many of his northern contemporaries, DeForest nonetheless suggested that their brand of masculinity rested mainly on an overblown notion of virility and the sins of riotous and ungoverned living. "It seems to me," DeForest wrote during his Reconstruction experience in South Carolina, "that the central trait of the 'chivalrous Southron' is an intense respect for virility. He will forgive almost any vice in a man who is manly." To DeForest, this was not genuine manliness but only a respect for superficial qualities, the southern man's admiration of "vices which are but exaggerations of the masculine."[9]

Some northern doctors even suggested that the pugnaciousness and exaggerated masculinity of southern men was rooted in their nervous constitution, thus connecting southern men to the same hysteria-prone physique which nineteenth-century doctors frequently attributed to women. In short, they implied that southern men, like many women, had lost control of their bodily, and hence emotional, powers. "The great rebellion that has just closed," wrote Dr. A. P. Dutcher in a leading medical journal in 1866, "was precipitated upon the nation, in a great measure, by the high nervous temperament of the Southern people, particularly their leaders." Yet, if only a few northerners made Dutcher's argument, many still agreed that the outcome had been the same—that southern men engaged in an unmanaged and erratic style of living totally unlike the idealized notion of the free-laboring, northern man. *The Nation* thus agreed with the portrayal of southern men which John DeForest presented in one of his novels, especially his depiction of "their almost total lack of humor . . . their lofty belief in themselves, and their fanatical devotion to their dueling code, all of which are the natural products in sinful men of ignorance, idleness, and slight responsibility."[10]

Not all southern men earned such harsh criticisms. Perhaps more than most rebels, Robert E. Lee won praise and respect from northerners. Yet, to a great extent, Lee gained this admiration as he was judged to be an exception to the southern code of manliness. By surrendering to Grant, Lee had shown the control which other southern men lacked. And by retiring into an apparently quiet and serene postwar life, Lee again won northerners' approval for accepting defeat and taking himself out of the political limelight. In this spirit, the *New York Times,* on the occasion of Lee's death, criticized the Confederate general for his role in the war but praised him for his postwar behavior. "By his unobtrusive modesty and purity of life," the *Times* reflected, Lee "has won the respect even of those who most bitterly deplore and reprobate his course in the rebellion." Henry Field, a northerner who traveled in the South during the 1880s, made a similar observation about Lee's manly self-control fifteen years after the *Times* obituary. "Retiring to his home in Lexington," wrote Field, "and remaining there in quiet dignity, [Lee] gave an example of moderation and self-restraint" which helped to restore good feelings between the sections. And, by the end of the nineteenth century, when both northerners and southerners were wallowing in a national cult of Robert E. Lee, northern men still praised Lee as the exceptional southern man, as the one who possessed the masculine reserve which all others had apparently lacked. "Whatever real anquish Lee may have felt" at Appomattox, wrote one northern textbook writer, "he kept all emotion suppressed while the formal interview lasted; his manner was dignified and impassive."[11]

Lee epitomized the possibility of reformed southern manhood, how the southern man might be "northernized" in the context of the military defeat and the postwar settlement. Other southern men, evil as their sins might have been, also had been or still could be transformed by military force, by the strength of northern masculinity. Southern women, however, posed an entirely different problem to the northern mentality. According to northern observers, southern women displayed an attachment to the Confederacy, and a hostility towards the Union, that far surpassed the disloyalty of southern men. Indeed, as some northerners suggested, the trauma of the battlefield had at least partially transformed the thinking of southern men. "The men who did the fighting," remarked northern journalist Sidney Andrews, "are everywhere the men who most readily accept the issues of the war." The ladies of Dixie, on the other hand, who had been raised under a corrupted form of male leadership and had never experienced the defeat of the battlefield, apparently had shifted the war from the field to the homefront. As with the alleged weaknesses of southern men, the intransigence of southern women became a potent symbol in northerners' postwar political discourse, suggesting the bitterness and anger northerners would encounter in the postwar settlement. And, by connecting this intransigence to women, northern men also found a way to deride the lingering spirit of southern sectionalism.[12]

During and after the war, numerous northern soldiers and travelers frequently attested to the feminine anger and hostility that had gripped the southern states. Union General Benjamin Butler publicly castigated the ladies of New Orleans for the "repeated insults" which they heaped upon his troops during the Union occupation of the Crescent City. Whitelaw Reid, in his postwar tour of the South, found the bitter mood of the New Orleans ladies only slightly alleviated. The southern women, Reid observed, "are very polite to Yankee officers in particular, but very bitter against Yankees in general." John Dennett reported to the readers of *The Nation* that certain Union officers "tell me that some of the women still carefully gather up the folds of their dresses when they approach a man in the Federal uniform," thus showing their anger through the swish of their skirts. Sidney Andrews also detected insult and anger in the flounce of southern women's dresses. These women, he found, "much more than the men, have contemptuous notions for the negro soldiers; and scorn for Northern men is frequently apparent in the swing of their skirts when passing on the sidewalk."[13]

But the toss of southern women's skirts held more serious implications than a mere rebuff to Yankee authority. Postwar observers portrayed southern women as the very foundation of the Confederacy—its main supporters and defenders. Hence,

Sidney Andrews, who claimed to "have seen not a little of feminine bitterness since coming into the South," viciously attacked the "bitter, spiteful women whose passionate hearts nursed the Rebellion." In a society that held women's political participation in contempt, this notion of southern women's intense commitment to the Confederate cause only underscored the illegitimacy of that government. Moreover, postwar observers relied on the image of southern women's hostility to suggest that the locus of war had moved from the battlefield to the homefront. Men, it was implied, had accepted the outcome of the struggle; but the women, explained one *Lippincott's* writer in 1870, "would hear of no truce and no peace." When southern women derided Yankee rule and swished their skirts at Union soldiers, northerners knew that the battles may have been won but that the war to establish northern control was not yet over.[14]

Finally, this feminine sectionalism again confirmed the weakness of southern masculinity as it pointed to the failure of southern leaders to assert their control over their womenfolk. In this spirit, the *New York Tribune,* in an April 18, 1865, editorial, commented on "the fiendish spirit evinced by many southern women" who "had been told, and believed, that 'the Yankees' were the scum of mankind. . . . Hence they have often insulted and berated our soldiers as no savages on earth would have done." Apparently, the women had pushed the bitterness of the sectional conflict beyond even the horrors of the battlefield. Echoing the gender concerns of post–Civil War northerners, one textbook writer of the late nineteenth century implicated the weakness of the southern chivalry, especially their pandering to the feminine element, as the crux of the gendered disorderliness of the war and the postwar period. "Towards women of his own rank and race," explained textbook writer James Schouler, "the Southern gentleman was strongly chivalrous, and woman in return loved fondly and passionately, laying great store by her beauty and personal graces. That stronger enthusiasm with which woman threw herself into this struggle of masters, to inflame and encourage their efforts, has been well understood." As men thus fell victim to feminine passions, Schouler maintained, the womanly spirit ruled over the Confederacy. "Southern women inspired the cause of Southern secession," Schouler wrote, "and scarcely an order was seen emanating from Confederate generals for exciting hatred of the North that did not allude to the softer sex."[15]

White southern women, at least those of the upper classes, undoubtedly were staunch defenders of their social system and of the Confederacy. Having withstood destruction, devastation, and invasion by the enemy, one cannot wonder that southern women expressed a bitterness and antagonism that may not have been matched by northerners, men or women. Still, the images and accounts of female intransigence do not necessarily reflect the emotional state of white southern womanhood. Southern men, taking comfort in the notion that their womenfolk had vehemently taken up their defense in this hour of defeat and emasculation, may have embellished and exaggerated these accounts of angry southern ladies. Likewise, northern men did not offer neutral appraisals of enraged southern women, but used that notion as a symbol in their political rhetoric. By stressing southern women's intense allegiance to the southern system, they confirmed their idea of a feminized, and, therefore, illegitimate, Confederate government. And by suggesting that these women presented the main obstacle to the Yankees' postwar authority, they constructed a vision of the new terrain of postwar conflict that would now be waged on the southern homefront.[16]

But the figure who best exemplified the notion of feminine unruliness was not a woman at all, but a man in women's clothing. Just one month after Lee's surrender to Grant at Appomattox, Jefferson Davis's capture by Union troops helped to crystallize northern men's ideas about unmanly southern men and disruptive southern women. In effect, Davis's arrest became enmeshed in the broader postwar discourse which relied on gender to establish northern men's vision of political power and regional identity. On May 10, 1865, the Fourth Michigan Cavalry of the Union army tracked down Davis, who had fled from Richmond after its fall, in a secluded spot in southern Georgia. Five days later, the *New York Times* printed a dispatch from the commanding officer that summarized the unusual events surrounding the Confederate president's arrest:

> The captors report that [Jefferson Davis] hastily put on one of Mrs. Davis' dresses and started for the woods, closely pursued by our men, who at first thought him a woman, but seeing his boots while running suspected his sex at once. The race was a short one, and the rebel President was soon brought to bay. . . . He expressed great indignation at the energy with which he was pursued, saying that he had believed our Government more magnanimous than to hunt down women and children.

Historians have disputed the accuracy of these reports of Davis's unheroic departure and certainly Davis himself took pains to counter his enemies' charges. Most scholars, however, agree that Davis donned some form of disguise that may have belonged to his wife—most likely a cloak or shawl (or both) which were commonly worn by both men and women. What is significant here is not the accuracy of these accounts but the way in which northerners adopted, propagated, and embellished the tale of the Confederate president, fashioning an image that thoroughly confirmed their gendered conceptions of the postwar South.[17]

Davis certainly never wore a petticoat or a hoopskirt, yet these were the frequently mentioned adornments to the Confederate's disguise. Such decorations, obviously more feminine than a simple shawl or cloak, allowed artists and songwriters to thoroughly delineate Davis's unmanly demeanor and get a good laugh out of it as well. Songwriters paid homage to "Jeff in Petticoats" in which the Confederate leader explained, "To dodge the bullets, I will wear my tin-clad crinoline." Poetic accounts of the petticoated Davis abounded, again sounding the theme of exposing the southern man's false claim to manliness:

> Jeff Davis was a warrior bold,
> And vowed the Yanks should fall;
> He jumped into his pantaloons
> And swore he'd rule them all.
> But when he saw the Yankees come
> To hang him if they could,
> He jumped into a petticoat
> And started for the wood.[18]

During May and June of 1865, in magazines, museums, and even on private farms throughout the North, Davis could be found decked out in his crinoline and skirts, offering a symbolic display of northerners' view of southern gender confusion at the close of the war. The United States Sanitary Commission presented a wax figure of Davis dressed in the clothes of an old woman at their June fund-raising fair in Chicago. P. T. Barnum, always eager to take advantage of a cultural phenomenon, exhibited the unfortunate Confederate at his New York museum in a tableaux showing a hoopskirted Davis surrounded by his captor-soldiers. And countless cartoons and prints offered similar impressions of "Jeff's Last Shift," "The Chas-ed Old Lady of the C.S.A.," and "Jeffie Davis—the Belle of Richmond." The prints frequently displayed soldiers in the very act of exposing the Confederate president, often depicting a single Union soldier using his sword to lift Davis's skirt, thereby revealing the hoop-skirt and unseemly boots which had given him away. One print in particular left little to the viewer's imagination. Entitled "The Head of the Confederacy on a New Base," the cartoon pictured Davis with skirt drawn back, legs parted, a phallic-like sword between his legs, and a menacing Union soldier standing above him (Figure 1).[19]

The wide circulation of the cartoons, as well as Barnum's display, suggest ways in which an initially middle-class image of inadequate southern manliness reached a broader audience in the North. Some of the cartoons, of a less sexually explicit nature, appeared in journals such as *Harper's Weekly* and *Frank Leslie's News*. Most, however, circulated as separate-sheet cartoons and were sold as single prints. The cost of such prints (ranging from twenty-five cents to one dollar) probably precluded their widespread purchase by a working-class clientele. But they were accessible to the more highly paid artisans, professionals, and merchants, many of whom were shop-owners and saloon keepers who exposed their patrons, of both the working and middle classes, to these pictures of Davis and the emasculated Confederacy. As these images circulated, they drew on a pervasive hostility among northerners and a widespread desire among northern men to make a mockery of southern manhood.[20]

In this regard, Davis became a symbol for all the southern rulers' deceptive claims to manliness and chivalric courage. Davis proved false the assertions of southern leaders who had boasted

Figure 1. From The Confederate Image: Prints of the Lost Cause, *by Mark E. Neely, Jr., Gabor Boritt, and Harold Holzer. (The University of North Carolina Press, 1987. Reprinted by permission.)*

of their more civilized society, their greater concern for the weaker sex, their military prowess, and their manly courage. Because these assertions of masculinity had become defining characteristics of the southern aristocrat, a blow aimed at Jefferson Davis's manliness also targeted the southern "chivalry's" class pretenses. Northern observers thus noted the contrast between Davis the coward and Davis the southern aristocrat and the alleged upholder of the manly tradition of southern honor. "Who is yonder aged, lean-faced female, flying through the woods, with skirts lifted of the wind, and with cloven feet disclosed in boots?" the *New York Independent* pondered. "That is no other than the masculine hero who promised never to desert the fortunes of the Southern Confederacy." By allegedly dressing as a woman, Davis revealed the fiction of the southern aristocracy's assertion of manliness. Moreover, as many noted, he implicated the entire

Confederate leadership through his actions. In this way, northerners again drew on the theme of depraved southern manliness to establish their regional and political superiority in the postwar period. "We are going to have the president of the petticoat Confederacy imprisoned at this fort," wrote Union soldier Edward Morley to his wife from Fortress Monroe, Virginia. And *Harper's Weekly* suggested a "new interpretation of the initials C.S.A. [Confederate States of America]—Crinolinum Skirtum Absquatulatum."[21]

Southerners clearly recognized in the Davis imagery an assault on their manhood. John Dennett, a reporter for *The Nation* who visited the South in July 1865, encountered one southerner who was astounded to learn that "intelligent" northerners actually believed the story of Davis's disguise. As Dennett's informant explained, the Confederate captive had merely taken a precaution against his neuralgia by throwing on a cloak prior to his arrest. Numerous southern leaders squirmed at the implications of the capture accounts, as well as the other assaults on southern manliness, and launched their own reaffirmation of southern virility in their protection and idolization of Davis's daughter Winnie. Northern Democrats likewise took pains to defend Jefferson Davis's manhood. One Democratic paper, the *Cleveland Plain Dealer*, questioned the veracity of the Davis disguise dispatches and noted that "It is now said that Davis had no disguise on at all, but was found in his tent dressed in a morning gown—and he absolutely had his boots on,—two articles of dress common to other men, less notorious than the rebel President."[22]

But for most northern Republicans, Jefferson Davis had become the petticoated president. Seeing Davis as the symbolic representative of the Confederacy, they interpreted the cartoons and reports as a metaphorical unmanning of the southern aristocracy. Northerners thus linked gender and class in their postwar portrayal of the southern ruling class but, in doing so, they turned the assertions of southern men on their heads. Davis may have represented the southern "chivalry" but now northerners were told that this chivalry could no longer lay claim to courage or a protective posture toward their women. Now it was Mrs. Davis who did the protecting as she advised the Union soldiers "not to provoke the President, or he might hurt some of 'em." The *New*

York Herald believed that the very thought of Davis, coward in
women's clothes, harming brave Union soldiers, must have been
"received with shouts of laughter"; but, in extending the role
reversal, the *Herald* cast the Union soldiers as the truly chivalric
ones and so supposed that they might laugh but only when "the
lady's back was turned." Finally, to underscore the transformation of roles and the loss of the male aristocrat's power, the *Herald*
informed its readers that Mrs. Davis's actions proved her to be
"more of a man than her husband."[23]

These ludicrous scenes of "the last shift of the Confederacy"
not only challenged Dixie's manhood but also ridiculed the
position of southern women. On one level, these depictions of
Davis as a woman satirized the chivalric ideal and the cult of
southern womanhood. When northerners depicted the Confederate leader as an awkward and ungainly female and then proceeded to crown him as "the belle of Richmond," they explicitly
challenged the delicate and sentimental ideal of southern femininity, a notion which northerners had been familiar with since
the antebellum period. But northerners also read into the Davis
images the idea of southern women's commitment to the Confederacy, finding in these depictions further affirmation of the belief
that southern women had become the foundation of southern
sectionalism. After all, if southern women had been the mainstay
of the rebellion, then it seemed only natural for Jefferson Davis to
reveal himself as one of the Confederacy's diehard supporters.
The *New York Herald,* for example, combined the image of the
petticoated Davis with the notion of southern fakery and a
feminized Confederacy. They saw Davis as a true representative
of southern hypocrisy and applauded his appearance in feminine
disguise as it confirmed the contention that the Confederacy "was
mainly supported by women and was as hollow as a hoopskirt."[24]

Finally, by casting Davis as a spiteful southern female, northern
images found a way to stifle this feminine hostility, to squelch that
aspect of the rebellion that could not be defeated on the battlefield. Hence, Union officers often surrounded and looked
leeringly at "Jeffie D.," who was frequently identified as a "lone"
and "unprotected female" (Figure 2). In other accounts, soldiers
subdued the unruly "female" by stripping off her notorious skirt,
or some form of feminine apparel, which she had rudely swished

JEFFERSON DAVIS AS AN UNPROTECTED FEMALE!

"He is one of those rare types of humanity born to control destiny, or to accept, without murmur, annihilation as the natural consequence of failure."—*N. Y. Daily News, May 15, 1865.*

Figure 2. Harper's Weekly *May 27, 1865.*

at Yankee soldiers. Even that epitome of bourgeois respectability, the *Atlantic Monthly*, maintained that, while the Union soldiers treated their prisoner kindly and considerately, Davis had been "stripped of his female attire." In effect, once the southern enemy had been pictured as a woman, northerners could punish that enemy in any manner they saw fit, even if that meant a sexually aggressive behavior which came close to rape. Thus, while Figure 1 suggests castration, it also presents a picture of violent sexual domination over an apparent woman. In the form of a woman,

Davis had become the object of any and every type of northern
male abuse.[25]

Still, as most accounts revealed, Davis was neither a woman nor
a man, but some amalgamation of both. His capture, the *New York
Herald* suggested, demonstrated an extreme state of gender
confusion:

> When [Davis] was finally brought to bay, he remembered that he
> was a man and flourished a bowie knife. . . . [But] the appear-
> ance of a Colt's revolver drove all his courage out of his heart, and
> reminded him that he was only a poor, lone woman. Consequently,
> he dropped his skirts and his knife . . . and blushingly pro-
> claimed, in falsetto tones, his indignation at being so energetically
> pursued, saying that "he believed our Government more magnani-
> mous than to hunt down women and children." From this state-
> ment we infer that the redoubtable Jeff had confused ideas as to
> whether he was a woman or a child.

In effect, Davis had become a peculiar symbol of both southern
men and southern women, at one moment the depiction of
southern gentlemen's manly pretenses, and at another the representative of those "bitter, spiteful women" loathed by northern
journalists and Union soldiers. And, in this way, he became a
figure whose subjugation could prove northern virility in several
ways. Davis, as a man who might attack with his bowie knife, was
seized at gunpoint and defeated in a way that men subdue men.
Knowing that, despite his disguise, Davis was really not a woman,
northern soldiers could prove their superior prowess in bringing
down this dangerous fugitive. Still, because he was a southern
man, northern men also believed that Davis lacked the genuine
qualities of masculinity; he had been an imposter of manliness.
Hence, Davis, appropriately enough, was shown in a disguise, in
a costume which hinted at his questionable masculinity. His
cowardice, his false bravado, and his final "shift" showed the
Confederate leader to be more like a woman than a man, a
woman who had not fought on the battlefield but would viciously
snipe at northern men from the sidelines. And so, Davis-as-
woman had to be subdued again: "she" had to be stripped of her
attire or, when protrayed as a "lone" and "unprotected" female
"she" would be leered at by lecherous Union soldiers (Figure 2).

In any case, whether as sexual aggressors or as superior soldiers, northern men could prove themselves the manly superiors of Davis and all that he/she represented.[26]

These gendered images of the South, especially the depictions of a female-led and feminine-inspired Confederacy, offered northern men more than just a vehicle for subduing southern women's intransigence. Ultimately, these images pointed to the northern man's conception of power and regional identity in the postwar society. Whether pictured as a Confederate president in women's clothes or as those "spiteful women" who "nursed the Rebellion," the southern Confederacy had been implicated in a complex web of gendered imagery which, to northern men, demonstrated the weakness and the illegitimacy of that government. These metaphors follow a pattern, described by historian Joan Scott, in which "gender has been employed literally or analogically in political theory to . . . express the relationship between ruler and ruled." In the aftermath of the Civil War gender was used to signify relationships of power, in this case to reveal northern men's belief in the natural condition of control which they were to exercise over the South. In the immediate postwar period, these notions of gender and sectional power presented themselves as images of weakened southern men, hostile southern women, and a disguised Jefferson Davis, all of whom were ultimately suppressed by virile northern soldiers. In this way, northern men conveyed their understanding of political power in the postwar society; and, at the same time, they also extolled their superior masculinity, rooted in their distinct social and economic system, which they contrasted to the corrupted gender code of the south.[27]

Yet, within a few years, these images had been somewhat softened, pointing to the possibility of a more harmonious sectional reconciliation. Beginning in the 1870s and continuing into the twentieth century, countless novels, short stories, and plays offered a standard recipe of reconciliation, a romantic plot which saw the initially spiteful southern belle tamed and subdued by the love of a Union officer. The new image suggested a more peaceable truce between the two sections, but one in which the power relations were still clearly defined. Indeed, according to journalist John Trowbridge, this was more than a fictional device; it was part of the political solution of the post–Civil War crisis. Writing his memoirs in the early twentieth century, Trowbridge recalled his travels in the postwar South, offering a gendered interpretation of what he had seen. "I found those who had been in the Confederate ranks," Trowbridge wrote, "generally the most ready to resume their loyalty to the flag they had fought against." These were the men who, apparently, had experienced the might of northern manliness on the battlefield and could thus be reformed of their sinful ways. But, Trowbridge pointed out, "the female secessionists were bitterest of all" and "to appeal to their reason was idle." Still, reunion with southern women could be accomplished as surely as it had been with southern men for, as Trowbridge noted, "they were vulnerable on the side of the sentiments; and many a fair one was converted from the heresy of state rights by some handsome Federal officer, who judiciously mingled love with loyalty in his addresses, and pleaded for the union of hands as well as the union of States." Within this "union of hands" was a more general conception of power and the path towards a stronger and reunited nation. Marriage, signifying an arrangement of proper, well-ordered, and hierarchical gender relations, became the metaphor for the reunited states, for a nation of clearly defined laws and hierarchies in regard to both North and South and men and women.[28]

In both the antebellum and postbellum dialogue, gender served as a central metaphor in the sectional debate between the North and the South. Implicit in northern men's free-labor ideology, and their free-labor critique of the South, was an understanding of two competing notions of masculinity—one rooted in hard work and moral self-restraint, the other mired in slavery, aggression, and vice. The northern victory in the Civil War thus seemed to many as a final affirmation of northern men's superior model of manliness. In contrast, the southern system seemed to rest on a foundation of gender corruption where whining, nervous men marched into battle and spiteful, angry women set the political agenda. Even the president of the Confederacy had revealed that neither southern men nor southern women understood the proper boundaries for gender behavior. In this way, northern men relied on these images of gender to define their regional distinctiveness and, in the aftermath of the war, to establish their regional and political superiority. Ultimately, by softening their portrayal of southern women and by proposing a marriage between the sections, northerners introduced a new image of gender into their political discourse, one which allowed for a reconciliation with the South but maintained a clear and hierarchical relationship of power.

Chapter 17

XXXXXXXXXXXXXXXXXXXXXXXXXXX

Reconstructing Freedwomen

CATHERINE CLINTON

There is no telling tale, no single story to capture the forces unleashed at war's end. The conquered Confederacy did not so much surrender as let the battlegrounds come home. Conflict reconfigurated: from the streets to the statehouses, in kitchens and in courtrooms terrain remained contested.[1] Sexual dynamics, racial definitions, gender roles as well as the political economy underwent traumatizing transformations.

There are many layers to unpeel before we can even identify historical changes wrought by Reconstruction, much less assess the impact on the emancipated generation and their descendants. Decoding women's roles remains complex.[2] The memoirs from this period are sparse. We have some black autobiographies, but most narratives by women are from the antebellum era or deal with the period following Reconstruction. Some manuscript material in southern archives offers evidence, but these traditional sources have severe limitations as most are written by whites and tell us more about white views than black lives. Riveting insight can be gleaned from both the records of the Freedman's Bureau and black newspapers from the period, as both are rich with unexploited material.

The testimony of former slaves themselves provides us with poignant images and clues to historical change. An oration celebrating the first anniversary of black freedom on January 5, 1866, included the following remarks: "This is a day of gratitude for the freedom of matrimony. Formerly there was no security for domestic happiness. Our ladies were insulted and degraded with or without their consent. Our wives were sold and husbands bought, children were begotten and enslaved by their fathers, we therefore were polygamists by virtue of our condition. But now we can marry and raise our children and teach them to fear God, O! black age of dissipation, thy days are nearly numbered."[3] We know that many slaves took extreme measures to legitimate slave unions.[4] We have countless examples which testify to the strength of and regard for the marital bond.

At the same time, emancipated slaves defied the dictates of southern society to find their own paths to freedom. On this question of marriage blacks frequently evaded white laws during this period. First and most important, former slaves were not likely to adhere strictly to white interference with their choices in the marital realm considering the hypocrisy under which they suffered as slaves. If slaves rejected standards set by former slaveholders, it is understandable.

Further, southern legislatures dealt with the thorny issue of legitimating slave unions in a haphazard fashion. As Margaret Burnham has shown, four different means of dealing with the problem emerged. First, some states—Alabama, Mississippi, Tennessee, Texas, Virginia, and West Virginia—declared all slave "customary marriages" as legal. Kentucky, Louisiana, Maryland, and North Carolina required couples to register unions with the county clerk. Four other states demanded remarriage in order to legitimate children: Florida, Georgia, Missouri, and South Carolina. Other states expected courts to solve the question of the legality of unions and legitimacy of offspring on a case-by-case basis.[5] Although indeed thousands attempted to conform to state law, chaos threatened.

One Freedman's Bureau agent, H. C. Baker, reported his dilemma when freedwoman Susannah Hawkins appealed to him for help in March 1867. Hawkins had married a fellow slave, Jacob Jones, in 1863. The couple spent time in Pennslyvania during the war, but returned to Virginia in September 1866. Shortly thereafter Jones deserted Hawkins, returned to Pennsylvania, and married a white woman. Another agent, M. S. Hopkins, commented in exasperation, "the within case is a deplorable instance of one of the evils of slavery. To the laws of Virginia, there was no such relation known as man and wife among slaves and consequently their marriage not being legal and binding there is no power to make the man respect it. By a recent law of Virginia all colored persons who were cohabiting together as nominally on the 27th of February 1866 were made legally so. It appears these parties were not in this state at that time. The laws of Pennsylvania forbid blacks and whites intermarrying I think."[6]

The law played havoc, but most Bureau agents soldiered on. On September 1, 1865, Assistant Superintendent C. W. Buckley reported from Montgomery, Alabama: "I am pained daily at the connubial relations of the colored people. I am determined to change their condition in this respect, as far as I may be able, and am resolved to give this matter my personal attention and efforts. Husbands & wifes [*sic*] are separating at a fearful rate: and 'taking up' with other persons. Not unfrequently a man is living with two or three wifes. . . ." Buckley's complaint is part of a constant refrain from field agents, lamenting these developments. However, he does see a partial solution: "I could do much to encourage lawful marriage among this people but they are not able to pay two dollars for a license, the price charged by the county judges."[7] In January 1869 in Rosedale, Mississippi, agent J. R. Webster suggested that "it would be to the furtherance of Morality if the agents of the Bureau were authorized to perform the marriage ceremony and were ordered to do so free of charge."[8]

One plantation owner in Manchester, South Carolina, included in his "regulations for freed negro labourers" that "labourers must have but one wife, and they must be lawfully married."[9] Ex-slave T. W. Cotton told an interviewer that the Ku Klux Klan "come in on me once before I married. I was at my girl's house. They wanted to be sure we married. The principal thing they was to see was that you didn't live in the house wid a woman till you be married. I wasn't married, but I soon did marry her. They scared us up some."[10] White interference was rarely this innocuous.

Ex-slaves reported that before Emancipation masters prevented slave men from striking their wives—and agents revealed that they took on this paternalistic role after abolition. However, this is a much more complex dynamic when we consider that the very same masters who might "protect" slave wives from being struck by their husbands might also consider it *their own* right to strike the woman—to exert control and maintain authority on the plantation, a right they wished to maintain as employers.

Most freedwomen resisted bringing agents into domestic matters. They recognized the limited role the Bureau could play in their lives and the temporary nature of federal force—indeed, perhaps former slaves more than Union troops knew how short-lived this experiment of northern intervention might be. Reliance on bureau agents, allied by color with their former masters, was dangerous for blacks in the short term and might result in retaliation over the long haul. The long arm of paternalism— clothed in blue uniform or tattered grey—was grasped only under duress.

Women generally sought assistance when frantic or destitute, without alternatives. The desperate circumstances of most women is revealed by even a brief survey of the records. Looking at the petitions for relief in one Alabama county in 1867, almost 90 percent of the heads of household were women.[11] In January 1867 a petitioner asked the Bureau to help a family with a "43 year old mother raising her six children (from 2 to 12 yrs. old) and keeping her sixty-five year old blind mother."[12] Equally common is the complaint of women run off the land just before getting paid. Some women did report that their husbands ran out on them in times of economic crises—but not to force apprehension or punishment, merely to justify their claims for assistance.

Mothers were those most severely affected by Emancipation's adversities, as Jacqueline Jones has so eloquently demonstrated. First and foremost, the care and feeding of children were thrown onto women who had few and rapidly depleting resources for caring for their young. A Bureau agent reported from King Williams County, Virginia, that "there is little call for female help, and women with children are not desired."[13] This comment does not begin to convey the dimensions of this crisis. While hundreds of thousands of freedpeople were negotiating contracts and selling their labor, women with children could be discriminated against and might be "blackballed" by employers.

Mothers had few alternatives and little recourse. When Cornelia Whitley and her sick child were thrown out of the house of her employer, Allen Dickenson (of Orange County, Virginia), in September 1865, she complained to the Bureau. An agent reported that Mrs. Dickenson then assaulted Whitley for going to the agency for help.[14] Women were trapped and, in some cases, rendered senseless by the ordeal of survival.

In October 1868 Polly Jennings of Halifax County, Virginia, was sentenced to hang for infanticide. Her employer, a Mr. Jennings, told her not to have any more children as she was unmarried and already supported five offspring. He threatened her that if she bore another child, he would dismiss her—throwing Polly and her children even further along poverty's downward spiral. When she found herself pregnant again, she murdered her newborn, leaving it in the woods. A Bureau officer attempted to get her death sentence commuted to life imprisonment. Polly Jennings's sacrifice of one child for the good of the five older ones was dramatic and unusual.[15] But the fact that women were confronted with life-and-death issues on a daily basis is not.

We know that whites were unwilling to expand their prewar definitions of "manhood" and "womanhood" to include formerly enslaved persons. Although the law might dictate an African American woman could now be a person and a wife, and a black man a citizen and voter, Lost Cause ideologues promoted white supremacy with a vengeance both fierce and formidable. Emancipation and federal conquest created unprecedented levels of anxiety among former Confederates who sought to refight the war on ideological grounds.

Within this new battle, gender and sexual roles were rewrought in a complex tangle of conflict and compromise. Certainly white supremacists intended to reassert their dominance by playing on antebellum themes—the "Sambo" incompetence of the black male and the moral bankruptcy of black women. Both of these racist stereotypes were woven from white fears—that the black man might wish to exact vengeance against his oppressor for generations of inhumanity. Second that the growing segment of the black population labeled "mulatto" might not be a result of slave women's promiscuity, but rather of white sexual coercion. Simultaneously, ex-Confederates, especially veterans, concocted new and important projections of their own fears—none more complex and potent than the "black rapist."

Equally powerful within the ideological warfare was the de-feminizing mythology launched at black womanhood during this era. Certainly Angela Davis, bell hooks, Deborah White, and Patricia Morton have made important inroads into this historical field imbedded with landmines.[16] Emancipation created few opportunities for African American women in the political economy beyond freedom. Women nevertheless seized the opportunity to express themselves, pioneering new avenues for individual and collective identity.

In October 1866 Patience Thompson stated her case against a white man, Thomas Gross of Irwin County, Georgia. When she refused to sell him soap, Gross became verbally abusive and she replied in kind. He responded by beating her. When the case went to the grand jury, they refused to support her for fear that their support might then have to be extended to "every Negro who choose to come before them." Thompson was forced to pay court costs and requested to "make up with Gross." She paid her fine but would not "make up" as the court had ordered.[17] Thompson was a strong example of this new model of freed-woman.

In July 1868 in Prince Edwards County, Virginia, four black women were in their own house singing when John Schofield (a white man) went to them and asked them to stop. When they refused he entered the house and beat them with his fists, then took out a knife and cut one of the women on the hand.[18] Subsequently, Schofield got off with a $15 fine and no reprimand. In Clinch County, Georgia, Viney Scarlett was arrested and given sixty-five lashes for using abusive language to a white woman.[19] Both the character and tone of black women's challenges shifted during Reconstruction, and were met with mighty resistance from white individuals and white authority.

Black women, fighting against the labels attached to them by former slaveowners, not only challenged these stereotypes directly but might throw them back at whites—unleashing violence. One tragic outcome is revealed in Culpepper County, Virginia, in February 1866 when Jane Twyman, working for Isiah Perry and his son George, accused Perry's wife and daughter of sleeping with other men. Twyman made her accusations in front of other servants. Alerted, Isaiah Perry grabbed his gun and confronted the woman. He shot at her as she ran from the house. After Twyman was wounded, Perry apologized—saying he did not mean to shoot her, only to frighten her. Twyman said she believed him in front of witnesses, and the two appeared reconciled. But while Twyman was having the bullet removed, Perry's son, in a drunken rage, pistol-whipped Twyman and "stomped" all over her. The case ostensibly ended when Isiah Perry died, Jane Twyman died of her injuries, and apparently two other witnesses to these attacks disappeared before George Perry could be brought to trial.[20]

It is difficult to fathom the fear created by a black woman fighting back—a force so strong that, in this particular case, it caused one white man to shoot at her and another to beat her to death. Such vocal and direct black female resistance—in this and many other instances—combined with the fear of male retaliation to fuel white hysteria during the postwar era.

The mechanism by which the nation was physically linked by the end of the nineteenth century, the railroad, ironically supplied the means by which the country came to be divided ideologically: the railway coach.[21] An article in 1866 in *The Loyal Georgian* (Augusta) asks, "Why is it that the wives and daughters of freedmen, though they be chaste as ice, and pay the same fare that white people do on railways, are put into filthy freight cars and compelled to submit to all kinds of vulgar and insulting language . . . ."?[22] Many distorted interpretations of this and other evidence have led some scholars to suppose that blacks were preoccupied with sexual purity as a means of emulating those white paragons to which African Americans aspired. Perhaps indeed models of white womanhood were cherished—but most likely to protect black women from errant white males whose techniques ranged from teasing to threats to gang rape. The status of "lady" was a plea for gentlemanly behavior from white males who had corrupted the status of slave women to "bestial" and hoped to preserve this degraded status past emancipation.

Few were able to challenge the hypocrisy of the sexual double standard explicitly, but African American women openly demanded the protection and privilege afforded white women by law. In 1868, three "colored females" brought a case before the U.S. District Court because they were "put out of ladies car" at Gordonsville by the railroad "on account of color."[23] Ida Wells-Barnett, only twenty-two, had her dress torn being pushed off a train when she tried to board the ladies' car in 1884. Humiliated but not humbled, she struck back through the courts and won $500 in damages.[24] This formative experience launched her on a career of reform and protest.

We know according the title of "ladies" for black women of whatever class or wealth was considered by white supremacists as insult to all white women within southern society. When Federal troops occupied southern towns during and after the war, many white belles displayed the affectation of wearing black veils—as mourning for their beloved Confederacy and to deny Yankees the pleasure of viewing their faces. After emancipation, when black women adopted this ornamentation as well—certainly for their own very different reasons of style and symbol—white women quickly abandoned this habit. Being undifferentiated from freedwomen was a risk they were unwilling to take—even for the Lost Cause crusade.

Southern white newspapers chronicled the crime and ignorance among freedpeople, featuring any violence and depravity they might detect among African American women. This libel and certainly slander created a constant war of words and images. Both as assailants and assailed, black women were stereotyped in accounts of violence. On July 30, 1867, the *Raleigh Register* reported:

> Another Horrible Murder in Richmond—Richmond is excited over another horrible and mysterious murder. This time a colored woman is found dead in the suburbs of the city with signs of violence about her. At the coroner's inquest, strong circumstantial evidence was educed [*sic*], which implicates her paramour—a colored man—as the murderer, and he was arrested and committed for examination.[25]

A week later another headline screamed: "A Fiendish Nurse Poisons a Child":

> On Saturday last a negro nurse employed by Mr. Wm. A. Pettaway
> in Richmond County, N.C. poured laudanum down the throat of
> his child, causing its death. On the previous day the female fiend
> had attempted to kill it by making it drink indigo. She was
> arrested.[26]

During this same period the paper reported a black wife being
shot through the head by a jealous husband who then hoped to
conceal his crime by burning her body.[27] Whether victims or
perpetrators, black women were involved in brutish horrors
according to the sensationalizing aspects of the white press. They
were not accorded the dignity of mention as clubwomen, church-
women, educators, or reformers.[28]

The message was clear and consistent. Before and during the
war black women were portrayed as aggressive, unrestrained,
and pathological. In this way whites justified their custodial
care—they were preventing African Americans from destroying
one another. With Emancipation, as ex-Confederates lamented,
former slaves were thrust into a free state for which they were
unprepared.[29]

The white South spent time and energy discrediting freedwomen's campaigns for dignity. The courtesies or niceties afforded black women were the subject of parody. A copy of the
Black Republican and Office-Holder's Journal, a handwritten and
viciously racist lampoon of a Radical Republican newspaper,
contained the following article:

> WHITE OUTRAGE: Yesterday afternoon, in de ebening, about
> thirteen o'clock, a cupple ob colored ladies pushed a white gal off
> de sidewalk, when de purposterous white wench gib sass to dem
> two epectable colored ladies, and told dem dey ought to be
> ashamed!—We blush at the thought! We axes what was the police
> doing all dat time—where am de war power and de militia commis-
> sion?[30]

This form of humor was both crude and effective. Indeed,
during Reconstruction, these images filtered into the national
press, especially *Harper's Weekly*.

African Americans found these cartoons and jokes no laughing
matter. Spokesman Henry Turner fought back boldly:

It was also said, and Southern fanatics rode that hobby everywhere, "That if you free the negro he will want to marry our daughters and sisters," that was another foolish dream. What do we want with their daughters and sisters? We have as much beauty as they. Look at our ladies, do you want more beauty than that? *All we ask of the white man is to let our ladies alone,* and they need not fear us. The difficulty has heretofore been, *our ladies were not always at our own disposal.*[31]

Turner might well have added that the protection of black women remained at the core of black complaints following emancipation.

Black men hoped by establishing themselves as protectors of wives and daughters they would lay claim to manhood while improving the lives of their loved ones and kin. In Richmond in 1865 Jenny Scott's husband stood up to soldiers who struck her, and suffered a severe beating on account of his heroism.[32] The following year a freedman complained to a Bureau Commissioner that his wife was accused by a "white lady" of "having intercourse" with another man. When the wife lashed back with verbal abuse, she was arrested, tried, sentenced to pay $16 in court costs and fined sixty lashes in Clinch County, Georgia. The husband wrote to the federal officer "believing that the days for corporeal punishment of the colored race are past, and knowing that this is by far not an isolated case."[33]

The beating, whipping, abuse, and coercion of black women under slavery is, as I have argued elsewhere, underemphasized in historical accounts.[34] Evidence indicates that these practices continued to plague black women following emancipation. The casual way in which ex-slaves address these issues weighs in favor of its commonality. C. W. Hawkins of Little Rock, Arkansas, reported in the WPA Narratives on coercion of slaves: "The women were beat and made to go to them. They were big fine men and the master wanted the women to have children by them. And there were some white men, too, who joined the slave women to do what they wanted to. Some of them didn't want to stop when slavery stopped."[35] Indeed, many of these attacks appear more violent and brutal in the postwar era. Whether their motives were humanitarian or mercenary, it was in the interests of the planters to keep their slaves healthy and alive. As ex-slaves, freedpeople could be maimed or killed with minimal interference from the ruling elite. The violent fate which befell black resistance served to muzzle protest.

A Freedman's Bureau agent reported on September 10, 1866, that Rhoda Ann Childs of Henry County was "taken from her house, in her husband's absence, by eight white men who stripped her, tied her to a log, beat and sexually abused her."[36] An account of this incident appeared on October 13 in the *Loyal Georgian,* published in Augusta: "Myself and husband were under contract with Mrs. Amanda Childs of Henry County and worked from January 1, 1866 until the crops were laid by, or in other words until the main work of the year was done without difficulty. Then (the fashion being prevalent among the planters) we were called upon one night." In Rhoda Childs's personal testimony, we have evidence of a political conspiracy to deprive freedpeople of their share of their labor. But far more harrowing is Childs's account of sexual abuse.

After a severe beating, she was "thrown upon the ground on my back, one of the two men stood upon my breast, while two others took hold of my feet and stretched my limbs as far apart as they could while the man standing upon my breast applied the strap to my private parts until they were satisfied that I was more dead than alive. Then a man supposed to be an ex-Confederate soldier, as he was on crutches, fell upon me and ravished me. During the whipping one of the men had run his pistol into me, and said he had a great mind to pull the trigger . . ."[37]

In this and in many other cases, the wife of a former Union soldier or the wife of a labor activist might be selected as the victim for gang or individual assault. In some ways her rape might be viewed as "symbolic," but regardless of the motives for this violation, these remained acts of real violence against individual women. The black women who suffered these brutal and dehumanizing attacks in this bloody power struggle in the postwar South were not just symbols of their race, but persons subjected to torture.

The attack upon the black wife or daughter provided a threat to communities as well as families. Hannah Travis recalled that "the Ku Klux never bothered us. They bothered some people about a mile from us. They took out the old man and whipped him. They made his wife get up and dance and she was in a delicate state. They made her get out of bed and dance, and after that they took her and whipped her and beat her, and she was in a delicate state, too."[38] For all the horror Hannah Travis's neighbor endured, she still escaped with her life, and we hope that of her unborn child.

George Band's wife was not so lucky. Because her husband was a local leader, known as someone who could always defend himself, "the Klan came to his house, took his wife, hung her to a tree, hacked her to death with knives." Band got his revenge by killing fourteen of these vigilantes, surprising them with a Winchester rifle, but he was forced to flee the county.[39]

The bloody battleground of Reconstruction included sexual as well as political ideologies. Confederate sympathizer Myrta Lockett Avary in *Dixie After the War* (1906) confidently claims, "The rapist is a product of the reconstruction period."[40] Like almost all white Southerners and most white Americans until the modern period, Avary does not bother to assign race to get her meaning across: she clearly expects us to assume that the rapist is a black man and the victim is a white female. Her explanation of the "Crime Against Womanhood" (published in 1906 by a respectable New York publisher, Doubleday) reflected popular ideology about the era: the ruin of innocent women by bestial blacks—a horror that justifies lynching. Further Avary goes on to argue that this crime "was a development of a period when the negro was dominated by political, religious and social advisors from the North and by the attitude of the northern press and pulpit. It was practically unknown in wartime, when negroes were left on plantations as protectors and guardians of white women and children."[41] Avary, of course, damns the North for their indignation against southern lawlessness and "not one word of sympathy or pity for the white victim of negro lust."[42]

At the time of Reconstruction these sexual libels and attacks upon the North were popular and frequent. An 1868 article in the *Atlanta Constitution* reported in earnest "that Mrs. Harriet Beecher Stowe is going to establish a school in Aiken, Ga., for the benefit of mulatto children that have been born in the South since its invasion by Yankee school-marms."[43] While northern women were smeared, southern white women were allegedly elevated. Indeed the editors of the *Atlanta Constitution* even encouraged white women to fill the gallery of the Georgia Reconstruction legislature, commenting that "the ladies are welcome and we think their presence there will have a good effect upon that piebald body."[44] The moral superiority of southern white women allegedly stood in stark contrast to northern women—while southern ladies could pride themselves on their purity of blood, ex-Confederates proclaimed northern women as "a mongrel race."[45] Much of this anxiety over blood, race, and sex reveals the torrents of hypocritical rage among white Southerners at this juncture.

Unfortunately for southern black women, emancipation escalated the degree of sexual violence to which they might be subjected. Freedwomen struggled to avoid the daily harassments imposed by white men before slavery ended. The so-called withdrawal of women from the labor force was black women's attempt to shift their productive roles into the family economy whenever possible, escaping white overseers and employers who proved an enduring threat. Freedwomen did not have the luxury of being interested in the status assigned to women who were ensconced in the domestic realm; they simply sought protection. Black women wanted respectability and the public image of virtue first for survival and then as a foundation for building their own, but more likely, their children's success.

Ironically, African American women's strategies and struggles in the nineteenth century have created bitter debate in the twentieth century as we attempt to reconcile the matrifocality of black households with racist and sexist assumptions about the role of families within modern culture. Further, the abolition of slavery shifted notions of appropriate sexual conduct and gave black women, if not more opportunities to resist coercion, then the hope that their horizons could expand while sexual abuse diminished. Reconstruction in many ways offered black women their rights, but little means to exercise those legal privileges. It afforded women a voice, but denied African Americans a forum within which to speak and be heard without reprisals.

The sexual terrorism of race politics during Reconstruction is evident. White women's bodies became sacred territory over which ex-Confederates organized and battled, refighting the war and re-exerting regional and race pride. Black women's bodies were just as critical. For too long shame and silence cloaked their sexual violation. Almost all the scholarly literature published on the topic of rape in the South deals exclusively with white victims, even the works devoted to interracial rape. This reflects racism pervasive within both the academy and society at large. But indictments are finally emerging, as there is no statute of limitations for historians. Voices ring loud and clear, compelling us to listen, to examine our shortcomings, and to incorporate critical issues of gender and sexuality into our reconstructions of freedwomen.

Chapter 18

XXXXXXXXXXXXXXXXXXXXXXXXX

Reshaping the Bonds of Womanhood: Divorce in Reconstruction North Carolina

VICTORIA BYNUM

In recent years, scholars have increasingly studied the private world of the family to enhance our understanding of the contours of public institutions of power. By shifting the inquiry away from public institutions toward personal household relations, we have developed a more comprehensive view of the ways in which household and kin relationships underwrite the transmission of culture and wealth from one generation to the next. Analyses of gender roles, the way in which societies mediate women's and men's sexual and reproductive behavior within and outside the family structure, have proved especially illuminating with regard to how the private and public worlds intersect. Subjecting the private family to public scrutiny can reveal the true status of women and the dynamics of their daily lives.[1] Divorce patterns may also reflect the social effects of political arrangements of race and class, or of upheavals like war and depression, on "ordinary" people.

When contrasted with court divorce decisions rendered between 1840 and 1860 in North Carolina, court divorce rulings between 1860 and 1880 offer evidence of the disruptive impact of the Civil War and Reconstruction upon the private lives of couples. As instruments of the state, superior courts and the supreme court interpreted postbellum divorce laws within an emerging new social order. These courts had to resolve divorce suits in the context of broader social and economic stress and in accordance with important changes in the law during the 1871–72 legislative sessions.

Although the essential definitions of male and female social and marital roles did not change between 1860 and 1880, the relationship between individuals and the larger society did. Men gained greater rights of marital contract that reflected the shifting locus of social and political stability away from the family. To a lesser extent, women did, too, evidenced in expanded grounds for legal separation. Unlike men, however, women continued to be defined as members of a family unit, not as individuals.

The war and Republican Reconstruction had shattered the old patriarchal system, but by 1870, North Carolina Conservatives—a coalition of Democrats and a few former Whigs—had ousted the Republicans and gained control of the state legislature. This new Conservative legislature revised many statutes, including those related to divorce, during the 1871–72 session. First, the Redeemer legislature encouraged women to *remain* in marriages by allowing them to sue for alimony without suing for divorce or separation of bed and board.[2] Second, it revised the grounds for divorce in a way that favored husbands. Adultery and impotence remained the sole grounds for a full divorce (*a vinculo*), but the law now injected gender distinctions into its definition of adultery. Whereas either sex could be divorced for having committed adultery *and* having abandoned one's spouse, only a woman could be divorced simply for the act of adultery. A husband's adultery had to be combined with abandonment of his wife to be considered grounds for divorce.[3]

The legislature also expanded the grounds for a separation of bed and board (*a mensa et thoro*) and more clearly distinguished such grounds from those for absolute divorce. A spouse who had been abandoned, driven from home, treated "cruelly" or "barbarously" in a way that endangered his or her life, or subjected to "intolerable" and "burdensome" indignities, or whose partner was a habitual drunkard could petition for a legal separation.[4] The list of admissible grounds seemed aimed at alleviating suffering more commonly experienced by wives than husbands. The grounds for obtaining a legal separation were apparently designed for women much as absolute divorces were for men. A legal separation, however, brought only physical separation; it did not give one the right to remarry, and it was not necessary in order for a wife to be granted alimony. For many women, seeking this partial divorce was probably not worth the time and effort required.

Ultimately, then, postbellum divorce laws in North Carolina provided men, but not women, greater freedom to divorce than had antebellum divorce laws. The abolition of slavery and the growing national emphasis on individualism accounted for this change. In antebellum North Carolina, as in the slaveholding South generally, the institutions of slavery and the family were so intertwined that laws governing one influenced those governing the other. As Elizabeth Fox-Genovese has pointed out, the "family figured as a central metaphor for southern society as a whole."[5] If slavery—the backbone of the southern economy— were to remain stable, so must the family, which was the backbone of the southern political and social structure.

In keeping with this philosophy, the antebellum North Carolina Supreme Court, presided over by Chief Justice Thomas Ruffin from 1833 to 1852, had consistently discouraged divorce. Ruffin, one of the state's pre-eminent proslavery philosophers, emphatically rejected claims that individual "rights" to happiness—male or female—should take precedence over social stability. "Divorce from the bonds of matrimony is not to be granted merely because one or both of the parties wish it," he declared in 1836. "It is not simply a cause between the parties to the record; the country is also a party, and its best interests are at stake." So rarely did Ruffin find the "country's" interests served by divorce that he proclaimed in 1832 that "there is in general no safe rule but this: that persons who marry agree to take each other *as they are.*"[6]

Ruffin expressed the above opinion in response to a divorce petition by Marville Scroggins, who sued his wife Lucretia on grounds she had been pregnant by another man at the time of their marriage in 1828 and had since given birth to a mulatto child. In affirming the lower court's denial of a divorce to Scroggins, Chief Justice Ruffin argued that marriage was one of the most important inviolable relationships of North Carolina society. He emphasized that to require partners to reveal their "defects" to each other before marrying would set a "dangerous precedent." "It would be impossible to say where it would stop," he wrote. For a woman to disclose her premarital affair, particularly one that included a black man, would no doubt mean that "she loses that marriage, and places it in the power of the suitor to proclaim her shame, and preclude her from any other alliance, and from reformation."[7] Marriage and family were a woman's entire sphere, and she must not be prevented from attaining them, according to Ruffin, lest society be crippled simply to alleviate an individual man's shame.

Ruffin's reasoning should not be construed as a tolerance of miscegenation. He regarded the "degradation" of Lucretia Scroggins as "absolute," and he observed that the "abhorrence of the community against the offender and contempt for the husband is so marked and unextinguishable, that the Court has not been able, without a struggle, to follow those rules which their dispassionate judgment sanctions." For Ruffin, however, the sanctity of marriage preceded even the "purity" of race when it came to protecting the antebellum social order.[8]

The case of *Barden v. Barden,* decided in December of the same year, demonstrated how difficult it was to make this distinction. In this case, Jesse Barden also sued his wife for divorce on grounds that she had given birth to a mulatto child. The court agreed to grant a new trial in the lower court. Ruffin, in response to public criticism of his decision in *Scroggins v. Scroggins,* explained that the court's decision was "a *concession* to the deep-rooted and virtuous prejudices of the community upon this subject" (emphasis mine).[9]

Although Ruffin dominated the high court during his tenure as chief justice, dissenting opinions surfaced, especially after Richmond M. Pearson joined the state supreme court in 1848. Ruffin and Pearson represented competing views of how best to preserve order and good government in North Carolina. Ruffin came as close as any man to representing a "Southern aristocracy"; he possessed wealth, an illustrious genealogy, and a Princeton degree, and he considered himself a Jeffersonian Democrat. Pearson, on the other hand, hailed from a competing class of western North Carolina slaveholders. His ancestors were rising merchants and planters; politically, they were federalist Whigs. Thus, Ruffin represented a class that sought to retain its wealth and power by maintaining social and political stability. In contrast, Pearson represented the more entrepreneurial slaveholders and yeomen of the west who challenged the hegemony of the "Raleigh Clique" of politicians and lawyers to which Ruffin belonged.[10]

The personal and political differences between Ruffin and Pearson manifested themselves in court decisions regarding the legal status of women. Ruffin displayed a paternalistic, even chivalrous view of the rights of upper-class white women, while Pearson emphasized men's near-absolute authority rather than women's reciprocal rights to protection and deference. Differences in temperament and class backgrounds influenced their attitudes toward women, just as they shaped their political allegiances. Both men accepted without question that wives were subordinate to husbands, but Ruffin's view of women was embedded in an aristocratic ideology of *noblesse oblige* toward one's social "inferiors." Pearson's was much less so. After Ruffin's retirement from the bench in 1858, and the defeat of the Confederacy in 1865, Pearson's emphasis on women's rather than men's marital obligations increasingly predominated.[11]

In 1875, Justice Pearson explained without hesitation or apology the double standard applied to adultery by the 1871–72 legislature: "There is a difference between adultery committed by a husband and adultery committed by a wife—the difference being in favor of the husband." A husband who condoned or ignored a wife's adultery, he argued, would be "cuckolded" and "disgraced," while a wife who did so would only be "pitied." Society knew that a husband's behavior was largely beyond a wife's control, given her dependent status, Pearson pointed out.[12] Postbellum changes in the law recognized divorce as a reward for men's loss of authority over their wives in a way that antebellum laws and judges did not. Indeed, in a number of antebellum divorce suits appealed to the high court, Ruffin had held men responsible for their wives' misbehavior.[13] In the postbellum era, the right to rule one's wife increasingly became an end in itself, rather than one component of a hierarchical, organic society.

A divorce case appealed to the state supreme court in June

1877 underscored the changes in postbellum judicial reasoning. James C. Long sued his wife Teresa for an absolute divorce on grounds that she, without his knowledge, had been pregnant by another man at the time of their marriage. Citing the relevant statutes and the 1832 *Scroggins v. Scroggins* case as precedent, the high court affirmed the lower court's denial of a divorce to Long. Illuminating the changing legal thought was a lengthy dissent by Justice William Blount Rodman to the higher court's decision. Rodman supported men's individual marital rights and expressed his belief in women's responsibility for being "pure" when they married. Departing from the paternalistic logic of Chief Justice Ruffin in 1832, Rodman wrote that "if a bride be at the time of marriage pregnant by a stranger, she is incompetent . . . to fulfill her part of the contract in that sense which is its holiest and purest interpretation."[14] In other words, she must be sexually pure.

Instead of emphasizing the needs of the "country," Rodman stressed the rights and responsibilities of "contract." He also endorsed the pseudo-scientific theories of race that underlay an expanding system of racial segregation. Although Teresa Long had given birth to a white child, Rodman raised the specter that she, like Lucretia Scroggins in 1832, might have been carrying a mulatto child. Above all, he cited this possibility as a reason for making a wife's premarital pregnancy grounds for divorce. "As physiologists tell us," he wrote, "the blood of the woman . . . has been tainted by mingling with that of her first [mulatto] child, and she is incapable of bearing children that will not show mixture of African blood in appearance or character." He concluded that if divorce were not allowed in such cases, "man has lost the common right lawfully to continue his pure race."[15]

Rodman was the quintessential New South leader, willing to shift party allegiances temporarily and welcome northern capital in order to build a new order that preserved as many of the sexual, racial, and class prerogatives of the old as possible. He applied new standards of judgment to the institution of marriage when those of the past conflicted with the emerging system of racial segregation that had replaced slavery. His rejection of Ruffin's reasoning in *Scroggins v. Scroggins* testified to the ability of many Old South conservatives to accommodate their thinking to the demands of the New South. He pointed out the legal contradiction that compelled a man to remain married to the mother of a mulatto child, thus forcing whites and mulattoes to share a common "hearth," while racial segregation laws required "that the mulatto and his white brothers shall not attend the same school."[16]

After the abolition of slavery, racial control became the responsibility of public institutions rather than families. The effort to institute physical separation of the races, which could never have been considered while slavery existed, further contributed to changing ideas about the relationship of marriage and divorce to the larger society. In 1879, for example, the North Carolina legislature made a wife's pregnancy by someone other than her husband and without the latter's knowledge at the time of marriage grounds for an absolute divorce.[17]

To determine how changes in the law and judicial reasoning affected the domestic relations of ordinary men and women in postwar North Carolina, we must turn from decisions of the state supreme court to those of the county superior courts. In the latter, people expressed their needs and perceptions of their marital rights in this new order. In the case of Granville, Orange, and Montgomery counties, differences in social composition shaped contrasting patterns of divorce. In Granville, a former plantation county that had a large African American population, nearly as many African Americans (seven) sued for divorce as did whites (nine). Of the three counties, Orange, which was the most disrupted by Reconstruction and the subsequent backlash, had the most dramatic increase in divorces and the highest divorce rate. Montgomery County, more rural and isolated from centers of political power than either Granville or Orange, had the fewest divorces. As in Granville, its overall number of divorces did not increase. (See Table 1.)

An important contrast between antebellum and postbellum divorce petitions was the changing sex ratio of the litigants. Whereas twice as many women as men sought divorce prior to the Civil War, men who petitioned for divorce during and after the war outnumbered female petitioners by a three-to-one margin. In fact, the total number of men who sought divorce during and

Table 1. The Number of Petitions for Divorce Filed in the Superior Courts of North Carolina by County and Gender

	1840–1860			1860–1880		
	Male	Female	Total	Male	Female	Total
Granville	3	13	16	14	2	16
Orange	7	4	11	16	7	23
Montgomery	1	5	6	4	2	6
Total:	11	22	33	34	11	45

Source: Divorce records and Superior Court minutes of Granville, Orange, and Montgomery counties. North Carolina Department of Archives and History (NCDAH), Raleigh, North Carolina.

after the war tripled, while the total number of women who petitioned for divorce decreased by one-half. (See Table 1.)

How do we account for this profound shift in divorce patterns? In part, this shift reflected changing patterns of adultery. Prior to the Civil War, many more men than women were charged with this offense. Superior court records from Granville, Montgomery, and Orange counties for the period 1860–69 suggest, however, that adultery increased among wives who were temporarily separated from their husbands as a result of the war. Between 1866 and 1868, several male plaintiffs specifically blamed the war for their wives' adultery. For example, Orange County's John Bowling, who claimed that he and his wife Elizabeth had been perfectly happy before he joined the Confederate Army, complained that a year after his wartime departure, "his house had been converted into a brothel." Willie Couch, also of Orange County, lodged a similar complaint. He claimed that when he returned home from the army in May 1865, his wife had been transformed into a "lewd woman and common prostitute" who had given birth to another man's child. Granville County's Wyatt Belvin and Orange County's James Wells recounted similar good-wives-gone-bad stories in their 1866 divorce petitions.[18]

Of the ten divorce petitions filed by men between 1866 and 1868, six were so similar in their allegations that wives had become full-blown prostitutes that they seem rather formulaic. Elizabeth Bowling, Nancy Jane Wells, and Emma Couch were all described as "common prostitutes," and Sophia Anderson was referred to as a "notorious prostitute." According to the other petitions, Mrs. Micajah Lancaster had abandoned herself to "promiscuous prostitution," and Agnes Belvin had run off to Richmond where she "took lodgings with the keeper of a common whore-house."[19]

Like antebellum divorce petitions, those of the 1860s were filled with lurid details of the most degraded and extreme levels of adultery. Unlike the earlier petitions, however, these primarily contained accusations against women rather than men. Since no changes in divorce law had yet occurred to encourage men to believe that divorce would be any easier to obtain after the war than it had been before, male petitioners sensationalized the details of their wives' adultery for dramatic effect. They often cultivated the sympathy of judges by invoking the image of a patriotic soldier who returned home only to find himself shamed by his wife's behavior.[20]

The number of men seeking divorce may also have increased in response to an act passed by the Republican-dominated legislature of 1868–69 that made it easier to get authorization to sue as a pauper.[21] Acquiring pauper status relieved petitioners of paying court fees and allowed them access to counsel assigned by the courts. In Orange, Montgomery, and Granville counties, nine petitioners, seven of whom were male, sued for divorce as paupers between 1860 and 1880, whereas only two petitioners, both of whom were women, had done so between 1840 and 1860. A much higher illiteracy rate among male petitioners in the postbellum period also suggests that poor men, not poor women, increasingly sought divorce. (See Table 2.) In times of economic stress such as the 1870s, men, encouraged by lower court costs, were more likely to flee the responsibilities of marriage, while women were more likely to cling to marriage as security. Most women who had sought divorces in the antebellum period were from the slaveholding class; over half were from planter-dominated Granville County. In contrast, most postbellum male plaintiffs were from Orange County's white yeomanry or Granville's substantial African American population.[22]

The revisions of divorce statutes that followed the overthrow of Republican Reconstruction in North Carolina further encour-

Table 2. The Number of Petitions for Divorce Filed in the Superior
Courts of North Carolina According to Race, Pauperism, and Illiteracy

	1840–1860			1860–1880		
	Male	*Female*	*Total*	*Male*	*Female*	*Total*
African Amer.	1	0	1	8	0	8
Pauper	0	2	2	7	2	9
Illiterate	1	3	4	9	3	12

Source: Divorce Records and Manuscript Censuses, 1860, for Granville, Orange, and Montgomery counties, NCDAH.

aged dissatisfied husbands to seek divorces. Proving mere adultery was far easier than proving both adultery and abandonment. The fact that far less sensationalized accounts of spouses' adultery appeared in divorce petitions filed during the 1870s indicates that petitioners were now more confident that a single charge of infidelity would suffice to win a divorce.

For women, however, divorce remained as difficult to obtain as ever. Between 1872 and 1880, only three women from the three counties (compared with twenty men) petitioned for an absolute divorce, as opposed to a more easily obtainable legal separation of bed and board. Mary Jane Boothe, Minerva Caldwell, and Esther Brown, all from Orange County, received full divorces only after they proved that their husbands had abandoned them *and* had committed adultery. Orange County's Susan Roach and Montgomery's Lucy Lammonds applied only for separations of bed and board, although Roach accused her husband of having committed adultery and Lammonds produced witnesses who testified that her husband had beaten her with a stick and horsewhip, had driven her from her home, kept her personal property from her, and had once shot at her. In contrast, eleven men obtained full divorces during the 1870s on the sole basis of their wives' adultery with single individuals.[23]

As in the case of white couples involved in divorce cases, most African American litigants were male. At least eight, perhaps nine, of the thirty-four men who sued for divorce in Orange, Granville, and Montgomery counties between 1860 and 1880 were African American.[24] Not one of the eleven women who

petitioned for divorce during that period was African American.
(See Table 2.)

Although there was little difference between the petitions filed
by black and white men in superior courts during the 1870s, two
African American men's petitions, both filed in the Granville
superior court in 1876, contain curious similarities that suggest
racial stereotyping of what constituted a "bad" African American
wife. Both Smith Watkins and E. B. Bullock accused their wives of
adultery, and they accused them of asserting their broader right
to do whatever they pleased in the marriage. Watkins claimed
that when he caught his wife for the second time committing
adultery in the lot of the Colored Baptist Church, she retorted, "I
am my own woman and will do as I please!" Bullock also reported
that his wife "continually" committed adultery with another man
and that she "often remarked" that she was "her own woman and
would do as she pleased."[25]

It is tempting to conclude from the above evidence that Dink
Watkins and Jane Bullock were fiercely independent women who
were determined to live as free from male domination as from
slavery. African American women, after all, had reaped neither
the privileges nor the confinement of domestic womanhood.
They had worked for others under slavery, and most continued
to do so after emancipation. More often economic partners than
dependents of husbands, they had less reason than many white
women to accept domestic subordination.[26]

Bullock contested her husband's suit, however, by charging
that he had long been guilty of beating and neglecting her, and
that he had committed adultery.[27] Furthermore, the similarities
of place, time, and wording of the petitions suggests that these
two men found stereotyping their wives as aggressive "Sapphires"
as effective a boost to winning a divorce as white men's stereotyping of their wives as common prostitutes had been in the previous
decade.

Since North Carolina's divorce statutes were reformed by the
same Redeemer legislature that replaced the coalition of Carpet-
bagger, Scalawag, and black Republicans who governed the state
between 1868 and 1870, they were a part of a general effort to
reinforce male authority as well as white supremacy. These
interlocking goals put African American men and women in

conflict with white society and each other. The conflict between whites and blacks in the postbellum South has often been explored, but conflict between black men and women is only beginning to receive the attention it deserves.[28]

The suggestion that some African American men may have exploited negative racial and sexual images of black women for their own personal gain may make some people uncomfortable or may seem a case of "blaming the victim." As Susan Mann has recently pointed out, analyzing oppression within oppressed groups is fraught with tensions, both from within and outside these groups. Nevertheless, as bell hooks writes, "The damaging effect of racism on black men neither prevents them from being sexist oppressors nor excuses or justifies their sexist oppression of black women."[29] The small number of divorce petitions filed by African American men in Granville, Orange, and Montgomery counties makes it difficult to offer more than a tentative hypothesis, but it appears that black men, like white men, eagerly took advantage of sexually biased statutes to rid themselves of wives.

Additional evidence of conflicts between African American wives and husbands is scattered throughout the records of North Carolina's Freedmen's Bureaus, set up to facilitate the transition of former slaves from bondage to freedom. Black men and women appealed to agents of these bureaus to mediate their complaints of spousal abuse. For example, Alfred Gray of High Point asked General Daniel Sickles for help in removing his wife from the home of the white man for whom she worked. He appealed for help after Mrs. Gray reportedly struck him a blow when he tried forcibly to remove her. To Mr. Gray, the clearest evidence that he was no longer a slave may have lay in the right to claim ownership of his wife. "I consider her my property," he stressed to General Sickles.[30]

In another case, former slave Clary Blackburn sought protection of her own property rights from the Statesville subdivision of the Bureau through the intermediary of J. Cowles, a white man. She charged that her husband Rufus had forced her from their home, taken up with another woman, and proclaimed their own marriage void on grounds that it had been contracted under "Reb" law. In the meantime, he had taken possession of her furniture, cooking pots, and quilts. In response to Cowles's request on behalf of Mrs. Blackburn, Captain William Jones suggested that troops might be sent, if necessary, to force the return of her property by her husband.[31]

In the initial postwar years, Reconstruction governments and courts began to interpret in piecemeal fashion the legal rights of African Americans. Likewise, black husbands and wives were negotiating their rights and responsibilities within the family. After 1870, when North Carolina's Redeemer government captured control of Reconstruction, it defined those rights more clearly within the context of both white supremacy and male authority.

The white male ruling class of post-Reconstruction North Carolina seemed eager to sanction black males' authority over black women. Whereas the political economy of the antebellum South required the denial of patriarchal rights of authority over their kin to black males, the postbellum political economy depended on it. As long as black men were subordinate to white men and women, their control over black women and children facilitated the building of a stable new social order. North Carolina judges displayed a selective measure of respect for the authority of black men over black families, while they stripped African Americans of their basic rights of citizenship by sanctioning racial segregation.[32]

Taken as a whole, the divorce petitions filed between 1860 and 1880 are far less expressive of women's views than those filed between 1840 and 1860. During the antebellum period, white female petitioners protested organic family structures gone awry. They sought divorces and separations when their right to protection and support within the institution of marriage was destroyed by brutal, profligate husbands. Those few African Americans who were free seemed reluctant to bring their marital problems before courts dominated by white slaveholders. Conversely, between 1860 and 1880, growing numbers of white and black men fled marriages that had been crippled by war, social chaos, and economic depression. By the 1870s, politicians who sought to reinstitute old relations of power in a new setting helped men to shed wives who did not behave in the prescribed manner. In North Carolina, as in the New South in general, the enforcement of racial and gender norms of behavior increasingly became the responsibility of public institutions rather than private families.

The state thus concentrated more on enforcing norms of appropriate individual behavior rather than preserving the institution of the family. To strengthen the authority of husbands in society, courts granted them divorces from wives who had broken the vows of fidelity. The inability of wives to obtain divorces unless their husbands had effectively ended the marriage through abandonment meant that although the family was no longer inviolable, women's identity was still embedded in marriage. The courts awarded black men authority over black women as long as they did not challenge their racial subordination. The reshaped bonds of womanhood and race, interlocked as ever, grafted old hierarchical configurations of power onto the contours of a new social order.

Epilogue

The essays in this collection reveal the many individual experiences, the human faces of war, which cannot encompass but can help us to convey the momentous impact of war. The power conflicts between a plantation mistress, an overseer, and slave during the war, the view from the trenches of a Union soldier, the view from the parlor of Harriet Beecher Stowe, the meaning of shiny buttons to slave children: these and other fascinating glimpses highlight the intensity and variety of experience often missed by panoramic presentations of the Civil War.

In our volume, we have chosen pieces that highlight the centrality of gender as part of the Civil War experience. Our point has not been simply to add gender as another feature for examination, but to weave gender into the tapestry of the war, creating a more complete understanding of the social, political, and ideological nature of the conflict. In this regard, several essays also raise theoretical questions about the nature of war and about the nature of gender relations in nineteenth-century America. Wars, throughout history, have often brought issues of gender into bold relief, often calling on both men and women to perform unusual, yet gender-specific roles. But the American Civil War, as many of these essays have shown, also raised specific questions and created unique tensions for American men and women. As the central event of the mid-nineteenth century, the sectional crisis took shape amidst a unique configuration of gender roles and identities in both northern and southern societies. On the one hand, northern society saw the emergence, in the early nineteenth century, of a new middle-class culture which highlighted new roles for men and women and a new ideology of separate spheres and female domesticity. Southerners, to some extent, shared in this vision, but continued to be influenced by notions of male dominance, honor, and chivalry which had a specific place in this slave-based plantation region. As the Civil War crisis loomed, and as the war itself was fought, the experience inevitably was shaped by the attitudes about gender which had developed in these two sections. Moreover, the men and women in both regions inevitably reshaped their own personal experiences, and occasionally their ideas about gender, amidst the trauma and tension of the Civil War.

Ultimately, then, the questions raised by these essays compel us to reconsider our understanding of the male and female experiences in nineteenth-century America. David Blight and Reid Mitchell re-examine traditional notions of manhood and the impact of war on male gender roles, recasting and enhancing our appreciation of the severe and unsettling effects bloodshed might have on soldiers' estimation of themselves in relation to family and home. Michael Fellman's essay on guerrilla warfare highlights the ways in which notions of ladyhood and gentlemanly behavior had peculiar if not bizarre effects in wartime Missouri. How and in what way these critical moments reshaped individual, collective, and even sectional perceptions of gender identity might be pursued in future work. Scholars would profit from comparing prewar and postwar rhetoric and behavioral patterns, both North and South.

Along these lines, several essays push us to reassess southern women in the postwar period. In their essays, both Joan Cashin and George Rable suggest that Confederate women gained a certain independence and sense of assertiveness amidst the wartime crisis, one showing the ability of a southern mistress to run her own plantation, the other documenting the defiance of the New Orleans ladies. Yet one wonders what, if any, long-term effects this independence had. Did southern white women emerge from the war ready to take their place in public places and political activities, like many of their northern sisters? Victoria Bynum and Catherine Clinton would question this assumption, suggesting certain definite limits to female assertiveness in the postwar years. Both see a recommitment to male hegemony and a new determination on the part of southern men (white men in Clinton's essay and both black and white in Bynum's) to keep southern women in line.

Moreover, as Bynum's and Clinton's contributions imply, the issue of gender in the postwar South takes on unique implications for African Americans. In this regard, historians must continue to analyze the Emancipation experience, paying special attention to gender. Both Jim Cullen and Peter Bardaglio offer some thoughts on this score, with Cullen noting the black Union soldier's reappraisal of issues of manhood and Bardaglio observing how gender filtered the new experience of freedom for African American children. But again, one wonders about extending these questions into the postwar period. How, for example, did the relationship between black men and women change once Emancipation had encouraged a new view of male and female roles? Likewise, how did the relationship between black men and white society change if the war did indeed call attention to the manhood of African American males? In this regard, Martha Hodes and Catherine Clinton have pointed to a dangerous conflation of sex, race, and politics in the Reconstruction era. Both have found that southern white men launched a sexually charged assault against black men and black women in an attempt to curtail the ex-slaves' new sense of freedom.

Several essays in this collection also call attention to the circumstances of northern women in wartime, a group that is often overlooked in Civil War studies. Here, too, historians need to reconsider how the Civil War reshaped the female experience in light of the activism and independence which many northern women displayed. In other words, did wartime independence represent a brief and fleeting act of patriotism, one that was quickly suppressed in the period of postwar readjustment, or did it have a lasting impact on the political and social life of northern women? One wonders, for example, about the lady nurses discussed by Kristie Ross, the female volunteers analyzed by Jeanie Attie, and the women spies examined by Lyde Sizer, and the extent to which these women's wartime actions fed into the postwar political activism, especially the suffrage campaign, of northern women. In contrast, as Patricia Hill suggests, Harriet

Beecher Stowe appears to have withdrawn from the public platform of sectional politics in order to advance her position in
northern literary ranks. Certainly, Nina Silber's essay suggests
that northern men did not emerge from the war with any new
acceptance of female activism, as witnessed by their unceasing
denunciation of southern women's political proclivities. Did
northern men's posturing on issues of manliness contribute to a
postwar backlash against female political activity, in both the
North and the South?

Finally, historians will need to reconsider age-old histo-
riographic questions of the Civil War, paying new attention to
issues of gender. Both LeeAnn Whites and Stephanie McCurry
suggest that historians cannot continue to debate the causes of the
war without considering the role of gender in shaping the sectional ideologies of both northerners and southerners. Southern
yeomen, McCurry explains, saw their role in their society and
their relationship to the slaveholders (and thus to the Confederate cause) through a prism of property and gender relationships.
Likewise, Whites has found that both northerners and southerners often interpreted their hostilities to each other from the
standpoint of gender. In this regard, both suggest that the
ideologies which brought northerners and southerners into war
were rooted in attitudes not only about free labor and slavery, or
about states' rights and federal power, but also about gender.

And lastly, we have the ever-present debate concerning the
war's outcome—the southern defeat and the Union victory.
Again, several essays claim that an understanding of gender can
clarify some of these issues as well. Drew Faust suggests that
historians who seek to understand the reasons for the Confederate defeat should consider the alienation of southern women
from the cause. Hence, while George Rable has noted southern
women's defiance of the enemy, Faust has observed southern
women's annoyance with their own government, especially as
they were left hungry and defenseless in the time of Confederate
failure. Yet, Nina Silber's essay suggests that southern women, at
least in the eyes of Union men, seemed to be the most active
supporters of the southern system. Northern men may certainly
have given undue attention to the actions of southern women, but
one wonders about the impact of female intransigence on Union

soldiers or female alienation on the Confederate system. Likewise, it also seems legitimate to ask what role northern women
played in the Union's success. Did northern ideology, which
offered women at least a limited degree of independence within
their own sphere, allow the women of that section to make a more
decisive contribution to the Union victory? Historians may not
pin all the blame for the southern loss and the Union victory on
women's shoulders, but it does seem clear that each society's
understanding of gender contributed to each section's ability to
mobilize and sustain the war effort. In the end, the entire Civil
War experience—from its causes to its legacy—can best be understood if historians analyze how gender shaped the actions and the
attitudes of the participants in this central historic event.

XXXXXXXXXXXXXXXXXXXXXXX

Bibliography

The bibliography that follows provides a selection of some of the most noteworthy primary sources pertaining to gender and the Civil War. We have divided the sources into three categories which address the Union, Confederate, and African American experience. In turn, the three categories are themselves subdivided: the Union and Confederate into family, men, and women; the African American into general works (including secondary sources), men, and women. Also included is a section on Dissertations and Works in Progress.

Union Families

Austin, Anne L. *The Woolsey Sisters of New York: A Family's Involvement in the Civil War and a New Profession.* Philadelphia: American Philosophical Society, 1971.

Bacon, G. W., and E. W. Howland. *Letters of a Family During the War for the Union, 1861–1865.* Privately published, 1899.

Mohr, James C., ed. *The Cormany Diaries: A Northern Family in the Civil War.* Pittsburgh: Univ. of Pittsburgh Press, 1982.

Union Men

Ambrose, Stephen E., ed. *A Wisconsin Boy in Dixie: The Selected Letters of James K. Newton.* Univ. of Wisconsin Press, 1961.

Anderson, Mary Ann, ed. *The Civil War Diary of Allen Morgan Greer, Twentieth Regiment, Illinois Volunteers.* Denver: R. C. Appleman, 1977.

Boney, F. N. *A Union Soldier in the Land of the Vanquished: The Diary of Sergeant Mathew Woodruff, June–December, 1865.* University: Univ. of Alabama Press, 1969.

Carter, Capt. Robert Goldthwaite. *Four Brothers in Blue: Or Sunshine and Shadows of the War of Rebellion, a Story of the Great War from Bull Run to Appomattox.* Privately published, 1913. (Reprint: Austin, 1978).

Coe, David, ed. *Mine Eyes Have Seen the Glory: Combat Diaries of Union Sergeant Hamlin Alexander Coe.* Rutherford, N.J.: Fairleigh Dickinson Univ. Press, 1975.

DeRosier, Arthur H., Jr., ed. *Through the South with a Union Soldier.* Johnson City, Tenn.: East Tennessee State University, Research Advisory Council, 1969.

Donald, David Herbert, ed. *Gone for a Soldier: The Civil War Memoirs of Private Alfred Bellard.* Boston: Little, Brown, 1975.

Duncan, Robert, ed. *"Dearest Mother": The Civil War Letters of Robert Gould Shaw.* Athens: Univ. of Georgia Press, 1992.

Dunlap, Leslie W., ed. *"Your Affectionate Husband, J. F. Culver": Letters Written During the Civil War.* Iowa City: Friends of the University of Iowa Libraries, 1978.

Fatout, Paul. *Letters of a Civil War Surgeon.* [West Lafayette, Indiana], 1961.

Halsey, Ashley, ed. *A Yankee Private's Civil War by Robert Hale Strong.* Chicago: H. Regnery, 1961.

Harwell, Richard, and Philip N. Racine, eds. *The Fiery Trail: A Union Officer's Account of Sherman's Last Campaigns: The Journal and Letters of Thomas Ward Osborn.* Knoxville: Univ. of Tennessee Press, 1986.

Hatch, Carl E., ed. *Dearest Susie: A Civil War Infantryman's Letters to His Sweetheart.* New York: Exposition Press, 1971.

Jackson, Joseph Orwell, ed. *"Some of the Boys . . .": The Civil War Letters of Isaac Johnson, 1862–1865.* Carbondale, Ill.: Southern Illinois University Press, 1960.

Lanes, Mill, ed. *"War Is Hell!" William Sherman's Personal Narrative of His March Through Georgia.* Savannah: Beehive Press, 1974.

Loving, Jerome M., ed. *Civil War Letters of George Washington Whitman.* Durham: Duke Univ. Press, 1975.

Reidgreen, Marcia M., ed. *Henry Matrau of the Iron Brigade.* Lincoln: Univ. of Nebraska Press, forthcoming.

Roth, Margaret Brobst, ed. *Well Mary: The Civil War Letters of a Wisconsin Volunteer*. Madison: Univ. of Wisconsin Press, 1960.

Scott, Robert Garth, ed. *Fallen Leaves: The Civil War Letters of Major Henry Livermore Abbott*. Kent, Ohio: Kent State Univ. Press, 1991.

Throne, Mildren, ed. *The Civil War Diary of Cyrus F. Boyd, 15th Iowa Infantry, 1861–1863*. Millwood, N.Y.: Kraus Reprint Co., 1977.

Truxall, Aida Craig, ed. *"Respects to All": Letters of Two Pennsylvania Boys in the War of Rebellion*. Pittsburgh: Univ.of Pittsburgh Press, 1962.

Walton, Clyde, C., ed. *Private Smith's Journal: Recollections of the Late War*. Chicago: R. R. Donnelley, 1963.

Winther, Oscar Osborn. *With Sherman to the Sea: The Civil War Diaries and Reminiscences of Theodore F. Upson*. Bloomington: Indiana Univ. Press, 1958.

Union Women

A Few Words in Behalf of the Loyal Women of the United States by One of Themselves. New York: Wm. C. Bryant, 1863.

Ames, Mary. *From a New England Woman's Diary in Dixie in 1865*. Norwood, Mass.: Plimpton Press, 1906.

Botume, Elizabeth Hyde. *First Days Amongst the Contrabands*. New York: Arno Press, 1968.

Boyce, Amy, and Pat Lammers, "A Female in the Ranks," *Civil War Times*. January 1984.

Brockett, L. P., and Mary C. Vaughan. *Woman's Work in the Civil War: A Record of Heroism, Patriotism and Patience*. Philadelphia: Zeigler, McCurdy, 1867.

Brumgardt, John R., ed. *Civil War Nurse: The Diary and Letters of Hannah Ropes*. Knoxville: Univ. of Tennessee Press, 1980.

Bucklin, Sophronia. *In Hospital and Camp: A Woman's Record of Thrilling Incidents Among the Wounded in the Late War*. Philadelphia: John E. Potter, 1869.

Collis, Septima. *A Woman's War Record, 1861–1865*. New York: G. P. Putnam's, 1889.

Cushman, Pauline. *The Romance of the Great Rebellion: Or, The Mysteries of the Secret Service*. New York: Wynkoop & Hallenbeck, 1864.

Dannet, Sylvia. *Noble Women of the North*. New York: T. Yoseloff, 1959.

Edmonds, Emma. *Nurse and Spy in the Union Army*. Hartford: W. S. Williams, 1865.

Hammond, Harold E., ed. *Diary of a Union Lady, 1861–1865.* New York: Funk and Wagnalls, 1962.

Harvey, Mrs. Governor. *My Story of War: A Woman's Narrative of Life and Work in Union Hospitals.* New York: Longmans, Green, 1885.

Hass, Paul, ed. "A Volunteer Nurse in the Civil War: The Letters of Harriet Douglas Whetten," *Wisconsin Magazine of History* XLVIII (1964).

Haviland, Laura. *A Woman's Life Work.* Miami, Fla.: Mnemosyne, 1969.

Hoge, Mrs. A. H. *The Boys in Blue; or Heroes of the "Rank and File."* New York: E. B. Treat, 1867.

Holland, Rupert S., ed. *Letters and Diaries of Laura M. Towne, Written from the Sea Islands of South Carolina, 1862–1884.* New York: Negro Universities Press, 1969.

Holstein, Anna Morris Ellis. *Three Years in the Field Hospitals of the Army of the Potomac.* Philadelphia: J. B. Lippincott, 1867.

Hurn, Ethel Alice. *Wisconsin Women in the War Between the States.* Madison: Wisconsin History Commission, 1911.

Jaquette, Herietta S., ed. *South After Gettysburg: Letters of Cornelia Hancock, 1863–1865.* Philadelphia: Univ. of Pennsylvania Press, 1937 (reprint: Freeport, N.Y., 1971).

Krug, Mark M., ed. *Mrs. Hill's Journal: Civil War Reminiscences.* Chicago: Lakeside Press, 1980.

Livermore, Mary A. *My Story of the War: A Woman's Narrative of Four Years' Personal Experience.* Hartford: A. D. Worthington, 1890.

Logan, Mary Simmerson Cunningham. *Reminiscences of a Soldier's Wife: An Autobiography.* New York: C. Scribner's Sons, 1913.

McSherry, Frank, Jr., Charles G. Waugh, and Martin Greenberg, eds. *Civil War Women: American Women Shaped by Conflict in Stories by Alcott, Chopin, Welty and Others.* Little Rock: August House, 1988.

Michigan Civil War Centennial Observance Commission. *Michigan Women in the Civil War.* Lansing: privately published, 1963.

Moore, Frank. *Women of the War: Their Heroism and Self-Sacrifice.* Hartford: S. S. Scranton, 1866.

Myerson, Joel, and Daniel Shealy, eds. *The Journals of Louisa May Alcott.* Boston: Little, Brown, 1989.

Pearson, Elizabeth Ware, ed. *Letters from Port Royal, 1862–1868.* New York: Arno Press, 1969.

Reilly, Wayne E., ed. *Sarah Jane Foster, Teacher of the Freedmen: A Diary and Letters.* Charlottesville: Univ. Press of Virginia, 1990.

Richards, Caroline Cowles. *Village Life in America, 1852–1872, Including the Period of the American Civil War as Told in the Diary of a School-Girl.* New York: Henry Holt, 1913.

Souder, Emily. *Leaves from the Battle-Field at Gettysburg.* Philadelphia: C. Sherman, 1864.

Swint, Henry Lee, ed. *Dear Ones at Home: Letters from Contraband Camps.* Nashville: Vanderbilt Univ. Press, 1968.

Swisshelm, Jane Grey. *Crusader and Feminist: Letters of Jane Grey Swisshelm, 1858–1865.* Westport, Conn.: Hyperion Press, 1976.

Wittenmeyer, Annie. *Under the Guns: A Woman's Reminiscences of the Civil War.* Boston: E. B. Stillings, 1895.

Wormeley, Katharine Prescott. *The Cruel Side of War: Letters from the Headquarters of the United States Sanitary Commission During the Peninsular Campaign in Virginia in 1862.* Boston: Roberts Brothers, 1898.

Confederate Families

Bleser, Carol, ed. *The Hammonds of Redcliffe.* New York: Oxford Univ. Press, 1981.

Cuttino, George Peddy, ed. *Saddle Bag and Spinning Wheel, Being the Civil War Letters of George Peddy, M.D. and Kate Featherston Peddy.* Macon, Ga.: Mercer Univ. Press, 1959.

Huckaby, Elizabeth Paisley, and Ethel Simpson, eds. *Tulip Evermore: Emma Butler and William Paisley, Their Lives in Letters, 1857–1887.* Fayetteville: Univ. of Arkansas Press, 1985.

Long, Mary Alves. *High Time to Tell It.* Durham: Duke Univ. Press, 1950.

McDaniel, Ruth Barr, ed. *Confederate War Correspondence of James Barr and Wife Rebecca Ann Dowling Barr.* Taylors, S.C.: Faith Printing Co., 1963.

Myers, Robert Manson, ed. *The Children of Pride.* New Haven: Yale Univ. Press, 1972.

Rozier, John, ed. *The Granite Farm Letters: The Civil War Correspondence of Edgeworth and Sallie Bird.* Athens: Univ. of Georgia Press, 1988.

Smith, Daniel E., Alice R. Huger Smith, and Arney R. Childs, eds. *Mason Smith Family Letters, 1860–68.* Columbia: Univ. of South Carolina Press, 1950.

Trammell, Camilla Travis. *Seven Pines: Its Occupants and Their Letters, 1825–1872.* Dallas: Southern Methodist Univ. Press, 1986.

Welton, J. Michael, ed. *"My Heart is So Rebellious": The Caldwell Letters, 1861–1865.* Warrenton, Va.: privately published, 1991 (ISBN: 0-9630128-0-0).

Confederate Men

Barrett, John G., ed. *Yankee Rebel: The Civil War Journal of Edmund DeWitt Patterson.* Chapel Hill: Univ. of North Carolina Press, 1966.

Barrett, John G., and Robert K. Turner, Jr., eds. *Letters of a New Market Cadet.* Chapel Hill: Univ. of North Carolina Press, 1961.

Bassett, John S., ed. *The Westover Journal of John A. Selden, 1858–1862.* Northampton, Mass.: Smith College Studies in History, 1921.

Battle, William James, ed. *Memories of an Old-Time Tar Heel* [Kemp Plummer Battle]. Chapel Hill: Univ. of North Carolina Press, 1945.

Boggs, Marion Alexander, ed. *The Alexander Letters, 1787–1900.* Athens: Univ. of Georgia Press, 1980.

Cash, William M., and Lucy Somerville Howorth, eds. *My Dear Nellie: The Civil War Letters of William L. Nugent to Eleanor Smith Nugent.* Jackson: Univ. Press of Mississippi, 1977.

Cummer, Clyde Lottride, and Genevieve Miller, eds. *Yankee in Gray: The Civil War Memories of Henry E. Handerson with a Selection of His Wartime Letters.* Cleveland: Case Western Reserve Univ. Press, 1962.

Davis, Varina Howell. *Jefferson Davis, Ex-President of the Confederacy: A Memoir by His Wife.* New York: Belford Co., 1890.

Davis, William C., ed. *Diary of a Confederate Soldier: John S. Jackman of the Orphan Brigade.* Columbia: Univ. of South Carolina Press, 1990.

Dennis, Frank Allen, ed. *Kemper County Rebel: The Civil War Diary of Robert Masten Holmes, C.S.A.* Jackson: Univ. and College Press of Mississippi, 1973.

Dowdey, Clifford, and Louis H. Manarin, eds. *The Wartime Papers of R. E. Lee.* Boston: Little, Brown, 1961.

Fisk, Wilbur. *Anti-Rebel: The Civil War Letters of Wilbur Fisk.* Croton-on-Hudson, N.Y.: E. Rosenblatt, 1983.

Griffith, Lucille, ed. *Yours til Death: Civil War Letters of John W. Cotton.* University: Univ. of Alabama Press, 1951.

Hassler, William W., ed. *The General to His Lady: The Civil War Letters of William Dorsey Pender to Fanny Pender.* Chapel Hill: Univ. of North Carolina Press, 1965.

Jones, Terry L., ed. *Civil War Memoirs of Captain William J. Seymour: Reminiscences of a Louisiana Tiger.* Baton Rouge: Louisiana State Univ. Press, 1991.

Long, Augustus White. *Son of Carolina*. Durham: Duke Univ. Press, 1939.

MacKintosh, Robert Harley, Jr., ed. *"Dear Martha": The Confederate War Letters of a South Carolina Soldier, Alexander Faulkner Fewell*. Columbia, S.C.: R. L. Bryan, 1976.

Pickett, LaSalle Corbett. *The Heart of a Soldier as Revealed in the Intimate Letters of General George E. Pickett, C.S.A*. New York: Seth Moyle, 1913.

Pierson, William Whatley, Jr., ed. *Whipt'em Everytime: The Diary of Bartlett Yancey Malone, Co. H., 6th N.C. Regiment*. Jackson, Tenn.: McCowat-Mercer Press, 1960.

Racine, Philip N., ed. *Piedmont Farmer: The Journals of David Golightly Harris, 1855–1870*. Knoxville: Univ. of Tennessee Press, 1990.

Scarborough, William K., ed. *The Diary of Edmund Ruffin* (2 vols.). Baton Rouge: Louisiana State Univ. Press, 1972.

Taylor, E. Jay, ed. *Reluctant Rebel: The Secret Diary of Robert Patrick, 1861–1865*. Baton Rouge: Louisiana State Univ. Press, 1959.

Tower, R. Lockwood, ed. *A Carolinian Goes to War: The Civil War Narrative of Arthur Middleton Manigault*. Columbia: Univ. of South Carolina Press, 1984.

Confederate Women

Anderson, John Q., ed. *Brokenburn: The Journal of Kate Stone, 1861–1868*. Baton Rouge: Louisiana State Univ. Press, 1955.

Andrews, Eliza Frances. *The War-Time Journal of a Georgia Girl: 1864–65*. New York: D. Appleton, 1908.

Avary, Myrta Lockett, ed. *A Virginia Girl in the Civil War, 1861–1865*. New York: D. Appleton, 1903.

Burr, Virginia Ingraham. *The Secret Eye: The Journal of Ella Gertrude Clanton Thomas*. Chapel Hill: Univ. of North Carolina Press, 1990.

Cathey, Cornelius O., ed. *A Woman Rice Planter* [Elizabeth W. Allston Pringle]. Cambridge: Harvard Univ. Press, 1961.

Clift, G. Glenn, ed. *The Private War of Lizzie Hardin*. Frankfort: Kentucky Historical Society, 1863.

Coxe, Elizabeth Allen. *Memories of a South Carolina Plantation During the War*. Privately published, 1912.

Crabtree, Beth G., and James Patton, eds. *"Journal of a Secesh Lady": The Diary of Catherine Ann Devereaux Edmonston, 1860–1866*. Raleigh,

N.C.: Division of Archives and History, Department of Cultural Resources, 1979.

East, Charles, ed. *The Civil War Diary of Sarah Morgan*. Athens: Univ. of Georgia Press, 1991.

Fleet, Betsey, and John D. P. Fuller, eds. *Green Mount: A Virginia Plantation During the Civil War*. Lexington: Univ. of Kentucky Press, 1962.

Galbraith, William and Loretta, eds. *A Lost Heroine of the Confederacy*. Jackson: Univ. Press of Mississippi, 1991.

Gay, Mary Ann Harris. *Life in Dixie During the War*. Atlanta: DeKalb Historical Society, 1979.

Geary, Patrick J., ed. *Celine: Remembering Louisiana, 1850–1871* [Celine Fremaux Garcia]. Athens: Univ. of Georgia Press, 1987.

Green, Fletcher M., ed. *Memorials of a Southern Planter*. New York: Knopf, 1965.

Greenhow, Rose. *My Imprisonment*. London: R. Bentley, 1863.

Hampton, Ann Fripp, ed. *A Divided Heart: Letters of Sally Baxter Hampton, 1853–1862*. Spartanburg, S.C.: Reprint Co., 1980.

Henderson, Dwight Franklin, ed. *The Private Journal of Georgiana Walker, 1862–1865*. Tuscaloosa, Ala.: Confederate Publishing Co., 1963.

Jones, Katherine M. *Heroines of Dixie: Confederate Women Tell Their Story of the War*. Indianapolis: Bobbs-Merrill, 1955.

King, Spencer Bidwell, Jr., ed. *Ebb Tide: As Seen Through the Diary of Josephine Clay Habersham*. Athens: Univ. of Georgia Press, 1958.

Marszalek, John F., ed. *The Diary of Miss Emma Holmes, 1861–66*. Baton Rouge: Louisiana State Univ. Press, 1979.

McGee, Charles M., Jr., and Ernest M. Lander, Jr., eds. *A Rebel Came Home: The Diary and Letters of Floride Clemson*. Columbia: Univ. of South Carolina Press, 1989.

McGuire, Judith White Brockenbrough. *Diary of a Southern Refugee During the War* (2nd ed.). New York: E. J. Hale and Son, 1867.

Miers, Earl Schenck. *When the World Ended: Diary of Emma LeConte*. New York: Oxford Univ. Press, 1957.

Morrill, Lily Logan, ed. *My Confederate Girlhood*. [Kate Virginia Cox Logan]. Richmond: Garrett and Massie, 1932.

Putnam, Sarah A. Brock. *Richmond During the War: Four Years of Personal Observation by a Richmond Lady*. New York: G. W. Carleton, 1867.

Robertson, Mary D., ed. *Lucy Breckenridge of Grove Hill: The Journal of a Virginia Girl, 1862–64*. Kent, Ohio: Kent State Univ. Press, 1979.

Rowland, Kate Mason, and Mrs. Morris L. Croxall, eds. *The Journal of Julia Le Grand: New Orleans, 1862–63.* Richmond: Everett Waddey, 1911.

Saxon, Elizabeth Lyle. *A Southern Woman's Wartime Reminiscences.* Memphis: Pilcher Printing Co., 1905.

Smith, John David, and William Cooper, Jr., eds. *Window on the War: Frances Dallam Peter's Lexington Civil War Diary.* Lexington, Ky.: Lexington-Fayette County Historical Commission, 1976.

Woodward, C. Vann, ed. *Mary Chesnut's Civil War.* New Haven: Yale Univ. Press, 1981.

Wright, Loise Wigfall. *A Southern Girl in '61: The War-Time Memories of a Confederate Senator's Daughter.* New York: Doubleday, Page, 1905.

African American (General)

Berlin, Ira, Steven F. Miller, Leslie F. Rowland, et al. *Freedom: A Documentary History of Emancipation.* New York: Cambridge Univ. Press, 1982–.

Blackett, R. J. M. *Thomas Morris Chester, Black Civil War Correspondent: His Dispatches from the Virginia Front.* Baton Rouge: Louisiana State Univ. Press, 1989.

Campbell, Edward D. C., with Kym S. Rice. *Before Freedom Came: African-American Life in the Antebellum South.* Charlottesville: Univ. of Virginia Press, 1991.

Garnet, Henry Highland *A Memorial Discourse.* Philadelphia: J. M. Wilson, 1865.

Long, Richard, ed. *Black Writers and the Civil War.* Secaucus, N.J.: Blue and Grey Press, 1988.

McPherson, James, M. *The Negro's Civil War.* Urbana: Univ. of Illinois Press, 1965.

Miller, Randall M., ed. *"Dear Master": Letters of a Slave Family.* Athens: Univ. of Georgia Press, 1990.

Quarles, Benjamin. *The Negro in the Civil War.* Boston: Little Brown, 1969.

Rawick, George. *The American Slave* [W.P.A. narratives]. Westport, Conn.: Greenwood Press, 1977.

African American Men

Adams, Virginia, Matzke, ed. *On the Altar of Freedom: A Black Soldier's Civil War Letters from the Front* [Corporal James Henry Gooding]. Amherst: Univ. of Massachusetts Press, 1991.

Brown, William Wells. *The Negro in the American Rebellion: His Heroism and His Fidelity*. Boston: R. F. Wallcut, 1865.

Browne, Junius H. *Four Years in Secessia*. Hartford, Conn.: O. D. Case, 1865.

Califf, Joseph M. *Record of the Services of the Seventh Regiment, U.S. Colored Troops, from September 1863 to November 1865*. Providence: L. L. Freeman, 1878.

Guthrie, James M. *Campfires of the Afro-American: Or the Colored Man as a Patriot, Soldier, Sailor, and Hero in the Cause of Free America*. Philadelphia: Afro-American Publishing Co., 1899.

Lee, William M. *History of the Life of Rev. William Mack Lee, Body Servant of General Robert E. Lee*. Norfolk: Virginia Smith Print Co., 1918.

Rollin, Frances A. (published under the name of Frank). *Life and Public Services of Martin R. Delany*. Boston: Lee and Shepard, 1868.

African American Women

Alexander, Adele Logan. *Ambiguous Lives*. Little Rock: Arkansas Univ. Press, 1991.

Leslie, Kent A. *Woman of Color, Daughter of Privilege*. Athens: Univ. of Georgia Press, forthcoming.

Romero, Patricia W., ed. *A Black Woman's Civil War Memoirs* [Susie King Taylor]. New York: M. Wiener, 1988.

Stevenson, Brenda, ed. *The Journal of Charlotte Forten Grimké*. New York: Oxford Univ. Press, 1988.

Dissertations and Works in Progress

In addition to the sources listed above we have come into contact with much new and exciting scholarship on gender and the Civil War. The most notable recent and forthcoming work is Cita Cook, "Growing Up White, Genteel, and Female in a Changing South, 1845–1917" (Ph.D. dissertation, University of California at Berkeley, forthcoming); Laura

Edwards, "The Politics of Manhood and Womanhood: Reconstruction in Granville County, North Carolina" (Ph.D. dissertation, University of North Carolina, 1991); Donna Rebecca Dondes Krug, "The Folks Back Home: The Confederate Homefront During the Civil War" (Ph.D. dissertation, University of California, Irvine, 1990); Megan McClintock, "Binding Up the Nation's Wounds: Civil War Pensions and American Families, 1861–1890" (Ph.D. dissertation, Rutgers University, forthcoming); Leslie Schwalm, "The Meaning of Freedom: African-American Women and Their Transition from Slavery to Freedom in Lowcountry South Carolina" (Ph.D. dissertation, University of Wisconsin, 1991); and Marli Frances Weiner, *Plantation Women: South Carolina Mistresses and Slaves, 1830–1880* (forthcoming).

XXXXXXXXXXXXXXXXXXXXXXXXXX

Notes

Foreword

1. Mark Twain and Charles Dudley Warner, *The Gilded Age* (New American Library ed., New York, 1969), 137–38; Albion W. Tourgée, "The Veteran and His Pipe," *Chicago Inter Ocean*, April 25, 1885.

2. Irwin Unger, ed., *Essays on the Civil War and Reconstruction* (New York, 1970); Charles Crowe, ed., *The Age of the Civil War and Reconstruction*, rev. ed. (Homewood, Ill., 1975).

3. Eric Foner, "Slavery, the Civil War, and Reconstruction," in Foner, ed., *The New American History* (Philadelphia, 1990), 73.

4. Roy P. Basler, ed., *The Collected Works of Abraham Lincoln*, 9 vols(New Brunswick, N.J., 1952–1955), VIII, 332; *The Diary of George Templeton Strong*, vol. 3, *The Civil War 1860–1865*, ed. Allan Nevins and Milton Halsey Thomas (New York, 1952), 449.

5. Barbara Hughett, *The Civil War Round Table: Fifty Years of Scholarship and Fellowship* (Chicago, 1990), 114.

6. Gerda Lerner, "Priorities and Challenges in Women's History Research," *Perspectives*, 26 (April 1988), 18.

7. Stephan Thernstrom, *Poverty and Progress: Social Mobility in a Nineteenth Century City* (Cambridge, Mass., 1964).

8. "Have Social Historians Lost the Civil War? Some Preliminary Demographic Speculations," *Journal of American History*, 76 (June 1989), 34–58.

9. Reid Mitchell, *Civil War Soldiers: Their Expectations and Their Experiences* (New York, 1988); Joseph T. Glatthar, *The March to the Sea and Beyond: Sherman's Troops in the Savannah and Carolinas Campaigns* (New York, 1985); Glatthar, *Forged in Battle: The Civil War Alliance of Black Soldiers and White Officers* (New York, 1990).

10. Gerald E. Linderman, *Embattled Courage: The Experience of Combat in the American Civil War* (New York, 1987); Earl J. Hess, *Liberty, Virtue, and Progress: Northerners and Their War for the Union* (New York, 1988); Randall C. Jimerson,

The Private Civil War: Popular Thought During the Sectional Conflict (Baton Rouge, 1988).

11. Orville Vernon Burton, *In My Father's House are Many Mansions: Family and Community in Edgefield, South Carolina* (Chapel Hill, 1985); Steven Hahn, *The Roots of Southern Populism: Yeoman Farmers and the Transformation of the Georgia Up-country, 1850–1890* (New York, 1983); J. William Harris, *Plain Folk and Gentry in a Slave Society: White Liberty and Black Slavery in Augusta's Hinterlands* (Middletown, Conn., 1985); Wayne K. Durrill, *War of Another Kind: A Southern Community in the Great Rebellion* (New York: 1990).

12. Michael Fellman, *Inside War: The Guerrilla Conflict in Missouri During the American Civil War* (New York, 1989); Iver Bernstein, *The New York City Draft Riots: Their Significance for American Society and Politics in the Age of the Civil War* (New York, 1990).

13. George C. Rable, *Civil Wars: Women and the Crisis of Southern Nationalism* (Urbana, Ill., 1989); Phillip Shaw Paludan, *"A People's Contest": The Union and Civil War, 1861–1865* (New York, 1988); J. Matthew Gallman, *Mastering Wartime: A Social History of Philadelphia During the Civil War* (Cambridge, Mass., 1990).

14. Barbara Jeanne Fields, *Slavery and Freedom on the Middle Ground: Maryland during the Nineteenth Century* (New Haven, 1985); Clarence L. Mohr, *On the Threshold of Freedom: Masters and Slaves in Civil War Georgia* (Athens, Ga., 1986).

15. Ralph L. Rusk, ed., *The Letters of Ralph Waldo Emerson* (New York, 1939), V, 251.

Chapter 1. The Civil War as a Crisis in Gender

1. Harriet Beecher Stowe read this eyewitness account by the man who helped the escaping slave woman and her child ashore in an antislavery magazine. It formed the basis for an early incident in her novel. Harriet Beecher Stowe, *Uncle Tom's Cabin; or Life Among the Lowly* (New York, 1892 [1853]), xiii.

2. Catharine Beecher, *A Treatise on Domestic Economy* (Boston, 1842). See also Kathryn Kish Sklar, *Catharine Beecher: A Study in American Domesticity* (New Haven, 1973), and Jeanne Boydston et al., *The Limits of Sisterhood: The Beecher Sisters on Women's Rights and Women's Sphere* (Chapel Hill, 1988). The political and social implications of the expansion of women's domestic authority in the North during this period has been discussed by many scholars. See, for example, Barbara Welter, "The Cult of True Womanhood, 1820–1860," *American Quarterly* (Summer 1966) 151–74; Nancy Cott, *The Bonds of Womanhood: "Woman's Sphere" in New England, 1780–1835* (New Haven, 1977); Mary Ryan, *Cradle of the Middle Class: The Family in Oneida County, New York, 1790–1865* (New York, 1981); and Ann Douglas, *The Feminization of American Culture* (New York, 1977).

3. Jane Tomkins, in her work *Sensational Designs: The Cultural Work of American Fiction* (New York, 1985), argues that the emergence of this critical domestic voice actually constituted the most "politically subversive dimension of Stowe's novel, more disruptive and far reaching in its potential consequences than even the starting of a war or the freeing of slaves" (142).

4. In the first year of its publication, the novel sold 300,000 copies and within a decade it had sold more than 2 million copies. James M. McPherson, *Battle Cry of Freedom: The Civil War Era* (New York, 1988), 88–89.

5. As cited in McPherson, *ibid.*, 90. According to McPherson, Lincoln consulted Stowe's work, *A Key to Uncle Tom's Cabin*, when he was confronting the problem of slavery in the summer of 1862 (89).

6. Chesnut discusses Stowe's work on twenty separate occasions in her diary. Mary Boykin Chesnut, *Mary Chesnut's Civil War*, C. Vann Woodward, ed. (New Haven and London, 1981), 880.

7. Of course the middle-class northern household was supported by the labor of domestic servants and so it was hardly innocent of class tensions. However, Catharine Beecher's treatise on domestic economy was in part dedicated to rationalizing domestic labor so that the household could function as close to servantless as possible. See Catharine Beecher and Harriet Beecher Stowe, *The American Woman's Home: or, Principles of Domestic Science; Being a Guide to the Formation and Maintenance of Economical, Healthful, Beautiful and Christian Homes* (New York, 1869).

8. Chesnut, *Mary Chesnut's Civil War*, 245.

9. Nell Irvin Painter identifies a similar "maternal" attitude among the planter-class women in "The Journal of Ella Gertrude Clanton Thomas: An Educated White Woman in War and Reconstruction," in *The Secret Eye*, Virginia I. Burr, ed. (Chapel Hill, 1990).

10. *Mary Chesnut's Civil War*, 169.

11. Ella Gertrude Clanton Thomas, "Journal" (Special Collections, Perkins Library, Duke University, Durham), Jan. 2, 1858.

12. In her biography of the best known of all southern women abolitionists, the Grimké sisters, Gerda Lerner argues that the root of their abolitionist sentiment lay in their resentment of their treatment when compared with their brother's. It was, according to Lerner, Sarah Grimké's squelched desire to have the same educational and professional opportunities as her brother that led her to identify with the position of her family's slaves. Of course perhaps no other southern women went to the lengths that the Grimkés did in actually leaving the South in order to carry out their commitment to a different social order. Gerda Lerner, *The Grimké Sisters from North Carolina* (New York, 1967).

13. Rebecca Latimer Felton, *Country Life in the Days of My Youth* (Atlanta, 1919), 93.

14. *Ibid.*, 86–87, 101.

15. *Mary Chesnut's Civil War*, 169. Elizabeth Fox-Genovese, *Within the Plantation Household* (Chapel Hill, 1988), and Nell Irvin Painter, "The Journal of Ella Gertrude Clanton Thomas," have both discussed at greater length the ways in which planter-class women's gender interests were subordinated to their race and class privilege.

16. Mounting tension over the patriarchal powers of southern planter-class men in the decade before the outbreak of war has been discussed elsewhere at some length. See William R. Taylor, *Cavalier and Yankee: The Old South and American National Character* (Cambridge, Mass., [1957] 1979); Anne Firor Scott,

The Southern Lady: From Pedestal to Politics: 1830–1930 (Chicago, 1970), and "Women's Perspective on the Patriarchy in the 1950's," *Journal of American History* LXI (1974): 52–64; and Michael P. Johnson, "Planters and Patriarchy: Charleston, 1800–1860," *Journal of Southern History* XLVI (1980): 45–72. Suzanne Lebsock makes the case for a veritable gender backlash in the town of Petersburg in the 1850s. See *The Free Women of Petersburg: Status and Culture in a Southern Town, 1784–1860* (New York, 1984), 225–36.

17. Joseph Jones to Caroline Davis Jones (Joseph Jones Papers, Tulane University, New Orleans), Feb. 12, 1859.

18. *Ibid.,* March 6, 1859.

19. As Fredrika Bremer wrote to Harriet Beecher Stowe upon the original publication of the novel, "I wondered that the woman, the *mother,* could look at these things and be silent—that no cry of noble indignation and anger would escape her breast, and rend the air, and pierce to the ear of humanity. I wondered, and God be praised! It has come [in the form of Stowe's novel] . . . the woman, the mother, has raised her voice out of the very soil of the new world in behalf of the wronged ones, and her voice vibrates still through two great continents, opening all hearts and minds to the light of truth." Harriet Beecher Stowe, *Uncle Tom's Cabin,* xxvii–xxviii.

20. For a further discussion of the development of northern women's feminist and abolitionist politics see Barbara Berg, *The Remembered Gate: Origins of American Feminism* (New York, 1978); Ellen Carol DuBois, *Feminism and Suffrage: The Emergence of an Independent Women's Movement in America, 1848–1869;* Blanche Hersh, *The Slavery of Sex: Feminist Abolitionists in America* (Urbana, Ill., 1978); and Caroll Smith-Rosenberg, *Disorderly Conduct: Vision of Gender in Victorian America* (New York, 1985).

21. Augusta *Chronicle and Sentinel,* April 18, 1861.

22. *Mary Chesnut's Civil War,* 86. The question of war as an assertion of masculine identity has received considerable recent attention. See Nancy Hartsock, "Masculinity, Heroism and the Making of War," in *Rocking the Ship of State,* Adrienne Harris and Ynestra King, eds. (New York, 1989), 133–52. Sandra Gilbert, "Soldier's Heart: Literary Men, Literary Women and the Great War," *Signs* 8, no. 3 (1983): 422–50; Carol Cohn, "Sex and Death in the Rational World of Defense Intellectuals," *Signs* 12, no. 4 (1987): 687–718; and Jean Bethke Eltshain, "Women as Mirror and Other," *Humanities in Society* 5, no. 1–2 (1982).

23. Here Wyatt-Brown means to refer to *white* southern men who saw the challenge to their right to own slaves from the North as a denial of *their* liberty, of *their* prerogatives as free men. Bertram Wyatt-Brown, *Southern Honor: Ethics and Behavior in the Old South* (New York, 1982), 35. See also Gerald Linderman, *Embattled Courage: The Experience of Combat in the American Civil War* (New York, 1987), 8–16.

24. For a further discussion of the manner in which black men perceived participation in the war as "masculinizing," see James McPherson, *The Negro's Civil War: How American Negroes Felt and Acted During the War for the Union* (New York, 1965) and *The Struggle for Equality: Abolitionists and the Negro in the Civil War and Reconstruction,* as well as Joseph T. Glatthaar, *Forged in Battle: The Civil War Alliance of Black Soldiers and White Officers* (New York, 1990).

25. As cited in Steven A. Channing, *Crisis of Fear: Secession in South Carolina* (New York, 1974), 287.

26. Discussion of the cause of the Civil War was intense for many generations afterwards; see Thomas J. Pressly, *Americans Interpret Their Civil War* (New York, 1962), for a treatment of this discourse. Despite this lengthy tradition, the possibility that the war might have a gendered face has received scant attention until recently. See Jean Bethke Eltshain, *Women and War* (New York, 1987), 94–101; and LeeAnn Whites, "Gender and the Origins of the New South: Augusta, Georgia, 1860–1900" (forthcoming, Chapel Hill).

27. As cited in David W. Blight, *Frederick Douglass' Civil War: Keeping Faith in Jubilee* (Baton Rouge, 1989), 13.

28. McPherson, *Negro's Civil War*, 131.

29. See Blight, *Frederick Douglass' Civil War* for a more extended discussion of this point.

30. McPherson asserts that northern blacks met this response "everywhere they turned." *Negro's Civil War*, 22.

31. *Ibid.*, 162.

32. Eric Foner, *Free Soil, Free Labor, Free Men: The Ideology of the Republican Party Before the Civil War*, discusses how Republican hostility toward the "slave-power" was in part a displacement of northern men's fears of the erosion of their status as economically independent, and therefore "free men," in the face of northern economic development.

33. This collapse of the southern social order from within is discussed by James L. Roark, *Masters Without Slaves: Southern Planters and the Civil War and Reconstruction* (New York, 1977); Ira Berlin et al., *Freedom: A Documentary History of Emancipation: 1861–1867*, and by Clarence Mohr, *Masters and Slaves in Civil War Georgia* (Athens, 1986).

34. See, for example, J. L. Underwood, *The Women of the Confederacy* (New York, 1906); Matthew Page Andrews, *The Women of the South in Wartimes* (Baltimore, 1920); Francis Butler Simkins and James Welch Patton, *The Women of the Confederacy;* H. E. Sterkx, *Partners in Rebellion* (Cranbury, N.J., 1970); and Bell Wiley, *Confederate Women* (Westport, Conn., 1975); and perhaps most recently, George C. Rable, *Civil Wars: Women and the Crisis of Southern Nationalism* (Urbana, 1988).

35. As originally cited in H. E. Sterkx, *Partners in Rebellion*, 5, and then later by Bell Wiley, in *Confederate Women*. In a break with this line of argument, Drew Gilpin Faust has suggested that the war may have been lost because its "paternalist" assumptions appeared increasingly meaningless to Confederate women as the war progressed and the loss of life and disruption of domestic life in general mounted. See Drew Gilpin Faust, "Confederate Women and the Narratives of War," in this volume.

36. Julia Cumming, who saw all four of her sons enlist in the first six months of the war, confessed privately to her daughter of how the loss weighed on her, casting a "very peculiar shade of gloom on my spirits," but even then she immediately went on to berate herself for her lack of faith, saying say that she knew she should have "more confidence and serenity than I now feel." Julia Bryan Cumming to Emily Cumming Hammond (Hammond, Bryan, Cumming Col-

lection, Caroliniana Library, University of South Carolina, Columbia), May 24, 1861.

37. Joseph Jones to Caroline Davis Jones, Oct. 8, 1861.

38. Caroline Davis Jones to Joseph Jones, Nov. 12, 1861.

39. Simkins and Patton, *The Women of the Confederacy*, 8–9.

40. Sterkx, *Partners in Rebellion*, 42.

41. Augusta *Chronicle and Sentinel*, April 25, 1861.

42. *Ibid.*

43. Mary Elizabeth Massey makes this point in *Bonnet Brigades* (New York, 1966), 367.

44. Augusta *Chronicle and Sentinel*, Sept. 22, 1862.

45. *Ibid.*, May 7, 1861. Julia Bryan Cumming wrote to her daughter of the humiliation her son did in fact feel at his failure to enlist at the time. "Poor Jule, The Guards have gone without him and how immensely more painful is his state, than that of any of them, who have gone to face the horrors of honorable warfare." Julia Bryan Cumming to Emily Cumming Hammond, May 24, 1861.

46. This propensity to sacrifice for the cause led some women to strip their own households virtually bare. According to Mary Elizabeth Massey, this was an important reason why the domestic population suffered from serious shortages. Mary Elizabeth Massey, *Ersatz in the Confederacy* (Columbia, 1952), 31. See also Simkins and Patton, *The Women of the Confederacy*, 27.

47. Augusta *Chronicle and Sentinel*, June 7, 1861.

48. *Ibid.*, Aug. 13, 1861.

49. Rebecca Latimer Felton, "Temperance," n.d., Felton Papers (Special Collections, University of Georgia, Athens). Looking back many years after the war, Felton claimed that it was the root of southern women's emergence as public figures. "The change stirred something in them—perhaps a murmur of the independence that was to echo down the corridors of future decades." Felton, *The Romantic Story of Georgia's Women* (Atlanta, 1930), 23. A position most forcefully argued by Scott, *Southern Lady;* as well as by Massey, *Bonnet Brigades,* and Wiley, *Confederate Women.*

50. Augusta *Chronicle and Sentinel*, Jan. 9, 1863. Amy Clark fought on until she was wounded twice and taken prisoner. Her sex finally discovered, she was required to "don female garb" in federal prison.

51. *Ibid.*, June 10, 1862.

52. Sarah Morgan Dawson, *A Confederate Girl's Diary*, James I. Robertson, ed. (Bloomington, 1960), May 9, 1862.

53. William G. Deloney to Rosa Deloney (William Gaston Deloney Papers (Special Collections, University of Georgia, Athens), March 13, 1862.

54. *Ibid.*, March 16, 1862.

55. M.D.D. to Rosa Deloney, Nov. 6, 1863.

56. Anne Scott has argued that the Civil War "opened every door" to women, giving women entree into wage labor and public organizations in the postbellum period, but Suzanne Lebsock has subsequently argued that the war opened those doors only in the context of poverty and personal loss and no white southern women felt that load more heavily in the postwar period than women widowed by

the war. Anne Scott, *The Southern Lady*, 106–33; and Suzanne Lebsock, *Free Women of Petersburg*, 237–49.

57. By the last year of the war, Frank Coker was urging his wife to borrow money rather than suffer for enough to eat and wear. He counted on his ability to make money after the war was over to bail them out of debt. Frank Coker to Sarah Coker, Feb. 1, 1865. Two weeks later she wrote to tell him that she was hiring out more of their slaves because she lacked the resources to support them. Sarah Coker to Frank Coker, Feb. 18, 1865.

58. Jacqueline Jones, *Labor of Love, Labor of Sorrow: Black Women, Work and the Family, from Slavery to the Present* (New York, 1985), 44–78; Susan Archer Mann, "Social Change and Sexual Inequality: The Impact of the Transition from Slavery to Sharecropping on Black Women," in *Signs* 14, no. 4 (Summer 1989), pp. 133–57.

59. Augusta *Chronicle and Sentinel*, April 4, 1865.

60. Susan Cornwall, "Journal" (Southern Historical Collection, University of North Carolina, Chapel Hill), May 29, 1866. For a more extended discussion of the way in which the family closed around both white men and women after the war, see Jean Friedman, *The Enclosed Garden: Women and Community in the Evangelical South, 1830–1900* (Chapel Hill, 1985), 92–109.

61. There are many first-hand accounts of widespread depression among white men of the South after defeat. See, for example, John T. Trowbridge, *The Desolate South: 1865–1866*, Gordon Carroll, ed. (New York, 1956); John Richard Dennett, *The South As It Is, 1865–1866*, Henry M. Christman, ed. (Athens, 1986); Whitelaw Reid, *After the War: A Tour of the Southern States, 1865–1866*, C. Vann Woodward, ed. (New York, 1965). Contemporary historians have discussed it as well. See Dan Carter, *When the War Was Over: The Failure of Self-Reconstruction in the South* (Baton Rouge, 1985), and James Roark, *Masters Without Slaves*. For a discussion of this depression as a more explicitly gendered expression of the loss of the war as a failure of their manhood, see Gaines M. Foster, *Ghosts of the Confederacy: Defeat, the Lost Cause and the Emergence of the New South* (New York, 1987).

62. Susan Cornwall, "Journal," Aug. 22, 1865. This sentiment was intensified by the widespread ridicule of southern white manhood in defeat in the northern press. See Nina Silber, "Intemperate Men, Spiteful Women, and Jefferson Davis," in this volume.

63. "Burial Services for John Francis Shaffner, M.D.," Fries and Shaffner Papers (Southern Historical Collection, University of North Carolina), Sept. 20, 1908. Charles Reagan Wilson discusses the importance of religion as a source of consolation for defeated ex-Confederate men in *Baptized in Blood: The Religion of the Lost Cause* (Athens, 1980).

64. Stowe, *Uncle Tom's Cabin*, 467.

Chapter 2. Politics of Yeoman Households

1. William Elliott to Wife, Paris, Sept. 20, 1855, Elliott-Gonzales Papers (Southern Historical Collection, University of North Carolina, Chapel Hill, hereafter SHC).

2. Grand Jury Presentments, Charleston District, May Term, 1851, General Assembly Records, South Carolina Department of Archives and History (hereafter SDCAH); Anonymous, *Preamble and Regulations of the Savannah River Anti-Slave Traffick Association* (n.p., Nov. 21, 1846). For the laws against trading with slaves, see H. M. Henry, *The Police Control of the Slave in South Carolina* (1914; New York, 1968), 28–51, 79–94. Patterns in their irregular enforcement can be traced in Grand Jury Presentments, 1820–1865; and in Branchville Vigilant Association and Detective Police, [Orangeburg District], Minute Book, 1860–63 (SCL). Accusations were usually made of more marginal "poor white" lowcountry men: tenants, peddlers, grog shop keepers, petty traders, and boatmen. Price, however, was a landowner and farmer. William Elliott to Ralph Elliott, Beaufort, July 12, 1856, Elliott-Gonzales Papers (SHC).

3. William Elliott to Ralph Elliott, Paris, Oct. 1, 1855, Elliot-Gonzales Papers (SHC). The legal decision in the case is not recorded in the collection, but there is a later notation that Price sold out and moved away. See William Elliott to Ralph Elliott, Beaufort, July 12, 1856, Elliott-Gonzales Papers (SHC).

4. A similar episode is recounted in Lacy K. Ford, Jr., *Origins of Southern Radicalism: The South Carolina Upcountry, 1800–1860* (New York, 1988), 67.

5. For an illuminating discussion of household property and labor relations, see Elizabeth Blackmar, *Manhattan for Rent, 1785–1850* (Ithaca, 1989), 1–71. For a social and spatial definition of rural households, see Christopher Clark, *The Roots of Rural Capitalism: Western Massachusetts, 1780–1860* (Ithaca, 1990), 21. Other historians have pointed to the household as the basic unit of antebellum southern society. See particularly Elizabeth Fox-Genovese, "Antebellum Southern Households: A New Perspective on a Familiar Question," *Review* 7 (Fall 1983): 215–53, and *Within the Plantation Household: Black and White Women of the Old South* (Chapel Hill, 1988), 37–99; Steven Hahn, *The Roots of Southern Populism: Yeoman Farmers and the Transformation of the Georgia Upcountry, 1850–1890* (New York, 1983).

6. William Elliott, *Carolina Sports by Land and Water: Including Incidents of Devil-Fishing, Wild-Cat, Deer and Bear Hunting, Etc.* (1846; New York, 1967), 166, 170, 172, and on public recognition of common rights, see 168–69. On the comparative history of common rights, see Steven Hahn, "Hunting, Fishing, and Foraging: Common Rights and Class Relations in the Post-bellum South," *Radical History Review* 26 (1982): 37–64. And on his proslavery unionist politics, see William Elliott, *Address to the People of St. Helena's Parish* (Charleston, 1832); Mrs. Elliott to Caroline Elliott, n.d. [1859], Elliott-Gonzales Papers (SHC). Elliott remained a unionist until 1859.

7. Extant court records and petitions to the legislature sustain the conclusion that this was the single most frequent source of community conflict by the 1840s and 1850s. See Petitions to the Legislature, 1820–1865, General Assembly Records (SCDAH), and the trespass cases cited below.

8. Elliott, *Carolina Sports*, 167–69. For a revealing example of the rulings in trespass cases, see *State v. Thomas Dawson*, Coosawhatchie, Spring Term, 1835, in W. R. Hill, *Reports of Cases at Law Argued and Determined in the Court of Appeals of South Carolina*, III (Columbia, 1841), 100–123.

9. What follows builds on the literature on southern households, but differs from it in the emphasis placed on the political meaning, not simply of the independence of yeoman household heads, but of the domestic relations of power and dependency out of which that independence was constructed.

10. See *John Porteous v. Joseph Hazel and Joseph Jenkins*, Charleston, May Term, 1824, in William Harper, *Reports of Cases Determined in the Constitutional Court of South Carolina*, Second Edition, I (Columbia, 1841), 332–33.

11. *E. D. Law v. J. Nettles*, Darlington, Spring Term, 1831, in H. Bailey, *Reports of Cases Argued and Determined in the Court of Appeals of South Carolina*, I, 447–48; *State v. Thomas Dawson*.

12. *A. S. Rhodes v. Lydia Bunch et al.*, Charleston, February Term, 1825, in David J. McCord, *Reports of Cases Argued and Determined in the Court of Appeals of South Carolina*, III (Columbia, 1826), 66–71; *John Marsh v. Iverson L. Brooks and Others*, Edgefield, Spring Term, 1834 in W. R. Hill, *Reports of Cases Argued and Determined in the Court of Appeals of S.C.*, II (Columbia, 1835), 427–30.

13. Virtually everything written on slavery, the planter class, and antebellum southern politics sustains this point. A few examples will suffice: Eugene D. Genovese, *Roll, Jordan, Roll: The World the Slaves Made* (New York, 1974); William Cooper, *The South and the Politics of Slavery, 1828–1856* (Baton Rouge, 1978); Fox-Genovese, *Within the Plantation Household;* William W. Freehling, *The Road to Disunion: Secessionists at Bay, 1776–1854* (New York, 1990).

14. J. Mills Thornton, III, *Politics and Power in a Slave Society: Alabama, 1800–1860* (Baton Rouge, 1978); Hahn, *The Roots of Southern Populism;* J. William Harris, *Plain Folk and Gentry in a Slave Society: White Liberty and Black Slavery in Augusta's Hinterlands* (Middletown, Conn., 1985); Ford, *Origins of Southern Radicalism.*

15. Ezekiel Stokes, Beaufort County, File 6662, Box 238, Record Group 217, Southern Claims Commission Records (National Archives). Yeoman households are thus quantitatively defined as those owning land and nine or fewer slaves, the number reflecting in part the disproportionate representation of women and children in small slaveholding units in the lowcountry. Moreover, contrary to the assumptions of many historians, yeoman households constituted the majority of white households in the coastal parishes of South Carolina, as they did in the middle districts and upcountry. For a more detailed discussion, see McCurry, "Defense of Their World: Gender, Class, and the Yeomanry of the South Carolina Low Country, 1820–1860 (Ph.D. dissertation, State University of New York at Binghamton, 1988), 43–130 (quotation, 86). This gender pattern among small slaveholdings has been confirmed for the entire South in an earlier period by Michael P. Johnson and David C. Rankin, "Southern Slaveholders, 1790–1820: A Census," paper presented at the Annual Meeting of the Southern Historical Association, New Orleans, November 1990.

16. For suggestive treatments of the gender and generational power relations of the labor systems of petty proprietors' households, see Daniel Vickers, "Working the Fields in a Developing Economy: Essex County, Massachusetts, 1630–1675," in Stephen Innes, ed., *Work and Labor in Early America* (Chapel Hill, 1988), 46–69; Jacqueline Dowd Hall et al., *Like a Family: The Making of a Southern Cotton*

Mill World (Chapel Hill, 1987), 3–43; and Allen Tullos, *Habits of Industry: White Culture and the Transformation of the Carolina Piedmont* (Chapel Hill, 1989).

17. Gavin Wright, *Political Economy of the Cotton South: Households, Markets, and Wealth in Nineteenth Century America* (New York, 1978); Hahn, *Roots of Southern Populism;* Ford, *Origins of Southern Radicalism.*

18. This owes, in part, to the fact that women's labor has historically been obscured by the public representation of the household in the person of its male head (in the census, for example), and by definitions of work that focus on the value of market exchange. See Jeanne Boydston, *Home and Work: Housework, Wages, and the Ideology of Labor in the Early Republic* (New York, 1990); Nancy Folbre, "The Unproductive Housewife: Her Evolution in Nineteenth Century Economic Thought," *Signs* 16 (Spring 1991): 463–84. The slave South presents an intriguing point of contrast to Folbre's argument about the gendering of use value as female in the antebellum North.

19. O'Neall quoted in Ford, *Origins of Southern Radicalism,* 53; Pendleton Farmers' Society Records, Minutes, Oct. 12, 1827, Oct. 9, 1828, Aug. 13, 1829 (SCL); Black Oak Agricultural Society, Constitutions and Proceedings, Nov. 16, 1847 (SCL).

20. Mary Davis Brown Diary, Jan. 13, 1857 (quotation), July 29, 1857, April 25, Aug. 7, 31, 1858, and throughout (SCL); Elizabeth Finisher to Nancy H. Cowan, Aug. 23, 1846, and Eleibers Cowen and Martha Cowen to John Cowen, Feb. 1846, Nancy H. Cowan Papers (Perkins Library, Duke University).

21. *The Southron,* June 11 and May 21, 1856. On sale of butter to planters, see the receipts of July 2, Dec. 4, 1841, Nov. 17, 1842, Lawton Family Papers, (SCL); on store accounts, see Accounts of Rebecca Robertson, April 18–Nov. 21, 1821, Account of Elsey Edwards, March 7, 1821, and the Account of Jane Oram, May 30–Aug. 28, 1821, Anonymous, Account Book, Camden and Hanging Rock, Kershaw District, 1821–23 (SCL); Samuel K. Carrigan, Sales Book, 1859–60 (SCL); Lewis E. Atherton, *The Southern Country Store, 1800–1860* (Baton Rouge, 1949), 48–54, 87–91.

For discussions of the meaning of non-monetary and barter exchanges, see Michael Merrill, "Cash Is Good to Eat: Self-sufficiency and Exchange in the Rural Economy of the United States," *Radical History Review* 4 (Winter 1977): 42–71; Christopher Clark, "Household Economy, Market Exchange, and the Rise of Capitalism in the Connecticut Valley, 1800–1860," *Journal of Social History* 13 (Winter 1979): 169–89, and *Roots of Rural Capitalism;* and Hahn, *Roots of Southern Populism.*

22. Mary Davis Brown Diary, Oct. 9, 1858.

23. Frederick Law Olmsted, *A Journey in the Back Country, 1853–1854* (1860; New York, 1970), 298; Frances Trollope, *Domestic Manners of the Americans* (1832; Gloucester, Mass., 1968), 117, 243.

24. For the exception that proves the rule, see Samuel DuBose, *Address Delivered at the Seventeenth Anniversary of the Black Oak Agricultural Society, on Tuesday, April 27th, 1858* (Charleston, 1858), 21.

25. James F. Sloan Journals, June 24, 1854 to March 27, 1861 (SCL). I would like to thank Lacy Ford for drawing these journals to my attention.

Sloan's property-holdings are outlined in Ford, *Origins of Southern Radicalism*, 78–80.

26. Many rural historians would acknowledge that women worked in the field during harvest in yeoman households. But they typically treat that activity as an exception to an otherwise clear gender division of labor, as if harvesting were a crisis or an emergency, rather than a regular seasonal activity. See Wright, *Political Economy of the Cotton South*, 82–83; Hahn, *Roots of Southern Populism*, 30; Ford, *Origins of Southern Radicalism*, 78–80.

27. Sloan Journals, June 21, July 5, Sept. 15, 1856, and Sept. 8 to Nov. 30, 1858.

28. Sloan Journals, June 4, June 5, 1857, and July 7, 1858.

29. See the comments on the value of children's labor to yeoman households in Elizabeth Finisher to Nancy H. Cowan, Aug. 23, 1846, and William Benson to Mr. John Cowan, Aug. 13, 1841, Nancy H. Cowan Papers.

30. On the global identification of ploughing as primarily a male task see Esther Boserup, *Women's Role in Economic Development* (London, 1970), 19–34. Such gender assumptions went so deep in antebellum perceptions that when Frederick Law Olmsted came upon slave women ploughing in the lower South, he "watched them with some interest to see if there was any indication that their sex unfitted them for the occupation." Charles E. Beveridge and Charles Capen McLaughlin, eds., *The Papers of Frederick Law Olmsted*, II (Baltimore, 1981), 218–19. The idea has persisted that women, and even slave women, did not plow. But there is considerable evidence that slave women were plow hands on many plantations and that on yeoman farms where grown sons were in short supply, wives and daughters took their turns driving the plow. On slave women, see the list of field hands by task in James Henry Hammond, Plantation Records, Aug. 7, 1850, James H. Hammond Papers (SCL).

31. Sloan Journals, Oct. 14, March 8, 1859.

32. *The Southron*, July 6, 1859. On the male culture of country stores, see Inventory of the Estate of [merchant] Col. Elisha Rogers, Court of Probate, Inventories, and Sales Book, Darlington District, Oct. 21, 1826, and Jan. 6, 1827 (SCDAH); Anonymous, Account Book, Camden and Hanging Rock, Kershaw District, Aug. 19, Dec. 6, 1820, and throughout (SCL); Samuel K. Carrigan, Day Book, [Darlington District], 1858–60 (SCL); Samuel K. Carrigan, Sales Book, 1859–60 (SCL). On the location of polls, see General Assembly Records, House of Representatives, Election Returns, 1820–60 (SCDAH); for a few specific examples see returns of St. Paul's Parish, Colleton District, Oct. 13, 1824; Williamsburg District, Oct. 9, 1838, and throughout. Other polls were located at muster houses and grounds. On developments in the Northeast, see Karen Halttunen, *Confidence Men and Painted Ladies: A Study of Middle Class Culture in America, 1830–1870* (New Haven, 1982).

33. Sloan Journals, March 3, April 6, 1859, April 13, 1860.

34. *Ibid.*, Aug. 9, 1860. There is now a substantial body of literature on antebellum southern women but little, if any, of it treats the experience of yeoman women. For a sampling of the studies of planter women and slave women, see Anne Firor Scott, *The Southern Lady: From Pedestal to Politics* (Chicago, 1970); Catherine Clinton, *The Plantation Mistress: Woman's World in the Old South* (New

York, 1982); Suzanne Lebsock, *The Free Women of Petersburg: Status and Culture in a Southern Town* (New York, 1984); Fox-Genovese, *Within the Plantation Household;* Deborah G. White, *"Ar'n't I a Woman": Female Slaves in the Plantation South* (New York, 1985); Jacqueline Jones, *Labor of Love, Labor of Sorrow: Black, Women, Work and the Family from Slavery to the Present* (New York, 1985).

35. Mary Davis Brown Diary, July 14, 1859, April 25, 1858, Aug. 11, 1859. The close relationship between conversion and marriage is sustained by analysis of evangelical church membership records. See McCurry, "Defense of Their World," 241–322. The connections between womanhood, motherhood, and conversion are also evident, although with profoundly different meanings and consequences, in the evangelical culture of the antebellum Northeast. See, especially, Mary P. Ryan, *Cradle of the Middle Class: The Family in Oneida County, New York, 1790–1865* (New York, 1981); and Nancy F. Cott, "Young Women in the Second Great Awakening," *Feminist Studies* 3 (Fall 1975): 15–29.

36. The case for a gendered political history that transgresses the boundaries of formal politics and confounds conventional distinctions between public and private spheres has been made most explicitly by Joan Scott, *Gender and the Politics of History* (New York, 1989).

37. This argument is developed at greater length in McCurry, "The Two Faces of Republicanism: Gender and Proslavery Politics in Antebellum South Carolina," *Journal of American History* 78 (March 1992).

38. Here I find myself in disagreement with the interpretation of manhood and political culture offered by Paula Baker, "The Domestication of Politics: Women and American Political Society, 1780–1920," *American Historical Review* 89 (June 1984): 620–47, although the argument is suggestive in many important respects.

Chapter 3. A Northern Volunteer

I would like to thank Judith Hunter for lending me a copy of Daniel Walker Howe's article precisely when I needed to read it, and Liza Buurma for criticizing an earlier draft of this essay.

1. Mildren Throne, ed., *The Civil War Diary of Cyrus F. Boyd, Fifteenth Iowa Infantry, 1861–1863* (Millwood, N.Y., 1977), 6 (hereafter referred to as *Boyd*).

2. For example, in Utica, New York, in the 1850s, 40 percent of native-born males between the ages of fifteen and thirty still lived at home. Mary P. Ryan, *Cradle of the Middle Class: The Family in Oneida County, New York, 1790–1865* (Cambridge, Eng., 1981), 167; also Tables E.4 and E.5., 269. What term to use to describe these older boys and young men is problematic. Joesph F. Kett uses the terms "dependence" and "semidependence," although he prefers the latter term for youth who have left home temporarily but are still bound to it; another—contemporary—term, for those males in their teens or beyond who are still at home is "large boys." Kett also reminds us that physical maturation occurred later in the antebellum period than it does now; a male in his early twenties was more likely to be still growing. Finally, the period around the Civil War saw the rise of the notion of adolescence—without, however, the use of the word "adolescence."

Joseph F. Kett, *Rites of Passage: Adolescence in America 1790 to the Present* (New York, 1979).

3. Gerald F. Linderman, *Embattled Courage: The Experience of Combat in the American Civil War* (New York, 1987), 26.

4. *Boyd*, 13–21.

5. *Ibid.*, 16, 123. Accounts of drunkenness and prostitution run throughout Boyd's diary.

6. William Grilfillan Gavin, *Infantryman Pettit: The Civil War Letters of Corporal Frederick Pettit* (New York, 1991), 8. *Boyd*, 24–25. On middle-class youth adopting a policy of sexual restraint, see Ryan, *Cradle of the Middle Class*, 179–80.

7. For a discussion of the centrality of self-discipline to manliness, see E. Anthony Rotundo, "Learning About Manhood: Gender Ideals and the Middle Class Family in Nineteenth Century America," in J. A. Mangan and James Walvin, eds., *Manliness and Morality: Middle Class Masculinity in Britain and America, 1800–1940* (New York, 1987), 35–51; for its centrality to evangelical culture in the North, see Daniel Walker Howe, "The Evangelical Movement and Political Culture in the North During the Second Party System," *The Journal of American History*, March 1991, 1216–39. The importance of self-discipline and obedience in antebellum schooling is discussed by Carl F. Kaestle in *Pillars of the Republic: Common Schools and American Society, 1780–1860* (n.p., 1983), 75–103. For the feminine image of the South in the postwar period, see Nina Silber, "Intemperate Men, Spiteful Women, and Jefferson Davis," in this volume. The way nineteenth century northern discussion of manhood can set up "Women," "Negroes," "Slaves," "Children," "Indians," "Irish," or "Southerners"—to name only a few—in opposition to "True Men" is too complicated and troublesome to deal with in this essay.

8. *Boyd*, 10, 25.

9. *Ibid.*, 23–42.

10. *Ibid.*, 59.

11. *Ibid.*, 123–25.

12. George C. Lawson to wife, April 29, 1864. George C. Lawson Papers in Robert Shaw Collection (Atlanta Historical Society).

13. Sidney O. Little to Sarah P. Durant, Dec. 19, 1862, Little Letters, Schoff Collection (Clements Library, University of Michigan). Benjamen F. Ashenfelter to Father, Aug. 23, 1863, Benjamen F. Ashenfelter Papers, Harrisburg Civil War Round Table Collection (U.S. Army Military History Institute). Marcia M. Reid-Green, ed., *Henry Matrau of the Iron Brigade* (Lincoln, forthcoming). Wilbur Fisk, *Anti-Rebel: The Civil War Letters of Wilbur Fisk* (Croton-on-Hudson, N.Y., 1983), 306. Donald J. Mrozek, "The Habit of Victory: The American Military and the Cult of Manliness," Mangan and Walvin, eds., *Manliness and Morality*, 220–39.

14. Burage Rice Diary, Oct. 9, 1861 (New-York Historical Society). See George B. Forgie, *Patricide in the House Divided: A Psychological Interpretation of Lincoln and His Age* (New York, 1979), for extended discussion of the concept of the Union as a paternal legacy that in many ways burdened their heirs, the generation of 1861.

15. Henry H. Seys to Harriet Seys, Oct. 23, 1863, Henry H. Seys Letters, Schoff

Collection (Clements Library, University of Michigan). See Ryan, *Cradle of the Middle Class,* 155–65, for a discussion of just how much of the burden of character development middle-class thought placed on a son's mother. Also see Michael Grossberg, *Governing the Hearth: Law and the Family in Nineteenth-Century America* (Chapel Hill, 1985), for a discussion of the changing perception of the "republican family" in nineteenth-century America.

16. Fisk, *Anti-Rebel,* iii.

17. George W. Crosley to Edna, April 10, 1862. The Civil War Miscellany Papers (U.S. Army Military History Institute). Henry C. Metzger to sister, Aug. 25, 1864, Henry C. Metzger Letters, Harrisburg Civil War Round Table Collection (U.S. Army Military History Institute). Margaret Brobst Roth, ed., *Well Mary: Civil War Letters of a Wisconsin Volunteer* (Madison, 1960), 135–36. For a general discussion of northern images of the South—although one that does not use gender or familial terms—see Reid Mitchell, *Civil War Soldiers* (New York, 1988), 24–55, 90–147.

18. Mrs. C. E. McKay, *Stories of Hospital and Camp* (Freeport, N.Y., 1971—reprint of Philadelphia, 1876 edition), viii.

19. George M. Frederickson, *The Inner Civil War: Northern Intellectuals and the Crisis of the Union* (New York, 1965), 217–38; Linderman, *Embattled Courage,* 275–97.

Chapter 4. A Union Soldier's Experience

This essay is an abridged version of the introduction to *When This Cruel War Is Over: The Civil War Letters of Charles Harvey Brewster,* edited with an introduction by David W. Blight (Amherst, Univ. of Massachusetts Press, 1992).

1. Paul Fussell, *The Great War in Modern Memory* (New York, 1975), 6.

2. Bell I. Wiley, *The Life of Billy Yank: The Common Soldier of the Union* (Baton Rouge, 1952), 15; Bell I. Wiley, *The Life of Johnny Reb: The Common Soldier in the Confederacy* (Baton Rouge, 1943). For the growing literature on the social history of the common soldier and the Civil War era, see Maris A. Vinovskis, "Have Social Historians Lost the Civil War?: Some Preliminary Demographic Speculations," *Journal of American History,* June 1989, 34–58; Maris A. Vinovskis, ed., *Toward a Social History of the American Civil War* (New York, 1990); Joseph T. Glatthaar, *The March to the Sea and Beyond: Sherman's Troops in the Savannah and Carolinas Campaigns* (New York, 1985); Joseph T. Glatthaar, *Forged in Battle: The Civil War Alliance of Black Soldiers and White Officers* (New York, 1990); Reid Mitchell, *Civil War Soldiers: Their Expectations and Their Experiences* (New York, 1988); Phillip Shaw Paludan, *"A People's Contest": The Union and Civil War, 1861–65* (New York, 1988), 316–38; Randall C. Jimerson, *The Private Civil War: Popular Thought During the Sectional Conflict* (Baton Rouge, 1988); James I. Robertson, Jr., *Soldiers Blue and Gray* (Columbia, S.C., 1988); Michael Fellman, *Inside War: The Guerrilla Conflict in Missouri During the American Civil War* (New York, 1989); Warren Wilkinson, *Mother, May You Never See the Sights I Have Seen: The Fifty-seventh Massachusetts Veteran Volunteers in the Army of the Potomac, 1864–65* (New York, 1990); Michael Barton, *Goodmen: The Character of Civil War Soldiers* (University

Park, Penn., 1981); Earl J. Hess, *Liberty, Virtue, and Progress: Northerners and Their War for the Union* (New York, 1988); and Marvin R. Cain, "A 'Face of Battle' Needed: An Assessment of Motives and Men in Civil War Historiography," *Civil War History* 28 (March 1982): 5–27.

3. *The Hampshire Gazette and Courier* (Northampton, Mass.), April 23, 30, May 7, 14, June 11, 1861 (Forbes Library, Northampton); Alfred S. Roe, *The Tenth Regiment Massachusetts Volunteer Infantry, 1861–64* (Springfield, Mass., 1909), 378–84.

4. Roe, *Tenth Regiment*, 18–28.

5. Robert Hunt Rhodes, ed., *All for the Union: The Civil War Diary and Letters of Elisha Hunt Rhodes* (New York, 1991); Geoffrey C. Ward, with Ric Burns and Ken Burns, *The Civil War: An Illustrated History* (New York, 1990). For the creation of the brigade in which the Tenth served, see Frank J. Welcher, *The Union Army, 1861–1865: Organization and Operations*, Vol. I, *The Eastern Theater* (Bloomington, Ind., 1989), 8. On March 13, 1862, Brewster's brigade became part of the Fourth Corps of the Army of the Potomac, and from September 1862 until the end of their service in June 1864 they were part of the Sixth Corps. Roe, *Tenth Regiment*, 318–19.

6. Roe, *Tenth Regiment*, 295. When the regiment returned to Springfield in June 1864, only 220 of the original nearly 1,000 men remained on active duty.

7. *The Brewster Genealogy, 1566–1907: A Record of the Descendants of William Brewster of the Mayflower, Ruling Elder of the Pilgrim Church Which Founded Plymouth Colony in 1620*, vol. 2, comp. by Emma C. Brewster Jones (New York, 1908), 868–69. On the ordinary soldier escaping from ordinary life, see Philip Caputo, *A Rumor of War* (New York, 1977).

8. Brewster letters, June 15, July 12, and June 21, 1862, Charles Harvey Brewster Collection (Northampton Historical Society, Northampton, Mass.). Some 210 Brewster letters survive, 193 as originals, and 17 as transcribed into journals by Mary Kate Brewster in 1893. The originals and the journals (where some letters contain erasures and embellishments) are housed at the Northampton Historical Society. This essay is based exclusively on original letters, hereafter cited as CHB letter, date. On the importance of letters and connections to "home" see Reid Mitchell, "The Northern Soldier and His Community," In Vinovskis, ed., *Toward a Social History*, 78–92.

9. CHB letter, July 9, 1863.

10. CHB letters, Nov. 24, 10, 1861, Sept. 22, Nov. 6, 10, 17, 24, and Dec. 14, 1861. Also see letter, Nov. 21, 1861, where he describes himself as "cursed with ill luck all my life."

11. CHB letter, Jan. 9, 1862. Brewster was subsequently promoted to first lieutenant, Sept. 29, 1862, and as adjutant of the regiment, Dec. 1862. He was technically a staff officer and not a field officer.

12. CHB letter, Jan. 15, 1862.

13. Henry W. Parsons to Aunt Julia, Sept. ? 1861, Parsons Family Papers (Northampton Historical Society).

14. CHB letters, Nov. 25, 1862, Feb. 23, Nov. 21, 1863. On the social distance between civilians and soldiers, see Mitchell, "The Northern Soldier," in Vinovskis,

ed., *Toward a Social History,* 89; and Eric J. Leed, *No Man's Land: Combat and Identity in World War I* (New York, 1979), 213.

15. CHB letter, April 3, 1864.

16. CHB letter, June 15, 1864. For the cycles of selective memory among veterans, see Gerald Linderman, *Embattled Courage: The Experience of Combat in the Civil War* (New York, 1987), 266–97. Brewster's wartime letters presaged what Linderman aptly calls the "militarization of thought and the purification of memory" (p. 284). Also see Leed, *No Man's Land,* 12–33.

17. Linderman, *Embattled Courage,* 7–110.

18. William Manchester, *Goodbye Darkness: A Memoir of the Pacific War* (New York, 1979), 46–47. A growing literature exists on the questions of manhood, male tradition, and war-making. Helpful to me have been Linderman, *Embattled Courage;* E. Anthony Rotundo, "Body and Soul: Changing Ideals of American Middle-Class Manhood, 1770–1920," *Journal of Social History* (Spring 1983), 23–38; Kim Townsend, "Francis Parkman and the Male Tradition," *American Quarterly* (Spring 1986), 97–112; Peter G. Filene, *Him/Herself: Sex Roles in Modern America,* 69–112; and Edward O. Wilson, *On Human Nature* (Cambridge, 1978), 99–120. An important critique of Fussell's *Great War in Modern Memory,* and useful to understanding what may be peculiarly male about the experience of and writing about war, is Lynne Hanley, *Writing War: Fiction, Gender, and Memory* (Amherst, 1991), 18–37.

19. CHB letters, May 24, 25, 27, 28, 29, 31, and July 27, 1862.

20. Stephen Crane, *The Red Badge of Courage* (New York: Avon edition, 1979), 39–40; CHB letters, Dec. 15, 23, 1862.

21. CHB letters, April 30, May 26, 1864. From May 5 to 12, the Army of the Potomac suffered 32,000 casualties, killed, wounded, or missing. During the first seven weeks of Grant's campaign against Lee in Virginia northern casualties reached the appalling figure of 65,000, a daily cost in life and limb that Brewster's letters help document. These seven weeks also constitute almost exactly the final days of the enlistment of the Tenth Massachusetts, which was mustered out on June 22. These casualty figures were horrifying to northerners because of the devastation they brought to so many families in towns like Northampton, but also because they offered no clear sign of an end to the war; Lee's lines in Virginia had not been broken as the siege of Petersburg began, though his casualties had been proportionately as high as Grant's. See James McPherson, *The Battle Cry of Freedom* (New York, 1988), 732, 741–42.

22. CHB letters, April 23, May 7, 1862. Aitken quoted in Fussell, *Great War,* 174.

23. CHB letters, June 2, 5, 12, 15, 21, and May 10, 1862. Some researchers may wish to follow the theme of Brewster's many physical maladies and the variety of medical treatments and drugs he endured.

24. John Keegan, *The Face of Battle: A Study of Agincourt, Waterloo, and the Somme* (New York, 1976), 35–45, 320–43.

25. CHB letters, July 30, 1863, May 11, 13, 15, 1864. Many of Bierce's stories would serve as comparisons, but see, for example, "A Horseman in the Sky" and

"The Mocking-Bird" in *The Civil War Short Stories of Ambrose Bierce,* compiled by Ernest J. Hopkins (Lincoln, Neb., 1970), 97–108.

26. CHB letters, Oct. 23, Sept. 25, 1861, May 21, 1862, May 23, 26, 1864. Obituary, "The Death of Charles H. Brewster, *Daily Hampshire Gazette,* Oct. 9, 1893. After the war, Brewster became the first successful professional florist in the upper Connecticut River Valley. One can only imagine how much the old soldier reflected on his deep memories of life and death in the fields of Virginia as he nurtured the perennials in his greenhouses during the 1880s.

27. See Wiley, *Life of Billy Yank,* 109–15; Glatthaar, *Forged in Battle,* 11–12.

28. See Dudley T. Cornish, *The Sable Arm: Black Troops in the Union Army, 1861–65* (Lawrence, Kans., 1956), 24–25; Ira Berlin, ed., *Freedom: A Documentary History of Emancipation, 1861–67,* Series II, *The Black Military Experience* (New York, 1982), 1–7. In August 1861, Lincoln countermanded the order of General John C. Frémont that would have emancipated all slaves in Missouri. Sensitive about the disposition of the four border states remaining delicately in the Union, and mindful of northern racism, the President resisted converting the war into an abolition crusade until 1862, when emancipation as policy and reality transformed the war's purpose.

29. CHB letters, Nov. 17, 24, 1861.

30. CHB letter, Dec. 4, 1861.

31. CHB letters, Jan. 2, 15, 1862.

32. CHB letters, March 4, 5, 8, 12, 1862.

33. CHB letters, Jan. 15, 23, Feb. 9, 1862. Ralph Ellison, "What America Would Be Like Without Blacks," in *Going to the Territory* (New York, 1986), 109; Mark Twain, *The Adventures of Huckleberry Finn* (orig. pub. 1884, Penguin edition, New York, 1966), 282–83; and "Annual Message to Congress," Dec. 1, 1862, in Roy P. Basler, ed., *The Collected Works of Abraham Lincoln,* vol. 5 (New Brunswick, N.J., 1953), 537.

34. CHB letters, Aug. 20, Oct. 12, 1864. On recruiting black troops, see Glatthaar, *Forged in Battle,* 61–80; Berlin, ed., *Freedom,* 6–15. Brewster's appointment as a recruiter, signed by Governor John A. Andrew, July 23, 1864, is in Brewster Family Papers (Sophia Smith Collection, Smith College). Brewster was appointed Assistant Adjutant General on the staff of Colonel J. B. Parsons.

35. CHB letters, Sept. 16, Aug. 30, 1864.

36. CHB letters, Aug. 4, Oct. 5, 12, 1864. One of the murders Brewster describes is that of a "colored barber," who, while jailed with three white sailors, was thrown to his death from a third-story window. A year earlier in July 1863, as a newly organized company of the United States Colored Troops (USCT) marched through the streets of Norfolk, led by their lieutenant, Anson L. Sanborn, Sanborn was publicly assassinated by a prominent physician and secessionist. The physician was later executed, but the incident and others like it diminished recruiting efforts in the area for many months to come. On this incident, see Glatthaar, *Forged in Battle,* 69. As Brewster described these "occasional murders" that relatively no one paid attention to, he concluded that "it is just the difference between a state of war and a state of peace" (letter, Oct. 12, 1864).

37. CHB letter, Oct. 27, 1864. The two examples from a freedman's letters quoted here were not written by Brewster, but they come from the Norfolk recruiting area in 1864. See letters by black soldier Rufus Wright, Feb. 2, May 25, 1864, in Berlin, ed., *Freedom*, 661–63. Wright uses the phrase "give my love to" eight times in these two short letters, forming the very kind of example that Brewster found so memorable and educative. Abraham Lincoln, "Second Inaugural Address," in Basler, ed., *Collected Works of Abraham Lincoln*, vol. 8: 333.

38. Brewster obituary, *Daily Hampshire Gazette*, Oct. 9, 1893; letter, Aunt Mary to Mary Kate Brewster, Nov. 9, 1893, Brewster Family Papers (Sophia Smith Collection, Smith College). Brewster's real and personal estate was valued at approximately $15,000 at his death in 1893. Administrator's Estate Inventory, filed Oct. 26, 1893, Probate Court, Hampshire County, Northampton, Mass. Brewster's more than twenty land transactions are recorded in Register of Deeds, Hampshire County, Northampton, Mass.

39. CHB to "My Dear Children," Oct. 7, 10, 11, 1886, Brewster Collection (Northampton Historical Society). Linderman, *Embattled Courage*, 297. On the G.A.R. also see Stuart McConnell, "Who Joined the Grand Army? Three Case Studies in the Construction of Union Veteranhood, 1866–1900," in Vinovskis, ed., *Toward a Social History*, 139–70.

40. Mary Katherine Brewster, "Log Book" (diary), 1893–94, pp. 3–7, 19, 21, 26–27; letter Mary Kate Brewster to Gertrude, Jan. 9, 1894, Sydney, Australia, Brewster Family Papers (Sophia Smith Collection, Smith College); Brewster obituary, Mary K. Brewster obituary *Daily Hampshire Gazette*, Oct. 9, 1893, Jan. 7, 1951. Mary Kate Brewster wrote articles for local Massachusetts newspapers while at sea, and later in life became a playwright, theater critic, and local Northampton author. For the full significance of Brewster's letters see *When This Cruel War Is Over: The Civil War Letters of Charles Harvey Brewster*, edited with an introduction by David W. Blight (Amherst, 1992).

Chapter 5. Gender and African American Men

The author would like to thank Mari Jo Buhle, William Hart, Jacqueline Jones, and John Thomas for their comments and advice. My greatest debt is to Lyde Cullen Sizer.

1. Joan Scott, *Gender and the Politics of History* (New York, 1988), 41.

2. James McPherson, *The Negro's Civil War: How Americans Felt and Acted During the War for the Union* (Urbana, 1965), 22.

3. *Ibid.*, 33–34, 29.

4. *Ibid.*, 31.

5. This definition of manly—in contrast to masculine, which has more innate connotations—is developed in Gail Bederman, "Manly Civilization/Primitive Masculinity: Race, Gender, and Evolutions of Middle-Class American Manhood" (Ph.D. dissertation, Brown University, 1992).

6. *The Negro's Civil War*, 32–33.

7. *Ibid.*, 162.

8. On p. 230 of *The Negro in the Civil War* (Boston, 1969), Benjamin Quarles

estimated one-quarter of naval enlistments were black. More recent calculations show the figure to be around 9 percent.

9. *Ibid.*, 198; Ira Berlin, Joseph P. Reidy, and Leslie S. Rowland, eds., *Freedom: A Documentary History of Emancipation 1861–1867*, Series II: *The Black Military Experience* (New York, 1982), 14.

10. Leon F. Litwack, *Been in the Storm So Long: The Aftermath of Slavery* (New York, 1980), 72.

11. Douglass quoted in *Black Writers and the Civil War*, ed. Richard A. Long (Secaucus, 1988), 313.

12. *Been in the Storm So Long*, 74.

13. *Ibid.*, 66, 71; *Freedom*, 85.

14. *Freedom*, 77.

15. Joseph Glatthaar, *Forged in Battle: The Civil War Alliance Between Black Soldiers and White Officers* (New York, 1991), 9, 36. For the specific ways black officers were harassed, see documents in *Freedom*, 303–47.

16. *Forged in Battle*, 115.

17. *Freedom*, 387.

18. The inequality of the Union pay structure is well documented, and is discussed in much of the literature on African American soldiers in the Civil War. For one particularly good discussion, see McPherson's *The Negro's Civil War*, 193–204.

19. For documents pertaining to fatigue duty, see *Freedom*, 483–516; for figures on disease and explanations for the disparity between blacks and whites, see 633–37.

20. *Ibid.*, 153.

21. *Ibid.*, 385–86.

22. Willie Lee Rose, *Rehearsal for Reconstruction: The Port Royal Experiment* (New York, 1964), 267.

23. *Been in the Storm So Long*, 64, 101; *Forged in Battle*, 79.

24. For a discussion of such strategies, see William Taylor, *Cavalier and Yankee: The Old South and the American National Character* (New York, 1961).

25. *Freedom*, 757.

26. *Ibid.*, 97.

27. *Forged in Battle*, 130.

28. Thomas Wentworth Higginson, *Black Life in an Army Regiment* (1869; New York, 1984), 224.

29. *The Negro's Civil War*, 186–87; *Forged in Battle*, 133.

30. *The Negro's Civil War*, 191.

31. *Forged in Battle*, 134.

32. *Ibid.*, 137.

33. *Freedom*, 291–95.

34. *Ibid.*, 733.

35. *Been in the Storm So Long*, 102.

36. *Ibid.*

37. *Freedom*, 689–90. The owner of the girls wrote a letter to the commander of the Department of the Missouri asking that the soldier be forced to leave the state.

"To be insulted by such a black scoundrel is more than I can stand," he said, claiming he had always been a Unionist, and, as such, his property should be protected (p. 691).

38. James Oliver Horton, "Freedom's Yoke: Gender Conventions Among Antebellum Free Blacks," *Feminist Studies* 12, no. 1 (Spring 1986): 53. For the work strategies of African American women, see Jacqueline Jones, *Labor of Love, Labor of Sorrow: Black Women, Work and the Family from Slavery to Freedom* (New York, 1985).

39. See the discussion of gender roles in *Freedom*, 30–32.

40. Eric Foner, *Reconstruction: America's Unfinished Revolution* (New York, 1988), 288.

41. Hazel Carby, *Reconstructing Womanhood: The Emergence of the Afro-American Novelist* (New York, 1987); Gail Bederman, "Civilization, the Decline of Middle-Class Manliness, and Ida B. Wells's Anti-Lynching Campaign (1892–1894)," *Radical History Review* (Winter 1992).

42. W. E. B. Du Bois, *Black Reconstruction* (New York, 1935), 110.

43. *The Negro in the Civil War*, 199.

Chapter 6. Refined Women as Union Nurses

I am especially indebted to Jeanie Attie for her insightful and supportive criticism of an earlier draft of this article. I would also like to thank Karen Farrell and Joan Kenderick for their editorial suggestions and their insistence on clarification.

1. Katharine Prescott Wormeley to a friend, July 25, 1862, in Katharine Prescott Wormeley, *The Cruel Side of War: Letters from the Headquarters of the United States Sanitary Commission During the Peninsular Campaign in Virginia in 1862* (Boston, 1898), 205.

2. Wormeley to "A," July 3, 1862, and Wormeley to "A," July 10, 1862, in *The Cruel Side of War*, 180–81 and 194.

3. Georgeanna Woolsey Bacon, Journal, July 12, 1862, in Georgeanna Woolsey Bacon and Eliza Woolsey Howland, eds., *Letters of a Family During the War for the Union 1861–1865*, 2 vols. (Privately published, 1899), 2: 459.

4. Wormeley to "A," July 10, 1862, in *The Cruel Side of War*, 194.

5. Elizabeth Blackwell to Barbara Smith Bodichon, June 5, 1861, Elizabeth Blackwell Papers (Columbia University, New York).

6. "The Origin, Organization, and Working of the Women's Central Association of Relief," Oct. 12, 1861, No. 32, *Documents of the United States Sanitary Commission*, 2 vols. (New York, 1966), 1: 28–29; italics in text.

7. Eliza Howland to Joseph Howland, April 28, 1862, in Bacon and Howland, *Letters*, 1: 313.

8. The commissioners and the female volunteers frequently used the term "ladies" to refer to the women listed above. "Female nurses" usually referred to the socially undistinguished women who were being paid by the Commission.

9. Charles E. Beveridge, ed., *The Papers of Frederick Law Olmsted*, 4 vols. (Baltimore, 1983), 4: 27–33; Frederick Law Olmsted, *Hospital Transports* (Boston,

1863), passim; and Laura Wood Roper, *FLO: A Biography of Frederick Law Olmsted* (Baltimore, 1973), 190–206.

10. Georgeanna Woolsey to "Mother," May 2, 1862, in Bacon and Howland, *Letters*, 1: 326; Wormeley to no salutation, May 10, 1862, and Wormeley to "Friend," May 16, 1862, in *The Cruel Side of War*, 18 and 44.

11. Eliza Woolsey Howland to Joseph Howland, April 28, 1862, in Bacon and Howland, *Letters*, 1: 312–13. The four women on board were Eliza Howland, Georgeanna Woolsey, Christine Griffin, and Caroline Lane. The commissioners present were Frederick Law Olmsted, Frederick Knapp. Lewis Rutherford, George Templeton Strong, Dr. Cornelius R. Agnew, and Dr. J. M. Grymes.

12. Harriet Whetten to Kate, May 8, 1862, in Paul H. Hass, ed., "A Volunteer Nurse in the Civil War: The Letters of Harriet Douglas Whetten," *Wisconsin Magazine of History* 48 (1964): 135; and Wormeley to "Friend," May 16, 1862, in *The Cruel Side of War*, 44.

13. Wormeley to no salutation, May 14, 1862, in *The Cruel Side of War*, 32; and Whetten to Hexie, May 19, 1862, in Hass, "Letters of Harriet Douglas Whetten," 139.

14. Olmsted to John Foster Jenkins, May 25, 1862, in Beveridge, *The Papers of Frederick Law Olmsted*, 4: 351.

15. Georgeanna Woolsey Bacon, Journal, May 26, 1862, in Anne L. Austin, *The Woolsey Sisters of New York: A Family's Involvement in the Civil War and a New Profession 1860–1900* (Philadelphia, 1971), 64; and Woolsey, Journal, May 4, 1862, in Bacon and Howland, *Letters*, 1: 325–26.

16. Woolsey to "Mother," n.d., in Bacon and Howland, *Letters*, 1: 358; Wormeley to "Mother," June 10, 1862, in *The Cruel Side of War*, 126.

17. Wormeley to no salutation, May 14, 1862, in *The Cruel Side of War*, 35–36 and 32; and Whetten to Hexie, May 30, 1862, in Hass, "Letters of Harriet Douglas Whetten," 139; Wormeley to no salutation, May 14, 1862, in *The Cruel Side of War*, 32.

18. Kristie R. Ross, "War and the Search for Professional Identity: USSC Physicians and Army Medical Care," unpublished paper presented at the Convention of the Organization of American Historians (New York, 1986); Paul Starr, *The Social Transformation of American Medicine: The Rise of a Sovereign Profession and the Making of a Vast Industry* (New York, 1982), 30–59 and 79–99.

19. Olmsted, *Hospital Transports*, 62. Olmsted used very similar language when he wrote to John Foster Jenkins describing the shore hospital at White House, Virginia. "The greater part of the men are not very ill; with nice nourishment, comfortable rest, and good nursing, would be got ready to join their regiments in a week or two—but this is just what they are not likely to have." May 21, 1862, in Beveridge, *The Papers of Frederick Law Olmsted*, 4: 343.

20. Woolsey to Mother, June 3, 1862, in Bacon and Howland, *Letters*, 2: 383; and Wormeley to Mother, June 4, 1862, in *The Cruel Side of War*, 102.

21. Wormeley to "A," May 27, 1862, and Wormeley to Mother, June 10, 1862, in *The Cruel Side of War*, 84 and 126. Wormeley's remarks also reflect her discomfort with the prospect of citizenship for non-white soldiers.

22. Wormeley to Mother, June 10, 1862, in *The Cruel Side of War*, 126.

23. Katharine Prescott Wormeley, *The Other Side of War* (1889), 63, in William Quentin Maxwell, *Lincoln's Fifth Wheel: The Political History of the United States Sanitary Commission* (New York, 1956), 339; Woolsey, Journal, May 14, 1862, in Austin, *The Woolsey Sisters*, 60.

24. Olmsted to Henry W. Bellows, May 7, 1862, in Beveridge, *The Papers of Frederick Law Olmsted*, 4: 322; Wormeley to "A," May 27, 1862, in *The Cruel Side of War*, 85; Olmsted, *Hospital Transports*, 66; Whetten to Kate, May 8, 1862, in Hass, "Letters of Harriet Douglas Whetten," 136; Harriet Douglas Whetten to Maria Lydig Daly, in Charles P. Daly Papers (Box 11, New York Public Library); Whetten to Hexie, June 14, 1862, in Hass, "Letters of Harriet Douglas Whetten," 143.

25. Wormeley to Mother, June 22, 1862, in *The Cruel Side of War*, 165.

26. Letter frag., n.s., n.d., Box 20, United States Sanitary Commission Papers (New York Public Library).

27. Letter frag., n.s., n.d., Box 20, United States Sanitary Commission Papers (New York Public Library).

28. Woolsey to Mother, May, 1862, in Bacon and Howland, *Letters*, 1: 340–41; Whetten to Hexie, May 19, 1862, in Hass, "Letters of Harriet Douglas Whetten," 139; and Olmsted, *Hospital Transports*, 38.

29. Whetten to Hexie, June 14, 1862, in Hass, "Letters of Harriet Douglas Whetten," 144; and Wormeley to Mother, June 10, 1862, in *The Cruel Side of War*, 127.

30. Harriet Douglas Whetten, Diary, July 31, 1862, in Paul H. Hass, ed., "A Volunteer Nurse in the Civil War: The Diary of Harriet Douglas Whetten," *Wisconsin Magazine of History* 48 (1965): 211 and 213; and Jane Newton Woolsey to Georgeanna Woolsey and Eliza Howland, May 13, 1862, in Bacon and Howland, *Letters*, 1: 350–51.

31. Wormeley to Friend, July 25, 1862, in *The Cruel Side of War*, 205.

32. Olmsted was disappointed that the Commission's transports had failed to stimulate improvement in the government's own system of transport, but he admitted that the summer's work had "paid splendidly in lives saved and pain alleviated." Altogether the hospital ships transported 8,000 men. Olmsted to Henry W. Bellows, July 13, 1862, in Beveridge, *The Papers of Frederick Law Olmsted*, 4: 405.

33. Wormeley to Mother, June 10, 1862, and Wormeley to "A," June 12, 1862, italics in text in *The Cruel Side of War*, 128, 136; and Whetten to Hexie, June 27, 1862, in Hass, "Letters of Harriet Douglas Whetten," 145.

34. Wormeley to Mother, June 14, 1862, in *The Cruel Side of War*, 142.

35. Wormeley to "A," July 10, 1862, *ibid.*, 197.

36. Olmsted to Henry Whitney Bellows, July 13, 1862, in Beveridge, *The Papers of Frederick Law Olmsted*, 4: 404–6.

37. Olmsted to Henry W. Bellows, July 7, 1862, *ibid.*, 395.

38. Wormeley to Mother, July 8, 1862, and Wormeley to "A," July 10, 1862, in *The Cruel Side of War*, 193, 195–97.

39. Wormeley to Friend, July 25, 1862, *ibid.*, 206.

40. Charles Woolsey to the *New York Evening Post,* May 31, 1862, in Bacon and Howland, *Letters,* 2: 402.

41. Jane E. Mottus, *New York Nightingales: The Emergence of the Nursing Profession at Bellevue and New York Hospital, 1850–1920* (Ann Arbor, 1981); Susan M. Reverby, *Ordered to Care: The Dilemma of American Nursing, 1850–1945* (Cambridge, Eng., 1987); and Kristie R. Ross, "Nursing Reform at Bellevue Hospital in New York City, 1850–1875," Master's thesis, Columbia University, 1979.

42. Katharine Prescott Wormeley, *The United States Sanitary Commission* (Boston, 1863), 246.

Chapter 7. Narratives of Union Women Spies

With special thanks to Professors Mari Jo Buhle, John L. Thomas, and Jacqueline Jones and colleagues Bruce Dorsey, David Moore, Kate Monteiro, Kevin Gaines, and Louise Newman. My greatest thanks, as always, go to Jim Cullen.

1. Pauline Cushman, *The Romance of the Great Rebellion: Or, the Mysteries of the Secret Service* (New York, 1864), 7–9; published also as *The Thrilling Adventures of Pauline Cushman* (Cincinnati, 1864).

2. Oscar A. Kinchen, *Women Who Spied for the Blue and Gray* (Philadelphia, 1972), 5. Newspaper accounts include: New York *Herald,* Jan. 22, Feb. 11, July 14, Aug. 3, Nov. 21, 25, 29, Dec. 3, 1862, May 9, 1863, Oct. 15, Nov. 26, 30, 1864, Jan. 8, 1865; Washington *Chronicle,* May 16, 1865; *Frank Leslie's Illustrated Newspaper,* Aug. 9, 23, 1862; Philadelphia *Inquirer,* July 28, 1862; "Women Spies," Middletown, N.Y., *The Sibyl* 6, no. 2 (Aug. 1861): 973. See also Jane E. Schultz, "The Women Who Went to the War: Gender and Genre in Literature of the American Civil War" (Ph.D. dissertation, University of Michigan, 1988), 381–82.

3. C. Vann Woodward, ed., *Mary Chesnut's Civil War* (New Haven and London, 1981), 92.

4. Kinchen, *Women Who Spied,* 2–3.

5. For the notion of "cultural work" see Jane Tompkins, *Sensational Designs: The Cultural Work of American Fiction, 1790–1860* (New York, 1985).

6. See [Charles Wesley Alexander], *Pauline of the Potomac; or, General McClellan's Spy* (Philadelphia, 1862, 1864); [CWA], *Maud of the Mississippi. Companion to Pauline of the Potomac* (Philadelphia, [1863] and [1864]); [CWA], *General Sherman's Indian Spy: A Singularly Thrilling Narrative of Wenonah, a Young and Lovely Indian Girl* (Philadelphia, c.1865); for Cushman's acceptance as legitimate see Bell Wiley, *The Life of Billy Yank* (New York, 1951), 337. He calls her "the famous spy of Rosecrans' command." See also File no. 184934Y–1, "Women Who Served in Wars of the United States," Record and Pension Branch, A.G.O. Records; and File 132D, A.G.O. Records, "Remarkable Cases and Names," both in the National Archives.

7. The spy story, fictional and real, was a popular genre following the Civil War. See also Lafayette Baker, *History of the United States Secret Service* (Philadelphia, 1868).

8. This point is made also in my Brown University dissertation, "Between the Lines: Gender, Race and Politics in Women's Writing on the American Civil War." My understanding of gender difference greatly benefited from Mary Poovey's *Uneven Developments: The Ideological Work of Gender in Mid-Victorian England* (Chicago, 1988).

9. Estelle C. Jelinek, *The Tradition of Women's Autobiography: From Antiquity to the Present* (Boston, 1986), 78.

10. For common attributes of spy narratives, see Curtis Carroll Davis, ed., *Belle Boyd in Camp and Prison, Written by Herself* (South Brunswick, New York, London, 1968): 42–43.

11. Of particular use to me on African American women writers generally and slave narratives particularly were: Marion Wilson Starling, *The Slave Narrative: Its Place in American History* (Washington, D.C., 1988); Joanne M. Braxton, *Black Women Writing Autobiography: A Tradition Within a Tradition* (Philadelphia, 1989); Jean Fagan Yellin, *Women & Sisters: The Antislavery Feminists in American Culture* (New Haven, 1989); and Hazel V. Carby, *Reconstructing Womanhood: The Emergence of the Afro-American Woman Novelist* (New York, 1987).

12. See Nancy F. Cott, *The Bonds of Womanhood: "Woman's Sphere" in New England, 1780–1835* (New Haven and London, 1977); Frances C. Cogan, *All-American Girl: The Ideal of Real Womanhood in Mid-Nineteenth Century* (Athens, Ga., 1989).

13. For this sense of ambivalence see Mary Kelley, *Private Woman, Public Stage: Literary Domesticity in Nineteenth-Century America* (New York, 1984).

14. Throughout this essay I refer to Harriet Ross Tubman Davis with her culturally current (both then and now) name of Harriet Tubman.

15. F[erdinand] L. Sarmiento, *Life of Pauline Cushman, the Celebrated Union Spy and Scout* (Philadelphia, 1865), 13–14. [His emphasis.]

16. Of course, there's some artful sleight-of-hand here: in constructing writing as her duty, Cushman contains the extent of her gender violation. See Pauline Cushman, *The Romance of the Great Rebellion; Or, the Mysteries of the Secret Service* (New York, 1864), 3.

17. These are very rare, and only both available at the Western Union Reserve Historical Society Library.

18. This information was gleaned from Curtis Carroll Davis's Appendix, 405–6, 408.

19. Cushman, *The Romance*, 6.

20. *Ibid.*, 9.

21. *Ibid.*, 10–12. [Her emphasis.]

22. *Ibid.*, 18.

23. *Ibid.*, 23, 25.

24. Unlike Cushman, Sarmiento celebrates Cushman's experience primarily because she was a woman, rather than because she endured perilous adventures: he avoids Cushman's uncompromising stance, leaving out her mention of the scout she did not kill, and the bushwhacker she almost did. See Sarmiento, *Life of Pauline Cushman;* Cushman, *The Romance*, 38.

25. Emma E. Edmonds, *Nurse and Spy in the Union Army* (Hartford, 1865), 19. [Her emphasis.]

26. *Ibid.*, 18, 21. [Her emphasis.]

27. Lammers and Boyce, "A Female," 28.

28. Edmonds, *Nurse and Spy*, 125.

29. *Ibid.*, 113.

30. Edmonds (like the biographers of Tubman I will later pick up) demonstrated clearly the racial elements to normative gender conventions. She also may have shied away from describing her African American companions as men to avoid any suggestion of sexuality, which might have shocked her reader. For quote, see Edmonds, *Nurse and Spy*, 118.

31. *Ibid.*, 120–21.

32. *Ibid.*, 147.

33. *Ibid.*, 155.

34. *Ibid.*, 161.

35. This is one of the few times in the narrative that Edmonds explicitly identifies herself as a woman to the reader. *Ibid.*, 359.

36. *Ibid.*, 360, 364, 371, 370.

37. *Ibid.*, 384; Lammers and Boyce, "A Female," 30.

38. Judith Nies, *Seven Women: Portraits from the American Radical Tradition* (New York, 1977), 51–52.

39. Earl Conrad, *Harriet Tubman* (New York, 1943), 214, and chs. III to X; see also Nies, *Seven Women.*

40. "Speech of T. W. Higginson," in the Report of the 5th Anniversary Meeting of the New York Anti-Slavery Society, *National Anti-Slavery Society* 19, no. 2 (New York, May 29, 1858), 1.

41. *The Journals of Charlotte Forten Grimké*, Brenda Stevenson, ed. (New York, 1988), 442.

42. For Harriet Tubman's war experiences, see the Charles P. Wood manuscript, Pension Certificate No. 415, 288, House of Representatives, under Nelson Davis, her second husband; see Conrad, *Harriet Tubman*, 235. As I am interested in the literary and cultural legacy of the Tubman story, I have not included an analysis of it here.

43. For this point and a context of "as told to" slave narratives generally see Joanne Braxton, *Black Women Writing Autobiography: A Tradition Within a Tradition* (Philadelphia, 1989), 72, 73.

44. One story particularly common to Tubman described the dread of an escaping slave, and the joy that he expressed after crossing into Canada. This story was also told to Forten; see *The Journals*, 442.

45. [Frank Sanborn], *Boston Commonwealth* (Friday, July 17, 1863), no. 46, p. 1, cols. 2–3.

46. [Sanborn], *Commonwealth*, also in *Scenes in the Life of Harriet Tubman*, 85–87. Not included in *Moses.*

47. [Sanborn], *Commonwealth;* Bradford, *Scenes*, 87.

48. Bradford, *Scenes*, 42.

49. A discussion of the religious tension between Tubman and her biographer is an important part of her story, one that I analyze in my dissertation, "Between the Lines" (note 8 above).

50. Bradford, *Scenes*, 52, 55. Also in *Moses*, 137. [Emphasis his.]

51. Bradford, *Scenes*, 40.

52. *Ibid.*, 42.

53. "Speech of T. W. Higginson," *National Anti-Slavery Standard*, 1.

54. James B. Clarke, "An Hour with Harriet Tubman," *The African Times and Orient Review* (Sept. 1912), 89. I am indebted to historian Kevin Gaines for this citation. This article became a pamphlet in an effort to raise money for Harriet Tubman. See Conrad, *Harriet Tubman*, 222.

55. Sarmiento, *Life of Pauline Cushman*, see chs. 1 and 3.

56. See Marian Talmadge and Iris Gilmore, *Emma Edmonds* (New York, 1970), and Pat Lammers and Amy Boyce, "A Female in the Ranks," *Civil War Times*, Jan. 1984, pp. 24–30, as well as Edmonds's own narrative.

57. Talmadge and Gilmore, *Emma Edmonds*, 122.

58. Earl Conrad describes the fight for Harriet Tubman's pension in the final chapters of his book, *Harriet Tubman;* he never dates when she finally began receiving that pension ($20 a month), which could have been in 1899 or 1900. Mentioned also in Schultz, "Women at the Front," 300–301.

Chapter 8. Women of the Confederacy

The author thanks the National Endowment for the Humanities, the Indiana Committee for the Humanities, the American Association for State and Local History, the American Philosophical Society, and Anderson University for financially supporting the research for this essay.

1. J. H. Hexter, *Reappraisals in History: New Views on History and Society in Early Modern Europe* (New York, 1963), 194–95.

2. At a conference a few years ago, I overheard a well-known Civil War scholar huffily object to having a woman on a panel at a session on the Civil War. On the other hand, I also heard a young scholar in women's history quickly dismiss traditional military history as nothing but "those arrows on maps."

3. Yet the standard treatment of death in nineteenth-century America contains only two passing references to the Civil War. James J. Farrell, *Inventing the American Way of Death, 1830–1920* (Philadelphia, 1980).

4. Rome *Weekly Courier*, Sept. 3, 1861.

5. Sarah Morgan Dawson, *A Confederate Girl's Diary*, ed. James I. Robertson (Bloomington, 1960), 390; Nov. 22, 1861, Mary Ezell Diary, typescript in Edward Conigland Papers, Southern Historical Collection, University of North Carolina (hereafter cited as SHC); Mary Latta to Samuel R. Latta, Aug. 25, 1861, Samuel R. Latta Papers (Louisiana and Lower Mississippi Valley Collections, Hill Memorial Library, Louisiana State University; hereafter cited as LSU).

6. Dawson, *Confederate Girl's Diary*, 120.

7. Mary A. Bowen to John Letcher, May 10, 1861, Nannie G. Abbott to Letcher, July 7, 1861, Lucetta A. Clove to Letcher, Letcher Papers (Virginia State Library).

8. U. R. Brooks, ed., *Stories of the Confederacy* (Columbia, S.C., 1912), 23; Bess Dell to Kate C. Encks, May 10, 1861, Confederate Miscellany, ser. 1e (Robert W. Woodruff Library, Emory University).

9. For an exception and for a useful discussion of Butler, the women of New Orleans, and public life, see Mary P. Ryan, *Women in Public: Between Banners and Ballots* (Baltimore, 1990), 143–45.

10. George W. Cable, ed., "The War Diary of a Union Woman in the South," *Century Magazine* 38 (Oct. 1889): 34.

11. New Orleans *Daily Delta,* April 29–30, 1862; New Orleans *Daily Picayune,* April 29, 1862.

12. May 4, 8, 1862, Clara E. Solomon Diary (LSU).

13. W. C. Corsan, *Two Months in the Confederate States, Including a Visit to New Orleans Under the Domination of General Butler* (London, 1863), 29–30; Kate Mason Rowland and Mrs. Morris L. Croxall, eds., *The Journal of Julia LeGrand, New Orleans, 1862–1863* (Richmond, 1911), 39–40.

14. Elsie Bragg to Braxton Bragg, April 7, 29, 1862, Braxton Bragg Papers (Western Reserve Historical Society, Cleveland); Elsie Bragg to Braxton Bragg, April 20, 1862, Braxton Bragg Letters (Barker Texas History Center, University of Texas); May 26, 1862, Clara E. Solomon Diary (LSU); Dec. 2, 1862, Ann Wilkinson Penrose Diary (LSU).

15. May 15, 1862, Clara E. Solomon Dairy (LSU).

16. Thomas Ewing Dabney, "The Butler Regime in Louisiana," *Louisiana Historical Quarterly* 27 (April 1944): 502–4; Hans L. Trefousse, *Ben Butler: The South Called Him Beast!* (New York, 1957), 110; May 8, June 19, 27, 1862, Clara E. Solomon Diary (LSU). Some of these women no doubt played a double game. Novelist John W. De Forest described a young woman who could rail against Butler from sunup to sundown but could also quietly seek protection from the general by "plying her fine eyes and smiling and flattering." John W. De Forest, *Miss Ravenel's Conversion from Secession to Loyalty* (New York, 1867), 130.

17. Corsan, *Two Months in the Confederate States,* 28–29.

18. For a description of this incident and several others, see Benjamin F. Butler, *Butler's Book* (Boston, 1892), 415–21.

19. *Ibid.,* 418.

20. Thomas Butler to "Dear Sister," May 24, 1862, Thomas O. Butler and Family Papers (LSU); Beth Crabtree and James W. Patton, eds., *"Journal of a Secesh Lady": The Diary of Catherine Ann Devereux Edmondston, 1860–1866* (Raleigh, 1979), 180–81; May 21, 1862, Fannie Page Hume Diary (Manuscripts Division, Library of Congress); Rowland and Croxall, eds., *Journal of Julia LeGrand,* 84–85; John Q. Anderson, ed., *Brokenburn: The Journal of Kate Stone 1861–1868* (Baton Rouge, 1955), 111.

21. May 17, June 22, 1862, Clara E. Solomon Diary (LSU); Dabney, "Butler Regime," 513–14; Gerald M. Capers, *Occupied City: New Orleans Under the Federals* (Lexington, 1965), 68–69. Mary Ryan cogently observes that the running battles Butler and the women of New Orleans "did not break the masculine monopoly on the formal public sphere." Ryan, *Women in Public,* 145–46.

22. New Orleans *Daily Picayune,* May 29, 1862; Florence Cooney Tompkins,

"Women of the Sixties," *Louisiana Historical Quarterly* 2 (July 1919): 283–84; July 20, 28, 1862, Ann Wilkinson Penrose Diary (LSU); Butler, *Butler's Book*, 450–52.

23. New Orleans *Daily Picayune*, July 2, 1862; June 30, July 2, July 7, 1862, Ann Wilkinson Penrose Diary (LSU); *War of the Rebellion: A Compilation of the Official Records of the Union and Confederate Armies* (128 vols.; Washington: Government Printing Office, 1880–1901), ser. 1, vol. 15, pp. 510–11; July 3, 1862, Eugenia Phillips Journal, Phillips and Myers Family Papers (SHC). For her days in Washington see the variant version of a journal attributed to her but perhaps written by a daughter in the Clement Claiborne Clay Papers (Duke), and Rose O'Neal Greenhow, *My Imprisonment and the First Year of Abolition Rule at Washington* (London, 1863), 27–28.

24. July 7, 24, 1862, Eugenia Phillips Journal, Eugenia Phillips to Philip Phillips, July 5, 1862, Eugenia Phillips to ?, July 25, 1862, Phillips and Myers Family Papers (SHC); Trefousse, *Butler*, 117–18.

25. June 11, 21, July 3, 1862, Ann Wilkinson Penrose Diary (LSU); Marion Southwood, *"Beauty and Booty," the Watchword of New Orleans* (New York, 1867), 131–36; Rowland and Croxall, eds., *Journal of Julia LeGrand*, 151; Anderson, *Journal of Kate Stone*, 105.

26. Aug. 10, Sept. 29, 1862, Ann Wilkinson Penrose Diary (LSU).

27. Rowland and Croxall, eds., *Journal of Julia LeGrand*, 52–53.

28. Dec. 17, 23, 1862, Ann Wilkinson Penrose Diary (LSU); Fred Harvey Harrington, *Fighting Politician: Major General N. P. Banks* (Philadelphia, 1948), 94–95; New Orleans *Daily Picayune* May 9, 23, 1863; Capers, *Occupied City*, 201–2; Rowland and Croxall, eds., *Journal of Julia LeGrand*, 86, 233, 285.

29. Southwood, *"Beauty and Booty,"* 278–81; Adelaide Stuart Dimitry, "The Battle of the Handkerchiefs," *Confederate Veteran* 31 (May 1923): 182–83; "M" to Lise Mitchell, Feb. 27, 1863, Mitchell Papers (Howard Tilton Memorial Library, Tulane University); Feb. 21, 1863, Ann Wilkinson Penrose Diary (LSU).

30. Sept. 16, 1862, April 23, 1862, Ann Wilkinson Penrose Diary (LSU); Rowland and Croxall, eds., *Journal of Julia LeGrand*, 280–82.

Chapter 9. Women and Guerrilla Warfare

This essay is a slightly revised version of *Inside War: The Guerilla Conflict in Missouri During the American Civil War* (New York, 1989), 205–23.

1. Testimony of Lucy Jane McManus, Nov. 9, 1863, Provost Marshal File, Charges of Disloyalty File 2792, Record Group 393, Records of U.S. Army Continental Commands, 1821–1920, Department of the Missouri (National Archives, Washington, D.C.; hereafter cited as Record Group 393, NA.).

2. Samuel S. Hildebrand, *Autobiography of Samuel S. Hildebrand* (Jefferson City, Mo., 1870), 145. Chivalric honor is placed in interesting contexts in Bertram Wyatt-Brown, *Southern Honor* (New York, 1982), and in Dickson S. Bruce, Jr., *Violence and Culture in the Antebellum South* (Austin, 1979).

3. W. Anderson to the editor of the two papers in Lexington, to the citizens and the community at large, General Brown, and Colonel McFerran and to his petty hirelings, such as Captain Burris, the friend of Anderson, July 7, 1864, in *The War*

of the Rebellion: A Compilation of the Official Records of the Union and the Confederate Army, 130 vols. (Washington, D.C., 1880–1902), Series I, XL1(2): 76–77. (This series is hereafter cited as OR.)

4. See, for example, the postwar apologia of one guerrilla, William H. Gregg Manuscripts, Joint Collection, University of Missouri Bland-Harris Collection, Western Historical Manuscripts–Columbia, State Historical Society of Missouri Manuscripts (hereafter cited as JC), p. 67.

5. N. F. Carter to Jud Waldo, Camp Bragg, Arkansas, Nov. 26, 1863, Bland-Harris Collection (JC).

6. Entry for Feb. 14, 1862, in Margaret Mendenhall Frazier and James W. Goodrich, eds., "'Life is Uncertain . . . ,' Willard Hall Mendenhall's 1862 Civil War Diary," *Missouri Historical Review* LXXVII (July 1984): 444.

7. M. G. Singleton to Colonel James S. Rollins, Centralia, Feb. 9, 1863, James S. Rollins Collection (JC).

8. Deposition of Mrs. Mary Hall, Franklin County, May 11, 1865, Letters Received File 2593, Record Group 393 (NA). Hall made this deposition five days after the event to the Union Provost Marshal, of what she called "this Horrid Barbarity."

9. Court Martial of James Johnson, Jefferson City, May 18, 1863, Case MM 1021, Record Group 153, Judge Advocate General–General Court–Martial Records (NA).

10. Mrs. J. R. Roberts to General James B. Long, Quincy, Ill., April 7, 1864, Provost Marshal File Letters Received File 2786, Record Group 393 (NA).

11. Entry for Feb. 25, 1863, Forseyth, Arkansas, Timothy Phillips Diary (Wisconsin State Historical Society, Madison).

12. Entry for May 22, 1862, Dr. Joseph H. Trego Diary (Kansas State Historical Society, Topeka).

13. Major Jeremiah Hackett to Lt. Colonel Hugh Cameron, Cassville, June 15, 1864, OR, XXXIV (1): 993; entry for April 19, 1862, Henry Dysart Diary (Iowa State Historical Society, Iowa City).

14. Entries for April 20, 1862, July 9, 1863, Sardius Smith Diary (Illinois State Historical Library, Springfield).

15. Entry for Oct. 19, 1862, James H. Guthrie Diary (Iowa State Historical Society).

16. Entry for July 9, 1863, Sardius Smith Diary (Illinois State Historical Library).

17. Charles W. Falker to His Wife, near Warrensburg, April 5, 1865, Charles W. Falker Letters (Wisconsin State Historical Society).

18. Entries for April 6, Harrisonville; April 15, south of Springfield; April 19, Berryville, Arkansas; April 28, in northern Arkansas, Anne E. Hemphill, ed., "The 1864 Diary of Seth Kelly," *Kansas History* I (Autumn 1978): 189–210, at 194, 196, 197. For an analysis of northern and eastern images of such rural types see Michael Fellman, "Alligator Men and Card Sharpers: Deadly Southwestern Humor," *Huntington Library Quarterly* XLIX (Autumn 1986): 307–23.

19. Theodore Ritsmiller to his Wife, Benton Barracks, Aug. 31, 1862, The-

odore Ritsmiller Letters (Manuscript Department, William R. Perkins Library, Duke University, Durham.).

20. Entry for May 29, 1862, Dr. Joseph H. Trego Diary (Kansas State Historical Society).

21. Entry for Jan. 24, 1865, Diary of W. W. Moses (Kansas State Historical Society). Moses or someone else glued a piece of paper over this diary entry, sometime after the war.

22. Bazel F. Lazear to his Wife, Harrisonville, April 29, 1863; Warrensburg, May 13, May 27, 1863; Lexington, June 22, 1863; Jefferson City, July 27, 1863, Bazel F. Lazear Collection (JC). An expurgated version of most of these letters was edited by Vivian Kirkpatrick McLarty, "The Civil War Letters of Colonel Bazel F. Lazear," *Missouri Historical Review* XLIV (April, July 1950): 254–73; 387–401; XLV (Oct. 1950): 47–63.

23. Investigation of the St. Charles Street Prison for Women, St. Louis, Jan. 5, 1864, Two or More Name File 2653, Record Group 393 (NA).

24. Entry for March 19, 1863, Diary of Timothy Phillips (Wisconsin State Historical Society).

25. Mollie McRoberts to A. J. McRoberts, Circleville, Ohio, July 17, 1863, A. J. McRoberts Papers (JC).

26. Mrs. Edwin H. Harris to her Husband, Paris, Texas, Aug. 12, Sept. 7, 1862; Edwin H. Harris to his Wife, St. Clair, Oct. 3, 1862, Bland Collection (Jackson County Historical Society, Independence, Missouri).

27. George S. Avery to Lizzie Avery, Palmyra, March 12, 1862, George S. Avery Letters (Chicago Historical Society).

Chapter 10. Confederate Women and Narratives of War

This essay was originally published in the *Journal of American History* (March 1990), 1200–228. The author would like to thank John Boles, Anne Boylan, Evelyn Brooks, Elizabeth Fox-Genovese, Eugene Genovese, Steven Hahn, Jacquelyn Hall, Lynn Hunt, Michael Johnson, Anne Goodwyn Jones, Mary Kelley, Linda Kerber, Stephanie McCurry, James McPherson, Reid Mitchell, Sharon O'Brien, Philip Racine, Janice Radway, Armstead Robinson, Charles Rosenberg, Barry Shank, and David Thelen for their acute criticisms and helpful suggestions, many of which she admits to having been foolhardy enough to ignore.

1. Homer, *The Iliad of Homer*, trans. Richmond Lattimore (Chicago, 1951), 166. Margaret Randolph Higonnet et al., eds., *Behind the Lines: Gender and the Two World Wars* (New Haven, 1987), 4. See also Jean Bethke Elshtain, *Women and War* (New York, 1987); and Eric Leed, *No Man's Land: Combat and Identity in World War I* (New York, 1979).

2. Julia Ellen (Le Grand) Waitz, *The Journal of Julia Le Grand, New Orleans, 1862–1863*, ed. Kate Mason Rowland and Mrs. Morris L. Croxall (Richmond, 1911), 52. The special experience of Confederate women arose both from the newness of the kind of combat the Civil War produced and from the growing scarcity of southern resources. For comparisons, see Claudia Koonz, *Mothers in the Fatherland: Women, the Family, and Nazi Politics* (New York, 1987); Higonnet et al.,

eds., *Behind the Lines;* Joan Hoff Wilson, "The Illusion of Change: Women and the American Revolution," in *The American Revolution: Explorations in the History of American Radicalism,* ed. Alfred F. Young (DeKalb, 1976), 383–446; Linda K. Kerber, *Women of the Republic: Intellect and Ideology in Revolutionary America* (Chapel Hill, 1980); Mary Beth Norton, *Liberty's Daughters: The Revolutionary Experience of American Women, 1750–1800* (Boston, 1980); and D'Ann Campbell, *Women at War with America: Private Lives in a Patriotic Era* (Cambridge, Mass., 1984). On northern women during the Civil War, see Philip Shaw Paludan, *A People's Contest: The Union and the Civil War, 1861–1865* (New York, 1988), 156–60, 182–83, 327–30.

3. John Keegan, *The Face of Battle* (New York, 1977). For a similar ideological use of the "hegemony of gender," see Christine Stansell, *City of Women: Sex and Class in New York, 1789–1860* (New York, 1986). On yeoman dissent, see Paul D. Escott, *After Secession: Jefferson Davis and the Failure of Confederate Nationalism* (Baton Rouge, 1978); and Paul D. Escott, "The Cry of the Sufferers: The Problem of Welfare in the Confederacy," *Civil War History* 23 (Sept. 1977): 228–40. On the history and historiography of Confederate morale, see Richard E. Beringer et al., *Why the South Lost the Civil War* (Athens, Ga., 1986); and Drew Gilpin Faust, *The Creation of Confederate Nationalism: Ideology and Identity in the Civil War South* (Baton Rouge, 1988). On the greater vulnerability of southern men, see Maris Vinovskis, "Have Social Historians Lost the Civil War? Some Preliminary Demographic Speculations," *Journal of American History* 76 (June 1989): 39.

4. "Resolutions of Thanks," in *The Messages and Papers of Jefferson Davis and the Confederacy, 1861–1865,* comp. James D. Richardson (2 vols., New York, 1981), I, 176; *Laws of the State of Mississippi, passed at a called and regular session of the Mississippi Legislature. Held in Jackson and Columbus, Dec. 1862 and Nov. 1863* (Selma, 1864), 226.

5. An important departure from the celebratory historiographical tradition is George C. Rable, *Civil Wars: Women and the Crisis of Southern Nationalism* (Urbana, 1989). Monuments to Confederate women were planned in Mississippi, North Carolina, South Carolina, Arkansas, Tennessee, and Florida. See also Gaines M. Foster, *Ghosts of the Confederacy: Defeat, the Lost Cause, and the Emergence of the New South, 1865 to 1913* (New York, 1987), 175–79; and J. L. Underwood, *The Women of the Confederacy* (n.p., 1906); Mary Elizabeth Massey, *Bonnet Brigades* (New York, 1966); H. E. Sterkx, *Partners in Rebellion: Alabama Women in the Civil War* (Rutherford, 1970). For the poem by Henry Timrod, see H. M. Wharton, *War Songs and Poems of the Southern Confederacy, 1861–1865* (Philadelphia, 1904), 215. For the notion of "two armies," see *Charleston Daily Courier,* Nov. 28, 1861.

6. A popular work, dedicated by its author as a "monument" to female contributions to the Southern Cause, is Rita Mae Brown, *High Hearts* (New York, 1986). For a more scholarly consideration, see Janet E. Kaufmann, "'Under the Petticoat Flag': Women Soldiers in the Confederate Army," *Southern Studies* 23 (Winter 1984): 363–75. For examples of the new women's historiography, see Nancy A. Hewitt, "Beyond the Search for Sisterhood: American Women's History in the 1980s," *Social History* 10 (Oct. 1985): 299–321; Elizabeth Fox-Genovese,

Within the Plantation Household: Black and White Women of the Old South (Chapel Hill, 1988); Joan Wallach Scott, *Gender and the Politics of History* (New York, 1988); Koonz, *Mothers in the Fatherland;* and Nancy MacLean, "Behind the Mask of Chivalry: Gender, Race, and Class in the Making of the Ku Klux Klan of the 1920s in Georgia" (Ph.D. diss., University of Wisconsin, Madison, 1989).

7. "Educated Woman—in Peace and War," *Southern Field and Fireside,* April 11, 1863; *Augusta Weekly Constitutionalist,* July 17, 1861.

8. Sarah Katherine Stone, *Brokenburn: The Journal of Kate Stone, 1861–1868,* ed. John Q. Anderson (Baton Rouge, 1955), 17; Julia Le Grand to Mrs. Shepherd Brown, Nov. 17, 1862, in *Journal of Julia Le Grand,* ed. Rowland and Croxall, 52–53; Kate Cumming, *Kate: The Journal of a Confederate Nurse,* ed. Richard Barksdale Harwell (Baton Rouge, 1959), 38–39. See also C. W. Dabney to "My Dear Brother," May 1, 1861, Charles W. Dabney Papers (Southern Historical Collection, University of North Carolina, Chapel Hill).

9. Francis Butler Simkins and James Welch Patton, *The Women of the Confederacy* (Richmond, 1936), 22; Clara D. MacLean Diary, Aug. 9, 1861 (Manuscript Division, William R. Perkins Library, Duke University, Durham, N.C.); Greenville Ladies Association Records (South Caroliniana Library, University of South Carolina, Columbia); Ladies Relief Association, Spartanburg, 1861, *ibid.*

10. Sarah Lois Wadley Diary, Aug. 20, 1863 (Southern Historical Collection); Amanda Chappelear Diary, April 19, 1862 (Virginia Historical Society, Richmond); Clara to "My dear Friend Jesse," May 4, 1863, Warren Ogden, Collector, Miscellaneous Civil War Letters. (Manuscripts Section, Special Collections Division, Howard-Tilton Memorial Library, Tulane University, New Orleans, La.); *The Diary of Miss Emma Holmes, 1861–1866,* ed. John F. Marsalek (Baton Rouge, 1979), 251, 323; Sarah Morgan Dawson, *A Confederate Girl's Diary,* ed. James I. Robertson, Jr. (Bloomington, 1960), 119; Caroline Kean Hill Davis Diary, Feb. 13, 1865 (Virginia Historical Society). See also Mary Eliza Dulany Diary, June 10, 1862, *ibid.;* Cornelia McDonald, quoted in Douglas Southall Freman, *The South to Posterity: An Introduction to the Writings of Confederate History* (New York, 1939), 152.

11. Elizabeth Collier Diary, April 11, 1862 (Southern Historical Collection); Emma Walton to J. B. Walton, May 12, July 15, 1863 (Historic New Orleans Collection, New Orleans, La.); Sallie Munford, quoted in Freeman, *South to Posterity,* 109; Dawson, *Confederate Girl's Diary,* ed. Robertson, 318. For an example of a southern woman disguising herself as a man, see J. M. Fain to E. Fain, Dec. 10, 1861, Huldah Annie Briant Collection (Manuscript Division, William R. Perkins Library); and Annie Samuels et al. to James Seddon, Dec. 2, 1864, Letters Received, Confederate Secretary of War, RG 109, microfilm 437, reel 122, B692 (National Archives). For an extended fictional treatment, see Brown, *High Hearts.*

12. Alexander St. Clair Abrams, *The Trials of a Soldier's Wife: A Tale of the Second American Revolution* (Atlanta, 1864), 165.

13. Leila W., "Woman a Patriot," *Southern Monthly* 1 (Oct. 1861): 115; *Mobile Evening News,* Jan. 25, 1864; *Natchez Weekly Courier,* March 12, 1862. See also Faust, *Creation of Confederate Nationalism.*

14. Mary B. Clarke to Macfarlane and Fergusson, Sept. 21, 1861, Macfarlane and Fergusson Papers (Virginia Historical Society); *Augusta Weekly Constitutionalist*, Oct. 16, 1861.

15. Theodore von La Hache, *I Would Like to Change My Name: A Favorite Encore Song* (Augusta, Ga., 1863).

16. *Charleston Daily Courier*, Aug. 15, 1861; Davis quoted in unidentified newspaper clipping in George Bagby Scrapbook, vol. 2, p. 128, George Bagby Papers (Virginia Historical Society).

17. "Heart Victories," in *Songs of the South* (Richmond, 1862), 68–69.

18. "Our Mothers Did So Before Us," *ibid.*, 70–71; "The Dead," *ibid.*, 47–48.

19. *Record of News, History and Literature*, Sept. 3, 1863, 105; Chappelear Diary, May 19, 1862.

20. *Charleston Daily Courier*, Aug. 19, 1861.

21. "I've Kissed Him and Let Him Go," in clipping in George Bagby Scrapbook, vol. 5, p. 99, Bagby Papers.

22. J. M. Fain to Huldah Fain Briant, May 19, 1862, Briant Papers; Priscilla Munnikhuysen Bond Diary, June 29, 1862 (Hill Memorial Library, Louisiana State University, Baton Rouge).

23. *Huntsville Democrat*, Aug. 21, 1861; *Countryman*, March 18, 1862.

24. *Richmond Daily Enquirer*, Aug. 5, 1863. One in eight Confederate soldiers deserted, as contrasted with one in ten from the North. Vinovskis, "Have Social Historians Lost the Civil War?" 41.

25. Barnwell quoted in *Diary of Miss Emma Holmes*, ed. Marsalek, 101–2.

26. Margaret Beckwith Reminiscences, vol. 2, p. 10 (Virginia Historical Society); Chappelear Diary, July 2, 1862.

27. *Record of News, History and Literature*, July 16, 1863, 37; "Slap-By Klubs," in *Songs of the South*, 67; Catherine Cochran Reminiscences, vol. 1 (Virginia Historical Society); U.S. War Department, *The War of the Rebellion: A Compilation of the Official Records of the Union and Confederate Armies* (128 vols., Washington, 1880–1901), ser. 1, LII, pt. 2, pp. 667–68. Statistical information on the Confederate army is incomplete, and thus casualty estimates necessarily involve guesswork. These figures are James M. McPherson's revisions, made in a telephone conversation to Drew Gilpin Faust on Oct. 26, 1989, of numbers he offers in James M. McPherson, *Ordeal by Fire: The Civil War and Reconstruction* (New York, 1982), 18; and James M. McPherson, *Battle Cry of Freedom: The Civil War Era* (New York, 1988), 471, 854. For his computations, McPherson considers 18–40 to be effective military age.

28. Addie Harris to G. W. Randolph, Oct. 29, 1862, Letters Received, Confederate Secretary of War, microfilm 437, reel 53, H1166.

29. Amanda Walker to the Secretary of War, Oct. 31, 1862, *ibid.*, reel 79, W1106; Lucy Sharp to John Randolph, Oct. 1, 1862, *ibid.*, reel 72, S1000. It is important to recognize that many of these letters complaining about slave management were prompted by the passage of the Confederate law exempting slave managers from military service and thus were not simply disinterested cries of pain. Alice Palmer to Hattie Palmer, July 20, 1865, Palmer Family Papers (South Caroliniana Library).

30. Cumming, *Kate*, 191–92. See also Patricia R. Loughridge and Edward D. C. Campbell, Jr., *Women and Mourning* (Richmond, 1985); and Drew Gilpin Faust, "Race, Gender, and Confederate Nationalism: William D. Washington's *Burial of Latané*," *Southern Review* 25 (April 1989): 297–307.

31. *Richmond Daily Enquirer*, March 7, 1862; *Confederate Baptist*, Oct. 15, 1862; Phoebe Yates Pember, *A Southern Woman's Story: Life in Confederate Richmond*, ed. Bell Irvin Wiley (Jackson, Tenn., 1959), 25; C. Vann Woodward, ed. *Mary Chesnut's Civil War* (New Haven, 1981), 641. For expression of similar concerns in the North, see Susan M. Reverby, *Ordered to Care: The Dilemma of American Nursing, 1850–1945* (New York, 1987), 43–47.

32. Pember, *Southern Woman's Story*, 25; Simkins and Patton, *Women of the Confederacy*, 86; Cordelia Scales, "Civil War Letters of Cordelia Scales," ed. Percy L. Rainwater, *Journal of Mississippi History* 1 (July 1939): 173. On nursing, see also Rable, *Civil Wars*, 121–28.

33. Cumming, *Kate*, 65.

34. Phebe Levy to Eugenia Phillips, Sept. 13, 1863, Philip Phillips Family Papers (Library of Congress); Clara MacLean Diary, March 3, 1862, Clara D. MacLean Collection (Manuscript Division, William R. Perkins Library); Woodward, ed., *Mary Chesnut's Civil War*, 677.

35. *Augusta Daily Constitutionalist*, May 14, 1863.

36. W. Buck Yearns and John G. Barrett, eds., *North Carolina Civil War Documentary* (Chapel Hill, 1980), 237; "Proceedings of the 6th Annual Meeting of the State Education Association," *North Carolina Journal of Education*, 4 (Nov. 1861), 326. By the end of the war, the percentage of female teachers in North Carolina had risen from 7 percent to 50 percent. Yearns and Barrett, eds., *North Carolina Civil War Documentary*, 231.

37. Yearns and Barrett, eds., *North Carolina Civil War Documentary*, 244; *Sixth Annual Circular of Wytheville Female College* (Wytheville, 1861); *Minutes of the Bethel Baptist Association* (Macon, 1863). See also *Catalogue of the Trustees, Faculty, and Students of the Wesleyan Female College, Macon, Georgia* (Macon, 1862); and Farmville Female College, *The Next Term of This Institution*, broadside [n.p., 1863].

38. *Diary of Miss Emma Holmes*, ed. Marsalek, 172; Grimball quoted in Fox-Genovese, *Within the Plantation Household*, 46; *Proceedings of the Convention of Teachers of the Confederate States* (Macon, 1863), 4; *North Carolina Journal of Education* 7 (July 1864): 88. On teaching, see also Rable, *Civil Wars*, 129–31.

39. For a consideration of painting, see Faust, "Race, Gender and Confederate Nationalism."

40. [Augusta Jane Evans], *Macaria; or, Altars of Sacrifice* (Richmond, 1864). On Evans and women's fiction generally, see Anne Goodwyn Jones, *Tomorrow Is Another Day: The Woman Writer in the South, 1859–1936* (Baton Rouge, 1981); Nina Baym, *Woman's Fiction: A Guide to Novels by and about Women in America, 1820–1870* (Ithaca, 1978); and Mary Kelley, *Private Woman, Public Stage: Literary Domesticity in Nineteenth-Century America* (New York, 1984).

41. [Evans], *Macaria*, 116, 168, 183, 182, 183.

42. *Ibid.*, 141, 9, 13, 134, 167, 179.

43. *Ibid.*, 139, 137.

44. *Montgomery Daily Advertiser,* June 15, 1864.

45. A. Grima to Alfred Grima, Nov. 27, 1863, Grima Family Papers (Historic New Orleans Collection); Mary L. Scales to the secretary of war, Sept. 8, 1862, Letters Received, Confederate Secretary of War, reel 72, S890.

46. G. Glenn Clift, ed., *The Private War of Lizzie Hardin* (Frankfort, Ky., 1963), 17; Constance Cary Harrison, *Recollections Grave and Gay* (New York, 1911), 83; Elizabeth Preston Allan, *The Life and Letters of Margaret Junkin Preston* (New York, 1903), 148; Sarah Jane Sams to Randolph Sams, March 14, 1865, Sarah Jane Sams Collection (South Caroliniana Library); Waitz, *Journal of Julia Le Grand,* ed. Rowland and Croxall, 44–45; Margaret Crawford, "Tales of a Grandmother," in *South Carolina Women in the Confederacy,* ed. Mrs. A. T. Smythe, Miss M. B. Poppenheim, and Mrs. Thomas Taylor (2 vols., Columbia, S.C., 1903), I, 210; Emily Harris Diary, Nov. 18, 1864, David Harris Papers (College Library, Winthrop College, Rock Hill, S.C.).

47. Lila Chunn to Willie Chunn, May 19, 1863, Willie Chunn Papers (Manuscript Division, William R. Perkins Library); Myrna Lockett Avary, ed., *A Virginia Girl in the Civil War, 1861–1865* (New York, 1903), 41; Annie Upshur to Jefferson Davis, Jan. 24, 1863, Letters Received, Confederate Secretary of War, reel 114, U2. Cornelia McDonald, *A Diary with Reminiscences of the War and Refugee Life in the Shenandoah Valley* (Nashville, 1935), 165, 167, 114–15; Mary A. Blackburn to David B. Blackburn, Dec. 19, 1864, Point Lookout Letters, Miscellaneous Files, Adjutant General's Office, RG 109 (National Archives). On stress reaction among soldiers, see Drew Gilpin Faust, "Christian Soldiers: The Meaning of Revivalism in the Confederate Army," *Journal of Southern History* 53 (Feb. 1987): 83–86.

48. Ella Stuart to secretary of war, April 28, 1863, Letters Received, Confederate Secretary of War, reel 111, S312; Miranda Sutton to secretary of war, Jan. 28, 1864, *ibid.,* reel 140, S79; Harriet Stephenson to secretary of war, Jan. 18, 1864, *ibid.,* S47; Nancy Williams to Jefferson Davis, April 1, 1863, Oct. 29, 1863, *ibid.,* reel 116, W246; Frances Brightwell to Davis, March 17, 1862, *ibid.,* reel 31, B167.

49. Anonymous to Davis, May 14, 1864, *ibid.,* reel 118, A134; Mrs. M. L. Nelson to Davis, n.d., *ibid.,* reel 137, N77; Nelson to Seddon, Oct. 12, 1864, *ibid.,* N80; Almira Acors to Davis, March 23, 1862, *ibid.,* reel 29, A62; The appearance of the instruction "file" on letters describing such desperate circumstances is striking and is also noted by Rable, *Civil Wars,* 75.

50. In their growing discontent with their situation, some women even came to question the paternalistic justice of God. See Grace Brown Elmore Reminiscences, June 20, 1865 (South Caroliniana Library).

51. Yearns and Barrett, eds., *North Carolina Civil War Documentary,* 22, 97; M. Chichester to Capt. Arthur Chichester, May 2, 1864, Point Lookout Letters; Charles Fenton James to "Dear Sister," Feb. 13, 1864, Charles Fenton James Papers (Southern Historical Collection).

52. See, for example, the report of applicants requesting permission to leave the Confederacy, July 25, 1864, Letters Received, Confederate Secretary of War.

53. *Children's Friend,* Dec. 1862.

54. Dulany Diary, Aug. 10, 1862; Stone, *Brokenburn,* ed. Anderson, 277; Harrison, *Recollections,* 188.

55. *Countryman,* May 3, 1864. On bread riots and female violence, see Michael Chesson, "Harlots or Heroines? A New Look at the Richmond Bread Riot," *Virginia Magazine of History and Biography* 92 (April 1984): 131–75; Paul D. Escott, *Many Excellent People: Power and Privilege in North Carolina, 1850–1900* (Chapel Hill, 1986), 67; Victoria Bynum, "'War within a War': Women's Participation in the Revolt of the North Carolina Piedmont," *Frontiers* 9 (1987): 43–49.

56. Woodward, ed., *Mary Chesnut's Civil War,* 430; *Richmond Daily Enquirer,* Feb. 11, 1864; Minutes of the Tombeckbee Presbytery, April 8, 1865 (Historical Foundation of the Presbyterian Church, Montreat, N.C.); unidentified clipping in George Bagby Scrapbook, vol. 5, p. 131, Bagby Papers; James to "Dear Sister," Feb. 13, 1865, Charles Fenton James Collection.

57. Cumming, *Kate,* 4; Robert E. Lee quoted in Douglas Southall Freeman, *Lee's Lieutenants: A Study in Command* (3 vols., New York, 1972), II, 752. See also Rable, *Civil Wars,* 207; Waitz, *Journal of Julia Le Grand,* ed. Rowland and Croxall, 16.

Chapter 11. The Marriage of Kate and William McLure

1. See George C. Rable, *Civil Wars: Women and the Crisis of Southern Nationalism* (Urbana, 1989); Jean E. Friedman, *The Enclosed Garden: Women and Community in the Evangelical South* (Chapel Hill, 1985), Suzanne Lebsock, *The Free Women of Petersburg: Status and Culture in a Southern Town, 1784–1860* (New York, 1984); Anne Firor Scott, *The Southern Lady: From Pedestal to Politics, 1830–1930* (Chicago, 1970). I thank Henry Fulmer for discussions of the McLures.

2. Mary Bailey Butt, "Genealogy," "History of the Families of Thomas and William McLure," McLure Family Manuscript (South Caroliniana Library, University of South Carolina); Fifth Decennial Census of the United States, South Carolina, Pickens County, 273; Seventh Decennial Census of the United States, South Carolina, York County, Free Schedule, 218, Slave Schedule, n.p. Unless otherwise noted, all collections are located at the South Caroliniana Library.

3. James S. McLure to J. William McLure, Feb. 4, 1851, James S. McLure Papers. Something of William McLure's personality can be glimpsed in a photograph taken a few years later; his plain face is marked by luminous, burning eyes; see photograph of William McLure, n.d., McLure Family Manuscript. On secessionist activity, see William W. Freehling, *The Road to Disunion, Volume I: Secessionists at Bay, 1776–1854* (New York, 1990).

4. Seventh Decennial Census of the United States, South Carolina, Free Schedule, 338–39; Union County Historical Foundation, *A History of Union County, South Carolina* (Greenville, S.C., 1977); Amelia T. Rainey to J. William McLure, Oct. 8, 1850, May 4, 1852, W. A. Walker to J. William McLure, April 16, 1852, J. William McLure to Kate Poulton, June 21, 1852, McLure Family Papers; James S. McLure to J. William McLure, Dec. 18, 1850, James Stringfellow McLure Papers; Butt, "History of Families," McLure Family Manuscript. William McLure resembles the tough, headstrong men described in Bertram Wyatt-Brown, *South-*

ern Honor: Ethics and Behavior in the Old South (New York, 1982), rather than the cultivated gentlemen in Steven M. Stowe's *Intimacy and Power in the Old South: Ritual in the Lives of the Planters* (Baltimore, 1987).

5. Mary Bailey Butt, "Poultons in America," Poulton Family Manuscript; Butt, "Genealogy of the Family of John McLure," McLure Family Manuscript; "Recollections of Mary Poulton Dawkins, Widow of Judge Thomas N. Dawkins"; Seventh Decennial Census of the United States, South Carolina, Union County, Slave Schedule, 363; Free Schedule, 37; Mary P. Dawkins to Kate P. McLure, July 11, 1859, McLure Family Papers. Kate's only brother George returned to England.

6. Butt, "Poulton Family Genealogy," Poulton Family Manuscript; "Recollections of Mary Dawkins"; Mary C. Townsend to Mrs. T. N. [Mary] Dawkins, July 31, 1852, Poulton Family Manuscript; Butt, "Genealogy of the Family of John McLure," McLure Family Manuscript; Kate P. McLure to "Liddie" Wallace, April 29, 1853, McLure Family Papers. A photograph taken of her in the early 1850s shows a pale, raven-haired young woman looking timidly at the camera; see photograph, n.d., McLure Family Manuscript.

7. J. William McLure to Kate P. McLure, July 6, 1853, R. J. Gage to J. William McLure, April 9, 1855, McLure Family Papers; Butt, "Poulton Family Genealogy," Poulton Family Manuscript; Butt, "History of Families," McLure Family Manuscript; Eighth Decennial Census of the United States, South Carolina, Slave Schedule, 375; Free Schedule, 282. On filibustering, see Robert E. May, *The Southern Dream of a Caribbean Empire, 1854–1862* (Baton Rouge, 1973). Rachel N. Klein, *Unification of a Slave State: The Rise of the Planter Class in the South Carolina Backcountry, 1760–1808* (Chapel Hill, 1990), describes the plantation economy.

8. Appointment by Governor Francis W. Pickens, J. William McLure, Pacolet Guards, First Battalion, Thirty-seventh Regiment, South Carolina Militia, Jan. 25, 1861, J. William McLure to Kate McLure, April 24, July 9, 1861, Kate P. McLure to J. William McLure, April 25, May 20, 1861, McLure Family Papers. On the "paternalistic" race relations practiced by seaboard white women, see Joan E. Cashin, *A Family Venture: Men and Women on the Southern Frontier* (New York, 1991), 26–29. On whether white women supported the Confederacy, see Drew Gilpin Faust, "Altars of Sacrifice: Confederate Women and the Narratives of War," in this volume; Rable, *Civil Wars*.

9. J. William McLure to Kate P. McLure, April 24, Aug. 4, Sept. 18, 1861, McLure Family Papers; J. William McLure to Kate P. McLure, May 5, 1861, James Stringfellow McLure Papers.

10. J. William McLure to Kate P. McLure, Oct. 4, Nov. 9, 1861, McLure Family Papers. On the exercise of power by women, see Cecile Dauphin, Annette Farge, et al., "Women's Culture and Women's Power: An Attempt at Historiography," and "Comments," by Karen Offen, Nell Irvin Painter, Hilda L. Smith, and Lois W. Banner, *Journal of Women's History* 1 (Spring 1989): 63–107. On overseers, see William K. Scarborough, *The Overseer: Plantation Management in the Old South* (Baton Rouge, 1966).

11. Butt, "Name Index," McLure Family Manuscript, 17; Eighth Decennial Census of the United States, South Carolina, Union County, Free Schedule, 283.

Clarence L. Mohr, *On the Threshold of Freedom: Masters and Slaves in Civil War Georgia* (Athens, 1986), shows how some plantation mistresses had to concede some power to slaves in order to keep plantations running. Kate McLure shared authority with Jeff willingly, even eagerly, however, which suggests her esteem for him as well as her frustration with the overseer.

12. J. William McLure to Kate P. McLure, July 9, 25, Aug. 1, Nov. 1, 26, 1861, Feb. 1, 26, Oct. 10, 1862, McLure Family Papers; Rolls of South Carolina Volunteers in the Confederate Army, Provisional Army, 1861–65, Memory Book, Company M, Palmetto Sharpshooters, 417; Forage Issued to Public Animals by Capt. J. W. McLure, Quartermaster C. S. Army, Richmond, Virginia, Aug. 1862, Muster Roll, First Palmetto Sharpshooters, Jenkins Regiment, Archives of the State of South Carolina.

13. J. William McLure to Kate P. McLure, Sept. 1, 1861, Aug. 11, 1862, Kate P. McLure to Amelia T. Rainey, May 26, 1862. On miscegenation, see Catherine Clinton, "'Southern Dishonor': Flesh, Blood, Race, and Bondage," in *In Joy and in Sorrow: Women, Family, and Marriage in the Victorian South, 1830–1900*, ed. Carol Bleser (New York, 1991), 52–69.

14. J. William McLure to Kate P. McLure, Feb. 23, June 23, 1862; Kate P. McLure to Amelia T. Rainey, May 26, Sept. 1, 1862; B. F. Holmes to Kate P. McLure, July 5, 1862; J. William McLure to Kate P. McLure, July 27, Oct. 2, 8, Jan. 10, 1862, McLure Family Papers; Muster Rolls, First Palmetto Sharpshooters, Jenkins Regiment, 1861–64, Archives of the State of South Carolina.

15. Amelia T. Rainey to Kate P. McLure, Sept. 21, Dec. 3, 1862; J. William McLure to Kate P. McLure, Nov. 10, 29, 1862, McLure Family Papers.

16. J. William McLure to Kate P. McLure, Dec. 3, 5, 1862, March 13, Nov. 10, 1863; T. H. Dawkins to J. William McLure, Jan. 14, 1863, McLure Family Papers. Mabery was probably a member of one of ten yeoman families by that name who resided in Union County in 1860; Franklin Mabery, a farm laborer aged twenty-four who lived a few doors away from the McLures, is the most likely candidate. See Eighth Decennial Census of the United States, South Carolina, Union County, Free Schedule, 283, Slave Schedule, 376 (on Dawkins), Free Schedule, 282 (on Franklin Mabery). Elijah Dawkins owned 41 slaves in 1860. Mabery earned $500 a year; see T. H. Dawkins to J. William McLure, Jan. 14, 1863, McLure Family Papers. There is no information on Holmes's salary.

17. J. William McLure to Kate P. McLure, March 13, 16, 1863, Kate P. McLure to Amelia T. Rainey, March 16, 1863, Amelia T. Rainey to Kate P. McLure, May 13, 1863, Kate P. McLure to J. William McLure, April 22, 1863, J. William McLure to Kate P. McLure, Nov. 4, 10, 1863, McLure Family Papers.

18. Kate P. McLure to J. William McLure, Jan. 19, 29, Dec. 6, 14, 1864, J. William McLure to Kate P. McLure, March 18, 1864, McLure Family Papers.

19. J. William McLure to John A. Reidy, June 15, 1864, McLure Family Papers.

20. T. H. Dawkins to J. William McLure, July 31, 1864, J. William McLure to Kate P. McLure, Aug. 8, 1864, Kate P. McLure to J. William McLure, Aug. 18, 1864, Mary A. J. Kennedy to Kate P. McLure, June 24, 1864, McLure Family Papers. On the "domestic, anti-commercial values" of white southern women, see Rable, *Civil Wars*, 107. In the antebellum era, a bushel of corn typically sold for

sixty *cents* a bushel; see Lewis Cecil Gray, *History of Agriculture in the Southern United States to 1860,* 2 vols. (Gloucester, Mass., 1958), 812–13, 1039.

21. Kate P. McLure to J. William McLure, Dec. 2, 4, 10, 1864, Thomas H. Dawkins to Kate P. McLure, Jan. 29, 1865, McLure Family Papers. Few of the McLure slaves ran away during the war.

22. J. William McLure to Kate P. McLure, Jan. 25, 1865, McLure Family Papers. On the similar wartime struggles of another white southern couple, see *The Secret Eye: The Journal of Ella Gertrude Clanton Thomas, 1848–1889,* ed. Virginia Ingraham Burr, introduction by Nell Irvin Painter (Chapel Hill, 1990).

23. Butt, "History of Families," McLure Family Manuscript; Butt, "Genealogy of the Family of John McLure"; Bill of Sale, Jan. 15, 1868, for J. W. McLure by J. D. Kirkpatrick, McLure Family Papers.

Chapter 12. African American Childhood in Wartime

I would like to acknowledge the valuable assistance of Ben Karp in the research for this essay. A Mary Wilhelmine Williams Fellowship in the Social Sciences from Goucher College helped support the research and writing of this study.

1. Rupert Sargent Holland, ed., *Letters and Diary of Laura M. Towne* (Cambridge, Mass., 1912; reprint ed., New York, 1969), cited in Carolyn E. Wedin, "The Civil War and Black Women on the Sea Islands," in *Southern Women,* ed. Caroline Matheny Dillman (New York, 1988), 76.

2. *Freedom: A Documentary History of Emancipation, 1861–1867,* Series II: *The Black Military Experience,* eds. Ira Berlin, Joseph P. Reidy, and Leslie S. Rowland (New York, 1982), 689–90 (hereafter cited as *Black Military Experience*).

3. The two main exceptions are Elizabeth Daniels, "The Children of Gettysburg," *American Heritage* (May–June 1989), 97–107; and Rebecca J. Scott, "The Battle over the Child: Child Apprenticeship and the Freedmen's Bureau in North Carolina," in *Growing Up in America: Children in Historical Perspective,* eds. N. Ray Hiner and Joseph M. Hawes (Urbana, Ill., 1985), 193–207.

Valuable works on youngsters in other wars include Roger Rosenblatt, *Children of War* (Garden City, N.Y., 1983); George Eisen, *Children and Play in the Holocaust: Games Among the Shadows* (Amherst, Mass., 1988); and Kati David, *A Child's War: World War II Through the Eyes of Children* (New York, 1989).

4. For a good discussion of this point, see the introduction to *Growing Up in America,* eds. Hiner and Hawes, xiii–xxiii.

5. This piece focuses on two main bodies of evidence: (1) the documents gathered by Ira Berlin et al., in *Freedom: A Documentary History of Emancipation* (3 volumes at this point); and (2) the interviews with former slaves conducted by Fisk University in 1927–30 and the Federal Writers' Project in 1936–38 that are contained in George Rawick, ed., *The American Slave: A Composite Autobiography,* 19 vols., Series 1 (Westport, Conn., 1972, hereafter all references to this collection (Series 1) will include only the name of the state and part, volume, and page numbers).

The Rawick collection, in particular, offers a rich opportunity to examine the experiences of those ex-slaves who were children during the war years. Problems with interview techniques and racial dynamics, as well as the faulty memory of elderly informants, limit to some extent the usefulness of this material, but the fact that many of them were so young at the time of the war's outbreak is clearly an advantage for this study. Paul D. Escott, *Slavery Remembered: A Record of Twentieth-Century Slave Narratives* (Chapel Hill, N.C., 1979), notes that almost two-thirds of the informants in Series 1 of the Rawick collection were no older than fifteen by the time the war ended in 1865. See pp. 16–17.

6. Quoted in Brenda Stevenson, "Distress and Discord in Virginia Slave Families, 1830–1860," in *In Joy and in Sorrow: Women, Family, and Marriage in the Victorian South, 1830–1900*, ed. Carol Bleser (New York, 1991), 111.

7. Quoted in James Oakes, *Slavery and Freedom: An Interpretation of the Old South* (New York, 1990), 20. See also Jacob Stroyer's description in Willie Lee Rose, ed., *A Documentary History of Slavery in North America* (New York, 1976), 401–3. Contrary to Oakes, I believe that such incidents did not inevitably lead to a sense of "kinlessness," but rather revealed to the child the dilemma faced by the parents and solidified his or her hatred of slavery. Oakes, *Slavery and Freedom*, 21.

8. Eugene D. Genovese, *Roll, Jordan, Roll: The World the Slaves Made* (New York, 1974), 510–11; John W. Blassingame, *The Slave Community: Plantation Life in the Antebellum South* (New York, 1972), 98–100; and Stevenson, "Distress and Discord in Slave Families," 110–12, 115.

9. Willie Lee Rose, "Childhood in Bondage," in *Slavery and Freedom*, ed. William W. Freehling (New York, 1982), 41–42; and Stevenson, "Distress and Discord in Slave Families," 108–9.

10. Quoted in Mary Frances Berry and John W. Blassingame, *Long Memory: The Black Experience in America* (New York, 1982), 75. See also Thomas L. Webber, *Deep Like the Rivers: Education in the Slave Quarter Community, 1831–1865* (New York, 1978), 169–72.

11. Herbert G. Gutman, *The Black Family in Slavery and Freedom, 1750–1925* (New York, 1976), 220–21; Stevenson, "Distress and Discord in Slave Families," 107; and Webber, *Deep Like the Rivers*, 157–59, 239–40.

12. Orville Vernon Burton, *In My Father's House Are Many Mansions: Family and Community in Edgefield, South Carolina* (Chapel Hill, N.C., 1985), 164–65; Elizabeth Fox-Genovese, *Within the Plantation Household: Black and White Women of the Old South* (Chapel Hill, N.C., 1988), 148; Willie Lee Rose, *Rehearsal for Reconstruction: The Port Royal Experiment* (New York, 1964), 134–35; Webber, *Deep Like the Rivers*, 10–11; and Blassingame, *Slave Community*, 94.

13. Jacqueline Jones, *Labor of Love, Labor of Sorrow: Black Women, Work, and the Family from Slavery to the Present* (New York, 1986), 35; Deborah Gray White, *Ar'n't I a Woman? Female Slaves in the Plantation South* (New York, 1985), 92; Webber, *Deep Like the Rivers*, 15, 180, 184–85; and David K. Wiggins, "The Play of Slave Children in the Plantation Communities of the Old South, 1820–60," in *Growing Up in America*, eds. Hiner and Hawes, 175.

14. Jones, *Labor of Love*, 23; White, *Ar'n't I a Woman?*, 92–93; Webber, *Deep Like the Rivers*, 13–14; Wiggins, "Play of Slave Children," 177–80, 183; Blassingame, *Slave Community*, 95–96; Leslie Howard Owens, *This Species of Property: Slave Life and Culture in the Old South* (New York, 1976), 204; and Genovese, *Roll, Jordan, Roll*, 505–6, 515.

15. White, *Ar'n't I a Woman?*, 93; Escott, *Slavery Remembered*, 30–31; Jones, *Labor of Love*, 24; and Genovese, *Roll, Jordan, Roll*, 502–3.

16. Owens, *This Species of Property*, 202, 205–6; Webber, *Deep Like the Rivers*, 19, 22–23; Burton, *In My Father's House*, 165; Jones, *Labor of Love*, 32–33; Fox-Genovese, *Within the Plantation Household*, 155–57; and White, *Ar'n't I a Woman?*, 94–95.

17. Rose, "Childhood in Bondage," 47–48; Blassingame, *Slave Community*, 97; and Genovese, *Roll, Jordan, Roll*, 505, 516.

18. John W. Blassingame, ed., *Slave Testimony* (Baton Rouge, La., 1977), 130.

19. Booker T. Washington, *Up from Slavery: An Autobiography* (New York, 1975; originally published in 1901), 5.

20. *South Carolina Narratives*, pt. 1, vol. 2, p. 293; and Rawick, ed., *American Slave*, vol. 18: Fisk University, *Unwritten History of Slavery*, 4. See also *Arkansas Narratives*, pt. 1, vol. 8, p. 338; pt. 2, vol. 8, p. 122; and pt. 3, vol. 9, p. 143.

21. Washington, *Up from Slavery*, 5, 6. On the workings of the "grapevine telegraph" during the Civil War, see Bell I. Wiley, *Southern Negroes, 1861–1865*, 2nd ed. (New York, 1953), 17–19.

22. *Arkansas Narratives*, pt. 3, vol. 9, p. 179; and *Alabama Narratives*, vol. 6, p. 297. See also *Arkansas Narratives*, pt. 4, vol. 9, p. 1; pt. 6, vol. 10, p. 188; and *Georgia Narratives*, pt. 3, vol. 13, p. 6.

23. *South Carolina Narratives*, pt. 3, vol. 3, p. 186; pt. 2, vol. 2, p. 6; and Candis Goodwin, quoted in Wiggins, "Play of Slave Children," 184. See also *Texas Narratives*, pt. 3, vol. 5, p. 275.

24. *Arkansas Narratives*, pt. 7, vol. 11, p. 184.

25. *Oklahoma Narratives*, vol. 7, p. 51.

26. *Arkansas Narratives*, pt. 5, vol. 10, p. 205; and pt. 3, vol. 9, p. 21.

27. *Ibid.*, 119; and *South Carolina Narratives*, pt. 4, vol. 3, p. 78. "Bumping" involved rocking in a straightback chair. See also *Georgia Narratives*, pt. 3, vol. 13, pp. 5–6; *Florida Narratives*, vol. 17, p. 367; *Kansas Narratives*, vol. 16, p. 1; *Oklahoma Narratives*, vol. 7, p. 359; and *North Carolina Narratives*, pt. 1, vol. 14, p. 366; pt. 2, vol. 15, pp. 377–78.

28. Wiley, *Southern Negroes*, 4–7; Leon F. Litwack, *Been in the Storm So Long: The Aftermath of Slavery* (New York, 1980), 30–36; *Freedom*, Series I, vol. I: *The Destruction of Slavery*, eds. Ira Berlin et al. (New York, 1985), 41–42 (hereafter cited as *Destruction of Slavery*); *Oklahoma Narratives*, vol. 7, p. 221; and C. Peter Ripley, "The Black Family in Transition: Louisiana, 1860–1865," *Journal of Southern History* 41 (Aug. 1975): 372–73.

Examples of former slaves who recall becoming wartime refugees as children include *Arkansas Narratives*, pt. 2, vol. 8, p. 88; pt. 7, vol. 11, pp. 60, 85; *South Carolina Narratives*, pt. 1, vol. 2, p. 163; and *Tennessee Narratives*, vol. 16, p. 9.

29. Litwack, *Been in the Storm So Long*, 120–21; and *Arkansas Narratives*, pt. 3, vol. 9, p. 21; pt. 2, vol. 6, p. 348.

30. *Arkansas Narratives*, pt. 4, vol. 9, pp. 84, 88; and *North Carolina Narratives*, pt. 1, vol. 14, p. 197. For other examples, consult *Arkansas Narratives*, pt. 2, vol. 8, p. 322; pt. 7, vol. 11, p. 194; and *North Carolina Narratives*, pt. 1, vol. 14, p. 104; pt. 2, vol. 15, p. 313.

The shiny, metal buttons seemed to signify power and strength, giving the persons who wore them special standing in the eyes of the youngsters as well as the soldiers themselves. As a Georgia ex-slave reported, the black troops that liberated the bondsmen and bondswomen on his plantation at the end of the war sang the following song:

> Don't you see the lightning?
> Don't you hear the thunder?
> It isn't the lightning,
> It isn't the thunder,
> It's the buttons on
> The Negro uniforms!

See *Georgia Narratives*, pt. 4, vol. 13, p. 215.

31. *Arkansas Narratives*, pt. 4, vol. 9, p. 138; pt. 7, vol. 11, p. 239; and Litwack, *Been in the Storm So Long*, 122–23. See also *Arkansas Narratives*, pt. 6, vol. 10, p. 45; *Oklahoma Narratives*, vol. 7, p. 41; and *South Carolina Narratives*, pt. 1, vol. 2, p. 69.

32. *Arkansas Narratives*, pt. 2, vol. 8, p. 221; *Texas Narratives*, pt. 3, vol. 5, p. 107; and *Missouri Narratives*, vol. 11, p. 120. See also *Arkansas Narratives*, pt. 5, vol. 10, p. 100; pt. 6, vol. 10, p. 357; and *South Carolina Narratives*, pt. 2, vol. 2, pp. 85–86.

33. Ira Berlin, Steven F. Miller, and Leslie S. Rowland, "Afro-American Families in the Transition from Slavery to Freedom," *Radical History Review* 42 (Fall 1988): 89–90; Ripley, "Black Family in Transition," 372–74; and Peter J. Parish, *Slavery: History and Historians* (New York, 1989), 161.

34. Ripley, "Black Family in Transition," 375; and *Black Military Experience*, 29–30, 526.

35. Jones, *Labor of Love*, 47–49; and Thomas Wentworth Higginson, *Army Life in a Black Regiment* (Boston, 1962; originally published in 1870), 247.

36. *Black Military Experience*, 30.

37. *Oklahoma Narratives*, vol. 7, p. 41, 42–43; and *Destruction of Slavery*, 38–39.

38. *Black Military Experience*, 49; and *South Carolina Narratives*, pt. 3, vol. 3, p. 131. See also Wedin, "Black Women on the Sea Islands," 75.

39. Ripley, "Black Family in Transition," 376; Jones, *Labor of Love*, 50; *Black Military Experience*, 189, 658; *Destruction of Slavery*, 48, 410, 513; and *Freedom, Series I, Vol. III: The Wartime Genesis of Free Labor: The Lower South*, eds. Ira Berlin et al. (New York, 1990), 65 (hereafter cited as *Wartime Genesis of Free Labor*).

40. *Black Military Experience*, 244, 243. For other documentation of the ill-treatment of black soldier families by slaveowners, see *ibid.*, 240–42, 245–46, 268–69, 686–88, 697; and *Destruction of Slavery*, 615–16.

41. *Black Military Experience*, 195–97, 267–71, 275, 658–59, 715–17; *Destruction of Slavery*, 48, 51, 308–10, 513; *Wartime Genesis of Free Labor*, 63, 716–17, 786–89; Jones, *Labor of Love*, 50–51; and Gutman, *Black Family*, 371–74.

42. Parish, *Slavery*, 162; Gutman, *Black Family*, 18–22, 412–18; and Litwack, *Been in the Storm So Long*, 240–41.

43. John W. De Forest, *A Union Officer in the Reconstruction*, eds. James H. Croushore and David M. Potter (New Haven, 1948), cited in Litwack, *Been in the Storm So Long*, 230.

44. Ripley, "Black Family in Transition," 376–80; and Gutman, *Black Family*, 139–43, 204–7.

45. Rose, *Rehearsal for Reconstruction*, 85–88, 229–32; Litwack, *Been in the Storm So Long*, 472–76, 485–91; Wiley, *Southern Negroes*, 260–81; and C. Peter Ripley, *Slaves and Freedmen in Civil War Louisiana* (Baton Rouge, La., 1976), 140–45.

46. Gutman, *Black Family*, 226–28.

47. Eric Foner, *Reconstruction: America's Unfinished Revolution, 1863–1877* (New York, 1988), 87; *North Carolina Narratives*, pt. 1, vol. 14, p. 76; and *Oklahoma Narratives*, vol. 7, p. 51.

48. Litwack, *Been in the Storm So Long*, 235–37; and *Texas Narratives*, pt. 4, vol. 5, p. 120.

49. Carol Gilligan, *In a Different Voice: Psychological Theory and Women's Development* (Cambridge, Mass., 1982), 30.

50. On gender in the nineteenth-century South, see Bleser, ed., *In Joy and in Sorrow*.

51. *South Carolina Narratives*, pt. 3, vol. 3, p. 202; and Rose, *Rehearsal for Reconstruction*, 11–12. For similar reactions to the arrival of Union forces and the possibility of emancipation, see *Arkansas Narratives*, pt. 3, vol. 9, p. 227; and *South Carolina Narratives*, pt. 1, vol. 2, p. 125.

Chapter 13. Wartime Dialogues on Illicit Sex

1. [David Croly and George Wakeman], *Miscegenation: The Theory of the Blending of the Races, Applied to the American White Man and Negro* (New York, 1863).

2. *Ibid.*, 43–44, 51. This might well be a parody of free-love language.

3. *Ibid.*, 28.

4. James McPherson, *Battle Cry of Freedom: The Civil War Era* (New York, 1988), 789–91; Sidney Kaplan, "The Miscegenation Issue in the Election of 1864," *Journal of Negro History* 34 (1949): 274–343; Forrest Wood, *Black Scare: The Racist Response to Emancipation and Reconstruction* (Berkeley, 1968), ch. 4.

5. *Congressional Globe*, 38th Cong., 1st sess., pt. 2, March 17, 1864, p. 1157. In 1866, a Democratic senator from Kentucky announced that the establishment of the Freedmen's Bureau would mean that black men could marry white women in violation of his state's laws (*Congressional Globe*, 39th Cong., 1st sess., pt. 1, Jan. 25, 1866, p. 418).

6. *Congressional Globe*, 39th Cong., 1st sess., pt. 1, Jan. 10, 1866, pp. 179, 180. In 1868, a Michigan Republican asked if those who professed such fears would feel obliged to arrange a social visit "because your ballot and theirs had been mingled in the same box?" And, he elaborated, "should your ballot and that of a black man happen to be placed in juxtaposition, would you for that reason at once deem it incumbent on you to give your daughter in marriage to the 'American

citizen of African descent?'" (*Congressional Globe*, 40th Cong., 2nd sess., pt. 2, March 18, 1868, p. 1970).

7. Martha Hodes, "Sex Across the Color Line: White Women and Black Men in the Nineteenth-Century American South" (Ph.D. dissertation, Princeton University, 1991), esp. chs. 2, 3, 4.

8. Testimony of Captain Richard J. Hinton, American Freedmen's Inquiry Commission, Letters Received, Office of the Adjutant General, Main Series, 1861–70, Record Group 94, M619, reels 199–201 (hereafter AFIC), file #8 (National Archives, Washington, D.C.; hereafter NA); grammar and spelling have been altered slightly for readability in all quotations.

Hinton also served as an army correspondent in Kansas, Missouri, and Tennessee; wrote Abraham Lincoln's campaign biography; organized the Kansas Emancipation League in 1862 to aid 4,000 former slaves; admired John Brown; and wrote for the *National Anti-Slavery Standard*. See Herbert Gutman, *The Black Family in Slavery and Freedom, 1750–1925* (New York, 1976), 613 n.9; James McPherson, *The Struggle for Equality: Abolitionists and the Negro in the Civil War and Reconstruction* (Princeton, N.J., 1964), 20, 170, 424.

9. The commissioners were Samuel Gridley Howe, a Boston physician and advocate for the blind and deaf; James McKaye, a New York activist against slavery; and Robert Dale Owen, freethinker and advocate of birth control and sexual equality. On the purposes of the commission, see *War of the Rebellion: A Compilation of the Official Records of the Union and Confederate Armies* (Washington, D.C.: 1880–1901), ser. 3, vol. 3, pp. 73–74; and *Congressional Globe*, 38th Cong., 1st sess., 1864, pp. 2799–800. On recommendations of the commission, see: "Preliminary Report of the American Freedmen's Inquiry Commission," *War of the Rebellion*, ser. 3, vol. 3, pp. 430–54; "Final Report of the American Freedmen's Inquiry Commission," *War of the Rebellion*, ser. 3, vol. 4, pp. 289–382; John Sproat, "Blueprint for Radical Reconstruction," *Journal of Southern History* 23 (1957): 25–44; McPherson, *Struggle for Equality*, 182–87; Eric Foner, *Reconstruction: America's Unfinished Revolution, 1863–1877* (New York, 1988), 68–69.

10. AFIC, General index, file #8 index, file #7 index (NA).

11. James Redpath, *The Roving Editor, or Talks with Slaves in Southern States* (New York, 1859), vi, 2; Charles Horner, *The Life of James Redpath and the Development of the Modern Lyceum* (New York, 1926), 24, 40; McPherson, *Struggle for Equality*, 6, 127, 128n., 155, 388–89.

12. Redpath, *Roving Editor*, 2–3, 140–41, 184, 234–35, 257–58.

13. Testimony of James Redpath, AFIC file #9 (NA).

14. Testimony of Major George Stearnes, AFIC file #7 (NA).

15. Testimony of Samuel B. Lucille, AFIC file #7 (NA). Lucille also said: "I believe the instances at the South where a yellow woman breeds with a full-blooded black man are fewer than where a black man has breeded on a white woman." See also testimony of Dr. James H. Richardson, AFIC, file #10 (NA); J. P. Litchfield to Samuel Gridley Howe, Sept. 7, 1863, American Freedmen's Inquiry Commission Papers (Houghton Library, Harvard University; hereafter HL).

16. Slaveholders were known to send the children they had fathered by slave women to Oberlin College in the nineteenth century, and records indicate that Colonel Miner was one of them. See Robert Samuel Fletcher, *A History of Oberlin College From Its Foundation Through the Civil War* (Oberlin, Ohio, 1943), 528, 535–36; James Fairchild, *Oberlin: The Colony and the College, 1833–1883* (Oberlin, Ohio, 1883), 111.

17. Testimony of Richard Hinton, AFIC file #8 (NA).

18. *Ibid.*

19. Testimony of James Redpath, AFIC file #9 (NA). Incidentally, the confession of the Mobile woman who had intercourse with her slave on her wedding day included the information that the man "came up to tie her boots the morning of her marriage, and had connection with her before the ceremony."

20. According to Bertram Wyatt-Brown and Catherine Clinton, women of the planter class were under too much scrutiny to be able to commit sexual offenses, while poorer women had an easier time of it; see Wyatt-Brown, *Southern Honor: Ethics and Behavior in the Old South* (New York, 1982), 298; Clinton, *The Plantation Mistress: Woman's World in the Old South* (New York, 1982), 72–73. Wyatt-Brown also surmises that white women had heard so much about the ardent sexuality of black men that they were curious to see for themselves if it was true (*Southern Honor*, 316). Of planter-class white women, Elizabeth Fox-Genovese writes: "That some southern white women took black lovers could be freely acknowledged, for it was assumed that the women were lower class and disreputable. But ladies? Through the wall of silence seeped gossip and occasional hard facts. Liaisons between white ladies and black men may have occurred rarely, but they did occur, not only in cities . . . but on the plantations"; and: "a few committed the ultimate rebellion against the dominance of white males by having sexual relations with black men." See *Within the Plantation Household: Black and White Women of the Old South* (Chapel Hill, 1988), 208, 241.

21. While those white women did suffer from and lament the abuses of the men who ruled their households and plantations, they did not, for the most part, challenge that authority. See Fox-Genovese, *Plantation Household*, 145; also pp. 24, 49, 97–98, 101–2, 192–93, 243, 326, 334, 359; George Rable, *Civil Wars: Women and the Crisis of Southern Nationalism* (Urbana, 1989), ch. 2 and *passim*.

22. On black women and white men in the slave South, see Deborah Gray White, *Ar'n't I a Woman?: Female Slaves in the Plantation South* (New York, 1985), 33–46; Wyatt-Brown, *Southern Honor*, 237, 297–98, 307–15, 319–24; Eugene Genovese, *Roll, Jordan, Roll: The World the Slaves Made* (New York, 1972), 413–31, 461; Gutman, *Black Family*, 83–84, 386–96, 399–402; Clinton, *Plantation Mistress*, 211–20; James Hugo Johnston, *Race Relations in Virginia and Miscegenation in the South, 1776–1860* (Amherst, Mass., 1970), ch. 9; Richard Steckel, "Miscegenation and the American Slave Schedules," *Journal of Interdisciplinary History* 11 (1980): 251–63; Steven Brown, "Sexuality and the Slave Community," *Phylon* 42 (1981): 7–8; C. Vann Woodward, *American Counterpoint: Slavery and Racism in the North-South Dialogue* (Boston, 1964), 47–48, 75. For a primary source, see Harriet Jacobs, *Incidents in the Life of a Slave Girl, Written by Herself*, Jean Fagan Yellin, ed. (Cambridge, Mass., 1987).

23. Testimony of Richard Hinton, AFIC file #8 (NA).

24. *Ibid.*

25. *Ibid.*

26. Poorer white women who attempted to coerce black men could be held responsible for the illicit liaison. In an 1813 Virginia case, for example, a slave was pardoned after he went on a violent rampage in the home of a white family because he had been coerced into "a considerable intimacy" by the daughter over several years. See Letters to Governor James Barbour, Oct. 5, 1813, Executive Papers, Letters Received, Virginia State Library and Archives, Richmond (hereafter VSLA). In an 1825 Virginia case about a married white woman and a neighborhood slave, the man's master testified: "I have good reason for believing this man of mine has been disposed to forsake this woman, which has produced considerable discontent in her, and has been the cause of her often visiting my negro houses and staying all night in the quarters." The woman was censured, while the man suffered no public retribution. See Deposition of John Richardson, Jan. 18, 1825, Lewis Bourne Divorce Petition, Louisa County, Jan. 20, 1825, #8305, Legislative Papers (VSLA). See also Hodes, *Sex Across the Color Line*, ch. 2, 3.

27. Testimony of Richard Hinton, AFIC file #8 (NA).

28. Testimony of James Redpath, AFIC file #9 (NA).

29. Testimony of Richard Hinton, AFIC file #8 (NA).

30. Benjamin Sherwood to "B. S. Hedrick and family," speech delivered in Iowa, April 7, 1860, Benjamin Sherwood Hedrick Papers (William Perkins Library, Duke University, Durham; hereafter WPL).

31. Testimony of Richard Hinton, AFIC file #8 (NA); Linda Gordon, *Woman's Body, Woman's Right: A Social History of Birth Control in America* (New York, 1976; reprint, New York, 1977), 44.

32. Testimony of James Redpath, AFIC file #9 (NA). Failing access to effective birth control, planter-class women also resorted to infanticide to protect themselves and their partners. A black man told Hinton about a planter's daughter in Missouri who had given birth to a "black child," and refused to reveal the father's name until the man had escaped to Kansas. "The child was reported to have died," Hinton said, "but the man believes it was killed," AFIC file #8 (NA). See also Jacobs, *Incidents*, 52. For an earlier case of planter-class infanticide, see *King vs. Sarah Wiggins*, Secretary of State Court Records, Box #312, April–May 1772, Dobbs County, North Carolina Department of Archives and History, Raleigh.

33. It is illuminating here to apply Orlando Patterson's discussion of male slaveholders and female slaves to sexual liaisons between white women and black men. "I know of no slaveholding society in which a master, when so inclined, could not exact sexual services from his female slaves," Patterson writes, later adding: "What masters and slaves do is struggle: sometimes noisily, more often quietly; sometimes violently, more often surreptitiously; infrequently with arms, always with the weapons of the mind and soul." See Orlando Patterson, *Slavery and Social Death: A Comparative Study* (Cambridge, Mass., 1982), 173, 207.

34. Jacobs, *Incidents*, 52.

35. "Equality," in Augusta (Ga.) *Colored American*, Jan. 6, 1866.

36. Antebellum documents support the phenomenon of coercion by planter-class women less directly. See, for example, Benjamin Sherwood to "B. S. Hedrick and family," April 7, 1860, Hedrick Papers (WPL). For a case regarding a female slaveowner and her male slave, see *Armstrong vs. Hodges*, in Ben Monroe, *Reports of Cases at Common Law and in Equity Decided in the Court of Appeals of Kentucky*, Fall 1841, pp. 69–71.

37. See Ronald Walters, *The Anti-Slavery Appeal: American Abolitionism After 1830* (New York, 1978), ch. 5. Some elite white women joined in the chorus of voices about the depravity of southern white men; see Mary Chesnut, *Mary Chesnut's Civil War*, C. Vann Woodward, ed. (New Haven, 1981), 29, 169; Nell Irvin Painter, "The Journal of Ella Gertrude Clanton Thomas: An Educated White Woman in the Eras of Slavery, War, and Reconstruction," in *The Secret Eye: The Journal of Ella Gertrude Clanton Thomas, 1848–1889*, Virginia Ingraham Burr, ed. (Chapel Hill, N.C., 1990), 55–56.

38. Testimony of Richard Hinton, AFIC file #8 (NA). Confederate women felt they were responding in kind to insolent Yankee soldiers; see, for example, Laura Lee Diary, Winchester, Va., March 11, April 18, May 15, June 5, 7, 1862 (Earl Gregg Swem Library, College of William and Mary, Williamsburg, Va.); Amanda Chappelear Diary, April 19, 1862 (Virginia Historical Society, Richmond; hereafter VHS); Mary Rawson Diary, Sept. 6, 1864 (Atlanta Historical Society; hereafter AHS); Kate Hester Robson Memoirs (1910), 23 (AHS); George Rable, *Civil Wars*, 164; Drew Gilpin Faust, "Altars of Sacrifice: Confederate Women and the Narratives of War," *Journal of American History* 76 (1990): 1213 (reprinted in this volume).

39. Letter from L. B. Cotes, Oct. 31, 1863, AFIC Papers (HL).

40. Samuel Howe, *The Refugees from Slavery in Canada West: Report to the Freedmen's Inquiry Commission* (Boston, 1864), 333, 94; for the manuscript version of the report (almost the same), see AFIC, "The Self-Freedmen of Canada West, Supplemental Report A of the AFIC," May 14, 1864 (NA).

41. John C. Gorman Diary-Memoir, 1864, p. 55, John C. Gorman Papers (WPL). Southern white women also expressed disgust at the fraternization of white Yankee soldiers and black women; see, for example, Eliza Andrews, *The War-Time Journal of a Georgia Girl, 1864–1865*, Spencer King, ed. (Macon, 1960), 267, 306.

42. Testimony of Mayor Cross, AFIC file #10 (NA); see also testimony of John Kinney, Mr. Sinclair, and Col. W. W. Stephenson, file #10 (NA). In the North, black antislavery agitator David Walker said in 1829: "I would not give a *pinch of snuff* to be married to any white person I ever saw in all the days of my life. And I do say it, that the black man, or man of color, who will leave his own color (provided he can get one who is good for any thing) and marry a white woman, to be a double slave to her just because she is *white*, ought to be treated by her as he surely will be, viz; as a NIGER!!!" *David Walker's Appeal, with a Brief Sketch of His Life: By Henry Highland Garnet* (New York, 1848; reprint, New York), 19.

43. Testimony of Bishop Green, AFIC file #10 (NA); see also testimony of Rev. Dr. McCaul, file #10 (NA).

44. See Donna Spindel, *Crime and Society in North Carolina, 1663–1776* (Baton Rouge, La., 1989), 109; Philip Schwarz, *Twice Condemned: Slaves and the Criminal Laws of Virginia* (Baton Rouge, La., 1988), 21–22, 72, 82–84, 150–52, 155–64, 179–80, 202–10, 291–95. For lynchings of black men for the alleged rape of white women during the war years, see Columbus (Ga.) *Daily Sun*, Feb. 22, March 2, 29, Dec. 5, 1861; Athens (Ga.) *Southern Banner*, July 16, 23, 1862.

45. Abbie M. Brooks Diary, May 9, 1865 (AHS). See also Mary T. Hunley Diary, March 19, May 13, 1864 (Southern Historical Collection, University of North Carolina, Chapel Hill, N.C.; hereafter SHC); Ann Bridges to Charles E. Bridges, July 17, 1865, Charles E. Bridges Papers (WPL); Grace B. Elmore Diary, Oct. 1, 1865 (SHC).

46. See, for example, Emma J. Slade Prescott Reminiscences, 1881, vol. 2, p. 9 (AHS). On sexual violence against southern white women by Yankee soldiers see, for example, Sydney S. Champion to Matilda Champion, April 4, 1863, Sydney S. Champion Papers (WPL). See also Rable, *Civil Wars*, 161, 341n. 25. Some white women alluded to fears of a conspiracy between Yankee soldiers and black men; see Amanda Chappelear Diary, Aug. 24, 1862 (VHS); Louisa Quitman Lovell to Capt. Joseph Lovell, Feb. 7, 1864, Quitman Family Papers (SHC).

47. Testimony of Richard Hinton, AFIC file #8 (NA). Fox-Genovese has noted the contradictory images of the virile "Buck" and the docile "Sambo" attributed to black men by whites in the slave South; see *Plantation Household*, 291. Winthrop Jordan has traced perceptions of black men and women as bestial and lustful to early British accounts of West Africa, and before that to early modern European literature which connected Africans with lasciviousness; see *White Over Black: American Attitudes Toward the Negro, 1550–1812* (Chapel Hill, N.C., 1968; reprint, New York, 1977), 579; see also pp. 32–43, 151–62, 398–99. Fox-Genovese and Genovese, however, both correctly point out that the idea of black male hypersexuality fully formed in white minds only after emancipation; see Fox-Genovese, *Plantation Household*, 291; Genovese, *Roll, Jordan, Roll*, 422, 461–62. See also Leon Litwack, *Been in the Storm So Long: The Aftermath of Slavery* (New York, 1979), 265–66; Jacquelyn Dowd Hall, *Revolt Against Chivalry: Jessie Daniel Ames and the Women's Campaign Against Lynching* (New York, 1979), 131–32.

48. Testimony of Richard Hinton, AFIC file #8 (NA).

49. Hodes, *Sex Across the Color Line*, chs. 2, 3, 4, 6; see also Nell Irvin Painter, "A Prize-Winning Book Revisited," *Journal of Women's History* 2 (1991): 132–33.

50. Two extremely illuminating cases are those of Jordan Ware and Henry Lowther, both in Georgia. See *Testimony Taken by the Joint Select Committee to Inquire into the Condition of Affairs in the Late Insurrectionary States*, 42nd Cong., 2nd sess., no. 41, 1871 (hereafter *KKK Report*), pt. 6, pp. 21–22, 30–31, 44–46, 74–75, 130 (Ware); and pt. 6, pp. 356–63, 426, 430–31, 443 (Lowther). See also Testimony of John W. Long, Ku Klux Klan Papers (WPL). In the minds of Klansmen and their sympathizers, the rape of white women was the logical extreme to which black men would go without the institution of slavery to restrain them; see, for example, *KKK Report*, pt. 6, p. 124; pt. 7, pp. 833, 835–36, 842–45;

pt. 9, p. 1260; pt. 13, pp. 6–7, 14–15. See also Wyatt-Brown, *Southern Honor*, 453–54.

51. *KKK Report*, pt. 2, p. 434; see also pt. 7, pp. 1113–14.

52. *Ibid.*, pt. 2, p. 318.

53. Genovese notes that white convictions about the sexual promiscuity of black women took precedence over ideas about black male sexuality in order to excuse sexual exploitation by male slaveholders; see *Roll, Jordan, Roll*, 461–62. But whites' focus on the presumed depravity of black women was also crucially accompanied by convictions about the depravity of white women outside the planter classes; it was these beliefs that could overshadow ideas about the hypersexuality of black men in the antebellum South.

54. See, for example, *KKK Report*, pt. 2, pp. 371–72; pt. 6, pp. 108–9, 125, 291–92; pt. 7, pp. 920–21; pt. 10, p. 1854. Black men and women used the same language to describe white women; see, for example, *KKK Report*, pt. 6, p. 362, 407–8, 412, 472; pt. 7, p. 1010.

55. *KKK Report*, pt. 6, p. 431.

56. See, for example, *KKK Report*, pt. 2, pp. 4, 37; pt. 7, pp. 1007, 1022, 1096, 1120; pt. 8, pp. 476, 549–51; pt. 9, pp. 771, 956; pt. 12, pp. 652, 672, 823, 839, 870, 912, 922–23, 1075, 1144, 1165–66; pt. 13, p. 137. On the treatment of black women by Klansmen, see, for example, *KKK Report*, pt. 2, pp. 36–37, 49, 148; pt. 6, pp. 75, 140–41, 375–77, 387; pt. 7, pp. 914, 1004; pt. 8, pp. 79–80, 547, 553; pt. 9, pp. 930, 1188, 1189; pt. 11, pp. 38–39; pt. 12, p. 1084.

Chapter 14. Warwork and Domesticity in the North

I would like to thank Betsy Blackmar, Josh Brown and Kristie Ross for their careful readings of this essay. Each provided valuable insights and astute advice for refining my thoughts and my prose.

1. See Margaret Randolph Higonnet, Jane Jenson, Sonya Michel, and Margaret Collins Weitz, eds., *Behind the Lines: Gender and the Two World Wars* (New Haven, 1987), 1–7; and Nina Silber, "Intemperate Men, Spiteful Women, and Jefferson Davis: Northern Views of the Defeated South," *American Quarterly* 41 (Dec. 1989): 614–35 (reprinted in this volume), for discussion on how northern male leaders cemented their regional identity by depicting the South as weak, irrational, and feminine.

2. Richard Franklin Bensel writes that in attempting a full mobilization of national resources the North necessarily relied on "unregulated capitalist markets" and "voluntarist structures"; *Yankee Leviathan: The Origins of Central State Authority in America, 1859–1877* (Cambridge, Eng., 1990), 94, 187–88.

3. Jeanne Boydston demonstrates that one way in which the domesticity ideology operated during the transformation to industrial capitalism was to locate all value in the wage. Redefining the concept of economy to include only that labor which was cash-based meant excluding any value produced by housework. *Home and Work: Housework, Wages, and the Ideology of Labor in the Early Republic* (New York, 1990), 99–141, *passim*.

4. See Iver Bernstein, *The New York City Draft Riots: Their Significance for American Society and Politics in the Age of the Civil War* (New York, 1990).

5. Leonard D. White, *The Jacksonians: A Study in Administrative History 1829–1861* (New York, 1954), 187–205. White notes that a long-standing distrust of a standing army had left the War Department with meager funding and a skeletal staff; federal appropriations to the Department in 1860 were at the same levels as those of 1808.

6. States voluntarily assisted the national government by allotting funds to raise militias, provide uniforms and food, and purchase arms and munitions. Cities, counties, and states instituted taxes to fund their own bounties for local recruits, while communities raised funds to support the families of soldiers left behind. See Eugene C. Murdock, *Patriotism Limited, 1862–1865: The Civil War Draft and the Bounty System* (Kent, Ohio, 1967), 16; Fred Albert Shannon, *The Organization and Administration of the Union Army 1861–1865,* 2 vols. (Gloucester, Mass., 1965), 1: 15–148; Emerson David Fite, *Social and Industrial Conditions in North During the Civil War* (New York, 1963), 288–89.

7. The idea for a centralized depot for homefront donations was actually begun by upper-class and professional women in New York City. Dr. Elizabeth Blackwell set in motion the events that led to the Women's Central Relief Association. The WCRA was in existence for a few months when it was absorbed by the Sanitary Commission, created by male physicians, professionals, and the Reverend Henry Whitney Bellows, and given sanction by the White House. See "The Origin, Organization, and Working of the Woman's Central Association of Relief," Oct. 12, 1861, No. 32, pp. 6–8, vol. 1, *Documents of the U.S. Sanitary Commission,* 2 vols. (New York, 1966; hereafter *Documents*); Walter Donald Kring, *Henry Whitney Bellows* (Boston, 1979), 227. For a fuller discussion of the relationship between the female homefront and the Commission see my dissertation: Rejean Attie, "'A Swindling Concern': The United States Sanitary Commission and the Northern Female Public, 1861–1865" (Ph.D. dissertation, Columbia University, 1987).

8. George Fredrickson was the first to argue for the significance of the Sanitary Commission as a vehicle for class power and for reshaping welfare ideology: *The Inner Civil War: Northern Intellectuals and the Crisis of the Union* (New York, 1965), esp. in ch. 7.

9. The views of Sanitary elites conform to those of other mid-nineteenth-century Western elites during what Eric Hobsbawm has characterized as the heyday of liberal nationalism. E. J. Hobsbawm, *Nations and Nationalism Since 1780: Programme, Myth, Reality* (Cambridge, Eng., 1990), 37–38.

10. Henry W. Bellows to Frederick L. Olmsted, Aug. 13, 1863, Frederick Law Olmsted Papers (Library of Congress, Washington, D.C.).

11. "What They Have To Do," No. 50, p. 7, *Documents*, vol. 1.

12. Henry W. Bellows, *Historical Sketch of the Union League Club of New York* (New York, 1879), 5.

13. See Lori D. Ginzberg, *Women and the Work of Benevolence: Morality, Politics, and Class in the Nineteenth-Century United States* (New Haven, 1990), 36–66, on antebellum female benevolent work.

14. Boydston, *Home and Work*, 142–63.

15. Charles J. Stillé, *History of the United States Sanitary Commission: Being the General Report of Its Work During the War of the Rebellion* (Philadelphia, 1866), 39; L. P. Brockett, *Woman's Work in the Civil War: A Record of Heroism, Patriotism and Patience* (Philadelphia, 1867), 57.

16. *A Few Words in Behalf of the Loyal Women of the United States by One of Themselves*, Loyal Publication Society Pamphlet No. 10 (New York, 1863).

17. Maria Lydig Daly, *Diary of a Union Lady, 1861–1865*, Harold E. Hammond, ed. (New York, 1962), 12.

18. Jane Stuart Woolsey to "a friend," May 10, 1861, in G. W. Bacon and E. W. Howland, eds., *Letters of a Family during the War for the Union 1861–1865*, 2 vols. (privately published, 1899), 1: 66.

19. *The Mayflower*, May 15, 1861.

20. Alfred J. Bloor to Frederick N. Knapp, Sept. 9, 1864, Alfred J. Bloor Papers (New-York Historical Society, New York; hereafter N-YHS).

21. Joel Myerson and Daniel Shealy, eds., *The Journals of Louisa May Alcott* (Boston, 1989), 105.

22. Daly, *Union Lady*, 73; Agatha Young, *The Women and the Crisis: Women of the North in the Civil War* (New York, 1959), 96–98; Jane Ellen Schultz, "Women at the Front: Gender and Genre in the Literature of the American Civil War" (Ph.D. dissertation, University of Michigan, 1977), 272–73. Schultz notes that the 400 figure was based on women who sought war pensions; her research in the sources revealed many more who went "incognito" to the front.

23. Sarah Edwards Henshaw, *Our Branch and Its Tributaries* (Chicago, 1868), 19, 21; Sophronia E. Bucklin, *In Hospital and Camp: A Woman's Record of Thrilling Incidents Among the Wounded in the Late War* (Philadelphia, 1869), 33.

24. "To the Loyal Women of America," Oct. 1, 1861, No. 32, *Documents*, vol. 1; "Statement of the Object and Method of the Sanitary Commission—with Supplement," Dec. 7, 1863, No. 69, p. 49, *Documents*, vol. 2; Bellows, "Sanitary Commission," 73.

25. Henry Bellows, Notes, Henry W. Bellows Papers (Massachusetts Historical Society, Boston).

26. "Origin and Objects of the Sanitary Commission," Aug. 13, 1861, No. 22, *Documents*, vol. 1.

27. Sarah H. Bradford to Mrs. Marshall, Jan. 25, 1864, WCRA, Box 671, United States Sanitary Commission Papers (New York Public Library; hereafter USSC Papers).

28. E. S. Denroche to Mrs. Helen W. Marshall, Jan. 25, 1864, Box 671 (USSC Papers).

29. Alfred Bloor to Wm. A. Hovey, Oct. 18, 1864, Bloor Papers (New-York Historical Society).

30. Mrs. Proudfit, Feb. 26, 1863; Caroline Sherman to L. Schuyler, Jan. 24, 1863; Ophelia Wait to L. Schuyler, Jan. 30, 1863; Mrs. C. Dales, Feb. 3, 1863; Mrs. Alanson Tuttle, Jan. 29, 1863; Mrs. Folney, 1863, Box 669 (USSC Papers).

31. Bloor to Knapp, Sept. 9, 1864, Bloor Papers (N-YHS).

32. Introduction to L. P. Brockett and Mary C. Vaughan, *Woman's Work*

in the Civil War: A Record of Heroism, Patriotism and Patience (Philadelphia, 1867), 59.

33. Alfred Bloor, "Women's Work in the War: A Letter to Senator Sumner," Sept. 18, 1866, Bloor Papers (N-YHS).

34. Lori Ginzberg argues that the shift in rhetoric about female benevolence represented the triumph of a conservative, masculine version of philanthropy which united elite women and men in espousing the virtues of corporatism and scientific charity. See Ginzberg, *Women and the Work of Benevolence*, 172–73, 193–213.

35. William Leach, *True Love and Perfect Union: The Feminist Reform of Sex and Society* (New York, 1980), 6–13. Leach singles out Abby May (a former officer of the Boston branch of the Commission) as a postwar feminist who articulated the view of the state as a province of male power, writing in 1869, "The state has proven itself void of all positive worth."

Chapter 15. Harriet Beecher Stowe's Averted Gaze

1. Harriet Beecher Stowe to Calvin Stowe and children, Jan. 4, 1865, Beecher-Stowe Family Papers (Schlesinger Library, Radcliffe College). Stowe was careless about dating letters; the date on this letter is certainly wrong, as there was no cannonade in Boston in January of 1865. The probable date is February 4, 1865; Governor Andrew did order bell ringing and a hundred-gun salute the morning of February 2, 1865, in honor of Lincoln's signing of the Thirteenth Amendment prohibiting slavery in the United States. It is possible Stowe's mistake was in the year rather than the month, for Governor Andrew also ordered a hundred-gun salute on January 3, 1863, in celebration of the Emancipation Proclamation.

2. For a detailed account of Stowe's relationship to her publisher and of Fields's role as the paradigmatic "gentleman publisher," see Susan Coultrap-McQuin, *Doing Literary Business* (Chapel Hill, N.C., 1990).

3. Harriet Beecher Stowe to James T. Fields, n.d. [1864?], as quoted in James C. Austin, *Fields of the Atlantic Monthly* (San Marino, Calif., 1953), 280. The letter refers to the success of "House and Home Papers" and proposes a sequel, presumably "The Chimney Corner," for 1865.

4. Harriet Beecher Stowe to James T. Fields, Nov. 29, 1864, as quoted in Austin, *Fields of the Atlantic Monthly*, 281.

5. For discussion of this differentiation, see Karen Halttunen, *Confidence Men and Painted Women* (New Haven, Conn., 1982); Lawrence Levine, *Highbrow/Lowbrow* (Cambridge, Mass., 1988); and John F. Kasson, *Rudeness & Civility* (New York, 1990). On the role of elite journals in fostering the concept of high culture, see John Tomisch, *A Genteel Endeavor* (Stanford, Calif., 1971). On distinctions being drawn between the middle classes and manual laborers, see John Blumin, *The Emergence of the Middle Class* (Cambridge, Eng., 1989).

6. Before the Proclamation few abolitionists expressed any confidence in Lincoln; many remained skeptical, but most shared with Stowe a belief that this was a step toward universal abolition. Many continued to press Lincoln and Congress for immediate universal emancipation. Stowe, confident God would

bring the promise of the Proclamation to fruition, was less active, but her correspondence shows she followed politics closely, supporting Lincoln in 1864. On the politics of evangelical abolitionism (Stowe's version), see Victor Howard, *Religion and the Radical Republican Movement, 1860–1870* (Lexington, Ky., 1990). On female abolitionists who, less sanguine than Stowe, mounted a massive petition campaign for immediate abolition, see Wendy F. Hamand, "The Woman's National Loyal League: Feminist Abolitionists and the Civil War," *Civil War History* 32 (1989): 39–58. After the war, with slavery formally abolished, Stowe supported Garrison's controversial decision to suspend publication of *The Liberator*. Stowe remained concerned with the plight of freed slaves, but her "causes" in the postwar era were multiple, and much of her energy was devoted to shaping and reforming her own class.

7. Critics who have elaborated various aspects of this dynamic in *Uncle Tom's Cabin* include Elizabeth Ammons, "Stowe's Dream of the Mother-Savior," in Eric Sundquist, ed., *New Essays on Uncle Tom's Cabin* (Cambridge, Eng., 1986), 155–95; Gillian Brown, "Getting in the Kitchen with Dinah: Domestic Politics in *Uncle Tom's Cabin*," *American Quarterly* 36 (Fall 1984): 501–23, and *Domestic Individualism* (Berkeley, Calif., 1990); Myra Jehlen, "The Family Militant: Domesticity Versus Slavery in *Uncle Tom's Cabin*," *Criticism* 31 (1989): 383–400; and Jane Tompkins, *Sensational Designs* (New York, 1985).

8. Harriet Beecher Stowe, *The Pearl of Orr's Island* (Boston, 1862; rpt. 1979), 396.

9. Harriet Beecher Stowe, *Agnes of Sorrento* (Boston, 1862; rpt. Boston, 1896), 376.

10. Harriet Beecher Stowe, "A Reply to 'The Affectionate and Christian Address of Many Thousands of Women of Great Britain and Ireland to Their Sisters the Women of the United States of America,'" *Atlantic* 11 (Jan. 1863): 132–33.

11. For a broader discussion of Stowe's efforts to influence public opinion in Britain during the war, see Wendy T. Hamand, "'No Voice from England': Mrs. Stowe, Mr. Lincoln, and the British in the Civil War," *New England Quarterly* 61 (1988): 3–24.

12. Nathaniel Hawthorne to Harriet Beecher Stowe, quoted in Charles Stowe, *Life of Harriet Beecher Stowe* (Boston, 1889), 394.

13. For the felicitous phrase "aesthetic of acquisition," I am indebted to Jan Lewis's comment on an earlier version of this essay delivered at the annual meeting of the American Historical Association, New York, 1990.

14. Harriet Beecher Stowe, "The Chimney Corner. I," *Atlantic* 15 (Jan. 1865): 111.

15. *Ibid.*, 113.

16. See, for example, Rebecca Harding [Davis], "The Promise of the Dawn," *Atlantic* 11 (Jan. 1863): 10–25; and "Paul Blecker," *Atlantic* 11 (May 1863): 580–98; (June 1863): 677–91; 12 (July 1863): 52–69.

17. The standard study of social purity is David Pivar, *Purity Crusade: Sexual Morality and Social Control, 1868–1900* (Westport, Conn., 1973). See also William Leach, *True Love and Perfect Union* (New York, 1980).

18. Harriet Beecher Stowe, "The Chimney Corner. I," *Atlantic* 15 (Jan. 1865): 115.

19. Harriet Beecher Stowe, "The Chimney Corner. VIII. The Noble Army of Martyrs," *Atlantic* 16 (Aug. 1865): 232–37.

20. Harriet Beecher Stowe, "House and Home Papers. VII," *Atlantic* 14 (July 1864): 95.

21. All the Stowe quotations in this paragraph, and in the remainder of this essay, are taken from Harriet Beecher Stowe, "Sojourner Truth, the Libyan Sibyl," *Atlantic* 11 (April 1863): 473–81.

22. For a balanced assessment of whether Stowe's tale inspired Story, see Jan M. Seidler, *A Critical Reappraisal of the Career of William Wetmore Story (1819–1895), American Sculptor and Man of Letters* (Ann Arbor, 1985), 514–18. Seidler cites Charles Eliot Norton's eyewitness account of the breakfast recital by Stowe, and argues that Story considered the Sibyl a comment on American slavery; she quotes his characterization of the statue as "my anti-slavery sermon in stone" (511), and cites his proposal to do a bronze version as an Emancipation memorial (521).

23. For a rich account of theories of ideal sculpture and actual viewing practices of Victorian audiences, see the opening chapters of Joy S. Kasson, *Marble Queens & Captives: Women in Nineteenth-Century American Sculpture* (New Haven, Conn., 1990). Her study explores cultural meanings embedded in the preference shown by male and female sculptors alike for producing female figures.

24. Jan Seidler argues convincingly for the acuity of Stowe's judgment that Story had created a new manner; see *A Critical Reappraisal,* 459–72, 530–37. Jean Fagan Yellin, in *Women & Sisters* (New Haven, Conn., 1989), suggests instead that Story utilized a pose "assigned to defeated barbarians in Roman art" and drew on Dürer's *Melancholy* (84) and that Stowe's article and Story's sculpture both emphasize a passivity demeaning to black womanhood (87). Seidler claims Victorians adeptly supplied "a more venturesome interpretive context for the image than the actual actions of the figure presented or suggested" (489); similarly, Stowe's audience would not have read passivity in her portrait of Truth with its references to vigor, queenliness, and power.

Chapter 16. Intemperate Men, Spiteful Women, and Jefferson Davis

This essay was originally published in *American Quarterly* 41 (Dec. 1989): 614–35.

1. Carroll Smith-Rosenberg, *Disorderly Conduct* (New York, 1985), 11–52, 90–108; Michael Paul Rogin, *Andrew Jackson and the Subjugation of the American Indian* (New York, 1975); Joan Scott, "Gender: A Useful Category of Historical Analysis," *American Historical Review* 91 (Dec. 1986): 1053–75.

2. *The Diary of George Templeton Strong,* ed. Allan Nevins and Milton H. Thomas (New York, 1952), 4: 11; Whitelaw Reid, *After the War: A Southern Tour* (Cincinnati and New York, 1866), 63.

3. Bertram Wyatt-Brown, *Southern Honor* (New York, 1982), 20. In this work, and in *Yankee Saints and Southern Sinners* (Baton Rouge and London, 1985), Wyatt-Brown develops his argument in much greater complexity than I am able to

do here, noting especially the divergent moral and religious traditions of northern and southern upper-class men.

4. Eric Foner, *Free Soil, Free Labor, Free Men* (New York, 1970), 23–29. For more on the construction of middle-class masculinity in the antebellum North, see Charles Rosenberg, "Sexuality, Class and Role in Nineteenth Century America," *American Quarterly* 25 (May 1973): 131–53, and E. Anthony Rotundo, "Body and Soul: Changing Ideals of American Middle-Class Manhood, 1770–1920," *Journal of Social History* 16 (1983): 23–38.

5. Wyatt-Brown, *Yankee Saints and Southern Sinners*, 124–26.

6. William Taylor, *Cavalier and Yankee* (Garden City, N.Y., 1961), 123–55; Eric Foner, *Free Soil, Free Labor, Free Men*, 69–72.

7. John W. Phelps, John W. Phelps Papers, 7: 87, New York Public Library (NYPL); Letter of Oliver W. Holmes to Senator A. J. Beveridge quoted in Daniel Aaron, *The Unwritten War: American Writers and the Civil War* (New York, 1973), 166–67; *Chicago Tribune*, May 25, 1865, p. 2.

8. *Diary of George Templeton Strong*, 3: 583–84; John W. Phelps, Phelps Papers, 7: 87 (NYPL); quote of James M. Morey in Daniel Sutherland, *The Confederate Carpetbaggers* (Baton Rouge, 1987), 236.

9. *New York Tribune*, May 12, 1865, p. 4; John DeForest, *A Union Officer in the Reconstruction* (New Haven, 1968), 183, 185.

10. A. P. Dutcher, "A Lecture on the Temperaments," *Medical and Surgical Reporter* 15 (Dec. 1, 1866): 451–52. For more on nineteenth-century medical views of women's unstable biology see Charles Rosenberg and Carroll Smith-Rosenberg, "The Female Animal: Medical and Biological Views of Women," in Charles Rosenberg, *No Other Gods: On Science and American Thought* (Baltimore, 1976), 54–70. Review of *Kate Beaumont, The Nation*, March 21, 1872, 190.

11. *New York Times*, Oct. 13, 1870, 4–5; Henry Field, *Blood Is Thicker Than Water: A Few Days Among Our Southern Brethren* (New York, 1886), 49; James Schouler, *History of the United States of America, Under the Constitution*, Vol. 6 (New York, 1899), 600.

12. Sidney Andrews, *The South Since the War, as Shown by Fourteen Weeks of Travel and Observation in Georgia and the Carolinas* (Boston, 1866), 318.

13. Benjamin Butler, *Butler's Book* (Boston, 1892), 418. Mary Ryan's unpublished paper, "Of Handkerchiefs and Brickbats: Women in the Public Sphere," has helped me to put the Butler incident in perspective. Whitelaw Reid, *After the War*, 46; John Dennett, *The South as It Is, 1865–66* (Athens and London, 1986), 279; Andrews, *The South*, 9.

14. Andrews, *The South*, 320, 187; Marchmont, "Southern Society," *Lippincott's* VI (August, 1870), 123.1.

15. *New York Tribune*, April 18, 1865, 2; James Schouler, *History of the United States* 1: 319–20.

16. Drew Faust, "Altars of Sacrifice: Confederate Women and the Narratives of War," in this volume; Elizabeth Fox-Genovese, *Within the Plantation Household* (Chapel Hill, 1988), 334–71; Gaines Foster, *Ghosts of the Confederacy* (New York, 1987), 29.

17. Quoted in Chester D. Bradley, "Was Jefferson Davis Disguised as a Woman

When Captured?," *The Journal of Mississippi History* 36 (Aug. 1974): 246; for more on the debate regarding Davis's disguise see Bradley, "Was Jefferson Davis Disguised"; for another interpretation of the event, and an excellent collection of capture cartoons, see Mark E. Neely, Jr., Gabor S. Boritt, and Harold Holzer, *The Confederate Image* (Chapel Hill and London), 79–96.

18. "Jeff in Petticoats" words by Henry Tucker and music by George Cooper in Irwin Silber, ed., *Songs of the Civil War* (New York, 1960), 345; *Boston Evening Journal*, May 27, 1865.

19. *Chicago Tribune*, May 31, 1865, 2; Neil Harris, *Humbug: The Art of P. T. Barnum* (Chicago, 1973), 169; Neely, Holzer and Boritt, *The Confederate Image*, 79–96.

20. Neely, Boritt, and Holzer, *The Confederate Image*, 90.

21. *New York Independent*, May 18, 1865, 2; Letter of Edward Morley, May 18, 1865, Edward Morley Papers, Library of Congress; *Harper's Weekly*, June 3, 1865, 347.

22. Dennett, *The South*, 17–18; Foster, *Ghosts of the Confederacy*, 26; *Cleveland Plain Dealer*, May 16, 1865.

23. *New York Herald*, May 16, 1865, quoted in *Public Opinion* 7 (June 3, 1865): 571–72.

24. William Taylor, *Cavalier and Yankee*, 125–26; *New York Herald*, May 16, 1865, in *Public Opinion* 7 (June 3, 1865): 572.

25. Captain G. W. Lawton, "Running at the Heads: Being an Authentic Account of the Capture of Jefferson Davis," *Atlantic Monthly*, Sept. 1865, copy found in James D. and David R. Barbee Papers, Library of Congress.

26. *New York Herald*, May 16, 1865, in *Public Opinion* 7 (June 3, 1865): 571–72.

27. Joan Scott, "Gender: A Useful Category of Historical Analysis," 1070.

28. John Trowbridge, *My Own Story* (Boston and New York, 1903), 284.

Chapter 17. Reconstructing Freedwomen

1. This essay is part of a larger project which will examine plantation life during the Civil War and Reconstruction. I wish to acknowledge my research assistants over the years: Michael Melcher, Bennett Singer, Lisa Cody, Pilar Olivo, Kim Lamp, Laura Vazquez, Nicoletta Karam, Tiya Miles, and Kellie Magnus.

2. For important insight see Jacqueline Jones's *Labor of Love, Labor of Sorrow* (New York, 1985) and Herbert Gutman's *The Black Family in Slavery and Freedom* (New York, 1975) and Leslie Schwalm, "The Meaning of Freedom" (Ph.D. dissertation, University of Wisconsin, 1991).

3. *The Colored American* (Augusta, Ga.), Jan. 13, 1866.

4. George P. Rawick, ed., *The American Slave: A Composite Autobiography* (Westport, Conn., 1972; hereafter cited as *Rawick*), Vol. 4, pt. 2, pp. 225–27.

5. Margaret Burnham, "An Impossible Marriage: Slave Law and Family Law," *Law and Inequality* 5 (July 1987): 221.

6. The Bureau of Refugees, Freedmen and Abandoned Lands (National Archives) (hereafter cited as BRF&AL), E4058, Vol. 280, Va., March 5, 1867.

7. BRF&AL, M809, Reel 18, 0566–7, Reports, Sept. 1, 1865.

8. BRF&AL, M826, Reel 32, 0012.

9. BRF&AL, M869, Reel 7, 0615.

10. *Rawick*, Vol. 8, pt. 2, p. 41.

11. BRF&AL, 105/9W4/Row 11/Comp 5/Shelf E/Box 26/Entry 53.

12. BRF&AL, M798, Reel 15, Letters Received, Madison, Georgia, Jan. 2, 1867.

13. BRF&AL, M1048, Reel 10, 0580, June 30, 1866.

14. BRF&AL, M1048, Reel 12, 0073, Letters Received, Gordonsville, Va., Jan. 6, 1866.

15. BRF&AL, M1048, Reel 33, 0827–30.

16. See Angela Davis, *Women, Race and Class* (New York, 1981), bell hooks, *Ain't I a Woman* (Boston, 1981), Deborah White, *Aren't I a Woman* (New York, 1985), and Patricia Morton, *Disfigured Images* (Westport, Conn., 1991).

17. BRF&AL, M798, Reel 13, Murders and Outrages, Oct. 15, 1866.

18. BRF&AL, M1048, Reel 59, Murder and Outrages, July 1868.

19. BRF&AL, M798, Reel 13, Reports of Murders and Outrages, Aug. 8, 1866.

20. BRF&AL, M1048, Reel 12, 0220–0240.

21. Segregation legislation begins in Tennessee in 1881—a railway case. And the famed *Plessy v. Ferguson* case (1896) which sanctified segregation at the federal level stemmed from a railway case.

22. *The Loyal Georgian* (Augusta, Ga.), Feb. 17, 1866, p. 3.

23. BRF&AL, M1048, Reel 59, Murders and Outrages, Feb. 21, 1868.

24. See Paula Giddings, "Ida Wells-Barnett," in G. J. Barker-Benfield and Catherine Clinton, *Portraits of American Women* (New York, 1991).

25. *Raleigh Register*, July 30, 1867, p. 3.

26. *Ibid.*, Aug. 9, 1867, p. 3.

27. *Ibid.*, July 30, 1867, p. 3.

28. See also *Richmond Enquirer*, July 24, 1863, p. 3.

29. See Mrs. N. B. De Sassure, *Old Plantation Days: Being the Recollections of Southern Life Before the Civil War* (New York, 1909), 18.

30. *Black Republican and Office Holder's Journal*, Aug. 1865.

31. *The Colored American* (Augusta, Ga.), Jan. 13, 1866.

32. BRF&AL, M1048, Reel 59, 0120–0123, Richmond, Va., June 8, 1865.

33. BRF&AL, M798, Reel 13, Murders and Outrages in Georgia, July 2, 1866.

34. See "Southern Dishonor: Flesh, Blood, Race and Bondage," in Carol Bleser, ed., *In Joy and in Sorrow* (New York, 1991).

35. *Rawick*, Vol. 9, PB, p. 218.

36. BRF&AL, M798, Roll 14, Letters Received, Sept. 10, 1866.

37. *Loyal Georgian* (Augusta, Ga.), Oct. 13, 1866, p. 3.

38. *Rawick*, Vol. 10, pt. 6, p. 350.

39. *Ibid.*, Vol. 6, pt. 2, pp. 134–36.

40. Myrta Lockett Avary, *Dixie After the War* (New York, 1906), 377.

41. *Ibid.*, 384.

42. *Ibid.*

43. *Atlanta Constitution*, June 27, 1868, p. 1.

44. *Ibid.*, July 18, 1868, p. 2.

45. *Ibid.*, June 18, 1868, p. 4.

Chapter 18. Divorce in North Carolina

1. Carol Smart, *The Ties That Bind: Law, Marriage, and the Reproduction of Patriarchal Relations* (London, 1983), xiii. On divorce patterns and their relationship to society, see especially Jane Turner Censer, "'Smiling Through Her Tears': Ante-Bellum Southern Women and Divorce," *American Journal of Legal History* 25 (Jan. 1981): 24–47; Linda Kerber, *Women of the Republic: Intellect and Ideology in Revolutionary America* (Chapel Hill, 1980), 159–84; Marylynn Salmon, "Equality or Submersion? Feme Covert Status in Early Pennsylvania," in Carol Berkin and Mary Beth Norton, eds., *Women of America: A History* (Boston, 1979), 92–111.

2. Act of 1871–72, Sec. 1286, c. 193, s. 39.

3. Act of 1871–72, Sec. 1286, c. 193, s. 35. Prior to the divorce acts of 1871–72, North Carolina would not grant full divorces to women or men unless their spouses had both abandoned them and committed adultery. For an overview of the evolution of divorce procedures in antebellum North Carolina, see Joseph S. Ferrell, "Notes and Comments," *North Carolina Law Review* 41 (1962–63): 604–16.

4. Act of 1871–72, Sec. 1286, c. 193, s. 36. Prior to 1872, the grounds for a separation of bed and board were cruelty and adultery. See Farrell, "Notes and Comments," 605.

5. Elizabeth Fox-Genovese, "Family and Female Identity in the Antebellum South: Sarah Gayle and Her Family," in Carol Bleser, ed., *In Joy and in Sorrow: Women, Family, and Marriage in the Victorian South, 1830–1900* (New York, 1991), 19.

6. *Whittington v. Whittington* 19 N.C. 65 (1836); *Scroggins v. Scroggins* 14 N.C. 567 (1832). In *Wood v. Wood* 27 N.C. 553 (1845), Ruffin declared that the "welfare of the community is to be consulted more than the wishes of the party." He also argued in *Hansley v. Hansley* 32 N.C. 365 (1848) that strict divorce laws were "intended to protect the public morals and promote public policy."

7. *Scroggins v. Scroggins* 14 N.C. 567 (1832). For a fuller analysis of the Ruffin court and divorce, see Victoria E. Bynum, *Unruly Women: The Politics of Social and Sexual Control in the Old South* (Chapel Hill, N.C., 1992), ch. 3.

8. *Scroggins v. Scroggins* 14 N.C. 567 (1832). On miscegenation in the Old South, see especially Catherine Clinton, "'Southern Dishonor': Flesh, Blood, Race, and Bondage," in Carol Bleser, ed., *In Joy and in Sorrow*, 52–68; Joel Williamson, *New People: Miscegenation and Mulattoes in the United States* (New York, 1980); and Bynum, *Unruly Women*, ch. 4.

9. *Barden v. Barden* 14 N.C. 580 (1832); Peter Bardaglio, "Sex Crimes, Sexuality, and the Courts in the Antebellum South," unpublished paper presented at the Second Southern Conference on Women's History, University of North Carolina, Chapel Hill, June 7, 1991, p. 11.

10. For biographical sketches of Ruffin and Pearson, see John Hill Wheeler, *Historical Sketches of North Carolina from 1584 to 1851* (Baltimore, 1964), 385–86; Samuel A. Ashe, ed., *Biographical History of North Carolina from Colonial Times to the Present* (Greensboro, N.C., 1906), V: 295–309. Upon Pearson's nomination to

the state supreme court in 1848, George C. Mendenhall, a piedmont Whig lawyer from a prominent Quaker family, wrote Governor Graham that he favored Pearson because he was "the least afraid of our Chief Justice [Ruffin] in North Carolina." See George C. Mendenhall to Governor Graham, April 8, 1848, Governors' Papers (Graham, NCDAH). On Pearson's challenge to the "Raleigh Clique," see also Mark Kruman, *Parties and Politics in North Carolina, 1836–1865* (Baton Rouge, La., 1983), 146.

11. Disagreements between Ruffin and Pearson over the rights of women are especially evident in *State v. Gibson* 32 N.C. 161 (1849); *Walter v. Jordan* 57 N.C. 558 (1852); and *Harris v. Harris* 53 N.C. 393 (1850).

12. *Horne v. Horne* 72 N.C. 489 (1875).

13. See especially *Whittington v. Whittington* 19 N.C. 65 (1836); *Moss v. Moss* 24 N.C. 44 (1841).

14. *Long v. Long* 77 N.C. 287 (1877).

15. *Ibid.*

16. *Ibid.* On Rodman's political career during Reconstruction, see Ashe, ed., *Biographical History of North Carolina*, III, pp. 342–54; Horace W. Raper, *William W. Holden: North Carolina's Political Enigma* (Chapel Hill, N.C., 1985), 109, 134, 289–90.

17. Act of 1879, c. 132.

18. *Bowling v. Bowling*, Spring 1866; *Couch v. Couch*, Fall 1867; both in Divorce Records, Orange County, North Carolina Department of Archives and History (hereinafter cited as NCDAH). *Belvin v. Belvin*, Fall 1866, Divorce Records, Granville County (NCDAH); *Wells v. Wells*, Spring 1866, Divorce Records, Orange County (NCDAH).

19. *Bowling v. Bowling*, Spring 1866; *Wells v. Wells*, Spring 1866; *Couch v. Couch*, Fall 1867; all in Divorce Records, Orange County (NCDAH). *Anderson v. Anderson*, Sept. 1867; *Lancaster v. Lancaster*, 1866; *Belvin v. Belvin*, Fall 1866; all in Divorce Records, Granville County (NCDAH). There were three divorce suits in Montgomery County during the 1860s. They do not contain references to wives' having become "common prostitutes." This illustrates that Montgomery County remained outside the mainstream of changing divorce patterns longer than did Granville and Orange. *Morton v. Morton*, Fall 1866; *Shaw v. Shaw*, Fall 1868; *Ingold v. Ingold*, Spring 1869; all in Divorce Records, Montgomery County (NCDAH).

20. *Wells v. Wells*, Spring 1866; *Bowling v. Bowling*, Spring 1866; *Herndon v. Herndon*, Spring 1867; *Couch v. Couch*, Fall 1867; all in Divorce Records, Orange County (NCDAH). *Belvin v. Belvin*, Fall 1866, Divorce Records, Granville County (NCDAH).

21. Acts of 1868–69, c. 96, s. 1, 3.

22. Divorce Records, Granville, Orange, and Montgomery counties (NCDAH); U.S. Federal Manuscript Censuses, 1860, Granville, Orange, and Montgomery counties.

23. *Boothe v. Boothe*, Fall 1875; *Caldwell v. Caldwell*, Fall 1878; *Brown v. Brown*, Spring 1877; *Roach v. Roach*, Fall 1875; all in Divorce Records, Orange County (NCDAH). *Lammonds v. Lammonds*, Fall 1875, Divorce Records, Montgomery

County (NCDAH). The cases in which men were granted divorces on the basis of wives' single affairs were *Trevan v. Trevan*, 1870; *Green v. Green*, 1871; *Hargrove v. Hargrove*, 1873; *Bullock v. Bullock*, Fall 1876; all in Divorce Records, Granville County (NCDAH). *Harward v. Harward*, Spring 1873; *Cheek v. Cheek*, Fall 1874; [*Allen*] *Atwater v.* [*Fannie*] *Atwater*, April 1874; [*Andy*] *Atwater v.* [*Alice*] *Atwater*, Spring 1875; *Emmerson v. Emmerson*, 1877; *Sandford v. Sandford*, Spring 1878; *Dickson v. Dickson*, Fall 1879; all in Divorce Records, Orange County (NCDAH).

24. For cases in which African American men sued for divorce, see *Anderson v. Anderson*, Sept. 1867; *Trevan v. Trevan*, 1870; *Green v. Green*, 1871; *Hargrove v. Hargrove*, 1873; *Watkins v. Watkins*, Aug. 1876; *McGehe v. McGehe*, 1876; *Bullock v. Bullock*, Fall 1876; *Wilson v. Wilson*, Fall 1879; all in Divorce Records, Granville County (NCDAH). *Chavers v. Chavers*, May 1877, Divorce Records, Orange County (NCDAH). James M. Day, who sued his wife Sarah Ellen for divorce in Orange County Superior Court in the spring of 1875, may also have been African American. The surname Day was common among Orange County free blacks before the Civil War; it was not common among Orange County whites.

25. *Watkins v. Watkins*, Aug. 1876; *Bullock v. Bullock*, Fall 1876; both in Divorce Records, Granville County (NCDAH).

26. On African American women and work during the nineteenth century, see Jacqueline Jones, *Labor of Love, Labor of Sorrow: Black Women, Work, and the Family from Slavery to the Present* (New York, 1985); Paula Giddings, *When and Where I Enter: The Impact of Black Women on Race and Sex in America* (New York, 1984); Deborah Gray White, *Ar'n't I a Woman? Female Slaves in the Plantation South* (New York, 1985); Suzanne Lebsock, *The Free Women of Petersburg: Status and Culture in a Southern Town, 1784–1860* (New York, 1984); and Herbert G. Gutman, *The Black Family in Slavery and Freedom, 1750–1925* (New York, 1977).

27. *Bullock v. Bullock*, Fall 1876, Divorce Records, Granville County (NCDAH).

28. On conflict between African American men and women, see especially Laura F. Edwards, "Sexual Violence, Gender, and Reconstruction in Granville County, North Carolina," *North Carolina Historical Review* 68 (July 1991): 237–60; Brenda Stevenson, "Distress and Discord in Virginia Slave Families, 1830–1860," in Bleser, ed., *In Joy and in Sorrow*, 103–24; Susan Mann, "Slavery, Sharecropping, and Sexual Inequality," *Signs* 14 (Summer 1989): 776–98; Christie Farnham, "'Sapphire?': The Issue of Dominance in the Slave Family, 1830–1865," in Carol Groneman and Mary Beth Norton, eds., *"To Toil the Livelong Day": American Women at Work, 1780–1980* (Ithaca, N.Y., 1987), 68–83.

29. Quoted in Mann, "Slavery, Sharecropping, and Sexual Inequality," 795.

30. Alfred Gray to Gen. Sickels [*sic*], April 12, 1867; A. Dilworth to Col. Edie, May 15, 1867; both in Records of the Freedmen's Bureau, ser. 2837, RG 105 (National Archives, Washington, D.C.).

31. J. Cowles to Capt. William Jones, July 23, 1867, Records of the Freedmen's Bureau, ser. 2837, RG 105 (National Archives, Washington, D.C.). For other evidence of paternalistic attitudes toward black women on the part of Freedmen's Bureau agents, see especially H. M. Waugh to Supt. Col. Stephen Moore, July 2, 1866, and W. H. Worden to Col. Edie, Aug. 27, 1866; both in Records of the Freedmen's Bureau, ser. 2837, RG 105 (National Archives, Washington, D.C.).

The latter document shows that not all agents displayed such paternalism, however. Worden complained to Edie that a neighborhood agent had told a black mother of six that "her husband can turn her away without any support."

32. Not only did two of the eight divorce petitions of African American men portray African American women as matriarchs bent on emasculating their husbands, but three of them contained assurances of the worthiness of the petitioner. James Wilson's attorney described him as a "deserving Negro," and Jordan Trevan's petition referred to him as "old and poor." The petition of James McGehe elicited sympathy for him as a former slave who had resided in Granville County for over 50 years. *Wilson v. Wilson*, Fall 1879; *Trevan v. Trevan*, 1870; *McGehe v. McGehe*, 1876; all in Divorce Records, Granville County (NCDAH).

About the Authors

Jeanie Attie is Assistant Professor of History at Washington University in St. Louis. She is currently completing a book on gender, voluntarism, and nationalism at the northern homefront during the Civil War.

Peter Bardaglio is Assistant Professor of History at Goucher College. His most recent publication is "'An Outrage upon Nature': Incest and the Law in the Nineteenth-Century South," in Carol Bleser, ed., *In Joy and in Sorrow: Women, Family, and Marriage in the Victorian South* (1991). He is currently completing a manuscript on families, sex, and the law in the nineteenth-century South.

David W. Blight is Associate Professor of History and Black Studies at Amherst College. He is the author of *Frederick Douglass' Civil War: Keeping Faith in Jubilee* (1989), and editor of *When This Cruel War Is Over: The Civil War Letters of Charles Harvey Brewster* (1992).

Victoria E. Bynum teaches history and women's studies at Southwest Texas State University. She is the author of *Unruly Women: The Politics of Social and Sexual Control in the Old South, 1840– 1865* (1992). Her current research is on gender and dissent in Civil War Mississippi.

Joan E. Cashin is Associate Professor of History at Ohio State University. She is the author of *A Family Venture: Men and Women on the Southern Frontier* (1991), *Our Common Affairs: Documents on the History of Southern Women* (forthcoming, 1993), and articles on the Civil War era. Currently she is working on a biography of Varina Howell Davis.

Catherine Clinton teaches in the Afro-American Studies Department at Harvard University. She is the author of *The Plantation Mistress* (1982) and *The Other Civil War* (1984), co-editor of *Portraits of American Women* (1991), and editor of *Stepdaughters of History: Southern Women and the American Past* (forthcoming).

Jim Cullen received his Ph.D. in American Civilization from Brown University in 1992. He is completing a study of how the Civil War is interpreted in twentieth-century popular culture.

Drew Gilpin Faust is Annenberg Professor of History at the University of Pennsylvania. She is author of *A Sacred Circle: The Dilemma of the Intellectual in the Old South* (1977), *James Henry Hammond and the Old South: A Design for Mastery* (1982), *The Creation of Confederate Nationalism: Ideology and Identity in the Civil War South* (1988), and *Southern Stories: Slaveholders in Peace and War* (1992). She is currently at work on a book about Confederate women.

Michael Fellman is Professor of History at Simon Fraser University in Vancouver, British Columbia. His most recent book is *Inside War: The Guerrilla Conflict in Missouri During the American Civil War* (1989). Currently, he is writing a study of the personality and values of William T. Sherman. During 1992–93, he is Martha Sutton Weeks Senior Research Fellow at the Stanford Humanities Center.

Patricia Hill is Associate Professor of History at Wesleyan University. The author of *The World Their Household* (1985), she is currently completing a cultural biography of Harriet Beecher Stowe.

Martha Hodes is Assistant Professor of History at the University of California, Santa Cruz. Her dissertation won the Nevins Prize in 1992. She is currently completing a project about sexual liaisons between white women and black men in the nineteenth-century South.

Stephanie McCurry is Assistant Professor of History at the University of California, San Diego. She is author of "The Two Faces of Republicanism: Gender and Proslavery Politics in Antebellum South Carolina," *Journal of American History* (March 1992), and *Masters of Small Worlds: Gender, Class, and the Yeomanry of the South Carolina Low Country, 1820–1860* (forthcoming).

James M. McPherson is George Henry Davis Professor of American History at Princeton University. His books include *Abraham Lincoln and the Second American Revolution* (1991), and *Battle Cry of Freedom* (1988), winner of the Pulitzer Prize in history.

Reid Mitchell teaches history at Princeton University and is the author of *Civil War Soldiers* (1988).

George C. Rable is Professor of History and Director of American Studies at Anderson University. He is the author of *Civil Wars: Women and the Crisis of Southern Nationalism* (1989), which won the 1991 Julia Cherry Spruill Prize and the 1989 Jefferson Davis Award. He is currently working on a book on the political culture of the Confederate States of America.

Kristie Ross is completing her doctoral dissertation at Columbia University on northern female nurses in the Civil War. She is currently living in Santa Fe, New Mexico.

Nina Silber is Assistant Professor of History at Boston University. She is currently completing a manuscript entitled *The Romance of Reunion: Northerners and the South, 1865–1900* (forthcoming).

Lyde Cullen Sizer will receive her Ph.D. in History from Brown University in 1993. She is completing a study on northern women writers during the Civil War era, and is the author of "A Place for a Good Woman: The Development of Women Faculty at Brown," in *The Search for Equity: Women at Brown University, 1891–1991* (1991), edited by Polly Welts Kaufman.

LeeAnn Whites teaches in the Department of History at the University of Missouri-Columbia. She is presently completing a manuscript on gender roles in the Civil War South. She is also working on a biography of Rebecca Latimer Felton.